# FOREWORD

There is a growing body of evidence that children starting strong in their learning and well-being will have better outcomes when they grow older. Such evidence has driven policy makers to design an early intervention and re-think their education spending patterns to gain "value for money".

*Starting Strong I* and *II* (2001, 2006) have set out the first international comparative works on early childhood education and care (ECEC) policy in OECD countries and suggest a list of comprehensive actions to expand access, ensure equity and enhance the quality of early interventions. Research emphasises that the benefits from early interventions are conditional on the "quality" of such interventions.

What does "quality" mean? Quality in ECEC may mean different things for different people (such as for children, parents and ECEC staff); it can be defined at different levels (such as at structural and system levels or at process or programme levels). Effective policy levers that can encourage "quality" may vary by country, considering country-specific contexts such as the political, financial and technical feasibility of implementing such levers. The OECD Education Policy Committee launched the project "Encouraging Quality in ECEC" to define or redefine quality from policy perspectives; review literature to identify effective policy levers; and set out different contexts under which such policy levers can be effectively implemented.

This publication is intended to be a quick reference guide for anyone with a role to play in encouraging quality in ECEC with a special focus on policy. Therefore, quality, as defined in this publication, is framed within characteristics that are more easily amenable to policy.

The analytical framework has been set up based on *Starting Strong I* and *II* as well as the latest findings from international literature reviews. With this analytical framework, five policy levers are suggested in *Starting Strong III*.

- Policy Lever 1: Setting out quality goals and regulations
- Policy Lever 2: Designing and implementing curriculum and standards
- Policy Lever 3: Improving qualifications, training and working conditions
- Policy Lever 4: Engaging families and communities
- Policy Lever 5: Advancing data collection, research and monitoring

Countries may be at different stages of policy development and implementation with varying focuses. Therefore, for each lever, different action areas are suggested in no particular order. Policy tools are presented to support actions, including research briefs, international comparisons, lists of country examples, policy questions for self-reflection and lessons learned from other country experiences.

Evidence is still dearth to suggest a certain course or a definite set of policy actions to encourage quality; and, therefore, an extensive list of country examples are presented. The list does not intend to suggest country examples as "policy recommendations": what works in one country may not necessarily work in others due to different political, institutional, historical and technical constraints. The list aims to be a practical guide, like "a menu of policy options", from which policy planners may get some food for thought and exposure to a wide range of country experiences (good practices and lessons learned). It is encouraged to interpret the policy implications from research briefs in terms of country contexts and broaden the perspectives by reflecting on whether other country examples could be transferred or applicable in your country.

The publication was drafted by the OECD Early Childhood Education and Care team: Miho Taguma (Project Leader), Ineke Litjens, Janice Heejin Kim and Kelly Makowiecki. Support was provided by consultant Matias Egeland and statistical assistant Claire Miguet. Members of the OECD Network on Early Childhood Education and Care provided country information and data as well as helped steer the development of this publication (see Annex for a list of Network members who have contributed[1]). Overall guidance was provided by Deborah Roseveare, Head of the Education and Training Policy Division, Directorate for Education, OECD.

International experts contributed to a great extent to the development of the toolbox. Ms. Wendy Jarvie (Australia), Mr. Jiaxiong Zhu (China), Ms. Kathrin Bock-Famulla (Germany), and Mr. Michael Anderson, Mr. Clive Belfield and Ms. Sharon Lynn Kagan (United States) helped to refine the survey instrument. Mr. Jeroen Aarssen, Mr. Hans Cohen de Lara and Ms. Karin Westerbeek (Netherlands), and Mr. William Steven Barnett and Ms. Ellen Frede (United States) contributed to the drafting of the research briefs. Ms. Wendy Jarvie (Australia), Ms. Claire Gascon Giard, Mr. Francisco Quiazua and Mr. Brennen Jenkins (Canada), Ms. Pamela Oberhuemer (Germany), Ms. Kiyomi Akita (Japan), Ms. Hyungsook Cho, Ms. Eunhye Park and Ms. Eunsoo Shin (Korea), Ms. Helen May (New Zealand), Ms. Anne Greve, Mr. Magne Mogstad and Mr. Thomas Moser (Norway), Ms. Júlia Formosinho and Ms. Teresa Vasconcelos (Portugal), Mr. Ramón Flecha (Spain), Ms. Sonja Sheridan (Sweden), and Ms. Megan Carolan and Mr. Danny Yagan (United States) commented on the drafts, which were finalised by the OECD ECEC team.

The online version of the toolbox can be found at: **www.oecd.org/edu/earlychildhood/toolbox**. The online toolbox will have additional information, such as a country materials page where actual documents from OECD countries are presented, including curricula, regulatory frameworks and data systems information. All information related to the OECD Network on Early Childhood Education and Care is available at: **www.oecd.org/edu/earlychildhood**.

---

[1] This document makes references to the "French Community of Belgium"; however, please note that, since May 2011, the official name has been changed to "Wallonia-Brussels Federation".

# Starting Strong III

## A QUALITY TOOLBOX FOR
## EARLY CHILDHOOD EDUCATION AND CARE

OECD

This work is published on the responsibility of the Secretary-General of the OECD. The opinions expressed and arguments employed herein do not necessarily reflect the official views of the Organisation or of the governments of its member countries.

This document and any map included herein are without prejudice to the status of or sovereignty over any territory, to the delimitation of international frontiers and boundaries and to the name of any territory, city or area.

**Please cite this publication as:**
OECD (2012), *Starting Strong III: A Quality Toolbox for Early Childhood Education and Care*, OECD Publishing.
*http://dx.doi.org/10.1787/9789264123564-en*

ISBN 978-92-64-12325-0 (print)
ISBN 978-92-64-12356-4 (PDF)

The statistical data for Israel are supplied by and under the responsibility of the relevant Israeli authorities. The use of such data by the OECD is without prejudice to the status of the Golan Heights, East Jerusalem and Israeli settlements in the West Bank under the terms of international law.

# TABLE OF CONTENTS

## Tables

## Figures

# EXECUTIVE SUMMARY

*Early childhood education and care (ECEC) can bring a wide range of benefits – for children, parents and society at large. But the magnitude of the benefits is conditional on "quality".*

A growing body of research recognises that early childhood education and care (ECEC) brings a wide range of benefits, for example, better child well-being and learning outcomes as a foundation for lifelong learning; more equitable child outcomes and reduction of poverty; increased intergenerational social mobility; more female labour market participation; increased fertility rates; and better social and economic development for the society at large.

But all these benefits are conditional on "quality". Expanding access to services without attention to quality will not deliver good outcomes for children or the long-term productivity benefits for society. Furthermore, research has shown that if quality is low, it can have long-lasting detrimental effects on child development, instead of bringing positive effects.

There is a general agreement that quality matters to gain significant pay-offs. In recent years, a growing number of OECD countries have made considerable efforts to encourage quality in ECEC; countries are at different stages of policy development and implementation. Regardless of which stage countries are at, research has suggested five key levers to be effective in encouraging quality in ECEC:

- Policy Lever 1: Setting out quality goals and regulations
- Policy Lever 2: Designing and implementing curriculum and standards
- Policy Lever 3: Improving qualifications, training and working conditions
- Policy Lever 4: Engaging families and communities
- Policy Lever 5: Advancing data collection, research and monitoring

*Setting out explicit quality goals and regulations can help align resources with prioritised areas, promote more co-ordinated child-centred services, level the playing field for providers and help parents make informed choices.*

Setting out explicit quality goals and minimum standards will help enhance quality in ECEC. Research has shown that setting out clear quality goals can help consolidate political will and strategically align resources with prioritised areas; anchor discussions between ministries for better government leadership in ECEC; promote more consistent, co-ordinated and child-centred services with shared social and pedagogical objectives; and provide guidance for providers, direction for practitioners and clarity for parents. In fact, many OECD countries set out specific quality-focused goals (such as improving qualifications of the workforce and setting out a child-centred curriculum).

Research has also shown that minimum standards can ensure conditions for better child development, support transparent regulation of the private sector, level the playing field for providers and help parents make informed choices. Many countries set minimum standards on structural indicators, such as staff-child ratios, indoor/outdoor space, staff qualification levels, and the frequency of contacts between staff and children or parents. In countries where the remit for early education and child care is "split" between different ministries, different standards are often set for different ECEC settings or for different age groups of children. In countries aiming to deliver "integrated" services, the same standards are applied in any ECEC settings.

In setting out quality goals, countries face such challenges as: i) building consensus on the goals; ii) aligning ECEC goals with goals of other levels of education or other child-focused services; and iii) translating the goals into action. With respect to minimum standards, common challenges include: i) securing financial resources for services to meet the quality standards; ii) lack of transparency among different providers under different regulations; iii) adapting to local needs and constraints; iv) implementation; and v) managing the regulation of private provision. To address these challenges, various strategies have been undertaken by countries that fit their country-specific contexts in terms of their financial viability as well as technical and political feasibility.

---

*Curriculum or learning standards can ensure even quality for ECEC provision across different settings, help staff to enhance pedagogical strategies and help parents to better understand child development.*

---

Curriculum and learning standards can have a positive impact on children's learning and development. They are of particular importance in ensuring even quality across different ECEC settings, supporting staff by giving them guidance on how to enhance children's learning and well-being, and informing parents about what the ECEC centres do and what they as parents can do at home.

Countries take different approaches in designing curriculum. There is a need to think beyond curriculum dichotomies (such as academic-oriented vs. comprehensive approaches, and staff-initiated instruction vs. child-initiated activities) and consolidate the "added value" of individual approaches. A focus on critical learning areas can facilitate customised curricula; and local adaptations of curricula in partnership with staff, families, children and communities can reinforce the relevance of ECEC services to local children and communities.

Almost all OECD countries have a curriculum or learning standards from age three up until compulsory schooling. In recent years, curricula or learning standards are often embedded within a life-cycle or lifelong learning approach, and a growing number of countries and regions have started to frame continuous child development from early childhood up to age eight, ten or eighteen. On the content, Nordic countries specify what is expected from staff rather than expected child outcomes, while Anglo-Saxon countries tend to take an outcome-based approach. Many OECD countries focus on literacy and numeracy in their learning framework. A growing body of recent research highlights the importance of "play"; some incorporate it as a separate subject area, while others embed it in other content areas. A few countries have included newly emerging elements, aligned with school curriculum, such as ICT.

Key challenges with respect to curriculum or standards include: i) defining goals and content; ii) aligning them with the school-level framework; iii) communicating it to relevant staff when it is created or revised; iv) implementing it effectively; and v) evaluating its contents and its implementation. To address these challenges, countries have undertaken strategies focusing on well-planned implementation, which includes stakeholder engagement, targeted outreach and professional staff development.

*ECEC staff play the key role in ensuring healthy child development and learning. Areas for reform include qualifications, initial education, professional development and working conditions.*

Higher qualifications are found to be strongly associated with better child outcomes. It is not the qualification *per se* that has an impact on child outcomes. What matters on the ground is the ability of the staff to create a high-quality pedagogic environment that makes the difference for children; that is, the critical element is the way in which staff involve children, stimulate interactions with and between children and use diverse scaffolding strategies. More specialised education and training of staff is found to be strongly associated with stable, sensitive and stimulating interactions in ECEC settings.

Countries have shown a wide range of qualifications for staff working in the ECEC sector. Kindergarten/preschool teachers generally have higher initial education requirements than care centre staff or family care staff, while some countries have a unified qualification for all workers. Initial education for kindergarten/preschool teachers is often integrated with that of primary school teachers to ensure smooth transition for child development. More professional development opportunities are available for kindergarten/preschool staff than for care centre staff, with only limited opportunities for family day care staff. Professional development tends to focus on: i) pedagogies and instructional practices; ii) curriculum implementation; iii) language and subject matters; iv) monitoring and assessment; and v) communication and management.

Working conditions can also improve the quality of ECEC services. Research has indicated that staff job satisfaction and retention – and therefore the quality of ECEC – can be improved by: i) high staff-child ratios and low group size; ii) competitive wages and other benefits; iii) reasonable schedule/workload; iv) low staff turnover; v) good physical environment; and vi) a competent and supportive centre manager.

Common challenges that countries face in encouraging a high-quality workforce include: i) raising staff qualification levels; ii) recruiting, retaining and diversifying a qualified workforce; iii) continuously up-skilling the workforce; and iv) ensuring the quality of the workforce in the private sector. Various strategies are undertaken to address these challenges using legal instruments, institutional rearrangements, financial incentives and data to inform policy and the public.

---

*Parents and communities should be regarded as "partners" working towards the same goal. Home learning environments and neighbourhood matter for healthy child development and learning.*

---

Parental and community engagement is increasingly seen as an important policy lever to enhance healthy child development and learning. Parental partnership is critical in enhancing ECEC staff knowledge about the children. Parental engagement – especially in ensuring high-quality children's learning at home and communicating with ECEC staff – is strongly associated with children's later academic success, high school completion, socio-emotional development and adaptation in society. Countries face such challenges as: i) lack of awareness and motivation on the parents' side; ii) communication and outreach of ECEC services with parents; iii) time constraints on the parents' side to be engaged; and iv) the increasing inequity and diversity among parents. Particular challenges are also associated with engaging ethnic minority parents. Countries take various strategies to tackle these challenges, using legal instruments, financial and non-financial incentives, as well as other support mechanisms.

Community engagement is also increasingly seen as an important policy lever. It can act as a "connector" between families and ECEC services as well as other services for children; a "social network" to support parents in reducing stress and making smart choices, especially for disadvantaged families; an "environment" to promote social cohesion and public order; and a "source of resources". Similar challenges are reported for community engagement as for parents, such as lack of awareness and motivation on the community's side as well as communication among communities and with ECEC services. There are also some unique challenges in community engagement, such as the challenges of managing dysfunctional communities and facilitating co-operation between ECEC services and other services as well as between ECEC and other levels of education. Various strategies are used to tackle these challenges. One element that is particularly helpful is taking a comprehensive view of community, *i.e.*, not simply seeing it as a "neighbourhood" or "municipality" but inclusive of non-governmental organisations, private foundations, religious organisations, libraries and museums, sports centres, police and other social services.

*Data, research and monitoring are powerful tools for improving children's outcomes and driving continuous improvement in service delivery.*

Data and monitoring can help establish facts, trends and evidence about whether children have equitable access to high-quality ECEC and are benefiting from it. They are essential for accountability and/or programme improvement. They can also help parents make informed decisions about their choice of services. Research suggests that better data systems and monitoring can improve child outcomes if they are developed and aligned with quality goals and if there are links between child-level data, practitioner-level data and programme-level data.

Country experiences have shown seven targets or purposes of monitoring: i) child development; ii) staff performance; iii) service quality; iv) regulation compliance; v) curriculum implementation; vi) parent satisfaction; and vii) workforce supply and working conditions. Various monitoring tools are used – depending on the purpose – such as interviews, observations, standardised testing and service quality ratings. The most commonly reported targets with difficulty in monitoring include: i) demand and supply of ECEC places; ii) workforce quality and working conditions; iii) financing and costs; iv) child development; and v) the quality of ECEC services. Countries also report challenges, such as ensuring that the data is consistent across services and regions as well as ensuring that the collected data is used to the full extent to enhance the quality of ECEC services. More and more countries and regions are making efforts to develop effective data systems – not simply for the sake of data collection or monitoring but by first defining a purpose.

Research can also be an influential tool to inform policy and practice. In ECEC, research has played a key role in explaining the success or failure of programmes; prioritising important areas for ECEC investment; and informing practices through evidence. Commonly used research types in ECEC include: country-specific policy research; large-scale programme evaluations; longitudinal studies; research on practice and process; participant-observation research; comparative, cross-national research; policy reviews; socio-cultural analysis; and neuroscience and brain research. There is a growing trend to use quantitative research methods, such as comparing the effectiveness of different programme types or different pedagogical strategies. However, there is also a growing recognition that qualitative research plays an essential role in informing practices with local values and democracy. Both quantitative and qualitative research are needed to advance research in ECEC.

Countries report challenges in advancing research, such as: i) a need for more evidence on the effects of ECEC and cost-benefit analysis; ii) under-researched areas or areas with newly growing interest; and iii) dissemination. In recent years, countries have focused their efforts so as to link research to policy and practice; to improve the quality and quantity of ECEC research; and to disseminate findings internationally.

# HOW TO USE THE QUALITY TOOLBOX

## Aim

The Quality Toolbox is intended to present "practical solutions" for anyone with a role to play in encouraging quality in ECEC. The toolbox will present five policy levers that are likely to enhance quality. Each lever is accompanied by supporting materials that serve as resources to help implement policy initiatives. The materials include research briefs, international comparisons, lists of strategy options compiled based on countries' implementation experiences, lessoned learned and self-reflection sheets.

These tools are described with accessible language and are designed to help you explore ways to improve ECEC services in your country. They can also be used as background materials for discussion with stakeholders.

## Structure

In recent years, a growing number of OECD countries[1] have made considerable efforts to encourage quality in ECEC, while others are focusing on other aspects of ECEC, such as access and affordability. Countries are at different stages of policy implementation to encourage quality in ECEC. Regardless of which stage countries are at, they might find it useful to learn about what research says and what other countries are doing.

Based on findings from international literature reviews, five policies have been identified as key levers to encourage quality in ECEC:

- Policy Lever 1: Setting out quality goals and regulations
- Policy Lever 2: Designing and implementing curriculum and standards
- Policy Lever 3: Improving qualifications, training and working conditions
- Policy Lever 4: Engaging families and communities
- Policy Lever 5: Advancing data collection, research and monitoring

Each chapter corresponds to each policy lever. For each policy lever, five action areas are presented.

- Action Area 1: Using research to inform policy and the public
- Action Area 2: Broadening perspectives through international comparison
- Action Area 3: Selecting a strategy option

- Action Area 4: Managing risks: learning from other countries' policy experiences

- Action Area 5: Reflecting on the current state of play

It is important to stress that these actions are not suggested in a particular order or in a fixed timeline. In the real world of policy development, policy can develop quickly or over years. Policy development and implementation can occur in a linear progression or go through an iterative process when Ministers and governments change or when the policy environment, public opinions and political imperatives change.

Frequently, advisors are asked to come up with new policy ideas, prepare analytic materials or design programme responses to emerging challenges at short notice. These five action areas have been identified to support them by focusing on the most frequently and urgently asked requests with short notice.

For each area, practical tools are presented as follows. These tools aim to help those developing policy to respond to government directions; be informed of other country responses to urgent priorities of their country; analyse most cost-effective actions; and examine trade-offs between long-term strategies and small, implementable steps ("quick wins"). To this end, the presented tools aim to provide a framework that prepares governments for action – to seize opportunities and help set policy agendas.

Each tool is intended to be a "stand-alone" document; therefore, some research findings, international comparisons, country experiences or figures may appear more than once in different tools. This way, each tool covers comprehensive information and does not require extracting information from different tools.

### Action Area 1: Using research to inform policy and the public

Questions frequently asked by policy makers, stakeholders or the media include, "Why is it important to take action on X or Y? What does research say? What research supports the decision?" To respond on what the research shows, the following tool has been prepared.

- Research brief

### Action Area 2: Broadening perspectives through international comparison

Other frequently asked questions may include, "How does our country compare with others in this selected policy area? Are we falling behind? Although it is domestically argued that this policy area needs more action, are we already doing enough in international comparison?" Or it might be necessary to raise the awareness of stakeholders of a need to move forward – without making them feel "imposed upon" by governments. To help manage these situations, the following tool has been prepared, bringing together international perspectives.

- International comparison

### Action Area 3: Selecting a strategy option

Other questions that arise are, "What kinds of challenges have other countries faced in implementing this policy lever? What strategies have they used to tackle the challenges? Is there anything we can learn from them? What would be some alternative strategy options that are politically feasible and financially sustainable within our own country context?" To help assess current strategies and identify alternative strategies, the following tool is presented.

- List of challenges and strategy options with country examples

### Action Area 4: Managing risks: learning from other countries' policy experiences

Another question that might be asked is "What can we learn from other countries as success factors and lessons learned to avoid policy failures?" The following tool will be a quick read about challenges and risks to consider when implementing policy initiatives.

- Policy lessons learned

### Action Area 5: Reflecting on the current state of play

Priorities are not often set strictly as a result of priority assessment exercises. Often times, a certain policy is to be implemented because it was part of an election package, and a political leader decided to pursue it. However, it is important to constantly reflect on the current situation and continuously make efforts for system improvements. Much reflection and constructive discussions with in-depth thinking will ultimately help prepare to justify a policy decision. To this end, the following tool is suggested.

- Self-reflection sheet

### Why does ECEC matter?

A growing body of research recognises that ECEC brings a wide range of benefits, including:

- Social and economic benefits.[2]
- Better child well-being and learning outcomes as a foundation for lifelong learning.[3]
- More equitable outcomes and reduction of poverty.[4]
- Increased intergenerational social mobility.[5]

These research findings have led education and social policy makers to re-think their investment patterns in children and families and to take a "life-cycle" view on child development and family support. In the last decades, this shift in thinking has been observed as visible action. Those OECD countries that spend significantly less on

ECEC compared to other levels of education have increased public spending on ECEC (OECD, 2011). Three broad rationales supported their actions:

1. ECEC has significant economic and social pay-offs.

2. ECEC supports parents to boost female employment.

3. ECEC is part of society's responsibility to educate children, a measure against child poverty and educational disadvantage.

Justifying more public spending on ECEC has been a challenge, even with "hard evidence" based on experimental studies with randomised trial controls. Children do not have votes or lobbying groups to voice their interest. Certainly, research has played a key role in making a case for them; but, oftentimes, it is not enough. Other factors are also at play.

*First*, political considerations get factored in. Although a growing body of research consolidates the knowledge base on the economic and social returns on investment in ECEC, such research is not often rigorously exploited by politicians in their agenda setting. A culture of evidence-based policy making is emerging in many OECD countries. However, policy making is a highly complex process; and a policy decision is often made not so much on the evidence base but influenced by election cycles, which appeal to voters, *i.e.*, highlighting short-term, visible gains. It takes decades to get gains from ECEC, and the short-term pay-offs are often found to be smaller.

*Second*, budgetary aspects play in. All ECEC costs are incurred up front, and providing high-quality ECEC can be expensive. Research has shown that structural indicators, such as staff-child ratios, qualified workforce and duration of the programme, are likely to influence child outcomes. Ensuring such quality indicators is not cheap. But school failure and its social costs later in life are far more expensive.

*Third*, benefits are conditional on "quality". The economic and social pay-offs depend on different quality indicators, such as staff-child ratios, duration and starting age. When quality indicators are low, research may indicate insignificant or null effects of ECEC.

Addressing these factors in linking research to policy making will require conscious efforts. It is not always clear how to encourage quality in ECEC and how to make a case for it. This toolbox aims to support readers by presenting practical tools and materials that could be use to encourage quality in ECEC.

The Quality Toolbox is also available at:
**WWW.OECD.ORG/EDU/EARLYCHILDHOOD/TOOLBOX**

# NOTES

1 When referring to integrated countries in this report, it means countries in which the responsibility for ECEC falls under one ministry at national level. These countries include: Chile, Denmark, Estonia, Finland, New Zealand, Norway, Slovenia, Slovak Republic, Sweden and the United Kingdom.

2 Heckman and Masterov, 2004; Vandell and Wolfe, 2000; CQO, 1995; Brooks-Gunn *et al.*, 1994.

3 National Centre for Education Statistics, 2009; Early Childhood Australia, 2009; Jalongo *et al.*, 2004; Heckman and Masterov, 2004; Vandell and Wolfe, 2000; NICHD, 1999; Blau, 1999; Shore, 1997; Barnett, 1995; Phillips *et al.*, 1987.

4 Mitchell, 2009; Heckman and Masterov, 2004; CQO, 1995.

5 OECD, 2009.

# REFERENCES

Barnett, W. S. (1995), "Long-term effects of early childhood programs on cognitive and school outcomes", *The Future of Children*, Vol. 5, pp. 25-50.

Blau, D. M. (1999), "The Effects of Child Care Characteristics on Child Development", *Journal of Human Resources*, Vol. 34, pp. 786-822.

Brooks-Gunn, J., M. C. McCormick, S. Shapiro, A. A. Benasich and G. W. Black (1994), "The Effects of Early Education Intervention on Maternal Employment, Public Assistance and Health Insurance: The Infant Health and Development Program", *American Journal of Public Health*, Vol. 84, pp. 924-931.

Cost, Quality, and Outcomes (CQO) Study Team (1995), "Cost, quality, and child outcomes in child care centers: Key findings and recommendations", *Young Children*, Vol. 50, No. 4, pp. 40-44.

Early Childhood Australia (2009), *Hands up for quality,* Early Childhood Australia Inc., Australia.

Heckman, J. J. and D. V. Masterov (2004), *The productivity argument for investing in young children*, New York: Committee for Economic development, Unites States.

Jalongo, M. R., B. S. Fennimore, J. Pattnaik, D. M. Laverick, J. Brewster and M. Mutuku (2004), "Blended perspectives: A global vision for high-quality early childhood education", *Early Childhood Education Journal*, Vol. 32, No. 3, pp. 143-155.

Mitchell, A. W. (2009), "Four good reasons why ECE is not just important, but essential", *Advocacy Exchange*, May/June 2009.

National Center for Education Statistics (2009), "The Children Born in 2001 at Kindergarten Entry: First findings from the kindergarten data collections of early childhood longitudinal study, birth cohort (ECLS-B)", US Department of Education.

NICHD Early Child Care Research Network (1999), "Child Outcomes When Child Care Center Classes Meet Recommended Standards of Quality", *American Journal of Public Health*, Vol. 89, pp. 1072-1077.

OECD (2011), *Doing Better for Families*, OECD, Paris.

OECD (2009), "Intergenerational Social Mobility", Working Party No.1 on Macroeconomic and Structural Policy Analysis [ECO/CPE/WP1(2009)4].

Phillips, D. A., K. McCartney and S. Scarr (1987), "Child-Care Quality and Children's Social Development", *Developmental Psychology*, Vol. 23, pp. 537-544.

Shore, R. (1997), *Rethinking the Brain: New Insights into Early Development*, New York, NY: Families and Work Institute, Unites States.

Vandell, D. L. and B. Wolfe (2000), *Child care quality: Does it matter and does it need to be improved?* Madison, WI: Institute for Research and Poverty, United States.

# POLICY LEVER 1

# SETTING OUT QUALITY GOALS AND REGULATIONS

*Quality-focused goal setting is one of the key policy levers to encourage quality in ECEC. Research has shown that, when explicitly set, they can help: i) consolidate political will and strategically align resources with prioritised areas; ii) anchor discussions between ministries and improve government leadership in ECEC; iii) promote more consistent, co-ordinated and child-centred services with shared social and pedagogical objectives; and iv) provide guidance for providers, direction for practitioners and clarity for parents.*

*Setting out clear regulations is another key policy lever. Research has shown that minimum standards can guarantee the health and safety of children in high-quality environments by: i) levelling the playing field to ensure the quality of all providers; ii) ensuring conditions of learning and care through structural indicators that can enhance child development; and iii) communicating with parents about the quality of services and helping them make informed choices.*

# ACTION AREA 1 – USING RESEARCH TO INFORM POLICY AND THE PUBLIC

This section contains the following research briefs:

- ECEC Quality Goals Matter
- Minimum Standards Matter

## ECEC QUALITY GOALS MATTER

### What are quality goals?

There are wide-ranging expectations for quality goals among specific populations. For governments, the primary goal may be school preparedness and healthy socio-emotional child development. For working parents, it may be easy access to high-quality child care. For communities, it may be shared values. For minority groups, it may be transmitting the native culture and language. Thus, arbitrating the priorities of diverse interest groups presents a major challenge in defining the terms of quality goals.

### What is at stake?

The objectives of centres are generally guided by the national (or local) quality goals, which set out the key goals of ensuring a quality early childhood system. These goals differ widely from country to country, and no doubt from decade to decade, but a common conviction is emerging across countries that broad quality goals should be set to stimulate further development and improvement of early childhood programmes. Fundamental differences in quality goals for child care and early education can characterise the ECEC sectors in countries operating split or two-tiered early childhood systems. The separation of "education" and "care" can, in some cases, undermine the delivery of quality goals. The result can be a lack of coherence for children and families, with a confusing variation in objectives, funding streams, operational procedures, regulatory frameworks, staff training and qualifications (OECD, 2006).

Competing ideas about childhood can help to explain the orientation of ECEC services. If the child is thought to be preparing for adulthood, early "child care" (generally, ages zero to three) is normally seen as the responsibility of parents with little government involvement (Dearing *et al.*, 2009). If, however, childhood is seen as an important stage of life, countries are more likely to integrate "child care" and "early education", which contributes to more holistic child development and greater clarity in objectives for centres, practitioners, parents and other stakeholders (Bennett, 2008; OECD, 2006).

## Why do quality goals matter?

Quality goals are important to give the "big picture" or bird's eye view of ECEC. They are able to consolidate political will, a key step to increasing core programme funding. Quality goals can also provide incentives for governments to improve ECEC leadership and strategically align resources with prioritised quality areas (Council of Australian Governments, 2009).

At the same time, quality goals can promote more consistent, co-ordinated and child-centred services through a national framework with shared social and pedagogical objectives. Quality goals can provide more coherent ECEC services at every level. They can anchor policy discussions between ministries, provide guidance for providers, direction for practitioners, purpose for students and clarity for parents (OECD, 2006). Common objectives leading to the development of the "whole person" can prevent the fragmentation of services, which can prevent early knowledge gaps and uneven child development (Eurydice, 2009).

## What matters most?

Goals give ECEC programmes their purpose and orientation. They should be specific but have enough flexibility for application (NIEER, 2004b; OECD, 2006). But on what subjects does research indicate it is important to set quality goals? Which aspects can impact ECEC quality?

### *Goals for leadership, governance and funding*

National governing bodies establish and reinforce ECEC quality goals. Integrated ECEC services – under a common authority – provide more co-ordinated and goal-oriented services (Bennett, 2008). A lead ministry or agency can increase the quality of provisions through direct funding, training practitioners and regularly evaluating programmes (CCL, 2006). At the same time, integrated services can better expand access to ECEC by raising public subsidies and reducing costs for families. The fragmentation of responsibility in split management systems can create inequality through uneven levels of quality provisions and the lack of coherent goals (OECD, 2001 and 2006).

Sustained public funding and regulation are necessary to achieve quality goals. First, generous core funding can ensure the recruitment of a highly professional staff who remain committed to improve children's performance towards cognitive, social and emotional goals. Second, investment in ECEC facilities and materials can support a child-centred environment for learning and development. In the absence of direct public funding or parent subsidies, there is a risk of uneven and poor quality provisions with high-quality ECEC limited to affluent neighbourhoods (OECD, 2006).

## Minimum standards

Through a regulatory framework, minimum standards can guarantee the health and safety of children in high-quality environments and ensure a minimum level of quality. National regulatory frameworks can better "level the playing field" by ensuring all children benefit from a minimum quality of education and care. They can also greatly improve the conditions of learning and care through standardised high-quality instruction that can improve reading, math and language skills (Burchinal *et al.* 2009; OECD, 2001). Minimum standards also communicate with parents about the quality of services and help them make informed choices (OECD, 2006).

## Curriculum

The national curriculum or curriculum framework normally elaborates ECEC key goals, including underlying concepts and values (OECD, 2006). Despite country-level differences, broad curriculum aims include *learning to be* (to be confident and happy with one's self); *learning to do* (experimentation, play and group interaction); *learning to learn* (specific pedagogical objectives) and *learning to live together* (respectful of differences and democratic values) (OECD, 2006; UNESCO, 1996).

It is generally agreed that more general goals (for well-being and socialisation) are appropriate for younger children, while specific cognitive aims are particularly useful for older preschoolers (Eurydice, 2009). A focus on skills rather than activities can help to make social and emotional goals more concrete (NIEER, 2004b).

## Workforce

The professionalisation of the ECEC workforce can increase the likelihood of achieving broad-based education and care quality goals. Better educated practitioners with specialised training are more likely to improve children's cognitive outcomes through larger vocabularies, increased ability to solve problems and increased ability to develop targeted lesson plans (NIEER, 2004a). Teachers' knowledge and ability to challenge children in their understanding is considered to be relevant for child development (Doverborg and Pramling Samuelsson, 2009). It is particularly important that ECEC staff understand the child's own perspectives in terms of strategies, approaches, communication and interplay. For example, a teacher who understands a child's interests and intentions for learning can match them with the goals of an ECEC curriculum (Sheridan, 2009).

Shonkoff and Philips (2000) find that the teacher's or caregiver's education and training are strongly associated with stable, sensitive and stimulating interactions. Educated staff are more likely to provide children with the stimulating, warm and supportive interactions that can lead to more positive social and emotional development outcomes (OECD, 2001). Education and training are also found to have an effect on the implementation and knowledge about the pedagogical approaches and curriculum (Elliott, 2006; Kagan and Kauerz, 2006).

## Parental and community involvement

Research found that there is a substantial need and demand for a parental component in ECEC services (Deforges and Abouchaar, 2003) and also shows that parental involvement in ECEC services can enhances children's achievements and adaption (Blok *et al.*, 2005; Deforges and Abouchaar, 2003; Edwards *et al.*, 2008; Harris and Goodall, 2006; Powell *et al.*, 2010; Sylva *et al.*, 2004; Weiss *et al.*, 2008). Furthermore, parental involvement is independently associated with school performance and achievement from childhood through to mid-adolescence (Glass, 2004). Parents with clear information on quality goals are better able to raise important questions and concerns with practitioners about their children's ECEC experience. They can also provide greater support and continuity for learning at home (NIEER, 2004b).

Harmonising policy goals on quality and parents' needs plays a critical role in building reliability and accountability in early childhood education. When the goals are not able to meet parental needs and expectations, there is a tendency to send children to private institutions for extra-curricular activities in addition to kindergarten or child care centre. This can result in heavy financial burdens for parents, regardless of government subsidies. Therefore, it becomes essential to reflect parents' voices in the process of establishing quality goals (Shin, Jung and Park, 2009).

Furthermore, a strong community can act as a social network that supports parents to reduce stress, maintain positive emotions and provide tools for raising their child. Moreover, a continuum between ECEC services, parents, neighbours and other civil society stakeholders can enhance co-operation between different services leading to a comprehensive services approach (Litjens and Taguma, 2010).

### Data collection, research and quality monitoring

There is increasing emphasis placed on ECEC data collection, research and quality rating systems aimed at achieving quality goals and raising standards. The evaluation of specific goals or outcomes can be important for policy makers, and child assessment can help identify special needs. However, child assessments can also unfairly rank young learners and lead to higher anxiety and lower self-esteem (OECD, 2001). To achieve evidence-based policy making, government administrations need to organise ECEC data collection in the ECEC field, conduct research on this topic and monitor the sector (OECD, 2006). Most ECEC programme evaluations focus on structural elements (funding, standards, staff, etc.) rather than children's learning outcomes through standardised tests and evaluation scales (OECD, 2006).

### What are the policy implications?

### Placing well-being, early development and learning at the core of ECEC

Children's well-being and learning are core goals of early childhood services, but services for children under age three are often seen as an adjunct to labour market policies, with infants and toddlers assigned to services with weak developmental agendas or goals. In some cases, it can be beneficial to focus more on the child and show greater understanding of the specific developmental tasks and learning strategies for young children. The ministry/ies in charge can address these issues with broad but realistic goals that focus on the child for all early childhood services (OECD, 2006).

### Developing a quality framework

Quality frameworks can include a broad range of elements, but, in general, they identify the key quality goals of early childhood services for a particular country or region. A systemic approach entails developing a common policy framework with consistent goals across the system and clearly-defined roles and responsibilities at both central and decentralised levels of governance (OECD, 2006). One policy option is the creation of an inter-departmental and/or intergovernmental co-ordination body to generate co-operative quality frameworks. Choi (2003) provides evidence that frameworks can work well when they are established for a specific purpose, for example, to co-ordinate a particular early childhood goal or to focus on a targeted quality issue.

### Concentrating efforts towards integrated services

The most successful ECEC systems have managed to integrate broad-based goals for "child care" with specific "early education" aims. Integrated systems are found to have increased public investment in ECEC and eliminate artificial age categories (Bennett, 2011). Adopting a more integrated approach to the field allows government ministries to organise agreed policies and goals and combine resources for early childhood services. Regulatory, funding and staffing regimes, costs to parents and opening hours can be made more consistent. Variations in access and quality can be lessened, and links at the services level – across age groups and settings – are more easily created. In integrated systems, a common vision of education and care can be forged with agreed social and pedagogical objectives and goals (NIEER, 2004b; OECD, 2001). The *Starting Strong* reports found that integrated ECEC services at governance level are better able to provide quality ECEC services.

It is important in this process that early childhood policy making should be placed in a ministry that has a strong focus on the development and education of young children.

### Delegating responsibility to local stakeholders

Devolution of tasks in the early childhood field can be needed or useful, not only as the concrete acknowledgement of the rights of families and local communities, but also for reasons of practical management. Numerous providers and fragmented provision patterns in the early childhood field can make it difficult for central governments to ensure quality and appropriate provision of services, especially in the absence of devolved local management. A shift towards more devolution can also be motivated by the desire to bring decision making and delivery closer to the families being served and to adapt services to meet local needs and circumstances (OECD, 2006).

Central authorities can delegate responsibility to centres and school-based institutions to manage a variety of tasks, including implementation, monitoring, evaluation and reporting. Local authorities can better co-ordinate with parents and communities to determine the appropriateness of national ECEC goals (Mahon, 2011).

### Strengthening institutional performance for improvement and accountability

Through generous core funding, the government and ECEC services are more likely to achieve quality goals: for example, ECEC providers can innovate curriculum to better meet local needs, hire more qualified practitioners, stimulate parental and community involvement, and advance data collection, research and monitoring (OECD, 2006). Ministries or local authorities may provide added financial incentives for ECEC providers to reach quality goals by making core funding contingent on achieving a specified quality goal. Financial tracking and monitoring of the achievement of quality goals is important, as it contributes to accountability, helps inform planning and resource allocation, and can contribute in the future to strengthening policy making (OECD, 2006).

### What is still unknown?

### Research on target quality aspects

The literature has helped to identify key areas where quality goals are likely to help improve quality in ECEC, as listed above. However, there is not sufficient research on "best practice" for each intervention. For example, workforce is the key factor in improving child outcomes. Experimentation with reward systems has been undertaken at the school level in the United States; however, little emphasis has been placed on ECEC. Research in this area has great potential to inform policy practice by answering questions, such as, "Does accountability in ECEC systems improve outcomes?", and, "If so, to what extent?"

Another example is curriculum. There is a general consensus that quality goals must be adapted to diverse needs namely for low-income, immigrant and ethnic groups (OECD, 2001). Broad-based adaptation is often considered expensive, and there is little information on the actual measures of adaptation in place in ECEC environments. More research is needed to answer questions such as, "Do current adaptation measures enable disadvantaged children to achieve shared quality goals?", and, "What still needs to be done?"

## REFERENCES

Bennett, J. (2008), "Early Childhood Education and Care Systems in the OECD Countries: the Issue of Tradition and Governance", *Encyclopedia on Early Childhood Development*, Centre of Excellence for Early Childhood Development and Strategic Knowledge Cluster on Early Child Development, Montreal, available at: www.child-encyclopedia.com/pages/PDF/ BennettANGxp.pdf, accessed 22 September 2011.

Bennett, J. (2011), "Introduction: Early Childhood Education and Care", *Encyclopedia on Early Childhood Development*, Centre of Excellence for Early

Childhood Development and Strategic Knowledge Cluster on Early Child Development, Montreal, available at: www.child-encyclopedia.com/pages/PDF/BennettANGxp1-Intro.pdf, accessed 22 September 2011.

Blok, H. *et al.* (2005), "The Relevance of the Delivery Mode and Other Program Characteristics for the Effectiveness of Early Childhood Interventions with Disadvantaged Children", *International Journal of Behavioural Development*, Vol. 29, pp. 36-37.

Burchinal, P. *et al.* (2009), "Early Care and Education Quality and Child Outcomes", *Child Trend*s, Washington, DC.

Canadian Council on Learning (CCL) (2006), "Why is High-Quality Child Care Essential? The link between Quality Child Care and Early Learning", *Lessons in Learning*, CCL, Ottawa.

Choi, S. (2003), "Cross-sectoral Co-ordination in Early Childhood: Some Lessons to Learn", Policy Brief No. 9, UNESCO, Paris, France.

Council of Australian Governments (2009), *National Quality Standard for Early Childhood Education and Care and School Age Care*, Early Childhood Development Steering Committee, Canberra.

Dearing, E., K. McCartney and B. A. Taylor (2009), "Does Higher Quality Early Child Care Promote Low-Income Children's Math and Reading Achievement in Middle Childhood?", *Child Development*, Vol. 80, No. 5, pp.1329-1349.

Desforges, C. and A. Abouchaar (2003),"The Impact of Parental Involvement, Parental Support and Family Education on Pupil Achievement and Adjustment: A Literature Review", Research Report No. 433, Department for Education and Skills, London.

Doverborg, E. and I. Pramling Samuelsson (2009), *"Grundläggande matematik"*, in S. Sheridan, I. Pramling Samuelsson and E. Johansson (eds.), *Barns tidiga lärande. En tvärsnittsstudie om förskolan som miljö för barns lärande*, Antologi, pp. 125-150, Göteborg: Acta Universitatis Gothoburgensis, available at: http://hdl.handle.net/2077/20404.

Edwards, C. P., S. M. Sheridan and L. Knoche (2008), *Parent Engagement and School Readiness: Parent-Child Relationships in Early Learning*, Lincoln, NE: University of Nebraska, available at: http://digitalcommons.unl.edu/famconfacpub/60.

Elliott, A. (2006), "Early Childhood Education: Pathways to Quality and Equity for all Children", *Australian Education review,* 50, 2006.

Eurydice (2009), Early Childhood Education and Care in Europe: Tackling Social and Cultural Inequalities, Eurydice, Brussels.

Glass, G. (2004), "More than Teacher Directed or Child Initiated: Preschool Curriculum Type, Parent Involvement, and Children's Outcomes in the Child-Parent Centres", *Education Policy Analysis Archives*, Vol. 12, No. 72, pp. 1-38.

Harris, A. and J. Goodall (2006), *Parental Involvement in Education: An overview of the Literature*, University of Warwick, Coventry.

Kagan, S. and K. Kauerz (2006), "Preschool Programs: Effective Curricula", *Encyclopedia on Early Childhood Development*, Centre of Excellence for Early Childhood Development and Strategic Knowledge Cluster on Early Child Development, Montreal, available at: www.child-encyclopedia.com/documents/Kagan-KauerzANGxp.pdf.

Litjens, I. and M. Taguma (2010), "Literature overview for the 7th meeting of the OECD Network on Early Childhood Education and Care", OECD, Paris.

Mahon, R. (2011), "Child Care Policy: A Comparative Perspective", *Encyclopedia on Early Childhood Development*, Centre of Excellence for Early Childhood Development and Strategic Knowledge Cluster on Early Child Development, Montreal, available at: www.child-encyclopedia.com/pages/PDF/MahonANGxp2.pdf, accessed 22 September 2011.

NIEER (2004a), "Better Practitioners, Better Preschools: Student Achievement Linked to Teacher Qualifications", *Policy Brief, NIEER, New Jersey.*

NIEER (2004b), "Child Outcome Standards in Pre-K Programmes: What Are Standards; What Is Needed To Make Them Work?", *Policy Brief*, NIEER, New Jersey.

OECD (2001), Starting Strong I: Early Childhood Education and Care, OECD, Paris.

OECD (2006), Starting Strong II: Early Childhood Education and Care, OECD, Paris.

Powell, D. R., S.-H. Son, N. File and R. R. San Juan (2010), "Parent-school relationships and children's academic and social outcomes in public pre-kindergarten", *Journal of School Psychology*, Vol. 48, pp. 269-292.

Sheridan, S., P. Williams, A. Sandberg *et al.* (eds.) (2009), *Barns tidiga lärande : en tvärsnittsstudie av förskolan som miljö för barns lärande* [Children's early learning: A cross-sectional study of preschool as an environment for children's learning], Göteborg Studies in Educational Sciences, 284, Göteborg, Sweden: Acta Universitatis Gothoburgensis.

Sheridan, S. (2009), "Discerning pedagogical quality in preschool", accepted for publication in *Scandinavian Journal of Educational Research*, Vol. 53, No. 3, pp. 245-261.

Shin, E., M. Jung and E. Park, E. (2009), "A survey on the development of the pre-school free service model", Research Report of the Korean Educational Development Institute, Seoul.

Shonkoff, J. P. and A. D. Philips (2000), *From Neurons to Neighbourhoods,* National Academy Press, Washington DC.

Sylva, K., E. C. Melhuish, P. Sammons, I. Siraj-Blatchford and B. Taggart (2004), *The Effective Provision of Pre-School Education (EPPE) Project: Final Report,* London: DfES and Institute of Education, University of London.

UNESCO (1996), *Learning: The Treasure Within,* J. Delors (ed.), Paris, Author.

Weiss, H., M. Caspe and M. E. Lopez (2008), "Family Involvement Promotes Success for Young Children: A Review of Recent Research" in M.M. Cornish (ed.), *Promising Practices for Partnering with Families in the Early Years,* Plymouth: Information Age Publishing.

## MINIMUM STANDARDS MATTER

### What are minimum standards?

Minimum standards are structural inputs that can enable "adequate" or "good enough" quality ECEC provisions. Structural requirements may define the quality of the physical environment for young children (*e.g.,* buildings, space, outdoors, pedagogical materials); the training levels for staff; staff-child ratios; work conditions; etc. (OECD, 2006). A certain minimum level of ECEC provision can be ensured by the clear formulation of standards and enforcement of legislation or regulations (OECD, 2006).

### What is at stake?

As ECEC expands outside the home, the regulation of services inevitably becomes a public responsibility. All OECD countries impose a preliminary health and safety check on centres or homes licensed to look after young children. However, as the *Starting Strong* reports point out, the extent and manner of regulation differs widely from country to country and often varies within countries according to region or the type of service concerned. Appropriate regulation not only helps define and enforce health, environmental and programme standards but can also ensure some degree of equity for parents and children in poorer neighbourhoods (OECD, 2001 and 2006).

It has been repeatedly shown in international studies, programme evaluations and quality measurements that ECEC programmes can have a positive effect on children's developmental outcomes on the condition that the level of quality of the service is high (Burchinal *et al.* 2010; OECD, 2001 and 2006; Sammons *et al.*, 2002; Shonkoff and Philips, 2000), although setting high-quality standards or raising standards can be costly. If providers raise costs to compensate for higher standards, provisions risk being unaffordable for low-income families. The added costs might also serve as a disincentive for providers to expand access, which can negatively impact the goal of increasing ECEC coverage. High standards may also invite non-formal providers with low quality to enter the market.

On the contrary, lower standards may reduce operating costs and might be an incentive for providers to expand access. However, research demonstrates that children are more likely to have language, social and development problems in low-quality provisions (OECD, 2001 and 2006). Children in high-quality ECEC centres, or programmes with high standards, perform better in literacy and mathematics. These positive effects are strongest for poor children and for children whose parents have little education (OECD, 2006).

Research also concludes that learning in one life stage begets learning in the next: investment in the foundation stage of early childhood increases the productivity of the next stage and so on (Cunha et al., 2005). The complementary effect of one stage on another can be weakened at any moment, for example, by a period of poor education and development. The early childhood stage of learning is of major importance since it forms the foundation of life-long development: in early childhood, positive (or negative) dispositions towards society and learning are absorbed and the basic life skills acquired, such as co-operation with peers and adults, autonomy, meaning making, creativity, problem solving and persistence.

Furthermore, remedial education interventions targeting young school drop-outs or adults with poor basic skills are far more costly than early interventions, such as ECEC and, according to research, are of limited benefit (Cunha and Heckman, 2010). Setting high minimum standards is therefore an investment not only in children but also in the future and society in general (OECD, 2006).

## Why do minimum standards matter?

Minimum standards can guarantee the health and safety of children in ECEC environments. They can ensure the conditions of learning and care by defining duration, staff qualification levels and curriculum to shape staff behaviour (Burchinal et al., 2009; OECD, 2001). National regulatory frameworks with appropriate minimum standards can better "level the playing field" by ensuring all children benefit from a minimum quality of education and care (Belsky, 2011; Eurydice, 2009; Vandenbroeck, 2011). Raising standards or setting minimum standards can help reduce knowledge gaps for all, although the effect is greater for low-income, immigrant and minority children (OECD, 2006 and 2011).

Although minimum standards can contribute to high-quality ECEC, countries do not *have* to set standards on all quality aspects; but this is rare. On what aspects countries need minimum standards depends on specific contexts, such as the current level of quality. Sweden, for example, is a country without minimum standards for, *e.g.*, space per child or staff-child ratio given that the level of quality is above the standard; it is indeed known as a country with a high-quality ECEC sector. The country has regulated minimum standards regarding staff qualification and a curriculum, which sets out goals for the quality of ECEC activities (OECD, 2006).

Due to increasing research on quality aspects and standards, there is now a considerable amount of data and information on which quality aspects matter most and influence quality – and through this, child development. The meta analyses of cost-effectiveness studies can shed insights into how different programme standards can produce different outcomes (Figure 1.1, Table 1.1). This needs to be interpreted within context, such as the family backgrounds of children who participated in the programmes.

**Figure 1.1. Returns on investment from high-quality ECEC programmes**

Based on model pre-primary programmes for low-income children

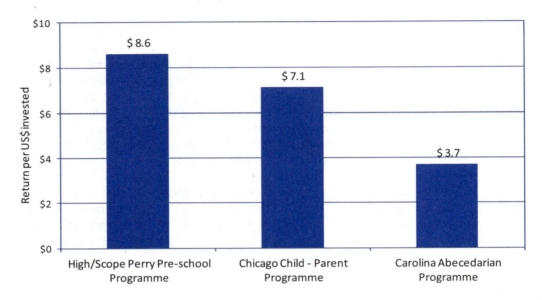

*Source*: Schweinhart, 2006; Heckmann *et al.*, 2009.

**Table 1.1. Features of high-quality ECEC programmes**

|  | High/Scope Perry Pre-school Programme | Chicago Child - Parent Programme | Carolina Abecedarian Programme |
| --- | --- | --- | --- |
| Age range | 3-4 years | 3-4 years | 0-5 years |
| Duration | 2 years | 2 years | 5 years |
| Maximum class size | 13 | 17 | 12 |
| Staff-child ratio | 1:6.5 | 1:8.5 | 1:6 |
| Teacher qualification | BA + certification | BA + certification | BA or equivalent |

*Source*: Schweinhart, 2006; Heckmann *et al.*, 2009.

## What aspects matter most?

There is no doubt that well-resourced ECEC systems have greater potential to systematically raise minimum standards (OECD, 2006), although the exact effect on children from regulating higher structural inputs cannot always be predicted. For example, it is difficult to know how teacher qualifications actually impact eventual teacher success. Individual staff factors, such as intelligence, motivation and job satisfaction, can combine with previous training to predict teacher quality. Having certain and uncertain factors in mind, policy makers still need to make a decision. The following section summarises the key research findings on ECEC structural inputs.

### Staff-child ratios and group size

Staff-child ratios play a key role in ensuring quality for better child development (OECD, 2006). It is generally the most consistent predictor of high-quality learning environments because it increases the potential for frequent and meaningful interactions (Pianta *et al.*, 2009; UNESCO, 2004). Children are found to perform better in cognitive areas at age 15 when enrolled in programmes of longer duration with high staff-child ratios and high per child expenditures (Figure 1.2). High staff-child ratios can also ensure safer environments for children since staff have a lower number of children to look after (Pianta *et al.*, 2009).

Besides staff-child ratios, small group size is considered as a predictor for more individualised attention and frequent interactions (NIEER, 2006; UNESCO, 2004). Younger and disadvantaged children tend to benefit more from smaller group sizes than older or more advantaged children due to increased attention from staff and more interactive dialogue opportunities. However, some studies have shown little relationship between group size and educational effectiveness, suggesting that other inputs may be more influential, such as the staff-child ratio (NIEER, 2004). For example, Chetty *et al.* (2011) have found a weak relationship between pre-primary group size and college attendance and no relationship with future earnings.

**Figure 1.2. Structural ECEC inputs improve student performance at 15 years**

Based on PISA 2009 results

Average score point difference associated with attending pre-primary education in school systems that:

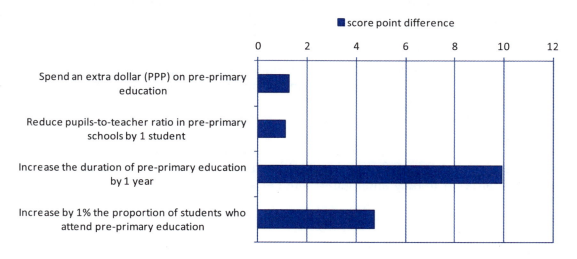

Note: The score point differences above are statistically significant.

*Source*: OECD, 2011.

## Staff qualification level and specialised training

Setting the minimum qualification level plays a key role in ensuring healthy child development. Most research claims that better educated preschool teachers with specialised ECEC training are more effective in providing stimulating staff-child interactions. It can lead to greater vocabularies and increased ability to solve problems in teaching staff. Besides this, qualified teachers are better able to engage children, elicit their ideas and monitor their progress (NIEER, 2006), and they tend to provide children with more stimulating, warm and supportive interactions leading to longer term positive impacts (OECD, 2001).

Striking the right balance between the level and quantity of a qualified workforce can be a challenge. On one hand, formal education standards need to be high enough to produce high-quality learning environments and lead to desirable, country-specific child outcomes. On the other, higher teacher qualifications might also lead to higher salary expectations. If standards surpass what ECEC providers are able to afford, this might negatively impact quality (Bender *et al.*, 2007).

A clear indication of the impact of practitioner quality comes from EPPE (Effective Provision of Pre-School Education) research in England (United Kingdom). This study found that higher proportions of staff with low-level qualifications were associated with poorer child outcomes on social relationships with peers and children's co-operation and were associated with higher levels of anti-social behaviour. Practitioners with specialised training and higher education were linked to positive child-adult interactions, including praising, comforting, questioning and responding to children (Elliott, 2006; Shonkoff and Philips, 2000). However, it is not the qualification *per se* that affects outcomes but the ability of the staff member to create a better pedagogic environment that makes the difference (Elliott, 2006).

## Staff salaries

Setting minimum wages for ECEC staff can increase the motivation of current staff and attract highly motivated and qualified professionals to the sector; indirectly, this can improve child development and outcomes (NIEER, 2003). Competitive wages attract a strong professional staff that is more likely to be satisfied with their jobs, perform well and make long-term career commitments leading to lower staff turnover rates. The latter generally results in stronger relationships between staff and children, calmer, less aggressive child behaviour, and improved language development (CCL, 2006). Staff with low wages are more likely to take on second jobs, lowering their performance through greater fatigue and less commitment (Centre for Families, Work and Well-being, 2000). A research study demonstrated that fully qualified pre-primary teachers who were given higher salaries equivalent to their primary education colleagues resulted in student performance that was two or more times larger in literacy and math (Pianta *et al.*, 2009).

## Programme duration

While there are mixed research findings about the impact of programme intensity (part-time or full-time), the duration of programme participation seems to be more consistently associated with long-term intellectual gains and future achievement (Love *et al.*, 2003; Melhuish *et al.*, 2004; Smith, 2003). Positive signs of increased duration include greater vocabularies, word analysis, math achievement and better memory (Belsky *et al.*, 2007; Glass, 2004). Higher "dose" programmes also have more visible long-term impacts, as they more often reduce "fade out" effects (Eurydice, 2009). As an example, the OECD PISA study found that an extension of participation in ECEC of one year leads to an improvement of ten score points in PISA[1], an international student assessment test at age 15 (OECD, 2011).

However, some literature has pointed to potential negative effects of non-maternal care on child attachment and security during the first months or years of a child's life, noting increased chances of externalising aggression and disobedience (Belsky *et al.* 2007; Belsky, 2011). However, such negative behavioural problems are relatively short-lived and can be reduced through good quality and consistent care (Love *et al.*, 2003).

## Curriculum

The presence of a curriculum, or learning and well-being standards, can help ensure more consistency among ECEC services in a country or region. Curricula help prioritise certain learning elements and provide common goals for educators and centres (OECD, 2006). This is particularly important in unregulated ECEC environments, which often serve the youngest children.

A well-planned and co-ordinated curriculum is crucial. First, it ensures that important learning areas are covered. Second, the curriculum can act as a tool to shape staff behaviour to ensure continuous child development from age zero to compulsory, or even beyond compulsory, schooling. Such curricula help to promote a more even level of quality across age groups and provision; guide and support professional staff in their practice; facilitate communication between staff and parents; and ensure pedagogical continuity between ECEC and school (OECD, 2006).

## Physical environment

Research demonstrates that the design, layout and space of ECEC environments can influence a child's learning, creativity, behaviour and cultural interests (Dearing *et al.*, 2009). Cross cultural studies of preschool quality highlight that the quality of conditions for children's learning depend on physical space in addition to staff-child ratios and staff working environment (Sheridan and Schuster, 2001; Sheridan *et al.*, 2009). Specifically, well-defined spaces and boundaries are associated with more positive classroom interactions and increased time spent exploring environments (CCL, 2006). Based on research findings, numerous countries have set minimum "space per child" benchmarks, which gradually decrease with age (Childhood Resource and Research Unit, 2004).

## Staff gender and diversity

Women represent the overwhelming majority ECEC teachers and care givers in OECD countries. But it is important for children – particularly boys – to have a strong male role model in the classroom or centre. A reinforced male presence is critical to counter traditional views of women in child rearing and ensure that school and learning remain gender neutral (OECD, 2006).

Among the predominantly female workforce, there are few teachers coming from minority and ethnic communities. The diversity of staff is beneficial for children to open their minds to new ideas, counter stereotypes and encourage respect for multi-cultural learning (OECD, 2006).

## What are the policy implications?

### Applying the common regulatory standards for all forms of ECEC provision

Creating and consistently enforcing standards at different levels of the ECEC system sets a guarantee that a minimum level of safety, health and quality for children is ensured. For equity reasons, regulations need to apply to all settings, whether they are publicly or privately operated, and should cover infant-toddler, preschool and out-of-school provision. At the same time, regulations should recognise that different settings and age groups may require different standards. In order to meet standards, provision will need to be supported by a strong infrastructure of co-ordinated national-, state- and local-level mechanisms to assure adequate financing at a level that attracts and retains highly-trained early childhood staff (OECD, 2006).

One major difference in policy is the degree to which private (for-profit and non-profit) provision is covered in legislation. This is of particular concern, as, in many countries, the majority of children under age three attend settings in the private sector or are in informal arrangements (OECD, 2001).

### Ensuring affordable universal access and minimum standards

Governments are often faced with a challenge to choose between targeted higher quality provisions for disadvantaged groups or relatively low-quality programmes that are available to all (Dearing et al., 2009). In theory, targeted programmes are justified in compensating for social and economic disparity. But, in practice, there are problems trying to track dynamic patterns of disadvantage (Currie, 2001). Thus, targeted programmes focused on family income disparity may not be the best way to reach the groups most in need (Pianta, 2010). Research suggests that governments should sufficiently invest in pre-primary programmes for children ages zero to six, providing all parents with consistent and affordable options for their children. However, there remain competing ideas on the extent of public responsibility for the youngest children (ages zero to three) (OECD, 2006).

A real advantage of encouraging universal coverage is that universally covered ECEC systems generally organise services more equitably, observe higher standards and employ more qualified personnel. Universal access does not necessarily entail achieving full coverage, as, at different ages and in different family circumstances, there will be variation in need and demand for ECEC (OECD, 2006).

### Promoting participatory processes in defining minimum standards

Defining and assuring quality should be a participatory and democratic process, involving different groups, including children, parents, families and professionals who work with children. The way in which quality is developed and the priorities and perspectives which are emphasised may vary across countries; and the enforcement of regulations is more likely to succeed when the authorities engage in consultative policy making and management and build up a general consensus about the need and relevance of standards (OECD 2001; 2006).

## What is still unknown?

### *Long-term impacts of minimum standards*

Which specific minimum standards have the strongest lasting impact on children later in life is unclear. Research needs to provide more conclusive evidence on specific quality inputs, especially those with mixed findings, such as the lasting impact of small ECEC group sizes or the importance of indoor versus outdoor space for children. There is a need for research on the learning environments and physical conditions for young children in ECEC centres, including research on spaces that focus on the needs of young children.

### *Research to reflect complex realities*

Policy makers, families and stakeholders need to have additional literature on key threshold levels where impacts are more or less often felt (Burchinal *et al.*, 2010). There is also little research on which structural inputs work best in combination to improve key cognitive areas and socio-emotional skills. There is also little information on how key inputs are "received" by target groups. For example, we know that younger children (as a whole) can benefit from smaller group sizes, especially disadvantaged children, but evidence is lacking for girls and other sub-groups.

### *Impact of a diverse workforce on child development*

There is no solid research base on the effects of having a diverse workforce on child outcomes. Longitudinal studies could shed light on the impacts of an all-female staff on the subsequent performance of boys and girls in primary school and beyond as well as the impact or relevance of having ECEC staff with immigrant backgrounds on child outcomes.

### *Optimal assurance of non-regulated care services*

There is very little data and there are few monitoring practices on informal child care services, particularly affecting the zero-to-three age group. It is therefore important to explore innovative ways to ensure a minimum level of quality or minimum standards in non-regulated environments for the health, safety and well-being of children.

# REFERENCES

Belsky, J., D. Vandell, M. Burchinal , K.A. Clarke-Stewart, K. McCartney, M.T. Owen and The NICHD Early Child Care Research Network (2007), "Are There Long-term Effects of Early Child Care?", *Child Development*, Vol. 78, No. 2, pp. 681-701.

Belsky, J. (2011), "Child Care and Its Impact on Young Children", *Encyclopedia on Early Childhood Development*, Centre of Excellence for Early Childhood Development and Strategic Knowledge Cluster on Early Child Development, Montreal, available at: www.child-encyclopedia.com/pages/ PDF/BelskyANGxp3-Child_care.pdf, accessed 22 September 2011.

Bender *et al.* (2007), "Teachers' Education, Classroom Quality, and Young Children's Academic Skills: Results From Seven Studies of Preschool Programmes", *Child Development*, Vol. 78, No. 2, pp. 558-580.

Burchinal, M. *et al.* (2010), "Threshold Analysis of Association between Child Care Quality and Child Outcomes for Low-income Children in Pre-kindergarten Programmes", *Early Childhood Research Quarterly,* No. 25, pp. 166-176.

Canadian Council on Learning (CCL) (2006), "Why is High-Quality Child Care Essential? The link between Quality Child Care and Early Learning", *Lessons in Learning*, CCL, Ottawa.

Centre for Families, Work and Well-being (2000), *You bet I Care! A Canada-wide Study on Wages, Working Conditions and Practices in Child Care Centres*, Centre for Families, Work and Well-being, Guelph.

Childhood Resource and Research Unit (2004), "Quality Targets in Services for Young Children", working document for the Quality By Design project, Childhood Resource and Research Unit, Toronto.

Chetty, R. *et al.* (2011), "How Does Your Kindergarten Classroom affect Your Earnings? Evidence from Project Star", *Quarterly Journal of Economics*, forthcoming.

Cunha, F., J. Heckman, L. Lochner and D.V. Masterov (2005), "Interpreting the Evidence of Life-Cycle Skill Formation", *IZA Discussion Paper Series 1575*, Institute for the Study of Labour (IZA), Bonn, Germany.

Cunha, F. and J.J. Heckman (2010), "Investing in Our Young People", *IZA Discussion Papers 5050*, Institute for the Study of Labor (IZA), Bonn, Germany.

Currie, J. (2001), "Early Childhood Education Programmes", *Journal of Economic Perspectives*, Vol. 15, No. 2, pp. 213-238.

Dearing, E., K. McCartney and B. A. Taylor (2009), "Does Higher Quality Early Child Care Promote Low-Income Children's Math and Reading Achievement in Middle Childhood?", *Child Development*, Vol. 80, No. 5, pp.1329-1349.

Elliott, A. (2006), "Early Childhood Education: Pathways to Quality and Equity for all Children", *Australian Education review,* 50, 2006.

Eurydice (2009), Early Childhood Education and Care in Europe: Tackling Social and Cultural Inequalities, Eurydice, Brussels.

Glass, G. (2004), "More than Teacher Directed or Child Initiated: Preschool Curriculum Type, Parent Involvement, and Children's Outcomes in the Child-Parent Centres", *Education Policy Analysis Archives*, Vol. 12, No. 72, pp. 1-38.

Heckman J. J., S. H. Moon, R. Pinto, P. A. Savelyev and A. Yavitz (2009), "The Rate of Return to the HighScope Perry Preschool Program", *Journal of Public Economics*, Vol. 94, No. 1-2, pp. 114-128

Love, J. M. *et al.* (2003), *Child Care Quality Matters: How Conclusions May Vary With Context*, Department of Child, Youth and Family Studies, University of Nebraska, Lincoln.

Melhuish, E. C. *et al.* (2004), "The Effective Provision of Pre-School Education (EPPE) Project: Findings from Pre-school to end of Key Stage 1", *Sure Start*, United Kingdom.

National Institute for Early Education Research (NIEER) (2003), "Low Wages = Low Quality: Solving the Real Preschool Teacher Crisis", *Policy Brief*, NIEER, New Jersey.

NIEER (2004), "Class Size: What's the Best Fit?" *Policy Brief*, NIEER, New Jersey.

NIEER (2006), "Increasing the Effectiveness of Preschool Programmes", *Policy Brief*, NIEER, New Jersey.

OECD (2001), Starting Strong I: Early Childhood Education and Care, OECD, Paris.

OECD (2006), Starting Strong II: Early Childhood Education and Care, OECD, Paris.

OECD (2011), PISA in Focus 1: Does participation in pre-primary education translate into better learning outcomes at school?, OECD, Paris.

Pianta, R. C., W. S. Barnett, M. Burchinal and K. R. Thornburg (2009), "The Effects of Preschool Education: What We Know, How Public Policy Is or Is Not Aligned With the Evidence Base, and What We Need to Know", *Psychological Science in the Public Interest*, Vol.10, No. 2, pp. 49-88.

Sammons, P. et al. (2002), The Effective Provision of Pre-School Education (EPPE) Project: Technical Paper 8a - Measuring the Impact of Pre-School on Children's Cognitive Progress over the Pre-School Period, London: DfES/Institute of Education, University of London.

Schweinhart, L. (2006), "Preschool Programmes", *Encyclopedia on Early Childhood Development*, Centre of Excellence for Early Childhood Development and Strategic Knowledge Cluster on Early Child Development, Montreal, available at: www.child-encyclopedia.com/pages/PDF/SchweinhartANGxp.pdf, accessed 22 September 2011.

Sheridan, S., J. Giota, Y. M. Han, and J. Y. Kwon (2009), "A cross-cultural study of preschool quality in South Korea and Sweden: ECERS evaluations. *The Early Childhood Research Quarterly*, *24*, 142-156.

Sheridan, S. and K.-M. Schuster (2001), "Evaluations of Pedagogical Quality in Early Childhood Education - A cross-national perspective", Department of Education, University of Gothenburg, Sweden, *Journal of Research in Childhood Education*, Fall/Winter 2001, Vol. 16, No. 1, pp. 109-124.

Shonkoff, J. P. and A. D. Philips (2000), *From Neurons to Neighbourhoods,* National Academy Press, Washington DC.

Smith, A. (2003), "School Completion/Academic Achievement-Outcomes of Early Childhood Education", *Encyclopedia on Early Childhood Development*, Centre of Excellence for Early Childhood Development and Strategic Knowledge Cluster on Early Child Development, Montreal, available at: www.child-encyclopedia.com/Pages/PDF/SmithANGxp.pdf, accessed 22 September 2011.

UNESCO (2004), "Curriculum in Early Childhood Education and Care", *UNESCO Policy Brief on Early Childhood,* No. 26, UNESCO, Paris.

Vandenbroeck, M. (2011), "Diversity in Early Childhood Services", *Encyclopedia on Early Childhood Development*, Centre of Excellence for Early Childhood Development and Strategic Knowledge Cluster on Early Child Development, Montreal, available at: www.child-encyclopedia.com/pages/PDF/VandenbroeckANGxp1.pdf, accessed 22 September 2011.

# ACTION AREA 2 – BROADENING PERSPECTIVES THROUGH INTERNATIONAL COMPARISON

This section contains international comparisons of:

- Policy goals
- Minimum standards

## POLICY GOALS

### Findings

- "Equity measures" is the most commonly cited policy goal of ECEC, followed by "public responsibility and investment". This indicates that governments aim to establish fair and inclusive ECEC systems, accessible for all children, and that they regard ECEC services as public goods. ECEC policy is designed as not only as part of education and child care policy but also labour market policy. In fact, "facilitating work-life balance" and "increasing maternal labour participation" are referenced as goals of ECEC. While ECEC is often referenced as a means to tackle falling fertility rates and respond to the needs of increasing immigrant children, only a few countries consider ECEC as a tool for "tackling demographic challenges" (Figure 1.3).

- The most frequently cited focus of quality goals in ECEC is related to learning standards, curriculum and pedagogy. They are considered effective tools to guide ECEC staff to improve their instruction strategies and, thus, enhance child development. Another frequently cited focus includes "workforce/working conditions", recognising the importance of staff to facilitate better child development. While it is difficult to steer by policy interventions, "parental and community engagement" is also cited as a quality goal by many respondents. Although "monitoring and evaluation" as well as "regulations" are typical government steering tools, they are less frequently cited than the formerly mentioned focuses. A few countries regard "equity" as part of quality goals. Some countries do not set out any quality-specific goals (Figure 1.4).

For more detail, see the Survey Response Table on "Policy Goals" (Excel$^{TM}$ file) in the online Quality Toolbox at **www.oecd.org/edu/earlychildhood/toolbox**.

**Figure 1.3. Overall policy goals for ECEC[2]**

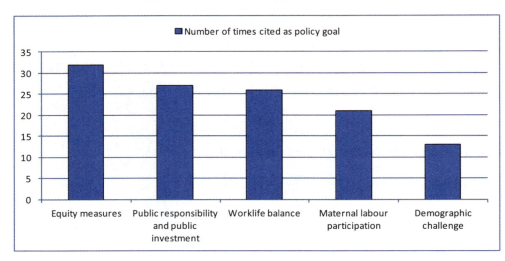

Note: Countries were given a list of example policy goals to choose from based on *Starting Strong II* (2006). Respondents may list more than one policy goal.

*Source*: OECD Network on Early Childhood Education and Care's "Survey for the Quality Toolbox and ECEC Portal", June 2011.

**Figure 1.4. Focus on quality goals in ECEC[3]**

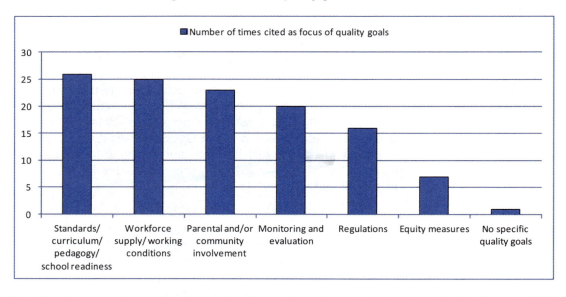

Note: Countries were given a list of example policy goals to choose from based on *Starting Strong II* (2006). Respondents may list more than one policy goal.

*Source*: OECD Network on Early Childhood Education and Care's "Survey for the Quality Toolbox and ECEC Portal", June 2011.

## Definitions and methodologies

**Policy goals** refer to the aims and expected outcomes of ECEC policies. They can give early childhood services their overall orientation but also contribute to specific areas. The OECD's *Starting Strong II* (2006) identified five overall ECEC policy goals, providing potential responses for the OECD survey (Figure 1.3):

1. **Maternal labour participation**: responds to the rise of the service economy and the influx of women into salaried employment.

2. **Work life balance**: reconciles work and family responsibilities, especially in a manner more equitable for women.

3. **Demographic challenges**: responds to changes in fertility rates and continuing migration/ immigration.

4. **Equity measures**: refers to the idea that the ECEC system should be fair and inclusive, acting against child poverty and educational disadvantage.

5. **Public responsibility and investment**: recognises ECEC as a public good.

The findings presented here are based on data from the OECD Network on ECEC's "Survey for the Quality Toolbox and ECEC Portal" (2011) and on the OECD's desk-based research. For each graph and table, the countries or regions for which data is used are listed.

## MINIMUM STANDARDS

## Findings

- Minimum standards are generally set for structural quality indicators, such as staff-child ratio and indoor and outdoor space. Different standards are often set for different ECEC settings or different age groups of children.

### *Staff-child ratio*

- Children in kindergarten and preschool (or children in the older age bracket[4]) tend to have less staff per child than those in care centres (or children in the age category zero to three[5]) (Figure 1.5). This goes well with the research finding that closer supervision and care matter more for younger children than older ones (see "Research Brief: Minimum Standards Matter").

- Across 19 OECD countries[6], on average, it is regulated that a kindergarten or preschool staff member can have, at most, 18 children; while a child care staff member, on average, can have only seven children at most in a child care centre

- Family or domestic care services tend to be regulated with stricter staff-child ratios than kindergarten/preschool or child care centres, and there is little data available on family day care. The average ratio, among the countries with available data, is five children per staff (Figure 1.6).

### *Space per child*

- In general, indoor space requirements are largest for family day care, followed by child care centres and kindergarten/preschool (Figure 1.7). The OECD average for regulated indoor space per child is set at 2.9m² per child for kindergarten/preschool, while it is 3.6m² for care centres. The OECD average outdoor space requirement per child is 7m² in kindergarten, while it is 8.9m² in child care (Figures 1.8).

- A wider range can be found across countries for outdoor than indoor requirements for both kindergarten and childcare centres.

## Figure 1.5. Regulated maximum number of children per staff member in ECEC

**Panel A: In kindergarten or preschool (three years to compulsory schooling age for integrated systems)**

**Panel B: In child care (zero-to-three-year-olds for integrated systems)**

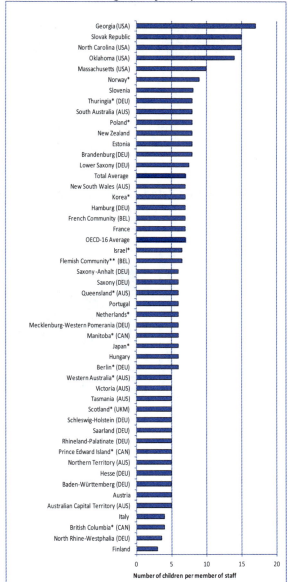

\* Jurisdictions with separate regulations for staff-child ratio for different age groups, the data given is based on: 3-6-yearolds attending for 5-7 hours per day regarding Berlin; and 4-year-olds regarding Korea.

\*\* The figure for Norway applies only to qualified kindergarten teachers, whereas regulation stipulates that if other staff will also be present in the kindergarten setting, the number of children per member of staff is effectively lower. The figure for Norway is based on regulation for 3-6-yearolds.

\* Jurisdictions with separate regulations for different age groups, the data given is based on: Berlin (DEU), 2-3-year-olds (attending 5-7 hours per day); British Columbia (CAN), 0-3-year-olds; Israel, 2-3-year-olds; Japan, 1-2-year-olds (while the country has different ratios in place for different ages: the ratio for age 0 is 1:3; age 1-2, 1:6; age 3, 1:20; and age 4, 1:30 – only data regarding 1-2-year-olds is included in the figure); Korea, 2-year-olds; Manitoba (CAN), 2-3-year-olds; Netherlands, 2-3-year-olds; Norway, 0-3-year-olds; Prince Edward Island (CAN), 2-3-year-olds; Queensland (AUS) 2-3-year-olds; Scotland (UKM), 2-3-year-olds; Thuringia (DEU), 2-3-year-olds; Western Australia (AUS), 2-3-year-olds. For Poland, when there is a disabled child in the playroom, the ratio is set at 1:5.

\*\*Subsidised facilities only

Note: Countries who reported averages for staff-child ratio instead of a minimum requirement in the Survey have not been included in the graphs, as averages do not constitute a regulated <u>minimum </u>requirement. When regulated ratios were indicated as maximum number per children per multiple staff members (*e.g.*, 2:15), the number included in the figure has been calculated based on the maximum number of children for one member of staff (*e.g.*, 2:15 has been re-calculated into 1:7.5).

Note on Panel A: OECD-19 Average is only based on data reported for OECD countries, excluding regions and territories, and is calculated based on data from: Austria, Czech Republic, Estonia, Finland, France, Hungary, Ireland, Israel, Italy, Japan, Korea, Netherlands, New Zealand, Norway, Portugal, Slovak Republic, Slovenia, Spain and Turkey.

Note on Panel B: OECD-16 Average is only based on data reported for OECD countries, excluding regions and territories, and is calculated based on data from: Austria, Estonia, Finland, France, Hungary, Israel, Italy, Japan, Korea, Netherlands, New Zealand, Norway, Poland, Portugal, Slovak Republic and Slovenia.

The Total Average is based on data for all countries and jurisdictions included in the respective figures.

*Source*: OECD Network on Early Childhood Education and Care's "Survey for the Quality Toolbox and ECEC Portal", June 2011.

**Figure 1.6. Regulated maximum number of children per care giver in family of domestic care**

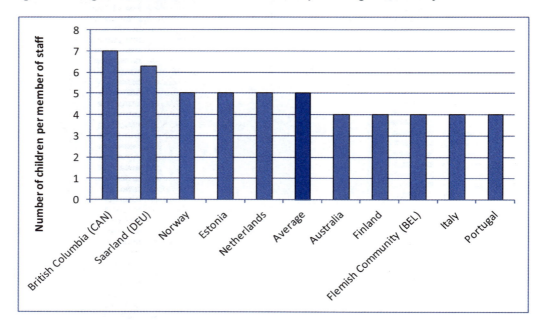

Note: Countries who reported averages for staff-child ratio instead of a minimum requirement in the Survey have not been included in the graphs, as averages do not constitute a regulated <u>minimum </u>requirement. For Australia, the figure is based on the maximum number of children per caregiver in family day care for children below the compulsory schooling age. For the Flemish Community of Belgium, data regards subsidised Family Day Care Centres only.

*Source*: OECD Network on Early Childhood Education and Care's "Survey for the Quality Toolbox and ECEC Portal", June 2011.

**Figure 1.7. Minimum required space per child across different types of ECEC**

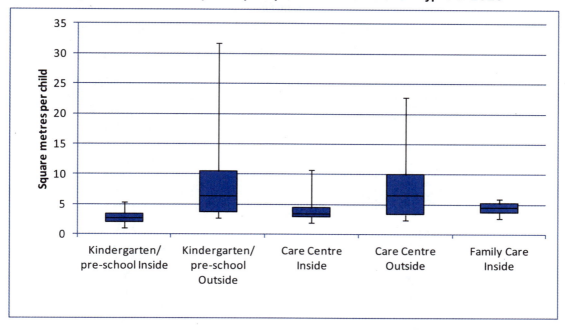

Note: Horizontal black lines mark the median value in minimum space; vertical black lines show the range (difference in smallest and largest value of minimum space requirement between countries). Reported averages in the Survey have not been included in the graphs, as they do not constitute a minimum requirement. Based on Survey responses from the following countries or regions:

— For Kindergartens Inside: Austria, Baden-Wurttemberg (DEU), Berlin (DEU), Czech Republic, Denmark, Estonia, Hamburg (DEU), Ireland, Israel, Italy, Lower Saxony (DEU), Manitoba (CAN), Netherlands, New Zealand, North Rhine Westphalia (DEU), Norway, Poland, Portugal, Saarland (DEU), Saxony (DEU), Slovak Republic, Slovenia, Thuringia (DEU) and Turkey.

— For Kindergartens Outside: Baden-Wurttemberg (DEU), Berlin (DEU), Czech Republic, Estonia, Israel, Italy, Lower Saxony (DEU), Netherlands, New Zealand, North Rhine-Westphalia (DEU), Norway, Prince Edward Island (CAN), Saarland (DEU), Saxony (DEU), Slovak Republic, Slovenia, Thuringia (DEU) and Turkey.

— For Care Centres Inside: Austria, Baden-Wurttemberg (DEU), Berlin (DEU), British Columbia (CAN), Estonia, Finland, Flemish Community (BEL), French Community (BEL), Hamburg (DEU), Ireland, Italy, Japan, Korea, Lower Saxony (DEU), Manitoba (CAN), Massachusetts (USA), Netherlands, New Zealand, North Rhine Westphalia (DEU), Norway, Poland, Portugal, Prince Edward Island (CAN), Saarland (DEU), Saxony (DEU), Scotland (UKM), Slovak Republic, Slovenia , Spain and Thuringia (DEU).

— For Care Centres Outside: Baden-Wurttemberg (DEU), Berlin (DEU), British Columbia (CAN), Flemish Community (BEL), Italy, Korea, Lower Saxony (DEU), Manitoba (CAN), Massachusetts (USA), Netherlands, New Zealand, North Rhine-Westphalia (DEU), Norway, Prince Edward Island (CAN), Saxony (DEU), Slovak Republic, Slovenia and Thuringia (DEU).

— For Family/Domestic Care: Estonia, French Community (BEL), Italy and Slovenia.

*Source*: OECD Network on Early Childhood Education and Care's "Survey for the Quality Toolbox and ECEC Portal", June 2011.

### Figure 1.8. Minimum space requirements as m² per child in kindergarten/preschool and child care centres

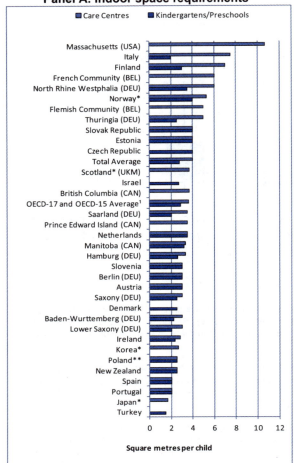

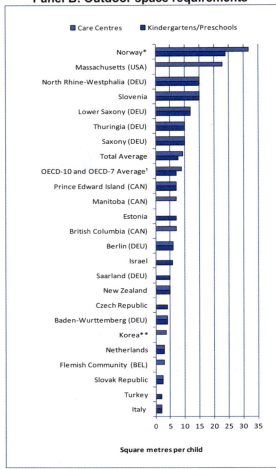

\* Jurisdictions with separate regulation for different age groups, the data given is based on: Ireland, 1-2-year-olds for care; Japan's data regards infants only; Norway, 0-3-year-olds for care, and 3-6-year-olds for kindergarten; Scotland 0-3-year-olds.

\*\* In Poland, the indoor space requirement for Care Centres and Kindergarten Points/Centres for a maximum of 5 children is set at 16m². For each additional child, the minimum indoor space requirement is 2.5m² per child. Kindergartens have higher and more detailed standards for public buildings, around 2.5 to 3m².

¹ OECD-17 Average refers to indoor space requirements for kindergarten/preschool; OECD-15 Average refers to indoor space requirements for child care.

Note: Japan's indoor requirements are set at 1.65m² per child for toddlers and 1.98m² per child for infants. In addition, space for kindergarten is regulated as 180m² per class and number of classes x180+100m² if the number is more than 2. Since the indoor space for kindergartens depends on the number of classes, the country is not included in this figure for kindergarten.

\* For Norway, the figure for care centres is based on regulation for 0-3-year-olds, whereas the kindergarten figure is for 3-6-year-olds. The minimum outdoor space requirement in Norway is six times the minimum requirement for indoor space.

\*\* Korea has a set space requirement per child for care centres but employs a formula for regulating space in kindergartens; therefore, only a minimum requirement for care has been included in the figure.

¹ OECD-10 Average refers to outdoor space requirements for kindergarten; OECD-7 Average refers to outdoor space requirements in child care.

Note: Japan's minimum outdoor requirements depend on the number of classes, and the country is therefore not included in this figure. The regulation of outdoor space for child care is referential standards. For kindergarten, it is regulated by the number of classes. If it is one class, 320m²; two, 420m²; three classes or more, 400m² +80x (the number of classes-3).

Note: Reported averages in the Survey have not been included in the graphs, as they do not constitute a minimum requirement.

Note on Panel A: OECD-17 Average regarding indoor space requirements for kindergarten/preschool is only based on data reported for OECD countries, excluding regions and territories, and is calculated based on data from: Austria, Czech Republic, Denmark, Estonia, Finland, Ireland, Israel, Italy, Netherlands, New Zealand, Norway, Poland, Portugal, Slovak Republic, Slovenia, Spain, and Turkey. OECD-15 Average regarding indoor space requirements for child care is based on the following countries: Austria, Estonia, Finland, Ireland, Italy, Japan, Korea, Netherlands, New Zealand, Norway, Poland, Portugal, Slovak Republic, Slovenia and Spain.

Note on Panel B: OECD-10 Average regarding outdoor space requirements for kindergarten/preschool is only based on data reported for OECD countries, excluding regions and territories, and is calculated based on data from: Czech Republic, Estonia, Israel, Italy, Netherlands, New Zealand, Norway, Slovak Republic, Slovenia and Turkey. OECD-7 Average regarding outdoor door space requirements for child care is based on the following countries: Italy, Netherlands, New Zealand, Norway, Slovak Republic, Slovenia and Turkey.

The Total Average is based on data for all countries and jurisdictions included in the respective figures.

*Source*: OECD Network on Early Childhood Education and Care's "Survey for the Quality Toolbox and ECEC Portal", June 2011.

For more detail, see the Survey Response Table on "Minimum Quality Standards" (Excel™ file) in the online Quality Toolbox at **www.oecd.org/edu/earlychildhood/ toolbox.**

## Definitions and methodology

Minimum standards are often referred to as structural inputs that can enable "adequate" or "good enough" quality ECEC provisions. The data is broken down into three major types of ECEC and can be defined as follows:

- **Centre-based day-care**: encompasses all child care that is provided outside the home in licensed centres. The services provided can be full- or part-time and are most commonly referred to as nurseries, day care centres, *crèches*, playschools and parent-run groups. All respondents enrol children from the age of zero in centre-based care services.

- **Family day care**: is traditionally provided in a home setting. This can be at the childminder's home or at the child's own home where a qualified or registered childminder looks after the child. Among respondents, all family day care services begin at birth (0+ years), with the exceptions of Mexico and Norway, where child care is available from birth but where most children start attending day care at the age of one.

- **Preschool early education programmes (Kindergartens):** includes centre- or school-based programmes designed to meet the needs of children preparing to enter primary education. In most countries, these programmes include at least 50% educational content and are supervised by qualified staff. With the exception of countries with an integrated ECEC system such as Norway, New Zealand and Sweden, which provide integrated pedagogical settings covering age zero or one to compulsory schooling age, almost all respondents enrol only an older age bracket in kindergartens/preschools – usually from three or four years of age until compulsory primary schooling starts.

The findings presented here are based on data from the OECD Network on ECEC's "Survey for the Quality Toolbox and ECEC Portal" (2011) and on the OECD's desk-based research. For each graph and table, the countries or regions for which data is used are listed (if not presented in the graph).

# ACTION AREA 3 – SELECTING A STRATEGY OPTION

This section contains lists of strategy options to tackle the following challenges:

- Setting quality goals
- Designing and implementing quality regulations and standards

## SETTING QUALITY GOALS

### Challenge 1: Building consensus on the goals

Building consensus among ECEC practitioners and managers, parents and policy makers on the goals for quality improvement or on the role or scope of ECEC can be challenging because they have differing views and expectations of "quality" in ECEC.

Policy makers may wish to design policies to improve quality based on research; however, there is often a lack of knowledge on which quality aspects matter in ECEC. Furthermore, there are often competing – not understood as complementary – views on what the focus of ECEC should be, for example, to support female labour participation, to address child poverty and disadvantages or to ensure granting it as public goods.

*Clarifying the role and scope of ECEC*

- **Flanders** (**Belgium**) is preparing a Child Care Decree (for zero to three years) which intends to lay down the economic, pedagogic and social role and concrete organisation of child care and is supposed to create clarity and coherence in child care provision by providing information on affordability, accessibility, monitoring, definition and scope.

- In **Norway**, the responsibility for ECEC/kindergartens was transferred from the auspices of the Ministry of Children and Family Affairs to the Ministry of Education and Research in 2006. By transferring the responsibility for kindergartens to the Ministry of Education and Research, the government acknowledged the role of kindergartens as a first step in lifelong learning and as part of an active policy to reduce differences in society. Important policy goals regarding ECEC since the current government took office in 2005 include: coverage of kindergarten places, maximum parental fees, equality in the financing of municipal and non-municipal kindergartens and aiming at stimulating high quality in ECEC.

- **Czech Republic** set the main objectives of preschool as follows: preschools should facilitate children's development and their ability to learn, enable children to acquire the basic values on which the Czech society is based, and enable them to learn how to become independent and express themselves as individuals in relation to their surroundings. The essential role of ECEC policy in the Czech Republic is equal access for all children, including those with special educational needs, children from problematic social backgrounds and foreigners. These objectives and goals were clearly stated to the ECEC sector and the general public.

- In **Finland**, the Government Resolution Concerning the National Policy Definition on Early Childhood Education and Care, issued in February 2002, sets out a definition and the key principles for ECEC. The document indicates that the primary responsibility for nurturing and educating children lies with their parents, but that it is society's role to support parents in exercising their responsibility in this area. The process of caring for, nurturing and educating children should form a seamless whole which flexibly supports the individual development of each child at every stage of the child's growth and education.

- In 2008, under the adoption of the School Act, **Slovak Republic** made kindergartens a part of the Slovakian school system. The term "day care centre" was also abolished and replaced with the term "preschool institution" for all forms of ECEC. This further clarifies and emphasises the educational goals the government has in mind regarding ECEC.

- **Sweden** emphasised the educational scope and goal of ECEC during the 1990s when preschooling and school-age child care were being integrated at the state level with primary school, and its responsibilities shifted to the Ministry of Education. The government made this decision because it wanted to move away from the idea of child care as a part of family policy and aimed at moving towards preschool as part of the education system with a stronger focus on development and learning.

*Encouraging inter-sectoral collaboration*

- The government of **Manitoba** (**Canada**) affirmed its commitment to children and families through the proclamation of the Healthy Child Manitoba (HCM) Act in December 2007. The HCM Act recognises that the health and wealth of Manitoba's future is directly tied to the quality of investments in children and youth; and it commits the provincial government to inter-sectoral government collaboration, evidence-based decision-making, and increased investments in prevention and early intervention, particularly in the area of early childhood. Healthy Child Manitoba represents a cross-departmental and child-centred approach to best meet the holistic needs of children and youth as they grow within their families and communities. The shared work of nine government departments, in collaboration with many community partners, is to develop, integrate, implement and evaluate policies, programmes and services to help its youngest citizens and their families achieve their fullest potential.

- The government of **Prince Edward Island (Canada)** affirmed its commitment to children and families through the establishment of the Children's Secretariat in 2000. The Children's Secretariat is a group of community and government representatives working across sectors, communities and departments as a collective voice to improve outcomes for children up to age eight. In essence, the Secretariat is "a network of networks" that links with other existing networks and coalitions who are working on behalf of young children and their families. The focus is on profiling healthy child development, promoting knowledge exchange and public education, inspiring action, and influencing policy. The Children's Secretariat membership includes representatives from seven government departments and 12 community networks.

## Challenge 2: Aligning goals to stimulate quality provision

Setting out goals is a common first step that countries take to explicitly express political commitment. It is used as a framework to harmonise actions across different stakeholders. However, setting out quality goals is one thing, while implementing them is another.

Goal setting with a bottom-up approach has strengths and weaknesses. There will be a sense of ownership among the group involved in setting out a particular goal for their sector; however, it may compete with another goal set by a different group for their sector. There should be a coherent framework so that all planned actions can move in an agreed upon direction without cancelling out the effects of each action.

Aligning ECEC goals with compulsory education reforms, which receive considerable policy attention and budgets, can be a driving force for implementation. However, goals set out for ECEC are often not well aligned with the goals set for primary or other levels of education.

### *Setting out comprehensive quality goals for the ECEC sector*

- All governments of states and territories in **Australia** agreed in July 2009 to an overarching National Early Childhood Development Strategy (Investing in the Early Years) to ensure that by 2020 all children have the best start in life to create a better future for themselves and for the nation. As part of this Strategy, all jurisdictions signed up to the National Partnership Agreement on the National Quality Agenda for Early Childhood Education and Care in December 2009 in specific recognition of the importance of high quality, accessible and affordable ECEC for children and families in achieving better outcomes for Australian children. The National Partnership Agreement sits under the umbrella of the broader National Early Childhood Development Strategy. Additionally, Australia has the Melbourne Declaration on Educational Goals for Young Australians.

- The **China** Development Research Foundation (CDRF) initiated, in collaboration with local governments in Ledu County (Qinghai Province) and Xundian County (Yunnan Province) a pilot programme on Early Childhood Development in September 2009, which has the goal to enhance early child development and fight poverty in poor rural areas. The programme was implemented in Early Education Centres. ECEC is used as an anti-poverty measure, and their goals are to improve nutritional conditions of infants and raise the early education coverage rate with sufficient quality in these areas.

- In 2008, **Manitoba (Canada)** launched Family Choices: Manitoba's Five-Year Agenda for Early Learning and Child Care, which includes the goals of Manitoba to improve the accessibility and universality, affordability and quality of child care throughout the province. Within the Family Choices agenda, Manitoba has explicitly set out to improve quality in ECEC centres since evidence-based research demonstrates that quality early learning environments result in improved outcomes for children and their families.

- **Spain** has set out the following policy goals: to provide free provision of ECEC to the second cycle of pre-primary education (three-to-six-year-olds), to establish minimum requirements for institutions offering ECEC to zero-to-three-year-olds, and to decentralise the curriculum. Additionally, a plan, called *Educa3*, has been developed to increase the number of ECEC places for zero-to-three-year-olds and promote the quality of materials and workforce in ECEC.

- In May 2010, the Province of **Prince Edward Island (Canada)** launched the Preschool Excellence Initiative: Securing the Future for Our Children. The overall aim is to build an early childhood system that is accessible, sustainable and quality-driven and also recognises the need for parental choice. The initiative addresses the needs of different actors in ECEC: children, parents, providers and staff. The specific goal is to help Island children by: providing a high-quality learning environment; stimulating and fostering creativity, discovery and a love of learning; ensuring indoor and outdoor play-based learning experiences; ensuring that all early childhood personnel are trained and certified; and expanding early learning opportunities for Island children with special needs. Besides this, the province stated it will try to help parents by moderating parent fees, providing new and expanded options for infant care in family home settings, and giving parents a voice through Parents' Advisory Committees. Needs of ECEC staff were met by aiming at increasing the wages for certified early childhood educators, developing and delivering new entry-level and one-year training programmes for all early childhood staff, and providing a new opportunity for early childhood educators to become self-employed through the establishment of Infant Homes. Lastly, regarding operators, the document includes goals, such as providing professional development and advisory support to supervisors and owner-operators and providing one-time funding to those who wish to retire their licences. These quality goals are expected to improve the level of quality of ECEC in Prince Edward Island and increase staff and parent satisfaction.

- **Korea** initiated two comprehensive mid-term plans in 2009 to reduce the parental burdens of child-rearing costs and provide quality education and care to young children: the *I-Sarang* (Child-Loving) Plan of child care and the Plan for the Advancement of Early Childhood Education. Under the vision of "building a future-oriented preschool where young children are happy", the latter plan by the Ministry of Education, Science and Technology manifested the provision of high-quality early childhood education for children and parents in a tangible way as the top priority goal. The *I-Sarang Plan* by the Ministry of Health and Welfare also places great emphasis on the nation's responsibility for quality child care. Furthermore, initiation of a common curriculum (*Nuri Curriculum*) for children age five in kindergartens and child care centres was announced in May 2011 and will be implemented from March 2012 to ensure high-quality education and care.

– The **French Community** of **Belgium** drafted the "Code of quality of care" at the community level that sets out the quality principles of care for children ages zero to twelve for all child care providers. The Code is laid down in the Decree of Government of the French Community of December 2003. It provides consistency of good qualitative child care. Every child care provider is required to implement quality aspects in accordance with the Code.

– In 2008, **British Columbia** (**Canada**) created a framework for early learning for children from birth to kindergarten entry that goes beyond overall policy for ECEC. This policy document, British Columbia Early Learning Framework, articulates a vision for young children's learning for all service providers working in the ECEC sector and creates greater understanding of the vital importance of early learning for all children.

– The Action Programme for Promotion of Early Childhood Education in **Japan** was formulated in October 2006 as a comprehensive action plan focusing on the educational requirements in recognised *kodomo-en* (child centres). In Japan, traditionally, policies have always been developed from the perspective of fulfilling the basic role of "equity in educational opportunities" and "maintenance and improvement of educational standards". With regard to nursery centres, an Action Programme to Improve the Quality of Nursery Centres was formulated in March 2008.

– The Ministry of Labour and Social Solidarity of **Portugal** launched the System for Quality Improvement of Social Services, which includes child care services. This system was created and implemented by the Institute for Social Security to promote high quality in the provision of social services. The programme's purpose is to ensure that citizens have access to quality social services that satisfy their needs and expectations. The system is based upon a number of criteria and specific requirements for the evaluation of quality and the client's degree of satisfaction. Another objective of this programme is to establish a series of minimum requirements for new buildings and for the adaptation of existing buildings, ensuring their safety and quality. Once all the requirements are fulfilled, the organisation may ask for certification and receive a "Quality Mark". There are three levels of certification (C, B and A) depending on the stage of development of the quality requirements. Level A corresponds to the highest quality.

*Introducing the quality goals at different education levels*

– In 2007, **Finland** developed a new Strategy for Special Needs Education for both pre-primary education and basic education. The Ministry of Education appointed a steering group to prepare a proposal for a long-term strategy for the development of pre-primary and basic special education. The quality goals for special education at both education levels have been streamlined in the new strategy.

- In April 2008, the government of **Prince Edward Island (Canada)** decided to integrate kindergarten into the public school system by September 2010 and to align the goals of pre-primary education and primary school to smooth the transition between the two education levels. With the integration of the two systems and aligning the goals, early education and primary schooling ensured a more continuous learning structure.

- Policies to promote high-quality ECEC services in **Norway** have, over the last five years, included policy development and legislation, monitoring and supervision, and strategic plans. Norway allotted means to raise the competence and support the recruitment of preschool teachers and qualified staff in the sector. By supporting research programmes, there has been an increase in the grants for research in the field of ECEC. The legislation on kindergartens from 2005 clarified the roles of owners, municipalities and county governors, regulated maximum parental fees and equal public financing of public and private institutions, and supported children's agency through a right to participation (*i.e.*, to have the right to express their views on the day-to-day activities of the kindergarten) for each child. This was followed by a revised Framework Plan for the Content and Tasks of Kindergartens. The plan describes the societal role of kindergartens and emphasises the importance of adults' attitudes, knowledge and ability to relate to and understand children, so that they can bring up children to participate actively in a democratic society. Legislation was followed by support material. The policy for quality also included grants to the National Center for Multicultural Education to initiate education in the field of multilingualism and multiculturalism.

## Challenge 3: Implementation – translating goals into actions

Translating goals into action is a challenge in virtually all OECD countries. First and foremost, successful implementation requires full support and buy-in from stakeholders who are at the front-line of implementation. Gaining their support and buy-in requires strategic thinking, a realistic timeline, sufficient funding and strong political leadership.

In reality, however, many countries report that there are not sufficient financial or human resources allocated for the implementation of goals. They feel they do not have sufficient knowledge on managing the implementation process; and they often find that the implementation plan is not realistically drafted under the pressure to complete it within the election cycle.

*Designing laws or policy papers to stimulate fulfilment of goals*

- In **Mexico**, to ensure that the goal of increased ECEC participation is being met, the national government reformed Articles 3 and 31 of the Mexican Constitution in 2002. The reform included a change to make preschool education compulsory. This increased participation in ECEC, especially among four- and five-year-olds.

- In 2009, the government of **Norway** presented a White Paper to the Parliament focusing exclusively on the quality of kindergartens in Norway.

Three main aims were presented in the paper: 1) ensuring equity and high quality in all kindergartens; 2) strengthening the kindergarten as an arena for learning and development; and 3) making sure that all children have the opportunity to participate actively in a safe and inclusive kindergarten environment. The paper describes the status and challenges in this field and makes propositions for actions toward the development of high and equitable quality in all kindergartens. Pending on the White Paper, two public commissions have been set up: one to give advice on the steering of the sector, another to propose different measures to secure high-quality, structured ECEC for all children.

- In **Poland**, in order to increase participation in ECEC, several reforms in the education system were introduced: the School Education Act of 1991 has been revised, leading to compulsory school education from age six onwards, whereas it used to be seven, and compulsory preschool education for five-year-olds. Additionally, new regulations were introduced allowing for the provision of ECEC services in institutions other than traditional kindergartens, such as kindergarten centres and points. These institutions have to implement the same standard curriculum but can operate on different hours than traditional kindergartens and are easier to establish. The changes in regulations led to an increase in the ECEC participation rate of three-to-five-year-olds from about 45% in 2006/07 to 65% in 2010/11.

- The White Paper on Education in **Slovenia** (1995) emphasises that the quality education and permanent professional training of professional workers in preschools represents a fundamental condition for their professionalism, autonomy and accountability. The White Paper served as the basis for systemic and legislative changes regarding quality enhancement in ECEC and education.

- States and territories in **Australia** signed the Melbourne Declaration on Educational Goals for Young Australians. The Declaration states the goals Australia aims to achieve for their youngest population group.

- In 2011, **Manitoba** (**Canada**) passed The Preparing Students for Success Act, requiring an early learning and child care facility to be included in all new schools and major renovations to existing schools. This Act contributes to the goal of Manitoba to ensure improved access and provision to ECEC for all children and families and ensures that new ECEC structures are being established.

*Allocating funding for implementation of quality goals*

- Municipalities in **Flanders** (**Belgium**) experienced a sharp increase in the number of pupils attending nursery and primary education, so extra teaching periods have been allocated to schools according to statutory funding tables. The extra teaching periods include an increase in funding for personnel/staff. A recalculation of funding allocation is performed as soon as the school's number of pupils in mainstream primary education experiences a rise of at least 12 pupils on the first school day of October 2010, in comparison with the year before. A decrease of 12 pupils and over is also deducted at a rate of one teaching period (with the allocated amount) per pupil from the teaching periods.

- In **Australia**, the government is investing funds to support the introduction of the new National Quality Framework for Early Childhood Education and Care. In addition, Australia is providing financial support in the form of one-off grants to Long Day Care services in disadvantaged areas to allow them to prepare for the National Quality Framework.

- **Spain** has set out to increase the number of places in ECEC for zero-to-three-year-olds (cycle one). To achieve this goal, the government has provided funding to open new public pre-primary schools, enlarge already existing facilities, and turn regular day care facilities into more education-oriented services for young children. A total of EUR 1 087 million has been budgeted for 2008-12 for this and for the improvement of the level of quality of these provisions by, for example, increasing the provision of training for ECEC professionals.

- **Korea** increased investment in ECEC to 0.62% of GDP in 2010. Compared to the government's investment in 2005, it has increased two-and-a-half times in early childhood education and three times in child care. Starting from March 2012, all five-year-olds, regardless of household income levels, will be entitled to free education and care.

- To encourage meeting the goal of increasing ECEC participation in **Mexico**, the Social Affairs Ministry developed a programme which stimulates access to and participation in child care for children of working mothers who did not have access to child care services offered by the Ministry of Education and Health. This service is called *Estancias Infantiles*. The programme, implemented in 2007, includes the establishment of care centres in urban areas for children of low-income, working parents.

- **Ireland** implemented the National Childcare Investment Programme (2006-10). This was a major programme of investment in child care infrastructure, which followed the Equal Opportunities Childcare Programme 2000-06 (EUR 500 million). The programme aimed at creating 50 000 new child care places, with the objective of assisting parents to access affordable, quality child care.

- **Norway** earmarked financial means to increase participation in ECEC since, in Norway, the right to a place in kindergarten for each child is considered an important quality goal. The financial means were earmarked grants for the establishment of new kindergarten places (to all kindergarten owners both public and private). Due to political time limits, an earmarked grant was introduced for the establishment of temporary places in kindergartens. The financing system also addressed the municipalities' need for extra grants to cover the costs that followed the expansion. The state grants for the sector were increased from 0.5 to 0.8 of the GDP from 2003-08 (NOK 4.5 billion in 2000 to NOK 24.3 billion in 2009). Besides this, in 2009, a legal right to a place in ECEC for each child over age one came into force.

- **Manitoba (Canada)** has invested in enhancing the quality and meeting their goals of early learning environments through the development of purpose-built space for early learning and child care. As part of Family Choices (Manitoba's agenda for early learning and child care), Manitoba has invested in a capital building fund for improving quality in early learning and child care centres. Since 2008, 114 projects have been approved for funding, including 54 new child care sites that have been approved to proceed or have already been completed. Many of the new sites are located in schools or on school property; and there is a partnership with the Department of Education, which supports the construction of non-profit early learning and child care centres linked to public schools. Family Choices also incorporates other initiatives that support meeting the goal to improve quality, such as efforts to strengthen the workforce through training and recruitment and retention strategies.

- **Sweden** implemented special targeted state grants to ensure meeting its goal of increasing ECEC participation and supply.

- In **Poland**, financial means were earmarked to increase the supply of and access to ECEC as well as overall participation rates. Poland received a significant amount of funding from the European Union, which was put towards the establishment of new kindergartens, new forms of kindergartens, and development and support of existing preschool facilities. For 2007-13, over EUR 305 million has been allocated to ECEC with special focus on the development of preschool facilities in rural areas where participation rates are lowest.

### Establishing an expert task force to guide implementation

- When kindergarten was being integrated with primary school in an effort to enhance quality in **Prince Edward Island** (**Canada**), a specialised Kindergarten Transition Team (KTT) had been established to guide the implementation. The team included staff from the Department of Education and Early Childhood Development, early childhood development staff and seven other partners. There were nine work groups created to deal with issues in the critical areas of transition. Each work group developed a Work Plan in co-operation with KTT, and each was given nine months to implement the transition. By September 2010, 1 410 young children in Prince Edward Island began kindergarten in public schools, and the transition was implemented very well. The costs of the plan were estimated at CAD 10 million. In addition, Prince Edward Island has established an Early Years Steering Committee to monitor the implementation of the Preschool Excellence Initiative. This committee is comprised of government and community stakeholders.

### Changing the school starting age to ensure fulfilment of participation goals

- In 2010, the government in **Slovak Republic** adopted the decision to make the final year of preschool education in kindergarten mandatory by the year 2014. This is expected to significantly increase ECEC participation.

- In 2002, the government in **Mexico** made preschool education compulsory. This was implemented in phases: in 2004/05, the third year of preschool became compulsory, while the second year of preschool became compulsory one year later in 2005/06. In 2008/09, the first year of preschool (three-to-four-year-olds) was made compulsory. The major positive effect has been increased enrolment rates of four-to-five-year-olds.

- In July 2008, **Prince Edwards Island** (**Canada**) lowered the age of school entry to age five by December 31 of the child's kindergarten year, which brought the age of school entry in line with most of the other Canadian provinces. It increased participation in early education and makes ECEC more accessible.

- In **Poland**, in order to increase participation in ECEC, the starting age of compulsory school education was lowered to age six, whereas it used to be seven, and preschool education for five-year-olds was made compulsory. This change led to an increase in ECEC participation rates of three-to-five-year-olds from 45% in 2006/07 to 65% in 2010/11.

- In **Spain**, the age for which education is free of cost has been reduced to age three as part of the National Education Plan 2008-10. This means that preschool education for all three-to-six-year-olds is free of charge, followed by free compulsory education from age six onwards. This initiative has greatly increased ECEC participation.

*Analysing or measuring the outcomes of implementation*

- The **China** Development Research Foundation (CDRF) analysed what outcomes their early childhood development projects in Xundian County had one year after implementation of the programme. The purpose was to analyse whether their goals of improving the health conditions of young children and the coverage rate of early education was being met. They found that both nutritional conditions and coverage improved: the anaemia rate for 6-to-24-month-olds dropped from 71.7% to 52.2%. The moderate to severe stunting rate dropped by 25%, and the coverage of early education was 89% over one year into the programme.

- **Spain** is planning to evaluate the implementation of their *Educa3* programme to analyse whether the goals of the programme are being met and what outcomes the programme has led to regarding the quality of ECEC provision for zero-to-three-year-olds.

## DESIGNING AND IMPLEMENTING QUALITY REGULATIONS AND STANDARDS

### Challenge 1: Securing financial means for quality enhancement in ECEC

There is increasing financial pressure on governments, especially in the time of economic crisis, which squeezes funding for ECEC in many OECD countries. When aiming at improving the level of quality of ECEC services, a question often arises about whether expanding access should be the priority instead of quality enhancement. There is a growing research body that indicates that "quantity without quality" could be harmful for child development, while it could boost female labour participation. However, the evidence is still limited.

Furthermore, funding is limited for ECEC to begin with. In some countries – if not all – where ECEC falls under the responsibility of the Ministry of Education, Ministry of Social Welfare or Ministry of Children, ECEC is often less of a policy priority than compulsory or tertiary education, and, therefore, less public spending is allocated per child; and resources and staff allocated to work in the Ministry unit are small compared to the resources and staff allocated to work on compulsory schooling. This can be due to the lack of awareness among policy makers of the importance and relevance of quality ECEC provision for better child development in later education outcomes, despite the fact that more and more research consolidates the evidence base for this.

*Revising quality standards in expanding access, raising participation and improving quality*

– Municipalities in **Flanders** (**Belgium**) with a population density of more than 1 500 inhabitants per square kilometre are now able to build new schools for mainstream nursery and primary education more quickly: the minimum distance requirement of two kilometres between schools has been reduced to 250 metres, stimulating the fulfilment of increasing provision of quality ECEC. In addition to this, the Flemish government decided to change the ratio of staff per ECEC places in subsidised day care from 1:7 to 1:6.8 in 2003; and they changed it again in 2005 to 1:6.5.

– **Korea** strengthened regulations on child care centres by amending the Childcare Act in 2005 to improve the quality of child care. A child care centre can serve 300 children maximum and should be located at least 50 metres away from any dangerous facilities. Additionally, regulated space for children increased from 3.64 to 4.29 square metres; the classroom space per child was changed to 2.64 square metres). Furthermore, the staff-child ratio was reduced from: 1:5 to 1:3 for under-one-year-olds; 1:5 for one-year-olds; 1:7 for two-year-olds; 1:20 to 1:15 for three-year-olds; and 1:20 for four- and five-year-olds. For better access to quality educational services, Korea is currently expanding public kindergartens in urban areas, while combining 322 small-scale kindergartens attached to elementary schools in rural areas to 112 kindergartens by 2012.

– **Manitoba**'s (**Canada**) minimum standards for ECEC are set in The Community Child Care Standards Act and Manitoba Regulation 62/86. As part of Family Choices (Manitoba's Five-Year Agenda for Early Learning and Child Care), the government committed to reviewing and modernising The Community Child Care Standards Act. In September 2009, new regulations came into force requiring all licensed child care facilities to have an inclusion policy with respect to children with additional support needs. Furthermore, in May 2010, The Child Care Safety Charter (an amendment to The Community Child Care Standards Act) came into force. Under the Safety Charter, all licensed child care facilities in Manitoba are now required to have approved safety plans and codes of conduct, including procedures for controlling visitor access. Further revisions in standards are planned for the future.

– In **Prince Edward Island** (**Canada**), the Early Learning and Child Care Act is in development to replace the Child Care Facilities Act, R.S.P.E.I. 1988 cap. C-5. The regulations to correspond with this new act are currently in the development and draft stage. Consultations with the child care sector were held about the changes in the new act, and further consultations will be taking place with the regulations in autumn 2011. Based on these consultations, revisions to regulations will be drafted and proposed, which should make regulations more up-to-date and stimulate quality in ECEC.

– An evaluation of current ECEC services in **Spain** shows that minimum standards for zero-to-three-year-olds are set at the regional level, and the level of quality for the youngest children greatly differs across the country. Because of these differences, Spain is planning to develop national minimum standards for the ECEC sector for zero-to-three-year-olds by revising the regional standards and setting out national minimum standards.

*Aligning quality enhancement of ECEC with that of compulsory education*

– In 2009, the **United States** allocated USD 4.35 billion for the Race to the Top (RTT) Fund, a competitive grant programme designed to encourage and reward states that are creating conditions for education innovation and reform, including education systems from preschool to primary and secondary education. In 2011, of the USD 700 million that will be awarded, USD 200 million will be used to improve K-12 education. USD 500 million will be awarded under a new competition, the Race to the Top-Early Learning Challenge (RTT-ELC), to states that plan to improve the quality of early learning and development programmes. Jointly administered by the Departments of Education and Health and Human Services, the competition calls for states to take a comprehensive approach to developing integrated, high-quality early learning systems, which in turn will help ensure that more children, especially children with high-needs, enter school ready and able to succeed. Specific competition requirements, priorities and selection criteria are still under development. However, consistent with the statute, applicant states will need to:

  – increase the number and percentage of low-income and disadvantaged children in each age group of infants, toddlers and preschoolers who are enrolled in high-quality early learning programmes;

  – design and implement an integrated system of high-quality early learning programmes and services; and

  – ensure that any use of assessments conforms to the recommendations of the National Research Council's reports on early childhood.

*Linking quality standards to public funding*

– Since more children in **Flanders** (**Belgium**) are participating in ECEC, providers need financial resources for meeting the standards on staffing. In some municipalities with a sharp increase in the number of pupils attending nursery education, schools are allocated additional "teaching periods". Schools receive funding based on teaching periods according to statutory funding tables. When more children attend, a nursery school receives more teaching periods, as well as more public funding, to meet the quality standards for staff-child ratio. Teaching periods and funding is recalculated as soon as the number of pupils enrolled in school increases with at least 12 pupils on the first school day of October 2010, in comparison with the first school day for the 2010-11 school year. A decrease of 12 pupils or more is deducted at a rate of one teaching period per pupil from the teaching periods, according to statutory funding tables. This is only valid for the education sector and does not apply to the care sector.

*Using international country examples to inform regulations and standards*

- **Australia** used international research evidence on the positive impacts of ECEC on the development of children to help convince stakeholders to adopt regulations and standards.

*Setting standards high on the policy agenda*

- *Kind and Gezin* in **Flanders** (**Belgium**) decided to give high priority to offering high-quality ECEC to all young children, which stimulated co-operation of politicians on improving quality in ECEC. The political commitment led to an increase in available funding.

- In **Czech Republic**, the government put revising standards for ECEC high on their political agenda and is currently preparing revision of legislative conditions relating to quality in ECEC. Since this is now a priority for the government, more political attention is given to ECEC.

## Challenge 2: Lack of transparency among different providers

Different ECEC services and often follow different regulations in many OECD countries, and, therefore, the sector seems fragmented. For example, staff-child ratios or group sizes are often regulated with uncoordinated standards for preschool and kindergartens, child care centres and family day cares. This is partly due to the fragmented responsibilities for ECEC sectors across different ministries as well as across different levels of governments.

The quality of different services – regulated by different standards – is often not transparent to parents and not well understood. When different regulations are in place, for example, regarding care and education, harmonising the regulations can be a great challenge. Finding an agreement on alignment can be difficult due to different views on what regulations should be in place: different developmental services have different opinions on this. Governance can further complicate the state of play, such as responsibilities for ECEC across different levels of government, or a split provision of care and education.

Furthermore, lack of child care places often invites non-regulated ECEC services in some countries. As they do not comply with regulations, the quality is determined only through the prices: the rich get high quality, the poor get low quality. This poses a policy concern of securing minimum standards as well as a question of affordability and, therefore, equity for children.

*Bringing policy coherence through co-ordinated or unified governance*

- In **Australia**, The National Partnership Agreement on the National Quality Agenda for Early Childhood Education and Care aims to foster a joint system of governance through the establishment of the Australian Children's Education and Care Quality Authority (ACECQA).

- In **Ireland**, in 2005, the Office of the Minister for Children and Youth Affairs (OMCYA) was set up to bring greater coherence to policy making for children and to work towards improving the lives of children (as part of the National Children's Strategy). The OMCYA is part of the Department of Health and Children. It is comprised of different child-policy related units, including the Child Welfare and Protection Policy Unit; Childcare Directorate; and the National Children and Young People's Strategy Unit. This co-location allows people to work side-by-side and provide a unified government approach to the development of policy and delivery of services for children.

- Since 2009, the three responsible institutions for ECEC in **Mexico** have been working together in a organisation called the National System of Day Care Centres (*Sistema Nacional de Guarderías, SNGEI*), which is directed by the Ministry of Health. The *SNGEI* was created by presidential decree as an organisation to foster co-ordination across the sectors to enhance the quality of ECEC services. Even though it is not a change in the governance structure or in the integration of ECEC services, it is a way to co-ordinate ECEC services more efficiently in a fragmented system.

- **Flanders (Belgium)** will bring together subsidised and independent child care in one single system of licensed child care, instead of splitting them into separate systems as was the case in the past.

- **Spain** has set up a network for education authorities, including the Ministry of Education and different regional education councils, to share information on the different regulations in their regions. Its long-term aim is to improve quality and share best practices among regions by raising awareness of regional differences in provision regarding the level of quality.

- **Turkey** established the General Directorate of Preschool Development in 1992 with the aim to support the development of children in preschool. Relevant regulations, programmes, space requirements, education materials and equipment were updated to provide quality education to young children and fell under the responsibility of the same government agency creating greater quality coherence.

### *Streamlining different standards in care and education*

- In the **Netherlands**, in 2010, a law on quality standards for *peuterspeelzalen* (playgroups for toddlers, a certain ECEC provision for mostly two- and three-year-olds) came into effect. Before this, there was no national quality standard framework for playgroups. The quality standards for these provisions differed between municipalities. When the new law came into effect, the national quality standards for day care (as in the Law on Day Care) became the standards for the playgroups as well. With this, a national quality framework came into existence. Playgroup managers now have the legal obligation to provide qualitative playgroup provision in line with the quality standards.

### *Setting up a framework to make "quality" transparent to users*

- In **Australia**, in December 2009, the Council of Australian Governments, comprising the Australian Government and all State and Territory Governments, signed a landmark agreement to drive higher quality education and care, recognising that giving children the best possible start in life provides the foundation for better education in school and later life, and delivers long-term social benefits. The National Partnership Agreement on the National Quality Agenda for Early Childhood Education and Care will create new national quality standards for ECEC and school age care services, including higher staff-child ratios and better trained carers and early childhood teachers with requirements to be phased in over the next decade, commencing 1 January 2012.

– A new regulatory framework for **New Zealand**, implemented in 2008, provides a clearer and more transparent statement of regulated requirements. The framework is comprised of legislation, regulations and a third tier of criteria used to assess compliance with the standards set out in regulations.

– **Turkey** developed a quality framework named Total Quality Management, which includes minimum quality standards for all Turkish preschools. Based on this framework, preschools are monitored, and their quality is evaluated.

## Challenge 3: Adaptation to local needs

Regional and local ECEC contexts can vary widely within one country, and at the national level there might be insufficient knowledge about local needs. Therefore, it is understood that it is most efficient if the standards are adopted to meet the local needs.

However, making regulations and standards relevant to different regional or local circumstances can run a risk of making uneven quality across the country. This poses a policy concern from the children's perspective: a child born in one region may have access to high-quality ECEC while a child born in another region may not because that region has adopted lower quality standards. Minimum standards should be defined at the national level and be followed, while adapting to the local needs.

### Delegating responsibilities to local authorities

– In **Belgium**, child care responsibilities were transferred to the different communities (Flemish, French and German speaking), resulting in different regulations for the different communities, which match the needs and views on child care of those communities.

– In **Finland**, decision-making powers have been increasingly delegated to the local level through the Local Government Act of 1995. With this, the autonomy of municipalities increased, and local authorities now have higher levels of freedom in terms of implementation of ECEC. Although the Finnish system is decentralised, the national legislation continues to set out clear requirements for municipalities on, for instance, access, the pedagogic goals, staff qualifications, adult-child ratios and day care fees.

– In 2000, a major decentralisation in the management of early education took place in **Slovak Republic**. The responsibility of kindergartens was transferred to cities and communities. With this change, municipalities became the founders of kindergartens as did, to a large extent, employers of the pedagogical staff and administrative staff in early education. With this shift, ECEC provisions could be more easily adapted to local needs.

- In 2008, **Korea** transferred the entire education budget to local authorities, including those of early childhood education. Consequently, local Offices of Education came to have more autonomy and responsibility in setting specific regulations under the general guidelines of the central government, thus accommodating local needs efficiently.

## Challenge 4: Implementation

Implementing standards and regulations and monitoring them can be challenging because of a lack of sufficient financial, human or time resources. There is also insufficient support or buy-in among stakeholders or a lack of knowledge and awareness on the standards and regulations. Besides this, a lack of expertise and know-how on how to implement or monitor the regulations can further complicate the challenge.

*Ensuring stakeholder buy-in by involving them in the design process*

- In **Australia**, a national Stakeholder Reference Group was established to act as a key consultation forum during the transition to and implementation of the National Quality Agenda (NQA). Members of the reference group represent the ECEC and school-age care sector and include peak bodies, unions, academics, training organisations and special interest groups. The Council of Australian Governments sought public comment on a series of options to improve the quality of ECEC. The general public was invited to give their comments and opinions on several proposed quality improvement measures, including changes in regulatory standards.

- Before standards in child care are set in the **Netherlands**, stakeholder organisations, such as the parent organisation BOinK and child care representatives, can have a say. Together, they advise the Minister about quality standards. Because of the involvement of these organisations in the process, there is not much resistance when new regulations are implemented.

- **Prince Edward Island** and **Manitoba** (**Canada**) used a consultative process for regulation changes to meet the needs of stakeholders and members of the early learning and child care field, and to reflect current best practices for educators and administrators of early learning and child care programmes. Prince Edward Island has a regulatory board, the Child Care Facilities Board, which monitors adherence to the Child Care Facilities Act and is comprised of members from the community at large, public education, government and the early childhood sector. In Manitoba, the Child Care Regulatory Review Committee was established, made up of representatives from government and stakeholder groups, including the Manitoba Child Care Association, an advocacy group working on behalf of the child care workforce. This committee has been successful in finding agreement on regulatory changes in a collaborative and consultative method for the improvement of licensed early learning and child care services in Manitoba.

*Allocating funding for implementation*

- The Flanders Participation Company in **Flanders** (**Belgium**) established an investment fund exclusively for the independent child care sector. The funding is called "Kidsinvest" and is targeted to independent child care providers. The target is to support them in order to avoid having financial problems that could threaten the existence of independent facilities. The aim is to avoid the decrease of independent child care facilities and, thus, the number of available places. From 2012, *Kind en Gezin* will guide one or more organisations as they develop a support project for quality and education in the independent child care sector.

- A new funding system, implemented in **New Zealand** in 2005, provides an incentive for ECEC services to increase the proportion of registered ECEC teachers employed. Since December 2007, teacher-led ECEC centres have been required to have at least 50% of their teachers with an ECEC qualification at diploma or degree level. The funding system supports ECEC centres in achieving this standard.

- **Prince Edward Island** (**Canada**) introduced in 2010 a new funding model for Early Years Centres, which ensures a wage grid for early childhood staff, regulated parent fees and viable operational costs. In addition, the province provided funding for the development and delivery of entry-level training for all uncertified staff working in Early Years Centres in both official languages. Infrastructure funds were also provided for the construction or renovations to existing space in primary schools to allow for starting/building an early years centre. Additional funds were made available to the remainder of early years centres for renovations or the purchase of materials as needed to meet the renewed criteria of an early years centre.

- In **Manitoba** (**Canada**), to assist with the implementation of the requirements under The Child Care Safety Charter, additional provincial funding was offered to support the physical changes to buildings so that facilities could comply with the requirements for controlling visitor access.

*Setting up an agency responsible for implementation*

- In **Australia**, a guidance authority, the Australian Children's Education and Care Quality Authority, has been set up to guide the implementation and management of the national regulatory system.

*Giving structural or financial incentives to service providers to follow the regulations*

- The Ministry of Labour and Social Solidarity of **Portugal** launched the System for Quality Improvement of Social Services, which includes child care services. One objective of this programme is to establish a series of minimum standards for new and existing buildings, ensuring a good level of safety and quality. Once all the requirements have been fulfilled, the provider can ask for a certification of good quality and safety and receive a "Quality Mark". There are three levels of certification depending on the stage of development of the quality requirements.

- **Ireland** provides a capitation grant to a wide range of ECEC service providers who meet specific quality criteria, including qualifications of preschool leaders and compliance with regulations. A higher capitation grant is available to preschool services that employ preschool leaders with ISCED Level 5 qualifications.

- **Korea** acknowledges kindergartens of high quality through official evaluation and provides financial support (*e.g.*, subsidies for teacher salary especially in private kindergartens) accordingly. The Korea Childcare Accreditation Council, a national agency, awards an official accreditation plaque to acknowledge child care centres which meet quality criteria.

### Providing training for staff and assessors

- As part of the full regulation renewal in 2007, education for licensing inspectors and the operators of facilities in **British Columbia** (**Canada**) was done by face-to-face all-day workshops with inspectors and included a training guide and video. All licensed child care facilities received an invitation to attend one two-hour information session.

- In **Manitoba** (**Canada**), to assist with the implementation of the requirements under The Child Care Safety Charter, the Province offered training and support to facilities in the development and approval of their safety plans and codes of conduct and reimbursed expenses (up to set maximums) for centre staff and home providers to attend training sessions on the new requirements and standards.

### Disseminating the new or revised regulations and standards widely

- In **Australia**, all key documentation, including the draft assessment and rating documentation and the draft regulations, have been made available on the Department of Education, Employment and Workplace Relations website for interested stakeholders to familiarise themselves with and comment on. Additionally, a range of other strategies are underway to engage and inform the sector about the new standards, including various public speaking engagements, more public consultation forums and targeted communications materials.

- **Flanders** (**Belgium**) designed the quality assurance manual, which is a written document setting out minimum standards. The document includes information on: 1) the quality assurance policy, including the mission, vision, objectives and values of the child care facility; 2) the elements of the quality system that the child care facility will develop, implement and maintain; 3) how the quality planning of the child care facility is organised; 4) who is in charge of the quality assurance policy; and 5) how the authorities can visit the facility to verify and evaluate its implementation of the regulations. The Flemish government made it compulsory for all subsidised child care provisions to have a quality assurance manual.

- **Korea** publishes the Childcare Guidebook annually and distributes it to all child care centres and family day care to inform providers of new regulations. Sixty-one Childcare Information Centres nationwide also disseminate new regulations and policy through their websites. For kindergartens, the Offices of Education in 16 provinces and cities and 178 District Offices of Education nationwide disseminate changes to regulations and guidelines in a written document and through their websites as well.

- All licensed child care facilities in **British Columbia** (**Canada**) were given an information packet that included Frequently Asked Questions, helpful tips and a copy of the new regulation.

- In **Manitoba** (**Canada**), the province developed and maintains a large assortment of publications and materials for use by the child care workforce. This includes a substantive Best Practices Licensing Manual for Early Learning and Child Care Centres. The aim is to help facilities in implementing legislative and regulatory requirements as well as to enhance their programmes beyond what is required by law.

- In **Poland**, a nationwide social campaign was carried out to share information about changes in the ECEC system and stress the importance of preschool education. The campaign information targeted the details on newly introduced kindergarten forms, practical guidelines on building regulations and impacts of preschool education. The means used include published guides, television and radio, articles in the press, supplements to popular magazines, websites, etc. Preschool education was also included as a topic of discussion in popular televisions programmes and series.

### Challenge 5: Managing private provision

Private provision can bring benefits, as well as challenges, for policy makers because the leverage of public policy is limited for data collection and quality control over unsubsidised private providers. When the private market delivers a significant proportion of ECEC services, a caution is needed for cases of "market failure". Action can be taken through regulation, giving incentives and monitoring.

*Streamlining different standards for public and private ECEC provisions*

- To ensure an equal level of quality across public and private institutions, in the Nordic countries, including **Finland**, **Norway** and **Sweden**, private providers must meet the same quality standards as publicly run institutions. The requirements are stated in the legislation and financing mechanisms.

- In **Korea**, most kindergartens offer various extracurricular activity programmes and programmes aimed at preparing children for elementary school curricula. However, there are no regulations on the teaching methodology or teacher qualifications of such extracurricular activity programmes. As a result, the quality of these programmes tends to vary considerably. Hence, the government decided to pilot the "Extracurricular activity programme recommendation system for full-day kindergartens" (2010-12) for quality management of such programmes, aligning the curricula of extracurricular programmes more with the regular kindergarten curriculum. Under this system, the appropriateness of extracurricular activity programmes for young children is being evaluated, and kindergartens are notified of the results. The pilot programme focuses on four areas: culture and arts; science and creativity; daily physical education; and language development.

*Steering private provisions through public funding*

- In 2009, the Seoul city government in **Korea** initiated a semi-public child care system (Seoul Childcare Centre) to enhance the service quality of private child care centres by providing financial support for the labour costs as well as applying the regulations and policies of public child care centres. As of 2011, there are 2 592 Seoul Childcare Centres, which make up 45.6% of child care centres in Seoul.

- Government subsidies in **Australia** are largely in the form of fee reimbursements to parents whose children participate in services that meet quality assurance requirements. These services may be operated by government authorities (local councils) or non-government providers (both for profit and not-for-profit).

*Managing private provisions through regulating market entry, monitoring and penalty*

- Child care provision in **Australia** has a strong emphasis on provision by private-for-profit and not-for-profit providers. One of the largest private providers used to be ABC Developmental Learning Centres, which was founded in 1998 and targeted long day care centres with children ages zero to five. By 2008, it made up 25% of long day care market. Due to financial difficulties, ABC was placed in voluntary administration in late 2008. Because of this, many children and families faced the prospect of losing their place in ECEC, and staff members faced losing their job and income. The government intervened to keep the services operating until alternative operators could be secured through a sale process. The government also provided a loan – to be fully repaid at no cost to taxpayers – to GoodStart, a consortium of not-for-profit organisations who acquired the majority of these services and are now the largest single child care provider in Australia. To prevent this from happening again, Australia set new regulations for private provisions seeking to enter the market. New private operators now need to demonstrate that they are suitable (also financially) to operate a child care centre; operators must give 42 days' notice before closing a child care centre; providers are monitored more often; and a new civil penalty regime has been introduced. Additionally, large long day care providers with 25 or more services must report annually on their financial situation.

*Setting up an information system to help parents make informed choices*

- As part of the Plan for the Advancement of Early Childhood Education, **Korea** is currently establishing the "information disclosure system" to help parents choose a quality kindergarten based on correct information.

- The Early Childhood Development Association of **Prince Edward Island** (PEI) (**Canada**) has published "A Parents' Guide to Quality Child Care on PEI". This guide assists parents in selecting the best possible match for them and their child when selecting child care.

*Conducting analyses on private providers*

- **Australia**'s National Quality Agenda sets out to encompass all types of services, whether delivered by government or non-government (for profit and not-for-profit) providers. Given the diversity of services in the ECEC sector, however, the agenda will incrementally incorporate service types starting with the largest and most regulated. Non-mainstream services such as indigenous playgroups and rural care services are often provided by non-profit organisations in communities where the market would otherwise fail to deliver. These services are generally subject to relevant children's services state and territory regulations, but they were not affected by the proposed national staff qualifications or staff-child ratio in the initial stages implementing the National Quality Framework. It was decided that governments would undertake work to determine how other ECEC services, such as non-mainstream services, will be incorporated into the National Quality Framework over a number of years.

# ACTION AREA 4 – MANAGING RISKS: LEARNING FROM OTHER COUNTRIES' POLICY EXPERIENCES

This section summarises country experiences as lessons learned from:

- Setting out quality goals and regulations

It aims to be a quick read about challenges and risks to consider when implementing policy initiatives.

## SETTING OUT QUALITY GOALS AND REGULATIONS

### Lesson 1: Prioritise and make the objectives SMARTT – Specific, Measurable, Achievable, Realistic, Timely and Time-bound

A key lesson learned from **Flanders (Belgium)** is that goals and objectives of ECEC must be made clear to all stakeholders, and they must be agreed upon if they are to be met. Flanders prioritised its goal to increase the use of child care by all children, including target groups, by making day care less expensive for parents through increasing the number of places with a means-tested fee. While this goal was prioritised, other projects were put on hold for two or three months.

### Lesson 2: Effectively communicate the need for high quality standards

**Slovak Republic** learnt that it is important to give and explain the arguments for high standards in preschool education and its positive effects on the general development of the child. Slovak Republic found it useful to organise conferences, seminars and media discussions on this. It increased support for the proposed changes in standards and also ensured involvement of different relevant stakeholders in the drafting process.

**Slovak Republic** also found it important to use the media to report on the debates and progress of finding an agreement between the government and ECEC providers on revising quality standards. Additionally, having the media in favour of the revisions positively influences the process of coming to an agreement.

A lesson learned from the **Czech Republic** is that it is highly relevant to explain why standards need to be regulated or revised. The country widely informed stakeholders of the need for high quality standards spelled out in a regulatory framework. The main reason for the regulatory framework was to help the early education sector adapt to new values, ideas and expectations of 21st century preschooling. Since the regulatory framework was expected to improve the level of quality and since the standards would be made relevant for modern society, stakeholders widely agreed on the regulatory framework for preschool provisions.

**Prince Edward Island** (**Canada**) pointed out that it is important to inform people about any plans you undertake in reaching your policy goals as well as the progress of the plan. In doing so, it is important to share the same message with all stakeholders. Progress reports informed people about where the plan was standing, which helped to ease stress and tension for people directly involved in or affected by the plan.

### Lesson 3: Be cautious in defining or re-defining at which government level minimum standards should be set

It is often debated whether the regulations should be set at the national level or at a different government level. **Finland** emphasises that minimum standards are necessary to safeguard the quality of service and safety of children at the national level while the administration is decentralised. Finland has learnt that when standards are set at the national level, legislation can ensure an even minimum quality level across ECEC institutions throughout the country.

### Lesson 4: Consult a wide range of stakeholders when changing curriculum goals or standards

**Australia** established a national Stakeholder Reference Group to act as a key consultation forum during the transition to and implementation of the National Quality Agenda. Members of the reference group represent the ECEC and school age care sector and include peak bodies, unions, academics, training organisations and special interest groups. Thorough consultation with a wide range of stakeholders was found to be necessary and important when seeking their engagement in implementation of the reform of the quality goals and standards. Consultation with these stakeholders also increased buy-in for implementation.

**New Zealand**'s Ministry of Education carried out intensive consultation with the ECEC sector on all regulatory proposals regarding standards from 2003 up to the implementation of the new regulatory framework in late 2008. In this way, the country achieved strong acceptance of proposals for regulatory change and workable mechanisms for implementation.

**Slovak Republic** has been organising meetings with ECEC providers to discuss pros and cons of current standards in Slovakian education and care. The evidence from the State School Inspection on the positive impacts of ECEC on disadvantaged groups of children has helped a lot in convincing providers to agree on proposed changes in regulations. Media were also engaged in the discussion. Slovak Republic has learnt that involving different stakeholder groups can create greater stakeholder buy-in.

**Spain** learnt that opening channels for information exchange and communication with stakeholders contributes to improved knowledge on Spanish ECEC provisions and a better understanding of structural, regulatory and curricular issues. It also supports decision making processes in policy design, which benefits quality in the education system as a whole.

**Sweden** set up a reference group when revising the curriculum. The country learnt that having a reference group with broad and different competences is highly relevant in finding suitable guidelines and goals reflecting the needs of different professionals and children with different backgrounds. Sweden also highlights the importance of involving researchers, as their input and consultation formed the essential basis of Sweden's revisions.

The **Netherlands** learnt that when different stakeholders are involved in the development or revision process of either goals or standards, there is very little resistance to new regulations. Before standards in child care were set in the Netherlands, field organisations were invited to share their opinion, as were the national parent organisation BOinK and representatives of the child care sector. These stakeholder groups advise the Minister about quality standards and goals. Due to their involvement, there was great support for quality standards in Dutch child care; and, in 2010, the Development Opportunities through Quality and Education Act came into force.

**Manitoba (Canada)** used a consultative process for regulation changes to meet the needs of stakeholders and members of the child care field as well as reflect best practices that encourage positive outcomes for children. They found that community consultation and engagement is an important and useful approach in finding agreement on changes in standards and finding commitment.

In **Prince Edward Island (Canada)**, individuals asked to serve on the Kindergarten Transition Team and Work Groups were either decision makers or had access to decision makers. Giving people the authority to get the job done ensured quick decision making, which is necessary when time and financial resources are limited. Additionally, involving experts and specialists and other key people related to ECEC helps ensure smooth implementation.

## Lesson 5: Allocate sufficient time to inform and implement changes

In **Japan**, kindergarten group size standards were changed by reducing the number of children in each class from 40 to 35. Instructions were given to systematically lower the number of children to 35 over a time period of ten years maximum. This ensured that providers had time to prepare themselves for the change regarding human and financial resources.

## Lesson 6: Provide supporting materials and tools for awareness-raising and implementation

**Portugal** found that distributing supporting equipment and materials, such as informative booklets, on the standards and the country's goals regarding ECEC improved the quality of preschool education. Staff and management were more aware of the standards that centres should meet and were more motivated to work towards meeting the quality goals.

**Korea** learnt that informing practitioners and parents of changes in regulations needs to take place through the use of various media forms, such as printed materials, websites, seminars, television advertisements and posters in the subways as well as by mobilising relevant institutions and local authorities. The *Childcare Guidebook*, published and distributed annually to all child care centres and family day care, is particularly efficient in providing highly detailed information about new regulations. City and provincial Offices of Education and 180 District Offices of Education disseminate changes in regulations swiftly through electronic mails to individual kindergartens.

**British Columbia (Canada)** learnt that it is important to train ECEC teachers and childminders about the revised regulations as well as the licensing inspectors and the operators of ECEC facilities. It was found that all day, face-to-face workshops in addition to training guides and videos were very useful in educating them about the changes.

**Slovenia** learnt that it is necessary to raise the quality of management to ensure a high level of quality in preschools, compliance with standards and attainment of goals. Headmasters of preschools have the possibility to regularly attend courses in management. This has been found to improve their management skills and knowledge of the standards and quality goals; and it has led to quality improvements in several preschools across the country.

## Lesson 7: Design a step-by-step action plan with the right balance between access, affordability, equity and quality

**Sweden** learnt that implementing new ECEC policies targeting certain children and families can be an effective method in meeting quality goals. In Sweden, mainly due to increasing parental costs of ECEC, unemployed or part-time working parents often opted out of using ECEC services for their children. Therefore, the goal of providing all children quality early education could not be met. As a result, in 2001, the government took the first step in reforming the ECEC sector and its costs. Children of unemployed parents received the right to preschooling, both in terms of obtaining a place and keeping a place they might already have. A year later, it was also extended to cover children whose parents were at home under the parental insurance scheme for taking care of another child. A year later, a maximum fee was introduced, and all municipalities introduced the fee even though it was not mandatory to do so. Through this reform package, ECEC became a truly fundamental part of general welfare that would benefit all children since fees were either low or non-existent. Additionally, it increased access to and participation in quality ECEC for children with different backgrounds.

**Prince Edward Island (Canada)** established the Public Kindergarten Commission in May 2008. The mandate of the Public Kindergarten Commission was to develop a detailed action plan for the smooth transition of kindergarten into the public school system. This plan was sent to all people in the Kindergarten Transition Team and Work Groups, who were responsible for guiding the implementation of integrating kindergarten into primary schooling. Clear mandates and responsibilities were described in the plan, which ensures that everyone is aware of their tasks. In addition, Prince Edward Island has established an Early Years Steering Committee to monitor the implementation of the Preschool Excellence Initiative. This committee is comprised of government and community stakeholders.

## Lesson 8: Plan to monitor when new or revised regulations are to be put in place

**Mexico** learnt that having a monitoring process can improve the level of quality in ECEC provisions. A monitoring process verifies whether providers and staff apply standards. In Mexico, when ECEC centres are unable to comply with standards, the Ministry of Education offers them additional strategies or initiatives which support them in complying with standards. This was found to benefit the level of quality of several ECEC centres.

Based on **Australia**'s experience, an important part of implementing new standards and regulations is assessing and monitoring compliance with the changes. The country notes the value of testing the assessment. When developing a new assessment and rating system, the government conducted trial assessments of about 200 ECEC services, which helped identify challenges and highlight any changes that should be made to contribute to quality improvement. Australia also learnt that they needed to strengthen monitoring of private for-profit providers after the collapse of ABC Learning Centres, which held the 25% share of Long Day Care (LDC) services at the time of closure in 2008. Australia's 2010-11 Budget announced plans to assess the financial viability of large LDC providers with 25 or more services and reassess the providers each year. There are also provisions to engage an expert to carry out an independent audit where a provider is found to be experiencing significant financial difficulty. Other steps taken in response to the collapse of ABC include: operators must give 42 days' notice before they close a child care centre; and a new civil penalty regime has been introduced.

## Lesson 9: Align incentives for successful implementation of new or revised regulations

In **New Zealand**, a range of teacher supply initiatives, including scholarships and grants, were put in place to encourage teachers to gain a recognised qualification. In addition, the early childhood education funding system provides a financial incentive to services to employ higher proportions of registered teachers. This helped providers meet the standards regarding staff-child ratio and have the minimum number of qualified staff in service.

## ACTION AREA 5 – REFLECTING ON THE CURRENT STATE OF PLAY

This sheet has been prepared based on international trends and is designed to facilitate reflection on where your country stands regarding:

- Quality goals and minimum standards

The aim is to raise awareness about new issues and identify areas where changes could be made; the aim is not to give marks on practices. Please reflect on the current state of play by circling a number on the scale from 1-5.

### QUALITY GOALS AND MINIMUM STANDARDS

| Quality goals | Not at all | | | | Very well |
|---|---|---|---|---|---|
| 1. Quality goals are set as SMART:<br>a) Specific | 1 | 2 | 3 | 4 | 5 |
| b) Measurable | 1 | 2 | 3 | 4 | 5 |
| c) Achievable | 1 | 2 | 3 | 4 | 5 |
| d) Relevant | 1 | 2 | 3 | 4 | 5 |
| e) Timely | 1 | 2 | 3 | 4 | 5 |
| f) Time-bound | 1 | 2 | 3 | 4 | 5 |
| 2. Quality-specific goals are aligned with the overall policy goals of ECEC. | 1 | 2 | 3 | 4 | 5 |
| 3. Quality-target goals are shared among relevant ministries and key stakeholders. | 1 | 2 | 3 | 4 | 5 |
| 4. Quality goals are aligned with sustained public funding and regulations. | 1 | 2 | 3 | 4 | 5 |

| Minimum standards | Not at all | | | | Very well |
|---|---|---|---|---|---|
| 5. Minimum standards include key quality indicators (*e.g.*, safety, space, staff-child ratio, staff qualification) in the regulatory framework. | 1 | 2 | 3 | 4 | 5 |
| 6. The minimum standards have been applied to all providers. | 1 | 2 | 3 | 4 | 5 |
| 7. Key quality indicators are monitored – not only structural indicators (*e.g.*, safety, staff-child ratio) but also process quality (*e.g.*, curriculum, staff-child relationship, staff-parent communication). | 1 | 2 | 3 | 4 | 5 |
| 8. Actions are taken as a result of monitoring, such as: | | | | | |
| a) making results available to parents | 1 | 2 | 3 | 4 | 5 |
| b) making results publicly available | 1 | 2 | 3 | 4 | 5 |
| c) implementing follow-up consequences to services that do not meet standards | 1 | 2 | 3 | 4 | 5 |
| d) linking to funding of services | 1 | 2 | 3 | 4 | 5 |
| e) providing additional services to support centres in raising standards | 1 | 2 | 3 | 4 | 5 |
| f) other option of your own country | 1 | 2 | 3 | 4 | 5 |

# NOTES

1   The PISA test assigns a score for students on a scale from 0 to 700.

2   Based on responses from: Australia, Austria, Flemish Community (BEL), French Community (BEL), British Columbia (CAN), Manitoba (CAN), Prince Edward Island (CAN), Czech Republic, Denmark, Estonia, Finland, Germany, Hungary, Ireland, Israel, Italy, Japan, Korea, Mexico, Netherlands, New Zealand, Norway, Poland, Portugal, Slovak Republic, Slovenia, Spain, Sweden, Turkey, England (UKM), Scotland (UKM) and United States.

3   Based on responses from: Australia, Austria, Flemish Community (BEL), French Community (BEL), British Columbia (CAN), Manitoba (CAN), Prince Edward Island (CAN), Czech Republic, Denmark, Estonia, Finland, Hungary, Israel, Italy, Japan, Korea, Mexico, Netherlands, New Zealand, Norway, Poland, Portugal, Slovak Republic, Slovenia, Spain, Sweden, Turkey and Scotland (UKM).

4   When referring to kindergarten or preschool in countries with an integrated ECEC system, data refers to the children in the older age bracket of ECEC, *i.e.*, children from the age of three to the age that primary schooling starts (unless indicated otherwise).

5   When referring to child care in countries with an integrated ECEC system, data refers to the children in the youngest age group of ECEC, usually zero-to-three-year-olds (unless indicated otherwise).

6   OECD averages are only based on data reported for OECD countries in the respective figures, excluding regions and territories. Data from jurisdictions and regions, as well as countries, are included in the Total Average.

# POLICY LEVER 2

# DESIGNING AND IMPLEMENTING CURRICULUM AND STANDARDS

*Curriculum and standards can reinforce positive impact on children's learning and development. They can: i) ensure even quality across different settings; ii) give guidance to staff on how to enhance children's learning and well-being; and iii) inform parents of their children's learning and development. Countries take different approaches in designing curriculum. There is a need to think beyond curriculum dichotomies (e.g., academic-oriented vs. comprehensive approaches, staff-initiated instruction vs. child-initiated activities, etc.) and consolidate the "added value" of individual approaches. Almost all OECD countries have a framework in place – either curriculum or learning standards – from age three to compulsory schooling. A growing number of countries and regions have started to address continuous child development from early childhood throughout older ages, such as eight, ten or eighteen.*

# ACTION AREA 1 – USING RESEARCH TO INFORM POLICY AND THE PUBLIC

This section contains the following research brief:

- Curriculum Matters

## CURRICULUM MATTERS

### What is curriculum?

Curriculum refers to the contents and methods that substantiate children's learning and development. It answers the questions "what to teach?" and "how to teach it?" (NIEER, 2007). It is a complex concept especially in ECEC, containing multiple components, such as ECEC goals, content and pedagogical practices (Litjens and Taguma, 2010).

### What is at stake?

There is growing consensus on the importance of an explicit curriculum with clear purpose, goals and approaches for zero-to-school-age children (Bertrand, 2007). Most OECD countries now use a curriculum in early childhood services, especially as children grow older, that is to say, that some structuring and orientation of children's experience towards educational aims is generally accepted. Currently, there is little pedagogical direction for younger children, although many neurological developments take place prior to age of three or four (OECD, 2006). Curricula are influenced by many factors, including society's values, content standards, research findings, community expectations, and culture and language. Although these factors differ per country, state, region and even programme, high-quality, well-implemented ECEC curricula provide developmentally appropriate support and cognitive challenges that can lead to positive child outcomes (Frede, 1998).

With trends toward decentralisation and diversification of policy and provision, there is more variation in programming and quality at the local level. A common framework can help ensure an even level of quality across different forms of provision and for different groups of children, while allowing for adaptation to local needs and circumstances. A clear view and articulation of goals, whether in the health, nutrition or education field, can help foster programmes that will promote the well-being of young children and respond adequately to children's needs (OECD, 2006).

Well-defined educational projects also serve the interests of young children. In infant-toddler settings with a weak pedagogical framework, young children may miss out on stimulating environments that are of high importance in the early years. At the programme level, guidelines for practice in the form of a pedagogical or curriculum framework help staff to clarify their pedagogical aims, keep progression in mind, provide a structure for the child's day, and focus observation on the most important aspects of child development (Siraj-Blatchford, 2004).

Debate remains widespread over the "correct curriculum approach" for the youngest and older children in ECEC. This raises important questions about aspects, such as the scope, relevance, focus and age-appropriateness of content; depth and length of descriptions; and input- or outcome-based descriptions. The learning areas that receive most focus in official curricula – particularly in countries where child assessments are used shortly after entry into primary school – are literacy and numeracy. Countries in the social pedagogy tradition do not exclude emergent literacy and numeracy but seek to maintain an open and holistic curriculum until children enter school and, sometimes, well into the early classes of primary school. On the other hand, countries in which early education has been part of, or closely associated with, primary school tend to privilege readiness for school and a more academic approach to curriculum and methodology.

## Why does it matter?

### Consistency and adaptation to local needs

A common ECEC curriculum can have multiple benefits. It can ensure more even quality levels across provisions and age groups, contributing to a more equitable system. It can also guide and support staff; facilitate communication between teachers and parents; and ensure continuity between pre-primary and primary school levels. However, a curriculum can remain unchanged for years and lack the necessary innovation to adapt to ever-changing "knowledge" societies. It can equally limit the freedom and creativity of ECEC staff (OECD, 2006).

Because ECEC centres are becoming more culturally diverse with children from different backgrounds and home environments, acknowledging that these children might have different needs is important for the effectiveness of a programme. Settings and activities that are designed to accommodate young children's different approaches to learning have been found to reduce disruptive and inattentive behaviour, like fighting with peers and unwillingness to respond to questions or co-operate in class (Philips *et al.*, 2000). The wide range of cultures, communities and settings in which young children grow up makes it essential to engage different stakeholders in developing and refining curricula and to adapt curricula, when needed, to local or cultural circumstances. This is to ensure that curricula actually meet children's needs and truly focus on the child and their development (NAEYC, 2002).

## Balancing diverse expectations

It is important that all stakeholders agree on the contents of the pre-primary curriculum. Governments and parents may share common objectives, such as preparing children for school; but they may also disagree on the appropriateness of specific pre-primary subjects for children, such as the integration of ICT in the classroom. In multicultural societies, governments may want to create a skilled and knowledgeable workforce and prioritise shared values for building a sense of community. Meanwhile, minority group families may be more concerned with transmitting native languages and customs to children while respecting specific beliefs on child rearing. Curricula can contribute to balancing different expectations of early childhood development in the curriculum and ensure that expectations and needs of different stakeholders are met (Bennett, 2011; Siraj-Blatchford and Woodhead, 2009; Vandenbroeck, 2011).

## Provides guidance, purpose and continuity

Curriculum can provide clear guidance and purpose through explicit pedagogical guidelines. A focused curriculum with clear goals helps ensure that ECEC staff cover critical learning or development areas. It can therefore equip children with the knowledge and skills needed for primary school and further learning and facilitate smooth transitions between education levels (UNESCO, 2004).

## Improves quality and reinforces impact

Curriculum can establish higher and more consistent quality across varied ECEC provisions; and having a steering curriculum is found to contribute to decreased class repetition, reduced referral to special education and better transitions to primary school (Eurydice, 2009). At the same time, a high-quality curriculum can reduce the fade-out effect of knowledge gained in preschool (Pianta *et al.*, 2009).

## Facilitates the involvement of parents

Curriculum can inform parents about what their children are learning in an education or care setting. It can act as a bridge between ECEC staff and parents for information sharing and needs-based interventions. Parental knowledge of the curriculum can be particularly important for children with special needs or learning difficulties to provide added support at home. One of the most effective approaches to increasing children's later achievement and adjustment is to support parents in actively engaging with children's learning activities at home (Desforges and Abouchaar, 2003; Harris and Goodall 2006). Activities that can be beneficially promoted include reading to children, singing songs and nursery rhymes, going to the library and playing with numbers.

## What aspect matters most?

### Thinking beyond curriculum dichotomies

Traditionally, ECEC curricula have been categorised into academic and more comprehensive models. An academic approach makes use of a staff-initiated curriculum with cognitive aims for school preparation. A comprehensive approach centres on the child and seeks to broaden the scope for holistic development and well-being (Bertrand, 2007; OECD, 2006). An academic approach can prescribe teaching in critical subject areas but can also limit a child-centred environment characterised by self-initiated activity, creativity and self-determination (Eurydice, 2009; Prentice, 2000). With more flexible aims, a comprehensive approach can better integrate social and emotional well-being, general knowledge and communication skills but risks losing focus of important education goals, as can be seen in Table 2.1 (Pianta, 2010; Bertrand, 2007; UNESCO, 2004).

It is argued that high-quality ECEC settings are related to curriculum practice in which cognitive *and* social development are viewed as complementary and of equal importance. Such integrated curriculum is believed to contribute to high-quality ECEC and improved social behaviour (Table 2.2) (Bennett, 2004; Siraj-Blatchford, 2010). As an example, Sweden is considered to have high-quality ECEC in part because its curriculum contents place the same value on social and cognitive learning (Sheridan *et al.*, 2009, Pramling and Pramling Samuelsson, 2011).

It should be noted that "mixed models" that combine different curriculum approaches are not always successfully integrated in practice. In some countries, the implementation of a mixed model curriculum has been found to be less effective than pure "academic" or "comprehensive" approaches. Nevertheless, a clear dichotomy between the "academic" and "comprehensive" approaches is not necessarily warranted. Instead of focussing on "type" of curriculum it may be beneficial to highlight a curriculum's 1) critical learning areas and 2) implementation (Eurydice, 2009).

**Table 2.1. Effects of academic and comprehensive curriculum models**

| Which "model" is most likely to improve a child's... | Academic | Comprehensive |
|---|---|---|
| IQ scores | X | |
| Motivation to Learn | | X |
| Literacy and Numeracy | X | |
| Creativity | | X |
| Independence | | X |
| Specific Knowledge | X | |
| Self-confidence | | X |
| General Knowledge | | X |
| Initiative | | X |
| Short-term outcomes | X | |
| Long-term outcomes | X | X |

*Source*: Pianta *et al.*, 2010; Eurydice, 2009; Laevers, 2011; Schweinhart and Weikart, 1997.

**Table 2.2. Different curriculum models' effect on school behaviours**

|  | Direct Instruction | Child Centred (constructivist) | Child Centred (social) |
|---|---|---|---|
| Misconduct at age 15 | 14.9 | 5.9 | 8.0 |
| Ever been expelled from High School | 16.0% | 5.9% | 8.0% |
| Total number of classes failed | 9.6 | 5.0 | 4.9 |

Note 1: For "Misconduct at age 15", the sum is out of 18 possible criteria of misconduct. For "Ever been expelled from High School", this is the percentage of sample group members that had been expelled from High School. For "Total number of classes failed", this is the number of classes failed by per member of sample group (asked at age 23).

Note 2: Results are from a study of different curriculum models impact on disadvantaged children in New Jersey. The sample groups are randomly selected and have comparable socio-economic backgrounds and other background characteristics.

Note 3: "Child Centred (constructivist)" is a High/Scope curriculum model, "Child Centred (social)" is a Nursery School programme with a focus on social skills. Both curriculum models place stronger weight on child-initiated activities.

*Source*: Schweinhart and Weikart, 1997.

## Critical learning areas

### Literacy

The importance of literacy is well-documented as the means through which all other subject areas are acquired (NIEER, 2006). Researchers continually point to the benefits of literacy for language development and reading outcomes (UNESCO, 2007). Literacy has also been consistently linked to improved school performance and achievement as well as higher productivity later in life. Evidence suggests literacy should focus on improving vocabulary and listening skills; building knowledge of the alphabetic code; and introduce printing (NIEER, 2006). The OECD has shown that children whose parents often read to them show markedly higher scores in PISA 2009 than students whose parents read with them infrequently or not at all (OECD, 2011). Research also shows that children quickly establish a stable approach to learning literacy. In order to do so, it is essential that they are exposed to texts, pictures, books, etc., in different communicative contexts. For example, structured play that is integrated into children's everyday interests can more easily introduce the fundamentals of written language (Mellgren and Gustafsson, 2011).

### Numeracy

There is a general consensus that early mathematics should be implemented on a wide scale, especially for disadvantaged children. Even the youngest children use abstract and numerical ideas (amounts, shapes, sizes) in everyday "play" (Björklund, 2008); and staff can use children's existing knowledge and curiosity to develop mathematical concepts, methods and language (Amit and Ginsburg, 2008). In everyday activities, numeracy should focus on "big ideas" to support mathematical competence, namely numbers and operations; shapes and space; measurement and patterns (Amit and Ginsburg, 2008; NIEER, 2009).

Developing early mathematical skills means that the child discerns relations in space, time and quantities and acquires an ability to use his or her understanding in communication with others when solving problems, in logical reasoning and in representation (Björklund, 2008 and 2010). Longitudinal studies on early numeracy show that a child's understanding of numbers and numeric relationships can predict later acquisition of arithmetical skills and mathematical competence (Aunio and Niemivirta, 2010; Aunola *et al.*, 2004).

## ICT

Computer-facilitated activities can have positive impacts on play and learning. They can tap into a child's creativity and motivate curiosity, exploration, sharing and problem solving (UNESCO, 2010). ICT can even eliminate boundaries between oral and written language and allow the visualisation of mathematical concepts and relationships (UNESCO, 2010). But while computer use is positively associated with achievement in math, it can be negatively correlated with reading. Some studies demonstrate that more frequent use of computers among low-achieving readers can hinder literacy progress since computers tend to replace face-to-face instruction, which is critical in literacy development (Judge *et al.*, 2006).

## Science

When a child experiences science-related courses early in life, he or she is found to be encouraged to ask questions, think more critically, experiment, develop his/her reasoning skills, read and write. Studies suggest that children become better problem solvers and even experience a raise in their IQ when they are taught principles of logic, hypothesis testing and other methods of reasoning. These dimensions are all tackled in science practices (Bybee and Kennedy, 2005).

## Art and music

Arts can boost children's attention, improve cognition and help children learn to envision, *i.e.*, how to think about what they cannot see. The ability to envision can help a child generate a hypothesis in science later in life or imagine past events in history class. Intensive music training can help train children for geometry tasks and map reading. However, there is little attention in research to children's use of art and music practices and its effect on developmental outcomes (Litjens and Taguma, 2010).

## Physical and health development

Motor skills, such as crawling, walking, gym classes or play time, are related to children's development of social skills and an understanding of social rules. Health education and hygiene practices are found to have positive effects for children and their parents. Children participating in ECEC programmes with specific hygiene and health guidelines have improved hygiene habits, which often result in healthy weight and height in comparison to children who do not benefit from such practices (Litjens and Taguma, 2010).

## Play

It is important to integrate exploration, play and peer interaction into the curriculum. Evidence suggests that "social pretend play" and "child-initiated play" lead to better co-operation, self-regulation and interpersonal skills (Bodrova and Leong, 2010; Nicolopoulou, 2010). Child-initiated play has been specifically linked to symbolic representation (Bodrova and Leong, 2010). Researchers point out that the combination of indoor and outdoor play – involving the use of media, role play, drawing and puppets – provides numerous high-quality development opportunities for children to create and negotiate (Aasen *et al.*, 2009).

### Choice, self-determination and children's agency

Research shows that children are more competent and creative across a range of cognitive areas when they are given the *choice* to engage in different well-organised and age-appropriate activities (CCL, 2006). A curriculum can stimulate this behaviour through including cross-disciplinary learning activities that trigger children's curiosity. Fun and interesting themes, such as "Alive!" (the study of living vs. non-living things), can make learning more personal and relevant for young learners (NIEER, 2007). Implementing such activities in small groups can encourage greater autonomy (Eurydice, 2009; Laevers, 2011) and provides more space for spontaneous or emergent learning (NIEER, 2007). Children's participation is not only important in order to facilitate effective learning of different curriculum elements but can be important in its own right and foster democratic values. When placing value on children's agency, it is considered important that children are allowed freedom of expression and that their modes of communication are recognised in everyday interactions (Bae, 2009).

### Children's perspectives

Research on ECEC curriculum confirms the importance of children's perspectives not only through their participation in activities but through their active input in decision making (Broström, 2010; Clark *et al.*, 2003; Sommer *et al.*, 2010). Evidence suggests that consultation with children (only when age-appropriate and possible) can increase their self-esteem and foster social competence (Clark *et al.*, 2003). It can also help ECEC staff and management reflect on their own practice and aspects such as the design of indoor and outdoor spaces (Pramling Samuelsson and Asplund Carlsson, 2008).

### Child-initiated learning

Children learn best when they are active and engaged; when interactions are frequent and meaningful; and when curriculum builds on prior learning (Kagan and Kauerz, 2006; NIEER, 2007). The ability of staff to create a chain of learning events over time with clear direction and concrete activities is also important for consistent development, especially in academic topics (Doverborg and Pramling Samuelsson, 2011).

Evidence suggests that a curriculum with a high level of child-initiated activities can have long-term benefits, including an increased level of community service and motivation to pursue higher education (Figure 2.1).

**Figure 2.1. Impact of different curriculum models**

On community involvement and motivation to pursue further studies

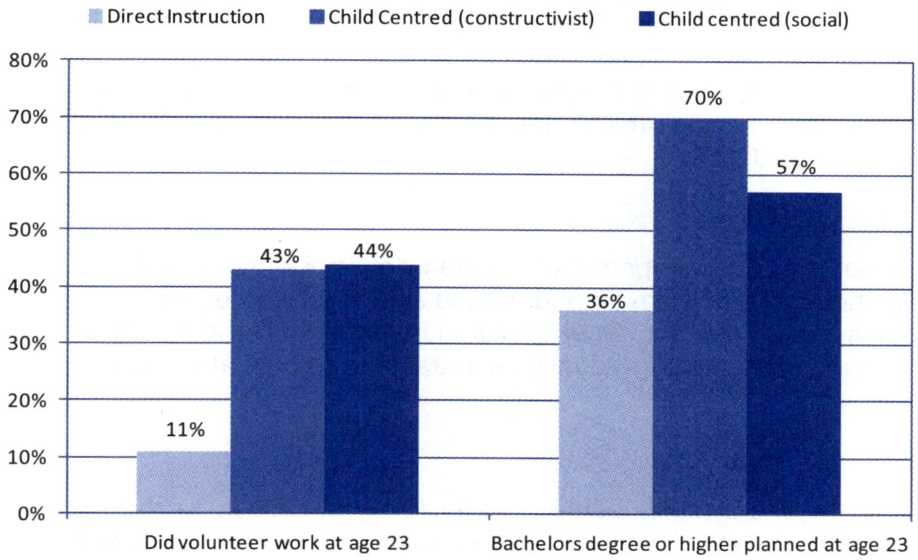

Note 1: Results are from a study of different curriculum models' impact on disadvantaged children in New Jersey. The sample groups are randomly selected and have comparable socio-economic and other background characteristics.

Note 2: "Child Centred (constructivist)" is a High/Scope curriculum model, "Child Centred (social)" is a Nursery School programme with a focus on social skills. Both curriculum models place stronger weight on child-initiated activities.

*Source*: Schweinhart and Weikart, 1997.

## *Teacher-initiated learning*

Research demonstrates that teacher-initiated learning (common in the academic approach) can reduce early knowledge gaps in literacy, language and numeracy. Numerous studies have concluded that high-quality academic programmes involving explicit teaching can have positive short-term effects on IQ scores, literacy and math (Pianta *et al.*, 2009) (Table 2.1). These skills have been found to be strong predictors of subsequent achievement (Brooks-Gunn *et al.*, 2007). However, as pointed out above, child-initiated learning can have long-term benefits and is highly important for children's future social development. In order to maximise learning, development and social outcomes, it is suggested that ECEC curricula should combine child-initiated with teacher-initiated contents and activities (Sheridan, 2011; Sheridan *et al.*, 2009).

## What are the policy implications?

## *Adapting curricula to local circumstances*

A greater extent of local adaptation of curricula can reinforce the relevance of ECEC services. This can be especially important when "national" values or ideas on early childhood development are not shared by all (Eurydice, 2009). Co-constructed responses developed in partnership with teachers, parents, children and communities can greatly enhance the local appropriateness of curriculum aims and objectives (OECD, 2001).

### Designing curriculum based on cognitive and neurological science

Cognitive developmental science and neurological research indicate that children learn certain things at particular ages, in a certain sequence. The "peaks" of brain sensitivity may vary across functions/skills as follows (Figure 2.2) (Council Early Child Development, 2010):

#### Emotional control and peer social skills

The brain sensitivity to development of emotional control starts from the middle level, increases to the high level from birth to around age one, and declines to the low level where it stays from age four. Peer social skills start with the low level, increase rapidly from ages one to two, gradually decrease and remain at a medium level from age four.

#### Language and numbers

Language development starts at the middle level, increases to the high level at around ages one to two, slightly decreases towards age four, and will continue to decrease towards the middle and low levels from then on. Numeracy starts with the low level, increases rapidly from ages one to three, gradually decreases but will be maintained at the high level from age four.

**Figure 2.2. Sensitive periods in early brain development**

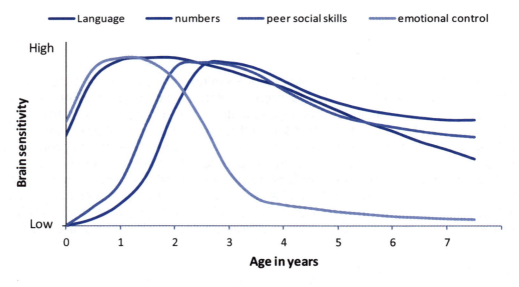

*Source*: Council for Early Child Development (2010).

### Recognising the "virtues" of complimentary curriculum models

In practice, comprehensive programmes are thought to better facilitate a child-centred environment where learning builds on existing knowledge from children's perspectives. Children's priorities can be identified in a number of ways, for instance, children can be engaged in taking photographs of the most important "things" in the classroom. Experiments like these have been able to identify the importance of friends, staff, food and outside play. Other information-gathering tools, such as interviews, questionnaires and role-play, reveal that children like to finish their activities and appreciate support for periods of transition between activities (Clark *et al.*, 2003). Children can benefit from teacher-led interaction and formal instruction (Eurydice, 2009). However, play-based, as opposed to "drill-and-practice", curricula designed with the developmental needs of children in mind can be more effective in fostering the development of academic and attention skills in ways that are engaging and fun (Brooks-Gunn, 2007).

### *Considering national characteristics and ECEC structural factors*

National characteristics and ECEC structural factors provide insight into the appropriateness of curriculum models. Where staff have little certification and training; and where ECEC provisions are fragmented, staff may benefit from added guidance and a more concrete curriculum. In countries encouraging child-centred activities and giving space to staff to create local innovations and adaptations, a child-centred model requires practitioners to be adequately qualified and trained to balance wide-ranging (and more abstract) child development areas. Thus, the chosen curriculum must be coupled with adequate staff training, favourable working conditions and appropriate classroom materials (OECD, 2001; 2006).

### *Ensuring sufficient and appropriate staff training*

To enhance children's learning and development, (additional) staff training is needed on curriculum in general, but also on specific areas in which staff might need additional training support, such as multicultural classroom management and adaptation of curriculum contents to diverse linguistic and cultural groups. Furthermore, in a rapidly changing society, knowledge on the use of ICT is becoming more relevant, which can also facilitate early development, especially in reading (Judge *et al.*, 2006).

### *Ensuring that curriculum or standards are well-aligned for children ages zero to six and beyond*

It is not only important that curriculum standards are present in ECEC environments but that they are well-aligned from ages zero to six, or even beyond: an aligned vision of ECEC contents can ensure more holistic and continuous child development.

### What is still unknown?

### *Comparative advantage of different curriculum models*

Table 2.1 compares the specific outcomes of "academic" and "comprehensive" curriculum models based on a selection of research findings. It remains unclear which of the two approaches produces the largest long-term benefits on health, college attendance, future earnings, etc. Geographical and political positioning has likely influenced the existing research: American researchers are more likely to support an academic ECEC approach, whereas the trend in Europe points to the importance of non-cognitive learning areas. More research is therefore needed to clarify the mixed research findings across different country-specific ECEC contexts.

### Pedagogical strategies to support "play"

Most researchers agree that children's "play" is important for cognitive, social and emotional development. It has been traditionally integrated into subject-based learning, improving literacy, math and science outcomes. However, there is little differentiation between types of "play" (*e.g.*, social, pretend, object) that serve different developmental purposes. A lack of evidence leads many to unfairly separate play ("child-initiated games with no purpose") from curriculum ("teacher-initiated practices with useful benefits") (Bodrova and Leong, 2010).

### Non-Western curriculum models and their effects

There is considerable literature on "academic" and "child-centred" curriculum models as seen in North America and Europe. But a Western child-centred curriculum focused on individual benefits can actually contradict other value systems, including those who privilege group interests (Kwon, 2004). Thus, there is a need to research and diffuse alternative national curriculum models that are locally adapted and implemented.

## REFERENCES

Aasen, W. *et al.* (2009), "The outdoor environment as a site for children's participation, meaning-making and democratic learning: examples from Norwegian kindergartens", Education 3-13: *International Journal of Primary, Elementary and Early Years Education*, Vol. 27, No. 1, pp. 5-13.

Amit, M. and H. Ginsburg (2008), "What is Teaching Mathematics to Young Children? A Theoretical Perspective and Case Study", *Journal of Applied Developmental Psychology,* Vol. 29, pp. 274-285.

Aunio, P. and Niemivirta, M. (2010), "Predicting children's mathematical performance in grade one by early numeracy", *Learning and Individual Difference*, Vol. 20, pp. 427-435.

Aunola, K. *et al.* (2004), "Developmental Dynamics of Math Performance from Preschool to Grade 2", *Journal of Educational Psychology*, Vol. 96, No. 4, pp. 699-713.

Bae, B. (2009), "Children's Right to Participate – challenges in everyday interactions", *European Early Childhood Education Research Journal,* Vol. 17, No. 3, pp. 391-406.

Bennett, J. (2011), "Introduction: Early Childhood Education and Care", *Encyclopedia on Early Childhood Development*, Centre of Excellence for Early Childhood Development and Strategic Knowledge Cluster on Early Child Development, Montreal, available at: www.child-encyclopedia.com/pages/PDF/BennettANGxp1-Intro.pdf.

Bennett, J. (2004), Starting Strong Curricula and Pedagogies in Early Childhood Education and Care, Directorate for Education, OECD, Paris.

Bertrand, J. (2007), "Preschool Programs: Effective Curriculum. Comments on Kagan and Kauerz and on Schweinhart", *Encyclopedia on Early Childhood Development*, Centre of Excellence for Early Childhood Development and Strategic Knowledge Cluster on Early Child Development, Montreal, available at: www.child-encyclopedia.com/documents/ BertrandANGxp.pdf.

Björklund, C. (2008), "Toddlers' opportunities to learn mathematics", *International Journal of Early Childhood,* Vol. 40, No. 1, pp. 81-95.

Björklund, C. (2010), "Broadening the horizon: Toddlers' strategies for learning mathematics", *International Journal of Early Years Education,* Vol. 18, No.1, pp. 71-84.

Bodrova, E. and D. Leong (2010), "Curriculum and Play in Early Child Development", *Encyclopedia on Early Childhood Development,* Centre of Excellence for Early Childhood Development and Strategic Knowledge Cluster on Early Child Development, Montreal, available at: www.child-encyclopedia.com/ documents/Bodrova-LeongANGxp.pdf.

Brodin, J. and P. Lindstrand (eds.) (2006). "Interaction in Outdoor Play Environments – Gender, Culture and Learning" (No. 47), Stockholm: Stockholm Institute of Education, Department of Human Development, Learning and Special Education.

Brooks-Gunn, J. *et al.* (2007), "School Readiness and Later Achievement", *Development Psychology*, Vol. 43, No. 6, pp. 1428-1446.

Broström, S. (2010), "A Voice in Decision Making young children in Denmark" in M. Clark and S. Tucker, *Early childhoods in a changing world*, Stoke-on-Trent, England: Trentham Publisher.

Bybee, R. W. and Kennedy D. (2005), "Math and Science Achievement", *Science*, Vol. 307, No. 5709.

Canadian Council on Learning (CCL) (2006), "Why is High-Quality Child Care Essential? The link between Quality Child Care and Early Learning", *Lessons in Learning*, CCL, Ottawa.

Clark, A., S. McQuail and P. Moss (2003), "Exploring the Field of Listening to and Consulting with Young Children", Research Report No. 445, Thomas Coram Research Unit, University of London.

Council Early Child Development (2010), from the World Bank, Investing in Young Children, an Early Childhood Development Guide for Policy Dialogue and Project Preparation, 2011.

Desforges, C. and A. Abouchaar (2003),"The Impact of Parental Involvement, Parental Support and Family Education on Pupil Achievement and Adjustment: A Literature Review", Research Report No. 433, Department for Education and Skills, London.

Doverborg, E., and I. Pramling Samuelsson (2011), "Early Mathematics in the Preschool Context", in N. Pramling and I. Pramling Samuelsson (eds.), *Educational encounters: Nordic studies in early childhood didactics*. Dordrecht, The Netherlands: Springer, pp. 37-64.

Eurydice (2009), Early Childhood Education and Care in Europe: Tackling Social and Cultural Inequalities, Eurydice, Brussels.

Frede, E. C. (1998), "Preschool program quality in programs for children in poverty", in Barnett, W. S. and S. S. Boocock (eds.), *Early Care and Education for Children in Poverty: Promises, Programs, and Long-term Outcomes*, Buffalo, NY: SUNY Press, pp. 77-98.

Harris, A. and J. Goodall (2006), *Parental Involvement in Education: An overview of the Literature*, University of Warwick, Coventry.

Judge, S. *et al.* (2006), "Closing the Digital Divide: Update From the Early Childhood Longitudinal Study", Heldref Publications, Tennessee.

Kagan, S. and K. Kauerz (2006), "Preschool Programs: Effective Curricula", *Encyclopedia on Early Childhood Development*, Centre of Excellence for Early Childhood Development and Strategic Knowledge Cluster on Early Child Development, Montreal, available at: www.child-encyclopedia.com/documents/Kagan-KauerzANGxp.pdf.

Kwon, Y.-I. (2004), "Early Childhood Education in Korea: Discrepancy between National Kindergarten Curriculum and Practices", *Educational Review*, Vol. 56, No. 3, pp. 297-312.

Laevers, F. (2011), "Experiential Education: Making Care and Education More Effective Through Well-Being and Involvement", *Encyclopedia on Early Childhood Development*, Centre of Excellence for Early Childhood Development and Strategic Knowledge Cluster on Early Child Development, Montreal, available at: www.child-encyclopedia.com/documents/LaeversANGxp1.pdf.

Litjens, I. and M. Taguma (2010), "Revised Literature Overview for the 7th Meeting of the Network on Early Childhood Education and Care", Paris: OECD.

Mellgren, E. and K. Gustafsson (2011), "Early Childhood Literacy and Children's Multimodal Expressions in Preschool", *Educational Encounters: Nordic Studies in Early Childhood Didactics*, Vol. 4, pp. 173-189.

NAEYC and NAECS/SDE (2002), Position statement "Early Childhood Curriculum, Assessment, and Program Evaluation—Building an Effective, Accountable System in Programs for Children Birth Through Age 8", NAEYC, Washington DC.

National Institute for Early Education Research (2006), "Early Literacy: Policy and Practice in the Preschool Years", *Policy Brief*, NIEER, New Jersey.

NIEER (2007), "Preschool Curriculum Decision-Making: Dimensions to Consider", *Policy Brief*, NIEER, New Jersey.

NIEER (2009), "Math and Science in Preschool: Policies and Practice", *Policy Brief*, NIEER, New Jersey.

Nicolopoulou, A. (2010), "The Alarming Disappearance of Play from Early Childhood Education", *Human Development*, Vol. 53, pp. 1-4.

OECD (2001), Starting Strong I: Early Childhood Education and Care, OECD, Paris.

OECD (2006), Starting Strong II: Early Childhood Education and Care, OECD, Paris.

OECD (2011), PISA in Focus Nr. 10: What can parents do to help their children succeed in school?, OECD, Paris.

Philips, D. *et al.* (2000), 'Within and Beyond the Classroom Door: Assessing Quality in Child Care Centers", *Early Childhood Research Quarterly*, Vol. 15, No. 4.

Pianta, R. C. *et al.* (2009), "The Effects of Preschool Education: What We Know, How Public Policy Is or Is Not Aligned With the Evidence Base, and What We Need to Know", *Psychological Science in the Public Interest*, Vol.10, No. 2, pp. 49-88.

Pramling, N. and I. Pramling Samuelsson (2011), *Educational encounters: Nordic studies in early childhood didactics*, Dordrecht, The Netherlands: Springer.

Pramling Samuelsson, I. and M. Asplund Carlsson (2008), "The playing learning child: Towards a pedagogy of early childhood", *Scandinavian Journal of Educational Research*, Vol. 52, No. 6, pp. 623-641.

Prentice, R. (2000), "Creativity: a Reaffirmation of its Place in Early Childhood Education", *the Curriculum Journal*, Vol. 11, No. 2, pp. 145-158.

Schweinhart, L. J. and D. P. Weikart (1997), "The High/Scope Preschool Curriculum Comparison Study Through Age 23", Early Childhood Research Quarterly, Vol. 12, pp. 117-143

Sheridan, S., I. Pramling Samuelsson and E. Johansson (eds.) (2009), *"Barns tidiga lärande. En tvärsnittsstudie av förskolan som miljö för barns lärande"* [Children's early learning: A cross-sectional study of preschool as an environment for children's learning] (Göteborg Studies in Educational Sciences, 284), Göteborg, Sweden: Acta Universitatis Gothoburgensis.

Sheridan, S. (2011), "Pedagogical quality in preschool: A commentary", in N. Pramling and I. Pramling Samuelsson (eds.), *Educational encounters: Nordic studies in early childhood didactics*, Dordrecht, The Netherlands: Springer, pp. 223-242.

Siraj-Blatchford, I. *et al.* (2004), "Effective pre-school and primary education", *Primary Practice*, Vol. 37, pp. 28-31.

Siraj-Blatchford, I. and M. Woodhead (2009), "Effective Early Childhood Programmes", *Early Childhood in Focus 4*, Open University, United Kingdom.

Siraj-Blatchford, I. (2010), "A focus on pedagogy: Case studies of effective practice", in K. Sylva, E. Melhuish, P. Sammons, I. Siraj-Blatchford and B. Taggart (eds.), *Early childhood matters: Evidence from the Effective Pre-school and Primary Education project*, pp. 149-165, London: Routledge.

Sommer, P. D., I. Pramling Samuelsson and K. Hundeide (2010), *Child perspectives and children's perspectives in theory and practice*, New York: Springer.

UNESCO (2004), "Curriculum in Early Childhood Education and Care", *UNESCO Policy Brief on Early Childhood,* No. 26, UNESCO, Paris.

UNESCO (2007), "Strong Foundations: Early Childhood Education and Care", *EFA Global Monitoring Report*, UNESCO, Paris.

UNESCO (2010), *Recognizing the Potential of ICT in Early Childhood Education - Analytical Survey*, UNESCO Institute for Information Technologies in Education, Moscow.

Vandenbroeck, M. (2011), "Diversity in Early Childhood Services", *Encyclopedia on Early Childhood Development*, Centre of Excellence for Early Childhood Development and Strategic Knowledge Cluster on Early Child Development, Montreal, available at: www.child-encyclopedia.com/documents/Vandenbroeck ANGxp1.pdf.

# ACTION AREA 2 – BROADENING PERSPECTIVES THROUGH INTERNATIONAL COMPARISON

This section contains an international comparison of:

- Curriculum frameworks and content

## CURRICULUM FRAMEWORKS AND CONTENT

### Findings

#### *Overall framework*

- Almost all OECD countries have some form of a framework – either in the form of a curriculum or standards. The age groups, which curricula are defined by, differ among countries (Figure 2.3).

- In a "split" system countries where child care and early education are governed and managed by different ministries:

    - The majority of countries and jurisdictions have created a learning framework for children in the older age bracket of ECEC: from around age two-and-a-half or three to compulsory schooling.

    - A few countries have parallel frameworks for child care (from age zero to compulsory schooling) and for early education (from age three to compulsory schooling), such as Japan and Korea.

- Many countries aiming to deliver "integrated" services use a framework that covers age zero or one to compulsory schooling (*e.g.*, Australia, New Zealand, Nordic Countries and Prince Edward Island [Canada]).

- Several countries aim to capture continuous child development in early childhood and beyond. This is reflected in the age coverage of the framework in, for example, Hesse (Germany), where there is a curriculum for children from age zero up to age ten, and in Scotland (United Kingdom), where the Curriculum for Excellence covers ages three to 18 – with age-appropriate content for different age groups.

### *Content and subjects*

- Curriculum descriptions can be, in general, categorised into "input"-based or "outcome"-based approaches. Most ECEC curriculum frameworks include "input from staff", *i.e.*, specific requirements as to what is expected of ECEC staff (Figure 2.4). "Values and principles" are also frequently included, while "child outcomes" and "input of the centres" are used by a fewer number of countries than others. Nordic countries tend to avoid using the term "child outcomes", while Anglo-Saxon countries favour the approach.

- Most OECD countries place a high importance on "literacy", "numeracy", "physical education", "science" and "arts" in their curriculum. "Music", "play" and "practical skills" are also popular content areas of the frameworks/guidelines. While several countries allocate time specific to "play" in their curriculum, some indicate that "play" is embedded into other content areas in order to stimulate learning such areas through play (Figure 2.5).

- Few countries have included newly emerging subject matters, which respond to changing needs in present-day society, such as ICT (*e.g.*, Spain), learning foreign languages (*e.g.*, Slovak Republic) and learning approaches (*e.g.*, Korea).

For more detail, see the Survey Response Tables on "Framework for Standards/Curriculum" and "Curriculum Contents" (Excel$^{TM}$ files) in the online Quality Toolbox at **www.oecd.org/edu/earlychildhood/toolbox**.

### Figure 2.3. Coverage of ECEC curriculum frameworks or guidelines by age group

| | |
|---|---|
| | Standards/curriculum for Care |
| | Standards/curriculum for Education and/or Education and Care |
| | No standard curriculum is in place for the specified age group |
| | Compulsory schooling |

| Age | 0 | 1 | 2 | 3 | 4 | 5 | 6 | 7 |
|---|---|---|---|---|---|---|---|---|
| Australia | Belonging, Being, Becoming - Early Years Learning Framework for Australia | | | | | | | |
| Austria | | | | | | | | |
| Belgium (Flemish Comm.) | | | 2.5y | Ontwikkelingsdoelen | | | | |
| Belgium (French Comm.) | | | 2.5y | | | | | |
| Canada (British Columbia) | British Columbia Early Learning Framework for 0-5 year olds | | | | | British Columbia Early Learning Framework for 5-6 year olds | | |
| Canada (Manitoba) | Early Returns Curriculum / Manitoba Kindergarten Curriculum | | | | | | | |
| Canada (Prince Edward Island) | Early Learning Framework | | | | | | | |
| Czech Republic | Framework Educational Programme for Pre-school Education | | | | | | | |
| Denmark | Preschool curriculum Læreplaner | | | | | | | |
| Estonia | 1.5y | | Framework Curriculum of Preschool Education | | | | | |
| Finland | National curriculum guidelines on early childhood education | | | | | | Core Curriculum for Pre-primary education | |
| France | | | 2.5y | National curriculum for école maternelle | | | | |
| Germany (Baden-Württemberg) | Orientierungsplan für Bildung und Erziehung für die baden-württembergischen Kindergärten | | | | | | up to 10 | |
| Germany (Bavaria) | Bildung, Erziehung und Betreuung von Kindern in den ersten drei Lebensjahren | | | Der Bayerische Bildungs- und Erziehungsplan für Kinder in Tageseinrichtungen bis zur Einschulung | | | | |
| Germany (Berlin) | Berliner Bildungsprogramm für die Bildung, Erziehung und Betreuung von kindern in Tageseinrichtungen bis zu ihrem Schuleintritt | | | | | | | |
| Germany (Brandenburg) | Grundsätze der Förderung elementarer Bildung in Einrichtungen der Kindertagesbetreuung in Brandenburg | | | | | | | |
| Germany (Bremen) | Rahmenplan für Bildung und Erziehung im Elementarbereich | | | | | | | |
| Germany (Hamburg) | Hamburger Bildungsempfehlungen für die Bildung und Erziehung von Kindern in Tageseinrichtungen | | | | | | up to 15 | |
| Germany (Hesse) | Bildungs- und Erziehungsplans für Kinder von 0 bis 10 Jahren in Hessen | | | | | | up to 10 | |
| Germany (Mecklenburg-Western Pomerania) | Bildungskonzeption für 0- bis 10-jährige Kinder in Mecklenburg-Vorpommern | | | | | | up to 10 | |
| Germany (Lower Saxony) | Orientierungsplan für Bildung und Erziehung im Elementarbereich niedersächsischer Tageseinrichtungen für Kinder | | | | | | | |
| Germany (North Rhine-Westphalia) | Mehr Chancen durch Bildung von Anfang an - Grundsätze zur Bildungsförderung für Kinder von 0 bis 10 Jahren in Kindertageseinrichtungen und Schulen im Primarbereich in Nordrhein-Westfalen | | | | | | up to 10 | |
| Germany (Rhineland-Palatinate) | Bildungs- und Erziehungsempfehlungen für Kindertagesstätten in Rheinland-Pfalz | | | | | | up to 15 | |
| Germany (Saarland) | Bildungsprogramm für saarländische Kindergärten | | | | | | | |
| Germany (Saxony) | Sächsischer Bildungsplan - ein Leitfaden für pädagogische Fachkräfte in Krippen, Kindergärten und Horten sowie für Kinderttagespflege | | | | | | up to 10 | |
| Germany (Saxony-Anhalt) | Bildungsprogramm für Kindertageseinrichtungen in Sachsen-Anhalt | | | | | | | |
| Germany (Schleswig-Holstein) | Erfolgreich starten: Leitlinien zum Bildungsauftrag in Kindertageseinrichtungen | | | | | | up to 15 | |
| Germany (Thuringia) | Thüringer Bildingsplan für Kinder bis 10 Jahre | | | | | | up to 10 | |

**Figure 2.3. Coverage of ECEC curriculum frameworks or guidelines by age group (continued)**

| Age | 0 | 1 | 2 | 3 | 4 | 5 | 6 | 7 |
|---|---|---|---|---|---|---|---|---|
| Hungary | | | | National Core Programme of Kindergarten | | | | |
| Ireland | Early Childhood Curriculum Framework: Aistear | | | | | | | |
| Israel | | | | Framework Programme for preschool | | | | |
| Italy | 3 months | | | Guidelines for the curriculum | | | | |
| Japan | | | | Course of Study for Kindergarten | | | | |
| Japan | National curriculum of day care centers | | | | | | | |
| Korea | | | | National curriculum for kindergarten | | Nuri Curriculum | | |
| Korea | Standardized childcare curriculum | | | | | | | |
| Luxembourg | | | | Le plan d'études | | | | |
| Mexico | Childcare curriculum | | | Early childhood education curriculum | | | | |
| Netherlands | | | 2.5y | Development goals/competences | | | | |
| New Zealand | Te Whāriki | | | | | | | |
| Norway | Framework Plan for the Content and Tasks of Kindergartens | | | | | | | |
| Poland | | | | Core Curriculum for Preschool Education | | | | |
| Portugal | | | | The Curriculum Guidelines for Pre-School Education | | | | |
| Slovak Republic | | | | The National Education Programme | | | | |
| Slovenia | | National Curriculum for Pre-school Institutions | | | | | | |
| Spain | Early Childhood Curriculum | | | | | | | |
| Sweden | | Läroplan för förskolan Lpfö 98 | | | | | Läroplan för grundskolan, förskoleklassen och fritidshemmet Lgr 11 | |
| Turkey | | | | Pre-school education programme | | | | |
| United Kingdom (England) | Statutory Framework for the Early Years Foundation Stage | | | | | | | |
| United Kingdom (Scotland) | Pre-birth to three - staff guidelines | | | Curriculum for Excellence | | | up to 18 | |
| United States (Georgia) | | | | Georgia's Pre-K Content Standards | | | | |
| United States (Massachusetts) | | | | Guidelines for Preschool Learning Experiences | | | | |
| United States (North Carolina) | | | | Early Learning Standards for North Carolina Preschoolers and Strategies to Guide Their | | | | |
| United States (Oklahoma) | | | | Priority Academic Student Skills | | | | |

Note: For Poland, the compulsory school age was lowered from age seven to six in 2009 with a transition period of three years (until 2012), during which time, parents can choose if their child starts school at age six or seven. For Sweden, *Läroplan för förskolan* is the curriculum for the preschool; *Läroplan för grundskolan, förskoleklassen och fritidshemmet* regards the curriculum for the preschool class, compulsory school and out -of -school centres.

*Source*: OECD Network on Early Childhood Education and Care's "Survey for the Quality Toolbox and ECEC Portal, June 2011.

**Figure 2.4. Approaches of ECEC curriculum[1]**

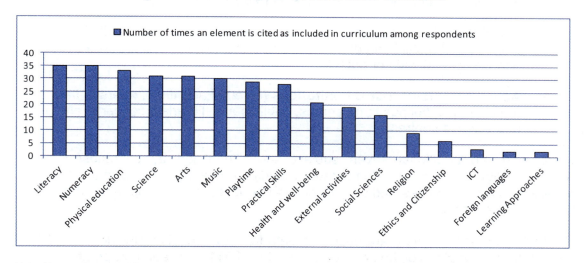

Input from staff

Values and principles

Input from centre

Child outcomes

0  5  10  15  20  25  30  35  40

■ Number of countries or jurisdictions citing the following as content of curriculum framework

Note: Respondents may list more than one content category.

*Source*: OECD Network on Early Childhood Education and Care's "Survey for the Quality Toolbox and ECEC Portal, June 2011.

**Figure 2.5. Content areas included in ECEC curriculum[2]**

■ Number of times an element is cited as included in curriculum among respondents

40
35
30
25
20
15
10
5
0

Literacy, Numeracy, Physical education, Science, Arts, Music, Playtime, Practical Skills, Health and well-being, External activities, Social Sciences, Religion, Ethics and Citizenship, ICT, Foreign languages, Learning Approaches

Note: Respondents may list more than one content category.

*Source*: OECD Network on Early Childhood Education and Care's "Survey for the Quality Toolbox and ECEC Portal, June 2011.

## Definitions and methodologies

A **curriculum framework** (**guidelines** or **standards**) is a tool which can guide the content of and approach to children's care and learning.

**Curriculum contents** can be organised into subject elements or areas. ECEC elements or subject areas highlight priorities and clarify how care, pedagogies and teachings are organised. In the OECD Network on ECEC's "Survey for the Quality Toolbox and ECEC Portal", countries were asked to choose from a list of nine ECEC elements or subject areas:

1. **Literacy**: refers to all subjects related to reading and writing, including language learning and development, and word recognition.

2. **Numeracy**: refers to all subjects related to numbering and counting, including calculations, number recognition, spaces and shapes.

3. **Science**: refers to all scientific subjects, such as geography and natural science.

4. **Arts**: refers to all subjects related to some form of art, including drawing, colouring, painting and handicrafts.

5. **Music**: refers to all subjects involving music, such as singing, playing musical instruments and dancing to music.

6. **Physical education**: refers to all instructed subjects that require physical effort or are related to physical well-being, such as gymnastics, sports and classes about food or hygiene.

7. **Practical skills**: refers to all practices related to practical skills not mentioned in one of the other subjects (*e.g.*, shoe-lacing).

8. **Playtime**: refers to the time children can play freely, *i.e.*, child-initiated play: the time that a child can decide for him- or herself what he/she wants to do and play with (inside or outside).

9. **Activities outside ECEC institutions** (external activities): refers to field trips, such as outings to museums, public parks, libraries, concerts, and art and science centres.

There were an additional seven subject areas identified by countries/regions, including religion, ethics and democratic citizenship; health, personal and/or social well-being; social sciences and/or inter-cultural education; ICT; languages (foreign); and learning approaches.

The findings presented here are based on data from the OECD Network on ECEC's "Survey for the Quality Toolbox and ECEC Portal" (2011). For each graph and table, the countries or regions for which data is used are listed.

# ACTION AREA 3 – SELECTING A STRATEGY OPTION

This section contains a list of strategy options to tackle the following challenge:

- Developing and implementing curriculum

## DEVELOPING AND IMPLEMENTING CURRICULUM

### Challenge 1: Defining goals and content

Defining goals and content is a challenge in many OECD countries due to the different visions of stakeholders on what the curriculum should aim at and include. Policy makers, researchers, ECEC professionals and parents consider that different subjects are important, and each has their own cultural values and ideas about early development.

Determining the degree of detail poses another challenge. Some staff members need and/or prefer the curriculum to include specific pedagogical guidance and a more detailed curriculum, while others are capable of effectively implementing a non-prescriptive curriculum with flexibility for interpretation and adaption to local and culturally specific needs and the individual child.

Furthermore, aligning the curriculum goals and contents with the future needs of society at large can be challenging, especially with changes, such as increasing migration and advances in information and knowledge economies.

*Setting out clear curriculum goals and guiding principles*

- In **Australia**, the Council of Australian Governments developed the *Early Years Learning Framework* (EYLF) *Belonging, Being, and Becoming* in July 2009. It aims to assist educators in providing young children with opportunities to maximise their potential and develop a foundation for future success in learning. In this way, the EYLF contributes to realising the Council of Australian Governments' goal of: "All children having the best start in life to create a better future for themselves and for the nation". The EYLF describes the principles, practice and outcomes essential to support and enhance young children's learning from birth to five years. It has a specific emphasis on play-based learning and recognises the importance of communication and language (including early literacy and numeracy) and social and emotional development. Broadly, the framework is set up in line with the Melbourne Declaration on Education Goals for Young Australians, which states that all young Australians should become successful learners, confident and creative individuals, and active and informed citizens.

- In **Scotland**, the *Pre-Birth to Three: Positive Outcomes for Scotland's Children and Families* has been developed. The document reflects the principles and philosophy which underpin the *Curriculum for Excellence* for ages three to eighteen. *Pre-Birth to Three* emphasises the importance of family and community engagement. Both curricula emphasise four key capacities: to become successful learners, confident individuals, responsible citizens and effective contributors to society. *Curriculum for Excellence* includes experiences that are planned for children and young people through their education. These experiences are grouped into four categories: curriculum areas and subjects; interdisciplinary learning; ethos and life of the school; and opportunities for personal achievement.

- The *Te Whāriki* curriculum for birth until school entry in **New Zealand** emphasises the critical role of socially and culturally mediated learning and of reciprocal and responsive relationships for children with people, places and things. Human relationships and positive well-being form the base principles of the curriculum as well as empowerment, holistic development and the family and community. The early childhood curriculum takes up a model of learning that weaves together intricate patterns of linked experience and meaning rather than emphasising the acquisition of discrete skills. The framework consists of four parts: 1) the principles of the curriculum; 2) its five strands; 3) goals for the early childhood years; and 4) examples of the links between early childhood education and the school years and the New Zealand Curriculum Framework for schools. The strands and goals are linked to each other and focus on well-being, belonging, contributions of children, communication and exploration. The content is age-appropriate for three different age groups within ECEC, namely infants (birth to eighteen months), toddlers (one to three years) and young children (two-and-a-half years to school entry age). The views on development for each of these age groups have been clarified in the curriculum.

- **Prince Edward Island** (**Canada**) introduced in September 2011 a new Early Learning Framework focusing on children from birth to school entry. It lays out a clear vision of the child as a competent contributor to their own learning; includes a set of values and guiding principles which recognise the family as having the most important role in the overall development and well-being of the child; and sets out clear learning objectives and goals, while being respectful of the diversity of the province's communities and understanding that the early childhood educator is key in this relationship. The Framework supports Prince Edward Island's move to a Social-Ecological Early Learning System, provides educators with strategies and reflections to guide their practice, and is based on three learning principles: relationships, environment and experiences.

- **Korea**'s new *Nuri Curriculum for Age 5* focuses on five objectives: 1) developing basic physical abilities and establishing healthy and safe daily routines; 2) learning how to communicate in daily life and developing good practices in terms of language use; 3) developing self-respect and learning how to live with others; 4) developing interest in aesthetics, enjoying arts and learning how to express yourself creatively and; 5) exploring the world with curiosity and enhancing children's abilities to solve problems by applying math and science in daily life. These five objectives are reflected in five curriculum areas: physical activities and health, communication, social relationships, arts and inquiry of nature. These five areas are broken down into 20 categories, 62 sub-categories and 136 detailed described contents/objectives, which children at age five should learn and develop. For instance, the area of communication includes four learning areas: listening, speaking, reading and writing. Speaking includes speaking in words and sentences, describing your feelings, and ideas and experiences.

- *Aistear* is the curriculum framework for all children from birth to six years in **Ireland**. The framework describes the types of learning that are important for children during this period in their lives, and as such, sets out broad learning goals for all children. *Aistear* does this using four broad and interconnected themes: well-being, identity and belonging, communicating, and exploring and thinking. Each theme identifies important dispositions, skills, attitudes and values, and knowledge and understanding.

- **Italy** developed the national Guidelines for the Curriculum (*Indicazioni per il Curricolo*) in September 2007. It is a framework of indications for Infant School (three to six years) and the first cycle of compulsory education (six to fourteen years). It contains the goals, content, pedagogical approaches and instructional practices as well as learning and well-being standards. The guidelines also indicate that education services should promote the development of identity, autonomy, competences, learning, well-being and citizenship of all children.

- The *Course of Study for Kindergartens* (curriculum) in **Japan** consists of three parts. The first part explains and formulates the curriculum, while the second part addresses the aims and content. The curriculum focuses on nurturing emotions, motivation and attitudes as a foundation for development. The goals and curriculum content are centred on five areas: health (mental and physical well-being), human relationships, environment, language and expression (feelings). These five areas are integrated into the curriculum and delivered in a comprehensive manner through specific activities. The third part of the curriculum describes points that kindergartens should take into consideration in the development of lesson plans. For day care centres, there is the *National Curriculum of Day Care Centres*, which is divided into seven chapters: general provisions, child development, nursery education content, planning and evaluating care, health and safety, supporting parents and staff training. The curriculum is centred on the same five areas as the kindergarten Course of Study.

- **Manitoba (Canada)** launched *Early Returns: Manitoba's Early Learning and Child Care Curriculum Framework for Preschool Centres and Nursery Schools* in 2011. This is the curriculum framework of Manitoba that supports staff at preschool centres and nursery schools to develop, describe and enhance their curriculum. It helps staff design play-based, developmentally-appropriate interactions, relationships, environments and experiences to allow all children to develop to their fullest potential.

–   In **Germany**, an important aspect of the curricula of all *Länder* is the emphasis on the development of individual competences, including social skills. Socialisation forms an important focus of the curricula, which is intended to stimulate democratic development and young children's early social and personal development. This is complemented by the learning competences young children should develop. The curricula include the goals a child should reach at a certain age and explains how staff can support children in reaching these goals. Additionally, curricula across Germany include aspects regarding stimulation of inter-cultural knowledge and acceptance and explain the expected roles of ECEC staff and parents with regard to the early education of their children.

–   In **Czech Republic**, in 2004, the Ministry of Education, Youth and Sports published the Framework Educational Programme (FEP) for the ECEC sector, which corresponds to new studies of the development of preschool-aged children. The FEP covers five areas: 1) the child and his/her body; 2) the child and his/her psyche (language and speech, cognitive abilities); 3) the child and the other; 4) the child and society; and 5) the child and the world. The FEP determines a suitable educational offering for each of these areas (teaching and learning methods), a list of expected outcomes, and a list of dangers (risks) that threaten successfulness in teaching and learning. On the basis of the FEP, each school develops its own educational programme in accordance with its special conditions (an obligation since September 2007).

–   The parliament of the **French Community** of **Belgium** adopted core skills and competencies for children ages two-and-a-half to six. All curricula must be developed based on these new standards and approved by the government of the French Community. Additionally, all new programmes developed by education providers and their representative bodies must be approved by the Ministry of Education after being subjected to a Commission of representatives from various education networks and inspectors. The ECEC sector for zero-to-three-year-olds does not have nationally set skills and competencies in place, but all providers for this age group are required by law to comply with the Code of Quality for Care, which spells out principles concerning the development and well-being of the child. Each care provider has to develop a plan which indicates how they will adhere to the code, and this plan has to be approved by the *Office de la Naissance et de l'Enfance* (*ONE* – Department for Birth and Childhood).

–   **Slovak Republic** merged three curricula from 1948 for three-to-four-year-olds, four-to-five-year-olds, and five-to-six-year-olds into one curriculum for three-to-six-year-olds in 2008. The new curriculum has undergone some changes since 1948 and now includes the content of education and care, which consists of four main topics: I am, people, nature and culture. Within each of the four themes, cognitive, motor and social-emotional skills are set out. Additionally, performance standards are defined, which should be achieved before entering primary school.

–   **Turkey** established its preschool curriculum in 2002 but revised it in 2006 by adding instructions and guidance on implementation of content and assessing child development. The aims and goals of the curriculum have been revised and further clarified, with the goal to improve school readiness. In addition, family participation has been included in the curriculum framework, aiming to improve children's development.

–   **Sweden** has revised its preschool curriculum, which was set to enter into force in July 2011. The pedagogical tasks of the preschool have been strengthened in the revised curriculum by clarifying the goals for language and communication, mathematics, natural science and technology. Furthermore, a new section for follow up, evaluation and development and a new section for the responsibility of the head of the preschool have been added. The responsibilities of preschool staff have also been clarified with new and revised guidelines. Philosophically, the curriculum builds on the idea of the child as competent learner, active thinker and involved doer. A strong orientation towards democratic values, continuous learning and development, connecting to the child's experiences, development in groups, and the pedagogical importance of both care and play underpin curriculum development and enactment in ECEC programmes.

–   Kindergartens in **Norway** aim at safeguarding the children's need for care and play and promote learning and formation as a basis for all-around development. In order to make it easier for kindergartens to plan a varied and comprehensive pedagogical programme, the content of kindergartens is divided into seven learning areas for children's experience, exploration and learning: 1) communication, language and text; 2) body, movement and health; 3) art, culture and creativity; 4) nature, environment and technology; 5) ethics, religion and philosophy; 6) local community and society; and 7) numbers, spaces and shapes. Each learning area covers a wide range of learning, and they rarely appear in isolation. The staff groups are free to choose methods in order to foster children's curiosity, creativity and thirst for knowledge. The plan indicates goals for what children shall experience. Assessment practices regarding the plan focus on staff pedagogical approaches – not individual performance of the child.

–   **Slovenia** set out clear goals and principles in its National Curriculum for Preschool Institutions (1999) while emphasising the importance of democracy, multiculturalism and pluralism. The curriculum sets out six areas of activities: movement, language, art, nature, society and mathematics. Additionally, examples of activities for different age groups are given, and the roles of staff are defined. It is regarded as an open framework aiming at ensuring equal opportunities for all children, respecting individual differences, and stimulating early learning and personal development. Developing standards or attainment targets are not defined. The Ministry of Education and Sport developed supplements to the national curriculum, such as the *Supplement to the Curriculum for Educational work with Roma children*, which give guidance and advice on specific pedagogical approaches to foster the development of Roma children and communication and partnership relations with parents of Roma children. The *Supplement to the Curriculum for Preschool Institutions in Nationally Mixed Areas* includes examples of learning activities for children living in nationally mixed areas, *e.g.,* Hungarian and Italian. The *Recommendations for adjusted programmes and additional help for preschool children with special needs* emphasises certain principles of working with special educational needs children.

- **England (United Kingdom)** specifies, in the *Practice Guide* for the *Early Years Foundation Stage,* expected goals for different age groups of children. The goals are made age-appropriate to fit the development stage of young children. Goals are established for birth to 11 months; 8 to 20 months; 16 to 26 months; 22 to 36 months; 30 to 50 months; 40 to 60+ months. They are grouped into six categories: dispositions and attitudes; self-confidence and self-esteem; making relationships; behaviour and self-control; self-care; and sense of community. The *Early Years Foundation Stage* is currently being revised based on the recommendations which were a result of the review that has been conducted on the Foundation Stage. Based on the results of this review, the areas of learning are being changed and the number of early learning goals reduced to meet the needs of staff and other stakeholders regarding implementation.

- The main goals of preschool education in **Poland** are defined by the Core Curriculum, which was last revised in 2008.[3] The overall aims of education are to be implemented through educational activities in 15 specified areas. A detailed list of learning outcomes, which children should gain by the end of preschool, are set for each area. The curriculum does not include specific teaching methods, but it emphasises play-based learning and outdoor activities. According to the revised curriculum, children are being prepared to read and write (reading and writing readiness); however, at least one-fifth of the time in preschool should be devoted to play and another one-fifth of the time to outdoor activities. Additionally, more attention has been put on continuity between primary and preschool education levels.

- In **Estonia**, the renewed national curriculum for preschool child care institutions was approved by the Government of the Republic in 2008 and was based on the preschool education framework curriculum that was enforced in 1999. A difference between the old and new curricula relates to the determination of the concept of learning. The addition of the concept of learning emphasises change, and the focus is now on the child instead of the teacher: a child is an active participant in education and schooling activities, whereas a teacher is the creator of an environment that supports the child's development. In the work of the preschool institution, co-operation between teachers and staff and inclusion of parents is of high importance, helping create a growing and learning environment supportive of children's development. The national curriculum presents the objectives and principles of education presents the objectives and principles of education and schooling activities and the presumed general skills (play, cognitive and learning, and social and self-management skills) and development results of children in seven fields of education and schooling activities: me and the environment; language and speech; Estonian as a second language (starting with three-year-olds, study is for all children whose home language is other than Estonian in all groups with Estonian or other language of instruction); mathematics; art; music; and movement.

## Developing standards or attainment targets

-   In the **Netherlands**, the University of Amsterdam has developed learning goals for young children. Based on this work, the National Expert Centre on Curriculum Development (*SLO*) is now in the process of developing competence levels and descriptors for the end of preschool (ages four/five) and the end of the second year of preschool, *i.e.*, the first year of compulsory schooling (ages five/six). Currently, goals exist for language, which includes three specific pillars: oral language skills, reading literacy, and language awareness and communication. Other planned pillars include maths and socio-emotional development. These three pillars will be supplemented with suggested pedagogical activities.

-   **New Zealand**'s *Te Whāriki* curriculum developed dispositions, also named learning outcomes, for each of its five strands: well-being, belonging, contributions of children, communication and exploration. These dispositions are encouraged rather than taught. For each strand, knowledge, skills and attitudes are described, and examples of experiences are given, which help to meet these outcomes. Since the curriculum emphasises social relationships and personal well-being, outcomes are formulated in terms of relationships and well-being. Examples of outcomes include: confidence and ability to express emotional needs, knowledge about how to keep themselves healthy, and a sense of responsibility for their own well-being and that of others.

-   For nursery education, developmental objectives have been developed in **Flanders (Belgium)** by the Ministry of Education. They are laid down in the Flemish Government Decree of 27 May 1997 and have been applicable from the school year 1998/99. They are the minimum objectives with regard to knowledge, insight, skills and attitudes, which the authorities consider to be desirable for children ages two-and-a-half to six.

-   **Scotland (United Kingdom)** clearly prescribes in their *Curriculum for Excellence* what children should know and experience at different educational levels. The outcomes and experiences are designed based on eight different subject areas, including expressive arts, health and well-being, languages, mathematics, religious and moral education, sciences, social studies and technologies. Taken as a whole, the experiences and outcomes differ per age group and embody the attributes and capabilities each child should achieve.

-   **England (United Kingdom)** covers six areas within the *Early Years Foundation Stage* (EYFS): personal, social and emotional development; communication, language and literacy; problem solving, reasoning and numeracy; knowledge and understanding of the world; physical development and creative development. Each area is described in terms of what children should know and be able to do by the end of the EYFS – before attending primary schooling. The areas of learning are currently being revised for implementation in September 2012.

-   The Ministry of Education in **Portugal** is setting *Learning Outcomes* for pre-school education (three-to-six-year-olds). Learning outcomes are acknowledged as the evidence of child performance, and they are defined in terms of child outcomes. They can be used as tools supporting teachers in their everyday work. The *Framework Law of Preschool* states the general objectives of preschool.

- The *Early Years Learning Framework* of **Australia** is outcome-based. The goals are designed to capture the integrated and complex learning of all children and include the following five goals and outcomes: 1) children should have a strong sense of identity; 2) children are connected with and contribute to their world; 3) children have a strong sense of well-being; 4) children are confident and involved learners; and 5) children are effective communicators.

- **Singapore** set out expected child outcomes by the end of their ECEC experiences. For example, the *Nurturing Early Learners: A framework for a kindergarten curriculum in Singapore* broadly spells out what children should be able to do by the end of their education in kindergarten: 1) having a sense of what is right and what is wrong; 2) be willing to share and take turns with others; 3) be able to relate to others; 4) be curious and willing to explore; 5) be able to listen and speak with understanding; 6) be comfortable and happy with themselves; 7) have developed physical co-ordination and healthy living habits; and 8) love their families, friends, teachers and school.

- The Infant Curriculum (part of the Primary School Curriculum [1999]) in **Ireland** sets out content objectives to guide children's learning in the first two years of primary school, at which stage children are between the ages of four and seven. The content objectives focus on skills, attitudes and values, concepts, and knowledge and understanding.

- **Prince Edward Island**'s (**Canada**) Early Learning Framework includes learning goals, which focus on learning dispositions and attitudes rather than discrete skills. There are four broad learning goals: 1) well being; 2) exploration and discovery; 3) expression and communication; and 4) social and personal responsibility, each with clearly stated objectives for children from birth to school entry. This approach is more in line with the 21st Century Education principles of the province.

### *Reviewing or analysing the curriculum to improve relevance*

- In **Korea**, the country has revised the *National Kindergarten Curriculum* seven times on a regular basis since the first edition in 1969: every revision was based on latest research findings. For each revision, the Ministry of Education commissioned a committee of experts and teachers to implement research in the revision of the curriculum. Based on research undertaken in 2010, the *National Kindergarten Curriculum* placed greater emphasis on creativity and character education. The *Standard Childcare Curriculum* for zero-to-four-year-olds was implemented for the first time in 2007, and a revision was undertaken in 2010 to improve the quality of child care services, diversify operation hours of child care in accordance with family needs, and strengthen the link between child care and elementary schooling. Revisions are based on latest research findings so as to meet changing family and societal needs; and the revised curriculum will be implemented in 2012. Additionally, in September 2011, the Ministry of Education, Science and Technology and the Ministry of Health and Welfare developed and launched the *Nuri Curriculum for Age 5* (*Nuri* means "world"), a common curriculum to improve the relevance of both care and education.

- ECEC staff in **Scotland** (**United Kingdom**) found their previous curricula for ages three to five and five to fourteen too descriptive, leaving insufficient room for local adaptation. Therefore, the curricula were revised, which resulted in a curriculum for children ages three to eighteen with less descriptive outcomes and practices.

- Some ECEC workers in **England** (**United Kingdom**) found the *Early Years Foundation Stage* (EYFS) too prescriptive, leaving insufficient room for innovation. Therefore, a review of the EYFS was conducted in 2010-11 to consider how the framework could be simplified, clarified and made less prescriptive. The review also recommended revising the EYFS to improve its accessibility to parents, and to promote action to respond to children progressing slower than expected.

- In **Turkey**, when the curriculum was being revised in 2006, the General Directorate of Preschool Education reported all the feedback it received from experts and teachers. The current preschool practices in Turkey and the revisions that were previously made in the primary education curriculum were reviewed. Other countries were analysed as well. Based on these analyses and reviews, further revisions were made to the framework.

- **Sweden** has reviewed and revised its preschool curriculum to increase and update their ECEC curriculum of 1998. The revised curriculum will come into force July 2011. The pedagogical tasks of the preschool have been strengthened in the revised curriculum by clarifying the goals for language and communication, mathematics, natural science and technology. Furthermore, a new section for follow up, evaluation and development and a new section for the responsibility of the head of the preschool have been added.

- **Ireland** has prioritised a review of the Infant Curriculum (for ages four to five), in light of the development of the common curriculum framework (for ages zero to five), which has been criticised for its over-crowded, play-free nature. Based on the review, the content will be adapted.

- In **Japan**, councils, composed of external experts, are set up to review standards of kindergarten education and nursery care as a way to link research to curriculum reform. Based on the reviews, curriculum is adapted when needed. The *National Curriculum of Day Care Centres* was established in 1965 and was last revised in 2008. The revised version provided clarification on minimum standards as issued by the Ministry of Health, Labour and Welfare and a generalisation of content (chapters 7 to 13).

- The 1979 Educational Programme for the Education and Care of Pre-school Children in **Slovenia** has been revised after analyses of the current situation, world trends on preschool education and recommendations from international organisations and the Council of Europe. The previous curriculum was found to be very strict. The new curriculum of 1999/2000 emphasised the relevance of using various methods and approaches in preschool, leading to more flexibility, and pointed out that the diversity of the age group should be taken into account.

*Supporting local initiatives in setting up their own curriculum*

- In the **Netherlands**, a national curriculum does not exist. Each provider is entitled to design their own curriculum. The national government provides centres with a "list" of recommended and nationally approved curriculum frameworks. The curricula on this list have been piloted and found to be effective in stimulating early development. Centres can either decide to implement a curriculum on this list or design their own. Many ECEC providers in the Netherlands chose the latter and design a framework which includes elements of different curricula that are found most relevant to local circumstances.

- In **Australia**, the *Early Years Learning Framework* is designed to guide early childhood educators in developing effective early childhood programmes. It is expected that, following a period of familiarisation, each early childhood service will develop their own strategy to implement the Framework, taking their own unique context into consideration.

- Staff in **Scotland** (**United Kingdom**) can set up their own curriculum to meet local or special development needs. The *Curriculum for Excellence* is less detailed and prescriptive than previous curriculum advice and can therefore be used as a basis for centres in setting up their own curriculum. The *Curriculum for Excellence* provides professional space for teachers and other staff to use in order to meet the varied needs of all children and young people.

- The objectives for nursery education in **Flanders** (**Belgium**) specify the minimum knowledge and skills children should encompass but do not indicate how to acquire them. Schools are free in the design and choice of curriculum. The curriculum is usually developed by the school board or the school's umbrella educational organisation and is afterwards assessed by the education inspectorate. Additionally, the Minister of Education has to approve the curriculum before schools can use their own curriculum.

- According to the Kindergarten Act in **Norway**, the owner of a kindergarten may adapt the national Framework Plan for Kindergartens to local conditions. The kindergarten's co-ordinating committee, consisting of staff, parents and owner, must establish an annual plan for the kindergarten's pedagogical activities. Staff members are expected to carry out the pedagogical programme in accordance with the national Framework Plan, local adaptation of the Framework Plan, and the annual plan.

- Each ECEC service in **New Zealand** develops its own curriculum, based on the early childhood curriculum, *Te Whāriki*, to meet the needs of its children, families, the specific setting and the local community. All curricula should be based on the principles of the early childhood curriculum and be planned in terms of the curriculum's strands and goals. *Te Whāriki* is designed to be adapted to local circumstances and children's special needs. Additionally, each curriculum should include aspects of the Māori language and culture to stimulate early knowledge and respect for the indigenous culture. Therefore, *Te Whāriki* is bilingual and protects the culture and language of the Māori.

- In **Korea**, each city and provincial education office is given autonomy in implementing the guidelines of the *National Kindergarten Curriculum* according to its own local needs. Based on the guidelines and kindergartens' needs, individual district education support offices prepare practice-oriented supervisory materials, which kindergartens can use. Each kindergarten then organises and implements the curriculum according to its own circumstances and specific wishes.

- In **Sweden**, centres are free to evolve their own local curricula and pedagogical methods from the principles outlined in the state curriculum (*Lpfö*) established in 1998. The national ECEC curriculum specifies broad goals and guidelines but does not specify the means by which these goals should be achieved.

- In **Germany**, there is no curriculum in place at federal level: each *Länder* creates its own curriculum framework. Within each *Länder*, ECEC centres and providers are encouraged to adapt the *Länder*'s curriculum framework to their own needs and the needs of the children attending their centre. However, if a centre adapts the curriculum framework to its own needs, this curriculum should be based on the *Länder* framework and explicitly refer to the framework in its curriculum.

- In **Italy**, each individual setting should develop a curriculum based on the objectives defined in the *National Indications for the Curriculum*. Teachers can draw up the curriculum, called the Educational Offer Plan (*POF*), including activities for each subject, the tools to be used, timeline and the assessment procedures. Since ECEC centres can develop their own *POF*, the plan can be in line with the needs of local community regarding time flexibility, immigrant children and parental needs. Each plan must be presented to the parents and community before receiving approval for implementation.

- The early childhood curriculum of **Spain** includes general guidelines. This approach allows staff to adapt the curriculum and work to the characteristics of the environment and community. They can develop and improve the programme to meet the needs of children, adapting to local social and cultural characteristics.

- In **Ireland**, *Aistear* is not prescriptive and does not subscribe to a particular pedagogical approach. It can be adapted at local level to support practice in a range of different types of settings, while at the same time, providing one set of learning goals to guide practitioners and children's work across all settings.

- Since the standards in the *Course of Study for Kindergartens* in **Japan** provide only a general outline, individual kindergartens are able to take a creative approach to formulating and implementing a curriculum, which meets the specific needs of a child's mental and physical development, the local area or the kindergarten itself.

- The Ministry of Education in **Mexico** created a framework syllabus to serve as a framework development guide. Each institution can use this guide to develop a curriculum meeting its own needs. This helps providers in developing a qualitative curriculum suitable for the children, parents and community in their region.

- In the **United States**, *Early Learning and Development Standards* (ELDSs) are created by individual states. These state-level expectations, guidelines or developmental milestones reflect state laws and the state's needs and wishes. Most ECEC providers, some of whom are private, are not required to use ELDSs, but states stimulate awareness on the existence, and encourage the voluntary use, of ELDSs across various settings by disseminating print and electronic copies of the standards.

- In the case of **Poland**, institutions offering preschool education are expected to develop their own curriculum based on the Core Curriculum, which presents general goals, learning outcomes and guidelines but does not define specific teaching methods. A centre's curriculum must define educational goals and the methods used to meet those goals as well as a methodology used to assess the school readiness of a child upon completion of preschool. Teachers can develop their own curriculum individually or as a team or use a curriculum prepared by other authors. The chosen curriculum must be approved by the kindergarten director after consultation with the board of teachers.

### *Involving stakeholders in the design process*

- In **Australia**, ECEC bodies and child development organisations were involved in the design process to ensure that different views and cultural perspectives were reflected in the curriculum. A country-wide network was in place to provide support and training to early childhood educators, and there was an agreement with universities and further education institutions to introduce the Framework.

- The *Curriculum for Excellence* in **Scotland** (**United Kingdom**) has built upon existing good practice across different sectors of Scottish education and takes account of research and international comparisons. It recognises the professionalism of staff in the development process. From the National Debate on Education in 2002 through to the drafting and preparation of the experiences and outcomes for publication, teachers were asked to contribute their knowledge and expertise to the process. One of the main responsibilities of development teams was to ensure that they drew on the expertise and advice of a wide range of staff in early years centres, schools, universities and colleges across all settings where learning takes place. They did this at meetings, events, seminars and focus groups, picking up ideas and case studies of good practice; and they maintained contact with subject networks and other specialist forums. Learning and Teaching Scotland, a non-departmental public body, published the proposed experiences and outcomes in draft format to give practitioners and wider stakeholders the opportunity to comment. There was further engagement during the refinement process leading to publication.

- **Korea** involves various stakeholders when revising a curriculum to reflect different perspectives and needs. Typically, a curriculum development/ revision team consists of 20 to 30 experts including representatives of academic associations. They undertake research in order to set directions, goals and content areas in collaboration with 150 to 200 people in consultation/working groups (professors, researchers, superintendents, practitioners in ECEC, elementary school curriculum experts, etc). As part of the process, national surveys for teachers and parents were undertaken to have an idea about their opinions and needs. After holding a series of seminars and public hearings, the curriculum framework and specifics have been finalised. It usually takes three years to revise a national curriculum and carry out piloting before implementing the revised version. For the *Nuri Curriculum* for five-year-olds, stakeholders from both early childhood education and child care sectors, as well as ministry officials, formed a task force team and collaborated on the design and content of the curriculum.

– **Finland** set up a steering group and working committee of policy makers and representatives of the ECEC sector to discuss and define the contents of an ECEC curriculum. A number of ECEC experts were also invited to contribute to the work and asked to comment on the draft guidelines.

– The National Agency for Education in **Sweden** was commissioned by the national government to draft a proposal for a revision of the current curriculum. Thereafter, the Ministry of Education established and consulted a reference-group with representatives from universities (researchers), municipalities (*e.g.*, head of preschool), trade unions and other stakeholders in the field. Researchers were also consulted and asked to give comments, which were incorporated in the revised proposal.

– A steering committee, which oversees all the changes in the curriculum, has been established in **Luxembourg**. The committee brings together different relevant stakeholders and their representatives and provides opportunities to share views, best practices and experiences. These opinions and views are noted and taken into account when changes in the curriculum are made.

– In **Spain**, the Ministry of Education and Science set up a process of public debate on education in September 2004 to discuss challenges in the education system and to agree upon solutions. The debate lasted six months, allowing key stakeholders to express pros and cons on different views and ideas. Autonomous Communities (regional governments) and the organisations representing school councils were also invited to express their views. Individuals and other stakeholder associations could send the Ministry of Education and Science their thoughts and suggested solutions. Based on the agreement, a media campaign was launched to make the approved Organic Law of Education known by the public and those working in the Spanish education system.

– **Norway** established new legislation concerning kindergartens in 2005. Essential intentions of the new kindergarten act were increased quality in kindergartens, children's right to participation and a new and expanded section concerning the content of kindergartens. The new act presupposed a revision of the Framework Plan. The Ministry of Education set up a working group, consisting mostly of researchers and practitioner, to draft a revised plan in accordance with a mandate given by the Ministry. After making some changes, the Ministry put the plan on a public hearing prior to establishing it as regulation. The public hearing included all stakeholders in the ECEC field, such as owners, parents, educators, researchers, other ministries, organisations and administrative bodies on various levels. Recently, a new public commission was set up to give advice on what all children should have experienced in kindergarten before they start school. Their report has been put to public hearing and will be considered in a future revision of the Framework Plan for the Content and Tasks of Kindergartens.

– In **Luxembourg**, the process of developing a new programme, based on a competency-based approach, was a participatory process. In December 2006, a first version of the cross-disciplinary skills that children must master at the end of the four basic education cycles was submitted for review to all staff members of preschool and primary education. Staff were invited to comment on the drafts and discuss whether the competences were defined as realistic. The Minister of Education met staff members personally at regional review meetings to hear their views and comments; their opinions were taken into account when revising the document.

– **Portugal**'s *Curriculum Guidelines* for three-to-six-year-olds were developed in a process of broad consultation involving preschool teachers and researchers. Official publication of the Curriculum Guidelines for Pre-School Education was preceded by a long discussion process involving the preparation of three drafts. The first draft was analysed by institutional partners: the Regional Directorates for Education, the Inspector-General of Education, Initial Teacher Training Schools, Teachers' Associations, Teachers' Unions, the Association of Private Education Providers and Parent Associations. A second draft was produced based on comments received from the institutional partners and was distributed among groups of preschool teachers for comments. Teachers were asked to apply the proposed guidelines prior to commenting. Comments from the teachers were incorporated into the final version of the Curriculum Guidelines. Portugal is in the process of developing curriculum guidelines for ages zero to three, in line with the guidelines for ages three to six. Relevant stakeholders, including local authorities, ECEC staff, teacher and parent associations, and researchers are involved in the design process. During a forum in June 2011, debates were organised with stakeholders discussing what should be included in the curriculum guidelines for ages zero to three and how it should be implemented.

– The Ministry of Education, Science, Research and Sport of **Slovak Republic** assigned the design of the curriculum to the State Pedagogical Institute, a ministerial institute. The institute subsequently involved ECEC experts in the design process. The State School Inspectorate and universities also played a significant role in the curriculum design. They were widely involved in discussions together with ECEC professionals.

– The *Te Whāriki* curriculum in **New Zealand** has been developed from, and builds on, experience with curriculum development by different early childhood services, together with findings in research, international literature, and the shared knowledge and agreed understandings that have emerged in New Zealand over the past two decades on child development. Feedback on the draft document from different stakeholders, including ECEC staff, local authorities, researchers and parents, has been taken into account when revising the draft version. The curriculum also considered findings from exploratory studies.

– In **Turkey**, the curriculum for preschool education was revised in 2006. The committee, consisting of international and national experts, competent departments of the General Directorate of Preschool Education, headmasters of kindergartens and preschool teachers were all involved in the revision process.

- **Prince Edward Island** (**Canada**), in 2011, established a stakeholder group that was the advisory committee overseeing the development of the Early Learning Framework, the new curriculum for early child development from birth until primary schooling.

- In the **United States**, *Early Learning and Development Standards* are created by individual states. The process usually involves input from a variety of stakeholders in the ECEC community.

## Challenge 2: Curriculum alignment for continuous child development

Ensuring continuous child development from birth to primary education is a key challenge in countries with a "split system" where child care and early education are administered by different ministries. In these countries, a lack of a curriculum framework for children ages zero to three is often non-existent; or, if it exists, is not aligned with the curriculum for children ages three to six. The rationale of the split system is often attributed to differences between the two sectors, such as historical roots, different goals and focus on contents.

Ensuring smooth transition from ECEC to primary education is also a challenge. Teaching approaches and practices that children experience are often disconnected in ECEC settings and compulsory schooling.

### *Aligning curriculum with broader quality goals and assessment practices*

- In **Australia**, educational programmes and practice in ECEC, including the implementation of the *Early Years Learning Framework*, is one of the National Quality Standards in the National Quality Framework. ECEC provisions are assessed on their curriculum practices, which should be in line with the broader quality goals of the National Quality Framework. This ensures delivery of nationally consistent and quality early childhood education programmes and practice across sectors and jurisdictions.

- In **Flanders** (**Belgium**), the developmental objectives set out for nursery education are used by the authorities as a tool for quality assurance. When conducting a school audit, the education inspectorate balances the pursuit of these objectives against school context and the characteristics of the pupil population.

- In **Norway**, **Sweden** and **Scotland** (**United Kingdom**), the curricula are aligned with international conventions, such as the United Nations Convention on the Rights of the Child (1989). In Scotland, these rights are one of the four key principles of the National Pre-Birth to Three Guidance. The legislative framework of Norway (the Kindergarten Act and the Framework Plan for the Content and Tasks of Kindergartens) states the expectations concerning the quality of kindergartens, including conditions for learning and well-being. Norway introduced a section in the Act giving "Children in kindergarten (...) the right to express their views on the day to day activities of the kindergarten". This is followed up in the Framework Plan for kindergarten. Children are seen as subjects or agents in their own right who should be met with respect in their diverse forms of communication.

- In **England** (**United Kingdom**), the *Early Years Foundation Stage* is part of a broader child care strategy, which includes effective earlier intervention where developmental problems become evident and support for parents who need it most.

- In **Ireland**, the *National Quality Framework for Early Education* (*Síolta*) consists of three distinct but independent elements. The first aspect of the framework is the national standards for quality in ECEC services; the second, the *Early Childhood Curriculum Framework* (*Aistear*); the third, assessment to provide information, which will allow for the dynamic development of *Síolta* so that it adequately meets the needs of ECEC services, children and families.

### Adopting a unified curriculum for care and early education

- In **Korea**, the Common Curriculum for age five, called *Nuri Curriculum*, will be implemented in February 2012. The *Nuri Curriculum* focuses on integrating two separate curricula from kindergarten and child care, so that it ensures fair quality of ECEC services for children in both provisions. The curriculum will emphasise children's well-being, safety, play activities and citizenship rather than cognitive, academic activities and will include five development areas: motor skills and health, communication, social relationships, art and science. Also, it aims to foster children's creativity through holistic development and will be aligned with the curriculum in primary school (grades one and two). A contest in which the public could come up with a title for the curriculum raised public awareness for the new curriculum.

- **Australia**'s Early Years Learning Framework *Belonging, Being, and Becoming* is developed for children from birth to age five and transition to compulsory schooling.

- The curriculum, *Te Whāriki*, in **New Zealand** has been developed for children from birth to school entry. However, to ensure the framework is age-appropriate, the content is made for three different age groups within ECEC: infants (birth to eighteen months), toddlers (one to three years), and young children (two-and-a-half years to school entry age).

- **England** (**United Kingdom**) developed the *Early Years Foundations Stage* for children from birth to five years, replacing three earlier frameworks for different age groups (*Curriculum Guidance for the Foundation Stage*; *Birth to Three Matters*; and *National Standards for Under 8 year-olds*).

- **Spain** has a curriculum framework for ages zero to six, but has split the framework into two development cycles for ages zero to three and three to six to make it age-appropriate. The curriculum for both cycles is organised around the same areas: 1) knowledge of self and personal autonomy; 2) knowledge of the environment; and 3) language development: communication and representation. These areas are adapted to the age and development level of the child.

- **Japan** is aligning the content and goals of its *National Curriculum of Day Care Centres* to its *Course of Study for Kindergartens*. Both frameworks will be made more consistent with one another to streamline transition from care to kindergarten.

- **Portugal** aims to design curriculum guidelines for ages zero to three, in alignment with the existing framework for ages three to six, to ensure continuous child development.

### *Aligning ECEC curriculum with other levels of education*

- The government of South Australia (Australia) has set up a framework for ages zero to eighteen. The *Länder* of Baden-Württemberg, Bavaria, Hessen, Mecklenburg-Western Pomerania, North Rhine-Westphalia, Sachsen, and Thuringia (Germany) have developed a framework for ages zero to ten, and Hessen is now considering extending the framework to age eighteen. The *Länder* of Hamburg, Rheinland-Pfalz, and Schleswig-Holstein (Germany) have aligned their ECEC curriculum with primary and lower secondary education: their curricula cover ages zero to fifteen.

- **Sweden** aims to promote continuity of learning from birth to age 20 guided by the same principles and values: democracy, inviolability of human life, individual freedom and integrity, equal value of all people, gender equality, solidarity with the vulnerable and respect for the environment.

- *Curriculum for Excellence* is **Scotland**'s (**United Kingdom**) curriculum for children and young people ages three to eighteen. It replaces the curricula for children ages 3-5 and 5-14 to ensure continuous development. Additionally, *Curriculum for Excellence* builds on the foundations developed in the critical years of pre-birth to three which is supported by the new *Pre-Birth to Three* national guidance.

- In the **United States**, there are neither national standards nor curriculum, but both exist at the state level. All 50 states plus the District of Columbia have their own *Early Learning and Development Standards* (ELDSs) for preschool children (ages three to five), and 24 states have developed or are developing ELDSs to support the development of infants and toddlers (ages birth to three). States can use ELDSs to ensure continuity between the skills children are building in preschool and the expectations for their further development as they transition to kindergarten, first grade and beyond, by aligning it with K-12 Common Core Standards.

- The *Te Whāriki* curriculum in **New Zealand** is linked to the country's Curriculum Framework for schools. The principles in the school curriculum are integrated into *Te Whāriki* as well. For each of the strands of the ECEC curriculum (well-being, belonging, contributions of children, and communication and exploration), links have been made with the learning areas and skills in the school curriculum to smoothen the transition from preschool to primary school.

- **Luxembourg** implemented a new competency-based curriculum approach in 2009 for its cycles of basic education. The curriculum defines the core skills for preschool education for three-to-four-year-olds, primary and secondary education. The curriculum includes the competencies to be developed during the four learning cycles and includes examples on how to achieve the skills.

- The Ministry of Education in **Portugal** is setting *Learning Outcomes for all education levels*, aiming at aligning the outcomes for different education levels. Although the implementation of the outcomes will not be mandatory, it is expected that teachers, children, students and families will start using the outcomes and regard them as a useful tool in curriculum implementation and early development.

- **Norway**'s new purpose clauses for kindergarten, schools and vocational training have the same structure and express the same value base. This is done to contribute to greater coherence between kindergartens, schools and training establishments. The purpose clause still reflects the uniqueness of kindergartens. Norway has also made a clear connection between the Framework Plan for ECEC and the Curricula for Norwegian Primary Schools. The learning areas are, to a great extent, the same since the subjects are similar in ECEC and primary school.

- In **Flanders** (**Belgium**), the aims of the different subjects in nursery and primary education are interrelated with one another, and the five subjects are the same for nursery and primary education. This enhances transparency and underpins continuous development across nursery and primary school.

- In **Ireland**, the **Netherlands** and **Sweden**, early education is often included as part of primary schooling. Preschool in the Netherlands is free of charge for four-year-olds, while compulsory education in kindergarten starts at age five. In Sweden, preschool is free from age three for 525 hours per year, although compulsory schooling does not start until age seven.

## Challenge 3: Dissemination and communication about the framework

Many countries experience challenges in informing ECEC staff and parents when a new or revised curriculum is set out. There is insufficient awareness and knowledge – among ECEC professionals – about what curriculum can do to help them ensure and enhance child development. This is the case especially among professionals with a lower qualification or working in remote areas.

Similarly, there is insufficient interest among parents in knowing what children are doing at ECEC centres through learning about the curriculum goals and content. This is the case especially among immigrant parents and families with a low social-economic or educational background.

A lack of established communication channels between the national government, local governments and ECEC staff, or between staff and parents, is one of the key factors that can explain dissemination challenges.

*Informing stakeholders about curriculum change through seminars and meetings*

- In **Italy**, curriculum changes were communicated to head managers of the ministerial Regional School Offices by the Ministry of Education, University and Research (*MIUR*). *MIUR* informed Inspectors of the changes; Inspectors disseminated the changes to headmaster and teachers; national seminars were organised for headmasters and teachers to address the changes on thematic areas; and the changes were posted on the ministry's website and described in emails to teachers.

– In **Korea**, large-scale public hearings and seminars have been held before and after announcing the revised versions of the *National Kindergarten Curriculum* and the *Standard Childcare Curriculum* to inform and discuss changes with a range of stakeholders, including local government officials, in-service teacher trainers, university professors, and representatives of kindergarten and child care centre associations. City and provincial education offices and Child Care Information Centres also organised meetings, seminars and conferences to communicate curriculum changes to teachers and directors at the local level.

– In **Scotland** (**United Kingdom**), ECEC staff members were informed about curriculum changes at meetings, events and seminars. Providers organised meetings for parents and explained the *Curriculum for Excellence* via PowerPoint presentations, developed by Teaching and Learning Scotland.

– The National Agency for Education in **Sweden** has been commissioned by the government to implement the curriculum changes. The agency will arrange conferences for municipality management and conferences for heads of preschools to inform them about the revisions in the curriculum.

– In **Luxembourg**, the College of Inspectors has an important role in the implementation of curricula since the college is, by law, responsible for ensuring compliance with laws and regulations. One of the main strategies chosen to reach people in the field are the mandatory regional meetings with inspectors and representatives of the department in which all new documents and programmes are going to be implemented. In these meetings, the new curricula are presented and explained, and institutions are informed about regulation requirements.

– The Ministry of Education in **Mexico** set up meetings with ECEC providers, organised conferences, forums and congresses to explain the changes in the curriculum. It also organised field visits to inform providers and staff about the changes.

– **Japan** organised a briefing session for those responsible for the administration of kindergarten education in all prefectural and city governments.

### *Communicating with staff through written forms of dissemination*

– **Ireland** sent copies of the Infant Curriculum to all providers and staff members. The ministry also provided information and support on a website developed for ECEC staff.

– The responsible ministries for ECEC in **Mexico** and **Sweden** developed brochures for the ECEC sector explaining the changes in the curriculum. These were sent to the providers and staff of ECEC centres.

- **Korea** is currently developing explanatory guidelines, a teaching manual, DVDs, CD-ROMs, PowerPoint presentations and websites in order to increase the level of familiarity of ECEC staff with the *Nuri Curriculum for Age 5*.

- **Japan** created explanatory guidelines that explain the content of the *Course of Study for Kindergartens* and the *National Curriculum of Day Care Centres* in simple wording for ECEC staff.

- The responsible ministries for ECEC in **England** (**United Kingdom**), **Italy**, **Luxembourg**, **Spain** and **Sweden** (National Agency for Education) developed online support websites for staff, providing information, guidance and support regarding curriculum changes.

### *Communicating with parents*

- **Korea** disseminated updated information on curriculum revisions to parents through the use of brochures, websites, and organising meetings and lectures.

- **Australia** distributed information about the *Early Years Learning Framework* for families, and made this information available online in 20 languages.

- In **Scotland** (**United Kingdom**), templates to support staff in creating or customising materials for communicating with parents are available online. Learning and Teaching Scotland, a non-departmental public body, also developed information sheets for parents on the importance of different curriculum subjects, including literacy, mathematics, transitions between different education systems and outdoor learning. In addition to this, a series of posters were distributed to providers, which can be used to raise awareness among parents about the *Curriculum for Excellence* for the early years.

- **England** (**United Kingdom**) developed a website to inform parents and others about the new curriculum and to support parents when choosing child care.

### Challenge 4: Effective implementation

Gaining wide support for curriculum and implementation is a challenge faced by many countries. Without buy-in from those who are to implement a change or a new idea, any reform may fail. And the buy-in or consensus cannot be built – without sufficient and strategic consultation – at the implementation stage.

It is also a challenge to implement the change or new idea without support. The kind of support required for effective implementation depends on various characteristics of the staff as well as contexts.

Furthermore, preparing conditions for staff to effectively implement the curriculum is another challenge. Insufficient guidelines and resources are likely to enhance difficulties, especially for inexperienced, new staff or staff with lower qualifications. Certain working environments, such as having too many children to look after, may hinder practising the pedagogy guided in the curriculum.

Monitoring or evaluation of effective implementation at the programme level is another challenge for national governments.

*Ensuring stakeholder buy-in by involving them in the design process*

- **Australia** involved ECEC bodies and organisations in the design process and prepared a national implementation plan of the *Early Years Learning Framework*. All states and territories agreed to follow the plan in their respective jurisdictions using an additional range of strategies. With stakeholders involved in the design process, the framework had their support upon implementation.

- In **Scotland** (**United Kingdom**), anyone with an interest in education was invited to be part of the feedback and revision process of the *Curriculum for Excellence*. The draft experiences and outcomes were published online and were accompanied by an online questionnaire for individuals, groups, schools and organisations to feed back their thoughts and views. Additionally, 37 focus groups were held, covering each curriculum area and involving practitioners, senior education managers, representatives from professional bodies, industry, parents and learners to discuss the draft experiences and outcomes. The University of Glasgow was commissioned to analyse the feedback on the draft experiences and outcomes.

- During the formulation process (1992-95) of the developmental objectives for nursery education in **Flanders** (**Belgium**), a number of measures were taken to create the largest possible support. In the development commissions which formulated the first proposals, academics, but also teachers and school management teams, were represented. After that, the proposals of the development commissions were checked by board groups in which teachers, school heads, advisors and inspectors gave feedback. Finally, a social debate was organised about the proposals. The wider public, individuals and organisations (*e.g.*, socio-cultural organisations, trade-unions, parent associations) had an opportunity to comment on the proposals by written communication and at discussion evenings. All reactions were taken into account when adapting the proposal.

- In **Slovenia**, at the time of curricular reform at the national level, particular attention was paid to the participation of all interested parties. First, a public call for comments on the draft version was organised, in which institutions, such as faculties, schools, societies, non-governmental organisations and others, took part. Curricular commissions, composed of 500 experts, were involved in revising the initial curriculum from preschools to upper-secondary education, taking into account the comments received. Another 300 experts were involved as reviewers or consultants. Furthermore, the curricular commissions held meetings with representatives of local governments, parents, and preschool and school representatives to present the proposals of the reform. Slovenian legislation stipulates that curriculum changes should be introduced gradually, which means that the number of preschool institutions and schools implementing the changes increased every year, *i.e.*, not all kindergartens implemented the changes at the same time. Institutions were eligible for implementation when they met certain requirements regarding human (in-service training) and other resources. Before the implementation of the new curriculum, each preschool institution and school had to appoint a team in charge of the introduction and implementation process to oversee the work.

– **Norway**'s revised Framework Plan for the Content and Tasks of Kindergartens is a regulation to the Kindergarten Act. Norway consulted intensively with stakeholders before revising the plan, therefore receiving large support for legislation of the plan.

### *Piloting before implementing nationwide/statewide*

– In the **Netherlands**, centres and municipalities are free to choose an ECEC programme. They may develop their own or adopt existing programmes. The *Piramide* programme is the most widely used programme based on the Van Kuyk-Slavin model, which uses a play-based curriculum giving flexibility for staff to adapt to children's needs. *Kaleidoscope* is the Dutch adaptation of the *High/Scope Preschool Programme* of the United States. Both programmes were piloted for three years in primary and preschools before implementation. The pilot evaluation concluded that: 1) both programmes offered a better work structure for the staff; 2) positive effects were found on cognitive and linguistic development of the participating children, although they are minor; and 3) the effects were largest for children who started the programmes from preschool. After the pilot period, other preschools were free to implement these "government approved" programmes. Funding is available for implementation.

– In **Australia**, the draft *Early Years Learning Framework* and its supporting documentation were trialled in 28 case study sites across Australia from February to April 2009 to test the Framework and its application in early childhood settings prior to implementation. The sites represented a wide variety of early childhood settings and services, including preschools, early childhood settings on school sites, Long Day Care Centres, Family Day Care, Multipurpose Aboriginal Children's Services, early intervention and occasional child care in metropolitan, regional and remote settings.

– More than 600 early years establishments and schools in **Scotland** (**United Kingdom**) took part in a formal trialling process to test specific experiences and outcomes from the *Curriculum for Excellence* in practice across all curriculum areas. Schools and centres chose experiences and outcomes to trial based on their planned programmes of work. They submitted reports containing detailed feedback, which was used to inform the revision process.

– **Luxembourg** published the new curriculum programme for basic education (including preschool) in June 2008. The document included the core skills children should achieve at the end of the four education cycles. Before nationwide implementation, it was tested in five schools. The opinions of these five schools were considered when revising the document.

– In **Mexico**, the Ministry of Education planned a pilot phase (from November 2010 to December 2011) for the implementation of the curriculum framework to ensure successful implementation.

- When revising the developmental objectives regarding "technology" in **Flanders** (**Belgium**), the attainment targets were first piloted in 17 settings before they were implemented nationally.

### *Providing "practical" support materials*

- Early Childhood **Australia**, the peak national, non-profit, non-government early childhood advocacy organisation in Australia, was contracted to develop support materials for ECEC centres and staff. All materials were developed with an Early Years Learning Framework (EYLF) and Educators' Guide to the EYLF focus. The Guide consists of two parts: the first focuses on curriculum decision-making, promotes reflective practice and inquiry and provides best practice examples and case studies; the second contains educators' stories and models of their plans for the outcomes of children's learning with questions to provoke thinking and generate discussion relative to the principles, practice and outcomes of the EYLF. The Department of Education, Employment and Workplace Relations developed a Remote Indigenous Professional Development support package for the EYLF, which includes a DVD, a book, a set of 50 cards to support learning outcomes, a set of posters and a CD ROM, to benefit locally engaged Indigenous staff.

- **Scotland**'s (**United Kingdom**) *Pre-Birth to Three* includes practical case studies, which staff can use for implementation. Additionally, a national implementation guide and accompanying staff support materials have been developed, including a DVD, a CD and a poster that are relevant for all adults working with and for babies and young children. This pack is issued to all early years establishments; and the interactive online version combines all materials contained in the pack. Scotland also developed a communication toolkit for staff with tools that address what *Curriculum for Excellence* means at different educational stages. The kit includes ready-made materials, such as posters, for use at ECEC centres and schools, a series of leaflets with the summary of a case study from the child's and the parent's points of view, a "pupil voice" video and a "practitioner voice" video as well as additional resources and links.

- In **England** (**United Kingdom**), a *Practice Guidance* for the *Early Years Foundation Stage* booklet has been made available. It includes non-statutory guidance, information on the areas of learning and development, and advice to professionals.

- The curriculum framework for ECEC in **New Zealand** provides professionals with examples of experiences that help meet the outcomes of the curriculum. The support guidance is divided in experiences helpful for infants, toddlers and young children to ensure practices and activities are age-appropriate. It provides ideas for activities and what is important to keep in mind for staff working with children. It also sets out questions for reflection for staff members, which help professionals analyse what they could improve when implementing the curriculum.

- **Mexico** created a guide on how to implement the new curriculum for staff in the initial training phase. The guides were used by a sample of teachers, and an evaluation showed that staff still had many questions about how to implement the new curriculum. While teachers are more prepared, 50% of them are not yet fully implementing the new curriculum; so further measures are being developed.

- In **Ireland**, the National Council for Curriculum and Assessment created the *Aistear Toolkit*, which includes tip-sheets, information leaflets, podcasts, presentations and activities and helps ECEC staff, as well as parents, to understand the framework. Ireland also prepared training videos for ECEC staff with an aim to inform them about curriculum changes and train them to effectively implement the changes.

- To support the implementation of its Framework Plan, **Norway** has issued guiding booklets on relevant themes, such as pedagogy for the youngest children, multiculturalism, children's agency and participation, language and language stimulation, numeracy, outdoor activities and gender equality. These booklets have been commissioned by the Ministry of Education and Research and were authored by experts. The intention behind the booklets is to promote reflection and discussion between staff on the Framework and the realisation of goals in local contexts.

- **Portugal** carried out a study to identify what areas are in need of materials to support the implementation of the curriculum guidelines. Based on the study, booklets were prepared for teaching literacy, maths and experimental science. Additionally, the Social Security Office developed a Guidance Manual for social security nursery care services. The manual gives guidance on implementing curricular practices and advises on pedagogical activities.

- In 2001, experts from **Slovenia** prepared a manual for the national curriculum, "The child in the preschool", with the purpose of offering starting points and examples of good practice for work in preschools.

- The National Agency for Education in **Sweden** publishes support material and General Guidelines with comments for guidance and supervision for municipality management, heads of preschools and staff in preschools.

- In **Japan**, explanatory guidelines accompany the *Course of Study for Kindergartens*, and a DVD accompanies the *National Curriculum of Day Care Centres*: they were prepared for all prefectural and city government officials.

- **Korea** is currently developing explanatory guidelines, a teaching manual, DVDs, CD-ROMs, PowerPoint presentations and websites in order to increase the level of familiarity of ECEC staff with the *Nuri Curriculum for Age 5*.

- In **Estonia**, the Ministry of Education and Research published handbooks for teachers and parents to support the implementation of the national curriculum for preschool child care institutions. The handbooks treat all fields of education and schooling activities and their organisation, the development of general skills in early ages, and the evaluation and support of children's development in a preschool child care institution. In 2010, a practical study material, "Values at preschool age: Education on values in preschool child care institutions", was issued on the initiative of the Ministry of Education and Research and in co-operation with the Centre for Ethics of Tartu University and the Institute of Educational Sciences of Tallinn University. In co-operation between the National Examinations and Qualifications Centre and Lasteveeb OÜ, an internet-based study material has been developed for supporting the learning of Estonian as a second language in preschool.

–   **Slovak Republic** and **Turkey** developed handbooks for ECEC staff that provide implementation support. Slovak Republic has the *Manual for the Design of School Educational Programmes*, while Turkey developed the *Preschool Education Curriculum Guidebook*. Slovak Republic also developed the *Methodology for Pre-Primary Education*, which includes methodological advice and recommendations for kindergarten teachers on how to develop key competences of children. Additionally, training videos were distributed to ECEC staff, informing them about curriculum changes and training them in how to implement the changes.

–   The responsible ministries of ECEC in **Flanders** (**Belgium**), **Luxembourg** and **Spain** developed guides and booklets on their (new) curriculum or changes in their framework to ensure staff had practical support tool for implementation.

### Setting out guidelines for materials or prescribing materials

–   Materials which staff and caregivers can use in the setting are prescribed by the national or regional authorities in **Australia**, **Italy**, **Japan**, **Korea**, **Luxembourg**, **Portugal**, **Spain** and **Turkey**.

–   In several states in the **United** States, local authorities prescribe which materials ECEC providers are allowed to use.

–   In **Manitoba** (**Canada**), Manitoba Education has developed a kindergarten-level resource for kindergarten teachers to improve and encourage language competences of children. *Listening and Speaking: First Steps into Literacy: A Support Document for Kindergarten Teachers and Speech Language Pathologists* (2008) assists kindergarten teachers in stimulating the oral language skills, strategies and attitudes of all kindergarten children.

### Revising initial education and providing demands-driven training

–   Before curricular reform took place, **Slovenia** extended the initial education programme of ECEC preschool teachers to improve quality in the preschools. After the introduction of the new preschool curriculum, selected topics were included in the initial study programme and in-service training of preschool teachers.

–   In **Italy**, universities that train future ECEC professionals embedded courses on the new curriculum into the initial education programme. Education institutes that provide initial ECEC education, organised workshops and activities for ECEC professionals to teach them about the curriculum changes. The national government also sent out training videos to staff to ensure all students are well informed on the new curriculum and prepared for implementation.

–   **Prince Edward Island** (**Canada**) provided developmental and implementation funding to allow for entry-level training of all uncertified staff working within Early Years Centres so they could be educated as an Early Years educator and learn about the new Learning Framework. The province also provides in-service training to early childhood directors and educators already working in the centres on the newly established Early Learning Framework, a curriculum document for the early childhood sector focusing on children from birth to school entry.

– Early Childhood **Australia**, a non-profit, non-government early childhood advocacy organisation, was contracted to provide nationwide training for early childhood educators in the implementation of the *Early Years Learning Framework* (EYLF). An online forum, master classes and an online newsletter about the framework have been developed as well. Australia also introduced the framework into undergraduate courses. Additionally, the network of Professional Support Coordinators, Indigenous Professional Support Units and Inclusion Support Agencies in each state provided EYLF support and training to early childhood educators.

– In **Luxembourg**, ECEC staff members are legally obliged to follow a certain minimum number of hours of continuous training. This in-service training provision informs staff about any changes in curriculum and furthers their professionalisation. There were also training courses organised on child observation and assessment when changes in the curriculum were made. Additionally, peers (ECEC workers) are trained to educate and inform their colleagues on, for example, changes in curriculum. This is found to be an effective method in training staff since they feel more comfortable asking questions to peers.

– Each year, **Flanders** (**Belgium**) allocates financial resources for in-service training to early education institutions. The government lays down priorities for the staff regarding in-service training initiatives that are necessary for supporting the implementation of educational reforms.

– In the **United States**, many states incorporate *Early Learning and Development Standards* (ELDSs) into professional education systems; and a large number of states offer training on the ELDSs and incorporate them into professional development systems.

– The Ministry of Education in **Mexico** developed a training course for staff to effectively implement the revised curriculum. Centres of Permanent Training were established to provide in-service training to ECEC workers and teachers. For the *Early Childhood Health and Care and Welfare Curriculum* framework, special training strategies were set up to ensure that it is properly implemented and that children will receive quality service.

– **Turkey** provided in-service training to practitioners, headmasters and education inspectors. Headmasters also provided training to teachers in their preschools.

– **Portugal** organises training sessions for ECEC staff working with children ages three to six on areas for which staff have indicated there is a need for training, including literacy, maths and experimental science.

– In **Norway**, project funding was made available for the revised Framework Plan by the Ministry of Education for improving staff competences and recruitment of staff from 2007-10. Grants were conditional upon municipalities establishing plans for competence development, as well as an implementation plan aligned with national priorities, which are pedagogical leadership, children's participation, language environment and linguistic stimulation, and collaboration and coherence between kindergartens and schools.

- **England** (**United Kingdom**) will develop training for ECEC staff to implement the revised *Early Years Foundation Stage*.

### Providing expert assistance to ECEC providers

- In **Slovenia**, educational advisers of the National Education Institute provided implementation assistance to ECEC providers. Project-team counsellors maintained ongoing contacts with preschools implementing the new curriculum and assisted them in solving problems encountered in practice.

- In **Australia**, the Professional Support Coordinators (PSC) and the Indigenous Professional Support Unit (IPSU) networks in each state and territory are funded by the national government to deliver training and mentoring services to ECEC services to support their implementation of the Early Years Learning Framework (EYLF). The Early Years Learning Framework Professional Learning Programme (EYLF PLP), developed for the government by Early Childhood Australia, also provides ongoing professional support and assistance to services as they engage in the EYLF implementation process. The programme is a national initiative that started in 2010 and continues through 2011. As part of this programme, ECEC professionals have access to an online interactive EYLF PLP Forum where they can raise questions, share ideas and interact with other educators implementing the EYLF. High-calibre early childhood experts and practitioners from across Australia are available on the Forum to respond to questions and conduct topical discussions – about issues raised by experts and practitioners via the forum and the national workshop programme – regarding implementation of the EYLF.

- Each educational network in **Flanders** (**Belgium**), an umbrella organisation of nursery schools/kindergartens and schools, has its own educational/pedagogical guidance service (*PBD*). This service provides professional internal support to kindergartens, and they are tasked with supporting education institutions in implementing their pedagogical projects.

- The Department of Education and Early Childhood Development in **Prince Edward Island** (**Canada**) has a support team to provide in-service and job-impeded support to early childhood educators and directors as they implement the newly introduced Early Learning Framework. This is a permanent team within the department, which supports the maintenance of the framework in addition to any further quality enhancement initiatives introduced by either the early learning and child care programme or the government.

### Improving working conditions to stimulate effective implementation

- In **Flanders** (**Belgium**), child care workers can assist kindergarten teachers in their work to reduce workload and provide a better staff-child ratio in a large classroom.

- Australia is progressively implementing changes to staff-child ratios, which should contribute to effective curriculum implementation. On 1 January 2012, Australia will start with the new 1:4 ratio for children from birth to two years.

- In Sweden, in 2004, a grant of SEK 2 billion increased state funding to local authorities for the employment of 6 000 additional preschool teachers and child assistants. The grant was intended to reduce class sizes and improve staff-child ratios to 1:5 on average for zero to six years to improve the quality of ECEC and qualitative curriculum implementation.

## Challenge 5: Systematic evaluation and assessment

Determining a curriculum's effectiveness and relevance is challenging for many countries due to a lack of capacity at the policy level for conducting evaluations, collecting valid, informative, credible information and data, and assessment procedures and instruments that combine efficiency and being informative.

### Integrating "curriculum" as part of the monitoring process

- **Slovenia** has developed a quality assessment model, taking into account system and process quality as well as curriculum quality. The model examined three levels of quality in preschool care and education: 1) structural quality (space, structure of activities, etc.); 2) process quality (co-operation among staff, parental involvement, professional development, satisfaction of staff, co-operation with other preschools, etc.); and 3) curriculum quality (design, implementation, routine activities, etc.). Monitoring results are presented in annual reports and serve as a form of assistance to preschool teachers and preschools. They also provide opportunities for changes in educational practice.

- In **Norway**, the municipal authorities are obliged to supervise/monitor kindergartens to see if the institution's practice is in accordance with legislation and the Framework Plan for the Content and Tasks of Kindergartens. A recent study by PricewaterhouseCoopers shows that 55% of the municipal authorities have developed local criteria for monitoring kindergarten content aligned with this legislation and framework. Municipalities report that they base monitoring activities on the following aspects: report of concern from parents and the public, advice from national authorities, the annual pedagogical plan produced by each kindergarten, and parents' responses to surveys on the quality of kindergarten.

- In **Flanders** (**Belgium**), regular assessments/evaluations are undertaken by the Inspectorate. Based on these audits, the government can retain, either in part or in full, funding or grants if the funded or grant-aided provider does not pursue the cross-curricular targets or developmental objectives. Operating budgets are at the disposal of kindergartens, enabling them to achieve attainment targets and developmental objectives for as many pupils as possible and to fund obligatory activities in the curriculum framework. Additionally, a process-oriented Self-evaluation Instrument for Care Settings (SICS) has been developed. It serves as a tool for self-assessment for staff in care settings, and it takes the child's experience in the care environment as the main focus when looking at quality. The instrument has been developed by a team based at the Research Centre for Experiential Education at Leuven University. SICS is designed to help settings gain awareness of their strengths and weaknesses when it comes to creating the best possible conditions for child development. The procedure for self-evaluation contains three steps. First, the actual levels of well-being and involvement are assessed. Second, the observations are analysed. Third, actions to improve quality are selected and implemented. A manual is designed to help users become familiar with SICS.

- **Portugal** has undertaken *Monitorisation and Supervision of Curriculum Development in Preschool Education* (2006). The Directorate General for Innovation and Curriculum Development hired the University of Oporto to carry out a case study with 20 kindergartens to collect data on the quality of actual practices of how curriculum guidelines have been used. The results of the study are practical: they call for more support materials; teacher training sessions on the assessment methods of children and their learning environments; more documentation; strategies to facilitate transition to the first cycle of primary education; and they identify target areas as experimental science, writing skills and maths.

- In **Australia**, from July to November 2010, a new assessment and ratings process was developed and implemented within around 200 education and care services across Australia. These will be assessed against the *National Quality Standards* and will be given a provisional rating. Communications and support materials have been developed for the sector and staff to support implementation of the new assessment and ratings process, including training manuals and operational guidelines. Self-evaluation kits for ECEC staff members have also been developed and distributed to all centres.

- In **Scotland** (**United Kingdom**), assessment is one of the strands of work in implementing *Curriculum for Excellence* and *Pre-Birth to Three*. As part of assessment, self-evaluations have been set up in centres as well as monitoring standards and outcomes over time. The framework of quality indicators set out in *How Good is Our School?* and *Child at the Centre* provides a focus for self-reflecting on professional practice and curriculum for improvement in schools and centres. Additionally, external inspections are organised to monitor curriculum and practices. The government is working with education authorities and other partners to develop processes for sharing assessment information so that education authorities can use the data to learn about the work of their schools and centres and, where appropriate, support changes in curriculum.

- **Slovak Republic** intensified co-operation with the State School Inspectorate, who is mandated to monitor the implementation of the school educational programmes. Inspections are now conducted on a regular, yearly basis. Slovak Republic also developed self-evaluation kits for staff, so teachers and carers can assess their own knowledge and skills.

- **New Zealand** implemented *Kei Tua o te Pae*, Assessment for Learning, in which teachers are expected to develop effective assessment practices that meet the aspirations of the curriculum *Te Whāriki*. The national government offers training on this assessment practice to ECEC staff. The curriculum programme is also evaluated in terms of its capacity to provide activities and relationships that stimulate early development. Children and parents can help in deciding what should be included in the process of assessing the programme and the curriculum.

- In **England** (**United Kingdom**), **Ireland**[4], **Italy**, **Mexico** and **Sweden**, self-evaluation kits have been developed so that ECEC professionals can evaluate their knowledge of the curriculum framework and their implementation of the framework.

### *Evaluating/reviewing the curriculum framework linked to quality improvement*

- In **Luxembourg**, all ECEC professionals are required by law to co-operate in teams and consult each other during regular team meetings. The law prescribes a minimum number of hours for team consultation. During these meetings, practices and implementation are evaluated and assessed, and experiences and advice are shared. The consultation teams and meetings are regarded as very useful by ECEC staff. Additionally, a national review of the revised curriculum for the four cycles of basic education is planned for the near future.

- Vestfold University College in **Norway** has conducted an evaluation of how the framework plan is implemented, used and experienced. The evaluation was commissioned by the Ministry of Education and Research. It consists of two quantitative and two qualitative investigations among groups involved in the work: children, parents, preschool teachers, assistants, head-teachers, municipalities as local kindergarten authorities and county governors. The report shows many positive results concerning the implementation, but it also points out some challenges, such as the understanding of documentation and the mapping of children's development and learning, the need for competence in the sector and limited resources for implementation.

- In **Australia**, a planned baseline study will establish a baseline of data on ECEC practice prior to the requirement to use the Early Years Learning Framework under the National Quality Framework from 1 January 2012. Evaluation of the Early Years Learning Framework will occur in 2014 with an aim to determine its effectiveness in raising the quality of ECEC.

- When an ECEC institution in the **Netherlands** develops a curriculum framework, these can be voluntarily screened and assessed by the National Youth Institute (NJI), a private organisation. The institute assesses whether the framework is suitable for young children and whether it stimulates quality early learning

- **Ireland's** National Council for Curriculum and Assessment has prioritised a review of the Infant Curriculum in light of the publication of the *Early Childhood Curriculum Framework* (*Aistear*).

- **England** (**United Kingdom**) carried out an independent review of the *Early Years Foundation Stage* (EYFS) in 2011. The government then consulted on its proposals for a revised EYFS and plans to implement in September 2012. The revised EYFS is simpler, clearer and less prescriptive. It will also reflect the latest evidence on child development. The government also proposes to improve the framework's accessibility to parents and to promote action to respond to children progressing slower than expected.

- **Luxembourg** has planned an assessment of its framework after three years of implementation.

- In **Slovenia**, the implementation of the new curriculum includes an evaluation of introduced changes.

# ACTION AREA 4 – MANAGING RISKS: LEARNING FROM OTHER COUNTRIES' POLICY EXPERIENCES

This section summarises country experiences as lessons learned from:

- Designing and implementing curriculum and standards

It aims to be a quick read about challenges and risks to consider when implementing policy initiatives.

## DESIGNING AND IMPLEMENTING CURRICULUM AND STANDARDS

### Lesson 1: Orient the curriculum reform to focus on "child" and "holistic development"

When revising its curriculum, **Italy** focused mostly on the child. The country believes it is important to keep in mind the individual personality of all children and the importance and influence of the parents as well as the social environment. Italy notes that focusing on the child and his/her personal development is crucial for successful implementation and stakeholder buy-in. They call it "the core of the process of building a curriculum".

**Flanders** (**Belgium**) learnt that it is important to offer children the opportunity to develop skills in situations that are realistic to them. Children learn from their own living environment and other people's environments. Harmonious personal development asks for well-balanced attention to all development zones of the child. Flanders indicated that not only cognitive and motor components but also socio-emotional aspects should be addressed when aiming to provide a broad education.

Inspired by article 12 of the United Nations Convention on the Rights of the Child, **Norway** introduced a section in the Kindergarten Act (2005) giving "Children in kindergarten (…) the right to express their views on the day to day activities of the kindergarten". This is followed up in the Framework Plan for the Content and Tasks of Kindergartens (2006). Children are seen as subjects or agents in their own right who should be met with respect in their diverse forms of expression. The plan emphasises the importance of adults' attitudes, knowledge and ability to relate to and understand children so that they can integrate children's participation in work on the content of kindergarten and bring up children to participate actively in a democratic society. The kindergarten shall, in collaboration with and close understanding of the home, safeguard the children's need for care and play and promote learning and formation as a basis for an all-round development.

## Lesson 2: Engage key stakeholders and relevant experts in the curriculum revision process

When reviewing the Infant Curriculum, **Ireland** worked directly with practitioners in infant classes, their principals, parents and children. National and international research was also used for review as well as consultation processes with the wider education sector. Ireland found this to be very useful in gaining wider awareness of the curriculum and stakeholder buy-in to support implementation.

**Mexico** found it effective to pursue a collaborative approach to reaching an agreement on a general curriculum framework, taking into account different points of view of organisations, parents and other stakeholders. When the draft curriculum was proposed, it reflected and respected the diversity of approaches as well as the views and needs of the population.

**Sweden** set up a reference group when revising the curriculum. The government learnt that having a reference group with broad and different competences is highly relevant to finding a suitable revised draft that reflects the needs of various professionals and children with different backgrounds. Sweden also believes it is important to involve researchers. Their input and consultation formed the essential basis of the revision.

In **Spain**, the period for feedback and opinions on draft proposals to improve quality in ECEC and compulsory education was found crucial for identifying principles that should govern the early childhood education system. Autonomous communities (regional governments), representatives of school councils and other stakeholders were invited to express their views and express their position on these proposals directly to the Ministry of Education. This stimulated open, public debate on quality in ECEC learning and contributed to improved curriculum design in Spain.

**Luxembourg** highlights the usefulness of involving foreign experts in the revision process. Facing challenges in linguistic areas due to the different languages spoken throughout Luxembourg, the involvement of foreign experts contributed to a revised curriculum focusing more on the regional context and needs of children.

**Korea** found it critical to collect different perspectives and identify the needs of various stakeholder groups (*e.g.*, parents, teachers, directors, academic associations and local and central authorities) by forming task force teams and review committees when revising or developing curriculum. Due to its split, market-driven ECEC system, Korea learnt that it is highly important to balance gathering opinions and reaching some consensus from the education and care sectors, especially in developing the *Nuri Curriculum for Age 5*.

## Lesson 3: Ensure coherency in learning and up-bringing for continuous child development

According to **Flanders** (**Belgium**), it is important to have horizontal coherence between the different learning areas within ECEC. The aims of different subjects should be interrelated. Flanders notes that this leads to a greater continuity in children's early learning and development.

In developing the *Nuri Curriculum for Age 5*, **Korea** emphasised the importance of both vertical and horizontal coherence and consistency in children's development and learning experiences regardless of the type of ECEC institution. Alignment of the *Standard Childcare Curriculum* to the elementary school curriculum, which tended to be relatively weak compared to the *National Kindergarten Curriculum*, will be strengthened. Furthermore, aligning the *Nuri Curriculum for Age 5*, the *National Kindergarten Curriculum* and the *Standard Childcare Curriculum* for ages three to four is being actively pursued.

**Japan** took into account the recent changes in children's environmental context when revising the Course of Study for Kindergartens and the National Curriculum of Day Care Centre Works in 2008. This included changes in the way children are being brought up, different lifestyle habits and family compositions, social norms and new methods of communication. This led to greater continuity in up-bringing between the home and learning environment. It also resulted in a clearer concept of kindergartens and day care centres and a greater awareness among stakeholders of the significance of early childhood services.

## Lesson 4: Plan sufficient time to raise awareness of the curriculum change and to implement the change; plan a feasible review exercise

**Luxembourg** learnt that good communication with all stakeholders is extremely important when implementing changes in a curriculum. This ensures consistency in the implementation of the changes. Communication on the changes should be well co-ordinated at the policy level to promote the revised curriculum. When communication is organised efficiently, it results in better understanding among practitioners and inspectors.

The priority of **Ireland** for the next two years is to continue raising awareness of the existence of its curriculum Aistear and to support the early childhood sector in its implementation. The country learnt that it is necessary to provide sufficient time for providers to use Aistear before planning a review, noting that it takes at least two years to properly implement the curriculum.

**Slovenia** learnt that it is important to implement curriculum gradually, taking sufficient time for centres to prepare. The number of preschool institutions and primary schools implementing the new curricula increases every year. For implementation, each preschool institution and school has to set up a team in charge of the introduction and implementation processes. Based on Slovenia's experience, gradual implementation results in more efficient implementation and correct usage of the curriculum.

**Prince Edward Island (Canada)** stated that the successful implementation of their Early Learning Framework, launched in September 2011, depends most largely on well-educated early childhood educators and pedagogical leadership from the director. These two aspects are key to successful implementation.

### Lesson 5: Ensure that ECEC centre leaders can effectively manage financial and human resources as well as pedagogic practices and, in addition, train staff for effective implementation

**Norway** emphasises that good management of ECEC centres is highly relevant for successful implementation of a curriculum. Norway learnt that resources should be well-managed and that the management team, including owners and head teachers, should inspire the rest of the staff in effective implementation. The management is also responsible for ensuring that their own and other staff's competences are sufficient and suitable for working in ECEC provisions and that staff work is goal-orientated. Additionally, management is responsible for meeting the legislative standards and regulations. Strong management with capable people in the management team was found to be key to successful implementation in Norway. Therefore, one of the national priorities on competence development in ECEC in Norway is pedagogical leadership.

In 2009, **Sweden** started the "Preschool Boost", which included in-service training (university courses) for preschool teachers (15 European Credit Transfer and Accumulation System [ECTS], 10 weeks) and child minders (5 weeks) in language/communication and mathematics. Pedagogical leaders for preschool were also offered university courses (30 ECTS, 20 weeks) in language/communication, mathematics and evaluation. Implementation conferences were organised by the National Agency for Education for municipality management and heads of preschools. This initiative gave staff and management more competence to work with the new, clarified goals in the Swedish curriculum.

### Lesson 6: Use simple and common language to draft the curriculum that can be easily understood by staff and parents

**Australia**, **Flanders** (**Belgium**), **Finland**, **New Zealand**, **Norway** and **Sweden** have learnt that it is useful and important to explain the curriculum in simple language, avoiding technical terms. When the curriculum is explained in understandable language, it is found that both staff and parents with different backgrounds have better knowledge about the curriculum. This also results in better implementation of the curriculum by educators and other ECEC staff. New Zealand found that it stimulates expanding the use of the curriculum by parents in home learning activities.

# ACTION AREA 5 – REFLECTING ON THE CURRENT STATE OF PLAY

This sheet has been prepared based on international trends and is designed to facilitate reflection on where your country stands regarding:

- Curriculum frameworks, standards and guidelines

The aim is to raise awareness about new issues and identify areas where changes could be made; the aim is not to give marks on practices. Please reflect on the current state of play by circling a number on the scale from 1-5.

## CURRICULUM FRAMEWORKS, STANDARDS AND GUIDELINES

| Alignment | Not at all | | | | Very well |
|---|---|---|---|---|---|
| 1. The curriculum is designed so that it is aligned with the overall ECEC goals. | 1 | 2 | 3 | 4 | 5 |
| 2. The curriculum is aligned with school curriculum to manage smooth transition from ECEC to compulsory school. | 1 | 2 | 3 | 4 | 5 |
| 3. The curriculum is aligned with assessment and monitoring, such as for child outcomes or the quality of services. | 1 | 2 | 3 | 4 | 5 |
| 4. The changes in the curriculum are aligned with the contents of the pre-service education for new graduates and on-going professional development for managers and practitioners for effective implementation. | 1 | 2 | 3 | 4 | 5 |
| 5. Curriculum implementation is aligned with regulatory requirements and funding arrangements. | 1 | 2 | 3 | 4 | 5 |

| Goals, scope and contents | Not at all | | | | Very well |
|---|---|---|---|---|---|
| 6. Curriculum goals and guiding principles are clearly set out. | 1 | 2 | 3 | 4 | 5 |
| 7. The scope of the age group for the curriculum is appropriately defined in your country's contexts. | 1 | 2 | 3 | 4 | 5 |
| 8. The content coverage of the curriculum is appropriately designed, consistent with parental expectations and societal future needs. | 1 | 2 | 3 | 4 | 5 |
| 9. The new/revised curriculum was developed in a participatory manner, taking into account the views of stakeholders (*e.g.*, practitioners, schools, private, voluntary and independent providers, academics, parents, local levels of government). | 1 | 2 | 3 | 4 | 5 |
| 10. There are opportunities for extra-curricular activities to complement what the curriculum does not cover. | 1 | 2 | 3 | 4 | 5 |
| 11. The curriculum is being used to promote an even level of quality across different types of provision. | 1 | 2 | 3 | 4 | 5 |
| 12. The curriculum is being used to guide and support professional staff in their practice. | 1 | 2 | 3 | 4 | 5 |
| 13. The curriculum is being used to facilitate communication between staff, parents and children. | 1 | 2 | 3 | 4 | 5 |
| **Training and staff support** | Not at all | | | | Very well |
| 14. The curriculum strikes an appropriate balance between giving concrete direction and specifics *versus* allowing space for staff initiative and local innovation. | 1 | 2 | 3 | 4 | 5 |
| 15. The curriculum is accompanied with useful materials for practitioners (*e.g.*, assessment toolkits, toys and books, other classroom materials). | 1 | 2 | 3 | 4 | 5 |
| 16. Specific training and support needs of practitioners (including managers and leaders) have been clearly identified. | 1 | 2 | 3 | 4 | 5 |

| | | | | | |
|---|---|---|---|---|---|
| 17. The training is designed to ensure relevance and practicality regarding:<br><br>a) contents and pedagogy | 1 | 2 | 3 | 4 | 5 |
| b) style and provision (*e.g.*, seminars, workshops, on-site coaching). | 1 | 2 | 3 | 4 | 5 |
| c) training approach (*e.g.*, cascading approach or train-the-trainer by practitioners, ECEC educators, government officers). | 1 | 2 | 3 | 4 | 5 |
| 18. Besides training and support materials, managers and practitioners have access to additional support (*e.g.*, telephone hotline/website, on-demand training). | 1 | 2 | 3 | 4 | 5 |
| **Implementation** | Not at all | | | | Very well |
| 19. Stakeholder buy-in has been established for the new/revised curriculum. | 1 | 2 | 3 | 4 | 5 |
| 20. Key elements of the curriculum and its implementation have been pilot-tested. | 1 | 2 | 3 | 4 | 5 |
| 21. The implementation plan presents clear and specific actions, a realistic timeframe and incorporates the key stakeholders. | 1 | 2 | 3 | 4 | 5 |
| 22. The language describing the curriculum is accessible to policy makers, practitioners, parents, etc. | 1 | 2 | 3 | 4 | 5 |
| 23. Multi-level governance and decentralised aspects of ECEC services have been taken into account. | 1 | 2 | 3 | 4 | 5 |
| **Monitoring, evaluation and quality assurance** | Not at all | | | | Very well |
| 24. The purpose of monitoring curriculum implementation is clearly defined, and the results of monitoring have been used to meet the purpose. | 1 | 2 | 3 | 4 | 5 |
| 25. Targets, approaches and instruments of monitoring have been carefully selected. Monitoring of curriculum implementation is embedded into the existing arrangements, if applicable. | 1 | 2 | 3 | 4 | 5 |

# NOTES

1   Based on responses from the following countries and regions: Australia, Austria, Bavaria (DEU), British Columbia (CAN), Czech Republic, Denmark, England (UKM), Estonia, Finland, Flemish Community (BEL), French Community (BEL), Georgia (USA), Hesse (DEU), Ireland, Israel, Italy, Japan, Korea, Manitoba (CAN), Massachusetts (USA), Mexico, Netherlands, New Zealand, North Carolina (USA), Norway, Oklahoma (USA), Poland, Portugal, Prince Edward Island (CAN), Scotland (UKM), Slovak Republic, Slovenia, Spain, Sweden and Turkey.

2   Based on responses from the following countries and regions:  Australia, Austria, British Columbia (CAN), Czech Republic, Denmark, England (UKM), Estonia, Finland, Flemish Community (BEL), French Community (BEL), Georgia (USA), Germany, Ireland, Israel, Italy, Japan, Korea, Luxembourg, Manitoba (CAN), Massachusetts (USA), Mexico, Netherlands, New Zealand, North Carolina (USA), Norway, Oklahoma (USA), Poland, Portugal, Prince Edward Island (CAN), Scotland (UKM), Slovak Republic, Slovenia, Spain, Sweden and Turkey.

3   Core Curriculum for Preschool Education for Kindergartens and Pre-school Classes in Primary Schools and Other Forms of Pre-school Education and Care; the Regulation of 23 December 2008 by the Minister of National Education (Dz.U.2009.4.17).

4   Only in place for the Infant Curriculum.

# POLICY LEVER 3

# IMPROVING QUALIFICATIONS, TRAINING AND WORKING CONDITIONS

*Staff qualifications, initial education and professional development contribute to enhancing pedagogical quality, which is – ultimately – highly associated with better child outcomes. It is not the qualification per se that has an impact on child outcomes but the ability of better qualified staff members to create a high-quality pedagogic environment. Key elements of high staff quality are the ways in which staff involve children, stimulate interaction with and between children, and use diverse scaffolding strategies.*

*Research has shown that working conditions can also improve the quality of ECEC services: better conditions will improve staff job satisfaction and retention. This will influence staff behaviour, encouraging more stable, sensitive and stimulating interactions with children, and thus, lead to better child development. Research has pointed to certain conditions that can impact the quality of ECEC services: i) high staff-child ratio and low group size; ii) competitive wages and other benefits; iii) reasonable schedule/workload; iv) low staff turnover; v) a good physical environment; and vi) a competent and supportive centre manager.*

# ACTION AREA 1 – USING RESEARCH TO INFORM POLICY AND THE PUBLIC

This section contains the following research briefs:

- Qualifications, Education and Training Matter
- Working Conditions Matter

## QUALIFICATIONS, EDUCATION AND TRAINING MATTER

### What are "qualifications, education and professional development" in ECEC?

ECEC qualifications indicate the recognised level and types of knowledge, skills and competencies that ECEC staff have received.[1] Formal education in ECEC refers to the level and type of education that ECEC staff pursue to acquire such knowledge, skills and competencies to work in the sector. Professional development provides opportunities for staff who are already working in the sector to update or enhance their practices; it is often referred to as "in-service training", "continuous education" or "professional training".

### What is at stake?

Recent social changes have challenged traditional views of childhood and child rearing: 1) the changing socio-economic role of women, 2) growing ethnic diversity of developed countries, and 3) changing views on (early) education and the purpose of (early) education. The last two changes have important consequences for what is expected of those who work with young children.

As pointed out by the OECD teachers' review (OECD, 2005), education systems need to invest in intensive teacher education and training if teachers are to deliver high-quality outcomes. This also refers to the ECEC sector (OECD, 2006). Specific knowledge, skills and competencies are expected of ECEC practitioners. There is a general consensus, supported by research, that well-educated, well-trained professionals are the key factor in providing high-quality ECEC with the most favourable cognitive and social outcomes for children. Research shows that the behaviour of those who work in ECEC matters and that this is related to their education and training. The qualifications, education and training of ECEC staff are, therefore, an important policy issue (OECD, 2006).

In spite of the consensus on the importance of well-trained staff, governments often fear the funding consequences of raising staff qualifications. Higher qualifications can be followed by increased wage demands, which, in turn, contribute significantly to the costs of services. Although the evidence is strong that improved training and qualification levels raise the quality of interaction and pedagogy in ECEC services – and similar evidence exists in favour of staff qualifications – governments often choose not to invest in raising qualifications or funding staff training (OECD, 2006). This might seriously affect ECEC quality, and with this, child development outcomes, since staff are not being optimally trained or educated to stimulate early learning and development.

Although research emphasises the high relevance of adequate staff initial education and continuous professional development opportunities, large differences occur between countries in terms of which qualifications are being asked of ECEC practitioners. Opportunities to participate in professional development and in-service training also vary greatly across countries and between education and child care in split systems. The qualification requirements vary from no formal education at all to a specialised bachelor's or even master's degree, and professional development and training ranges from being compulsory to being based on voluntary will in combination with no additional funding for training (OECD, 2006).

Often there is a difference between the qualifications required to work with very young children (up to three or four years of age) and the qualifications needed to be a teacher for children age four to primary school age. This is especially the case in countries with a so-called split system: children ages zero to three or four attend different ECEC institutions (often day care services) than those ages three or four to primary schooling age, who more regularly attend pre-primary services. In countries with an integrated system where all young children (age zero to primary school age) attend the same centres, all practitioners usually have to meet the same requirements in terms of education and training (Eurydice, 2009; OECD, 2006). The latter encourages continuous child development throughout the ECEC years and ensures greater professionalism of staff working with both younger and older children (Shonkoff and Philips, 2000).

## Why do qualifications, education and professional development matter?

Staff qualifications/education/professional development → pedagogical quality → child outcomes

The main importance of staff lies in their effect on the process and content quality of ECEC[2] (Sheridan, 2009; Pramling and Pramling Samuelsson, in press 2011). The training and education of ECEC staff affects the quality of services and outcomes primarily through the knowledge, skills and competencies that are transmitted and encouraged by practitioners. It is also considered important that staff believe in their ability to organise and execute the courses of action necessary to bring about desired results (Fives, 2003). Qualifications can matter in terms of which skill sets and what knowledge are recognised as important for working with young children. The skills and staff traits that research identifies as important in facilitating high-quality services and outcomes are:

- Good understanding of child development and learning;

- Ability to develop children's perspectives;

- Ability to praise, comfort, question and be responsive to children;

- Leadership skills, problem solving and development of targeted lesson plans; and

- Good vocabulary and ability to elicit children's ideas.

However, it is not the qualification *per se* that has an impact on child outcomes but the ability of better qualified staff members to create a high-quality pedagogic environment that makes the difference (Elliott, 2006; Sheridan *et al.*, 2009).There is strong evidence that enriched stimulating environments and high-quality pedagogy are fostered by better qualified staff; and better quality pedagogy leads to better learning outcomes (Litjens and Taguma, 2010). Key elements of high staff quality are the way staff involve children and stimulate interaction with and between children as well as staff's scaffolding strategies, such as guiding, modelling and questioning.

More specialised staff education and training on ECEC are strongly associated with stable, sensitive and stimulating interactions (Shonkoff and Philips, 2000). Other elements of high staff quality include staff's content (curriculum) knowledge and their ability to create a multi-disciplinary learning environment (Pramling and Pramling Samuelsson, in press 2011).

## What matters most?

### *Level of education and/or pedagogical practices*

Studies that have addressed the question of whether higher staff qualifications lead to better pedagogical practice have yielded mixed results. There are various studies showing that, generally, a higher level of education is associated with higher pedagogic quality in ECEC settings. One study found that preschool teachers with bachelor's degrees were the most effective practitioners. Their effectiveness was measured within the classroom and based on stimulation, responsiveness and engagement of the children in learning activities (Howes *et al.*, 2003). The results of the Effective Provision of Pre-school Education (EPPE) study from England (United Kingdom) have also shown that key explanatory factors for high-quality ECEC were related to "staff with higher qualifications, staff with leadership skills and long-serving staff; trained staff working alongside and supporting less qualified staff; staff with a good understanding of child development and learning" (Siraj-Blatchford, 2010). Higher proportions of staff with low-level qualifications were related with less favourable child outcomes in the socio-emotional domain (social relationships with their peers and co-operation).

However, the general conclusion that higher education of ECEC staff leads to higher pedagogical quality and, therefore, to better child outcomes is not supported by all studies. Early *et al.* (2007) emphasise that teacher quality is a very complex issue. There is no simple relationship between the level of education of staff and classroom quality or learning outcomes. They studied the relationship between child outcomes and staff qualifications and found no, or contradictory, associations between the two.

They argue that increasing staff education will not suffice for improving classroom quality or maximising children's academic gains. Instead, raising the effectiveness of early childhood education will likely require a broad range of professional development activities and support for staff's interactions with children. An area to improve pedagogical practices of ECEC staff includes supporting staff's competence to communicate and interact with children in a shared and sustainable manner (Sheridan *et al.*, 2009).

Research also points out that it is not necessary that all staff have high general levels of education. Highly qualified staff can have a positive influence on those who work with them and who do not have the same high qualifications. The EPPE study finds that the observed behaviour of lower-qualified staff turned out to be positively influenced by working alongside highly trained staff (Sammons, 2010).

## Specialised education and training

Not only the level of education but also the content of the staff's educational or training curriculum is important for the level of quality in ECEC. Specialised education is associated with better child outcomes and improved staff competences to provide suitable pedagogical learning opportunities. Specialisation can refer to "any education or training focusing on early childhood education, child development or similar, above and beyond general educational attainments" (Litjens and Taguma, 2010).

Initial education and training in areas such as early child development and early education increase the likelihood that practitioners are effective in promoting the educational, socio-emotional and healthy development of children.

The practitioners' ability to create rich, stimulating environments in ECEC is jeopardised when staff have inadequate, insufficient or incorrect content and pedagogical knowledge. When trained on matters related to early development and care, staff can better develop a child's perspective (Sommer *et al.*, 2010); are better able to integrate playing and learning into practice (Pramling Samuelsson and Asplund Carlsson, 2008; Johansson and Pramling Samuelsson, 2009); have increased ability to solve problems and develop targeted lesson plans; and have an improved vocabulary, which stimulates early literacy development (NIEER, 2004). Additionally, staff with higher education *and* specialised training engage in more positive teacher-child interactions including praising, comforting, questioning and being responsive to children (Howes *et al.*, 2003).

However, specialised education and training does not *guarantee* greater effectiveness (Hyson *et al.*, 2009). The quality of the education or training programme may be a more critical factor in staff's ability to stimulate children's development and learning. There is a strong need for good initial staff preparation; and there is a call for greater consistency across initial professional preparation programmes to enhance quality (Elliot, 2006).

Ongoing education and training are also important. Research shows that in order for staff to maintain their professional quality, they need to engage in ongoing professional development[3]. A well-trained practitioner does not only have a good initial level of education but makes sure that the effects of initial education do not fade out (Fukkink and Lont, 2007; Mitchell and Cubey, 2003). Ongoing professional development has the potential to fill in the knowledge and skills that staff may be lacking or require updating due to changes in particular knowledge fields. This is especially crucial in ECEC where new programmes are being developed continuously. The body of research on what works is growing, the discussions on quality in ECEC are ongoing, and the focus has changed to a developmental perspective.

In-service (ongoing) education and training can be conducted "on the job" or can be provided by an external source, such as training institutes or colleges. It can be provided through, for instance, staff meetings, workshops, conferences, subject training, field-based consultation training, supervised practices and mentoring. The key to effective professional development is identifying the right training strategies to help ECEC practitioners stay updated on scientifically based methods and curriculum subject knowledge so as to be able to apply this knowledge in their work (Litjens and Taguma, 2010). It also pointed out that it should continue over a longer period of time: staff should have long-term or regular opportunities for training (Sheridan, 2001). Only when learning experiences are targeted to the needs of staff and are true learning experiences with development opportunities can professional development have favourable outcomes (Mitchell and Cubey, 2003).

An effective way of improving knowledge and skills is found to be subject training. Field-based consultation can also be very effective, as it provides ECEC staff with the possibility to receive feedback on their practices. Furthermore, practitioners who do not have a degree, but who attend ECEC-relevant professional workshops are found to provide higher quality care than colleagues who do not attend (Burchinal *et al.*, 2002). However, in general, there is little clarity about what forms of professional development are *most* effective. One of the reasons is that staff have different needs: practitioners have very different backgrounds, and effective training methods should suit these differences (Elliott, 2006).

### *Leadership of managerial staff*

Managers play an important role in supporting professional development. Managers matter for the extent to which the centre supports, stimulates and subsidises professional development (Ackerman, 2006). Staff quality is maintained by leadership that motivates and encourages working as a team, information sharing and professional staff development (OECD, 2006). The quality of leaders and managers of ECEC services is also strongly related to their level of education and professional development, as found in the EPPE study (Sylva *et al.*, 2010).

### *Differences between education and training for educating different age groups*

The United States National Institute of Child Health and Development (NICHD) points out that, although staff education and training has an impact on infants and toddlers, staff's formal education is a stronger predictor for children of preschool age than for younger children (NICHD, 2000). For younger children (toddlers and infants), specialised and practical training seems to be more strongly associated with pedagogic quality and cognitive and social outcomes.

### Social equality and professional development

ECEC is often seen as a vehicle to give children from socially disadvantaged backgrounds a "head start" when commencing compulsory education. Early childhood educators come across increasingly complex social environments and encounter a multiplicity of family backgrounds and experiences. These factors create imperatives to adopt new pedagogies and organisational practices to accommodate this pluralism (Elliott, 2006). In various countries, this has led to knowledge and skills requirements for staff.

In line with the issues of integration and prevention of social inequality highlighted by politicians and professionals, current and emerging content for continuing professional development include: intercultural approaches, approaches to second languages, working with children with special needs, working with children at risk and special focus on language acquisition (Eurydice, 2009). However, little is known yet about the effectiveness of these approaches.

## What are the policy implications?

### Raising qualifications of ECEC practitioners

Highly qualified practitioners often provide better quality ECEC. This can yield better child outcomes, both socially and academically, not only in the short term but also in the long term. It is not necessary that all staff working in ECEC have high levels of education, which may also be impossible to realise and not desirable. However, those with lower levels of general education should work alongside those who are highly qualified.

### Providing ongoing professional development to ECEC staff

Ongoing professional development can lead to higher quality ECEC services and outcomes. Attending a workshop may be an easy way to realise means of professional development; however, high-quality subject training, field-based consultation training or supervised practices may be more effective. Ongoing professional development should not only be available, but it should be a requirement to stay and grow in the profession. Furthermore, professional development should be tailored to staff's needs.

### Providing specialised training courses for those working with young children

In-service training that provides possibilities for ECEC specialisation is considered beneficial: educating young children requires specialised skills and content knowledge, including a variety of subject and development areas.

## What is still unknown?

### Concept of quality in ECEC

Researchers are still debating the concept of "quality" in ECEC. Judgement of quality involves values. The effect of the education and training of teachers on the quality of

ECEC depends on the definition of quality and the instrument that is used to measure this quality. Children's developmental outcomes are often used as the most important dependent variable in assessing high-quality ECEC, but this leaves the debate open on *which* developmental outcomes should be studied.

### Content of training and education of ECEC staff

The debate around the concept of "quality" in ECEC also means that the content of the training and education of ECEC staff remains a point of discussion. Some early childhood specialists voice concerns about the suitability for young children of the emphasis on 1) standards and testing (performance rather than meaning making), 2) the teaching of predefined knowledge rather than play, discovery, personal choice and the responsibility of the child – the traditional tools of early childhood learning, and 3) the neglect in ECEC curricula of developmental readiness (see "Research Brief: Curriculum Matters").

### Effectiveness of the level of education and different in-service training strategies

Even though correlations have been found between the level of education and pedagogical quality, the exact relationship between the two is still unclear. Also, little is known about the effectiveness of different training strategies to help ECEC practitioners stay updated. More research is needed on how to engage staff in learning about and implementing evidence-based practices (Diamond and Powell, 2011).

### Knowledge, leadership and competences of managerial staff

Focus has been on the individual qualifications of staff. Knowledge, leadership and competences of the manager have also been found to be important. Research is needed that shows how important this is and why; what kind of qualifications and training would be most relevant for managers; what would be the most effective delivery of such training; etc.

### Ethnic diversity in training and education

The effectiveness of teacher training (both initial and in-service) in which special attention is devoted to social and ethnic diversity has hardly been evaluated. This is a growing issue of importance because of the greater ethnic diversity of the population many countries are facing.

## REFERENCES

Ackerman, D. (2006), "The costs of being a child care teacher: Revisiting the problem of low wages", *Educational Policy*, Vol. 20, No. 1, pp. 85-112.

Burchinal, M., D. Cryer, and R. Clifford (2002), "Caregiver training and classroom quality in child care centers", *Applied Developmental Science*, Vol. 6, No. 1, pp. 2-11.

Diamond, K. E. and D. R. Powell (2011), "An Iterative Approach to the Development of a Professional Development Intervention for Head Start Teachers", *Journal of Early Intervention*, Vol. 33, No. 1, pp. 75-93.

Early, D. *et al.* (2007), "Teachers' Education, Classroom Quality, and Young Children's Academic Skills: Results From Seven Studies of Preschool Programs", *Child Development*, Vol. 78, No. 2, pp. 558-580.

Elliott, A. (2006), "Early Childhood Education: Pathways to quality and equity for all children", *Australian Education Review*, Vol. 50, Australian Council for Educational Research.

Eurydice (2009), Early Childhood Education and Care in Europe: Tackling Social and Cultural Inequalities, Eurydice, Brussels.

Fives, H. (2003), "What is Teacher Efficacy and How does it Relate to Teachers' Knowledge? A Theoretical Review", Paper presented at the American Educational Research Association Annual Conference, Chicago.

Fukkink, R. G. and A. Lont (2007), "Does training matter? A meta-analysis and review of caregiver training studies", *Early Childhood Research Quarterly*, Vol. 22, pp. 294-311.

Howes, C., J. James and S. Ritchie (2003), "Pathways to effective teaching", *Early Childhood Research Quarterly*, Vol. 18, pp. 104-120.

Hyson, M., H. B. Tomlinson and C. A. S. Morris (2009), "Quality improvement in Early Childhood Teacher Education: Faculty perspectives and recommendations for the future", *Early Childhood Research and Practice*, Vol. 11, No. 1.

Johansson, E., and I. Pramling Samuelsson (2009), "To weave together: Play and learning in early childhood education", *Journal of Australian Research in Early Childhood Education*, Vol. 16, No. 1, pp. 33-48.

Litjens, I. and M. Taguma (2010), "Literature overview for the 7th meeting of the OECD Network on Early Childhood Education and Care", OECD, Paris.

Mitchell, L. and P. Cubey (2003), Characteristics of professional development linked to enhanced pedagogy and children's learning in early childhood settings. Report for the New Zealand Ministry of Education. Wellington: NCER.

NIEER (2004), "Better Teachers, Better Preschools: Student Achievement Linked to Teacher Qualifications", *Policy Brief*, NIEER, New Jersey.

NICHD Early Child Care Research Network (2000), "Characteristics and quality of child care for toddlers and preschoolers", *Applied Developmental Science*, Vol. 4, No. 3, pp. 116-135.

OECD (2005), Teachers Matter. Attracting, Developing and Retaining Effective Teachers, OECD, Paris.

OECD (2006), Starting Strong II: Early Childhood Education and Care, OECD, Paris.

Pramling Samuelsson, I. and M. Asplund Carlsson (2008), "The playing learning child: Towards a pedagogy of early childhood", *Scandinavian Journal of Educational Research*, Vol. 52, No. 6, pp. 623-641.

Pramling, N. and I. Pramling Samuelsson (in press 2011), *Educational encounters: Nordic studies in early childhood didactics.* Dordrecht, The Netherlands: Springer.

Sammons, P. (2010) "The EPPE Research Design: an educational effectiveness focus" in: Sylva *et al.* (eds.), *Early Childhood Matters: Evidence from the Effective Pre-school and Primary Education project,* Routledge, London/New York.

Sheridan, S. (2001), "Quality Evaluation and Quality Enhancement in Preschool - A Model of Competence Development", *Early Child Development and Care*, Vol. 166, pp. 7-27, (B).

Sheridan, S. (2009), "Discerning pedagogical quality in preschool", *Scandinavian Journal of Educational Research*, Vol. 53, No. 3, pp. 245-261.

Sheridan, S., I. Pramling Samuelsson and E. Johansson (eds.) (2009), *Barns tidiga lärande. En tvärsnittsstudie av förskolan som miljö för barns lärande* [Children's early learning: A cross-sectional study of preschool as an environment for children's learning], *Göteborg Studies in Educational Sciences*, Vol. 284, Göteborg, Sweden: Acta Universitatis Gothoburgensis.

Shonkoff, J. P. and D. A. Phillips (2000), *From Neurons to Neighborhoods: The Science of Early Childhood Development,* National Academy Press, Washington DC.

Siraj-Blatchford, I. (2010), in Sylva *et al.* (eds.), Early Childhood Matters: Evidence from the Effective Pre-school and Primary Education project, Routledge, London/New York.

Sommer, D., I. Pramling Samuelsson and K. Hundeide (2010), *Child perspectives and children's perspectives in theory and practice*, New York: Springer.

Sylva, K. et al. (2010), Early Childhood Matters: Evidence from the Effective Pre-school and Primary Education project, Routledge, London/New York.

# WORKING CONDITIONS MATTER

## What are "working conditions"?

Working conditions in ECEC settings are often referred to as structural quality indicators (*e.g.*, wages, staff-child ratio, maximum group size, working hours, etc.) and other characteristics (*e.g.*, non-financial benefits, team-work, manager's leadership, workload, etc.) that can influence the ability of professionals to do their work well and their satisfaction with the workplace, work tasks and nature of the job.

## What is at stake?

Attracting, training and retaining suitably qualified ECEC staff is a challenge. Good working conditions are strong incentives for qualified staff to enter the profession. Structural quality indicators have received ample attention because they can usually be regulated or guided at the national level. For staff quality, it is also crucial that practitioners are motivated and supported in applying what they have learned.

The European Commission's Early Matters symposium (European Commission, 2009) concluded that many research findings indicate that, in addition to training and education of staff, staff working conditions are important in providing safe, healthy and good learning environments for children. In spite of these findings, the ECEC sector is usually associated with relatively poor working conditions and poor compensation leading to high turnover rates. ECEC centres often experience turnover rates exceeding 40% annually, undermining the quality of care (Moon and Burbank, 2004).

## Why do working conditions in ECEC matter?

Research points out that the ability of staff to attend to the needs of children is influenced not only by their level of education and training but also by external factors, such as their work environment, salary and work benefits (Shonkoff and Philips, 2000). Working conditions can have an impact on staff job satisfaction and their ability to carry out their tasks; and their possibilities to positively interact with children, give them enough attention and stimulate their development.

Strongly associated with stable, sensitive and stimulating interactions with children are the context and conditions in which staff member works. One study found that low wages: i) effect the ways in which staff interact with children, and ii) are related to high turnover rates (Huntsman, 2008). High turnover rates can have a negative effect on ECEC quality since staff provision is less stable, which, in turn, can impact child development. When staff members regularly change within a group of children, staff and children are less able to develop stable relationships; and nurturing, stimulating interactions take place less often (CCI, 2006).

The body of research on the effects of working conditions on child development is not very extensive, and findings do not always point in the same direction. This is mainly because there is a complex inter-relationship between staff-child ratios, staff qualifications, quality and type of provision that makes it difficult to single out the effect of a particular characteristic of working conditions (Sammons, 2010).

## What matters most?

Firstly, it is important to point out that more research is needed in this area. Available research findings focus on the effects on staff satisfaction rather than on child development. Many aspects of working conditions are found to be related to the quality of ECEC services, while a few aspects have been found to be related to child development. Table 3.1 presents an overview of research findings, pointing to characteristics of working conditions that matter.

**Table 3.1. Which staff working conditions improve ECEC quality?**

| Optimal staff working conditions | Areas of improvement | |
|---|---|---|
| | ECEC services | Child outcomes |
| 1. High staff-child ratio and low group size | X | X |
| 2. Competitive wages and benefits | X | unclear |
| 3. Reasonable schedule/workload | X | unclear |
| 4. Low staff turnover | X | X |
| 5. Stimulating and playful physical environment | X | unclear |
| 6. Competent and supportive centre manager | X | unclear |

Note: Areas of improvement that remain "unclear" present important opportunities for future ECEC research.

*Source*: Ackerman, 2006; Burchinal *et al.*, 2002; De Schipper *et al.*, 2004; De Schipper *et al.*, 2006; De Schipper *et al.*, 2007; Diamond and Powell, 2011; Huntsman, 2008; Litjens and Taguma, 2010; Loeb *et al.*, 2004; Moon and Burbank, 2004; Sheridan and Shuster, 2001; Sheridan *et al.*, 2009; Torquati *et al.*, 2007.

### Staff-child ratio

Higher staff-child ratios, referring to a smaller number of children per staff, are usually found to enhance ECEC quality and facilitate better developmental outcomes for children (Burchinal *et al.*, 2002, De Schipper *et al.*, 2006; Huntsman, 2008; Torquati *et al.*, 2007). While there have been some older studies with contradictory results, the weight of evidence favours the conclusion that staff-child ratio in an ECEC setting is significantly associated with quality (Huntsman, 2008). Findings on "quality" can be summarised as follows.

#### Better staff-child interactions and less stress for staff

Larger staff-child ratios are associated with better working conditions and less stress. Staff are found to be more supportive when they are responsible for a smaller group of children (De Schipper *et al.*, 2006). A higher staff-child ratio improves working conditions within ECEC settings, as staff can give sufficient attention to different developmental domains and create more caring and meaningful interactions with children. As the number of children per staff member increases, staff spend more time in restrictive and routine communication with children and less in positive verbal interactions (Litjens and Taguma, 2010; Rao *et al.*, 2003).

### Better child development

Children become more co-operative in activities and interactions with larger staff-child ratios. They also tend to perform better in cognitive and linguistic assessments when staff-child ratios are higher. Furthermore, academic development seems to be enhanced by higher staff-child ratios, although there are not many (recent) studies that have investigated this topic (Huntsman, 2008; Sylva *et al.*, 2004). A limitation of the research mentioned above is that most findings are almost exclusively correlational, and there have been very few experimental studies (Huntsman, 2008). An experimental study carried out by Chetty *et al.* (2011) found that even though smaller staff-child ratios of three-to-four-year-olds improved outcomes, there were no long-lasting effects on adult earnings. However, the *overall* quality of the ECEC setting did have an effect on adult earnings.

High staff-child ratios are considered particularly important for younger children; there is evidence indicating that infants and toddlers especially benefit from high staff-child ratios (De Schipper, 2006). In many countries staff-child ratios have been regulated with higher staff-child ratios for the very young and lower ratios for older children (NICHD, 2002). Research is lacking, however, on exactly which ratio is most favourable to enhance teacher job satisfaction, ECEC quality and child outcomes. Nevertheless, many early childhood educators believe that anything less than a 1:3 or 1:4 ratio for children up to two years old is insufficient to allow staff to interact effectively with each child (Litjens and Taguma, 2010).

### Group size

#### Increased process quality, although the direct effect remains unclear

Group sizes are often regulated, prescribing the number of children to be arranged and supervised as a group. Not all studies find effects of group size on the quality of ECEC: effect sizes are usually small, and the "size" factor is often difficult to single out when staff-child ratios are included in the same analyses. Another research limitation on group size is that it rarely takes into account the age mixing of children, which may be an important factor (with homogeneous age groups being easier to handle). The overall research conclusion, however, is that group size has an effect on process quality (*e.g.*, staff-child relationship, staff-parent communication). If staff experience their working conditions as more pleasant, this will result in more caring and stimulating behaviour (Huntsman, 2008; Burchinal *et al.*, 2002; Clarke-Stewart *et al.*, 2002).

#### Classroom quality and staff job satisfaction

Research suggests that it is not only the staff-child ratio but also the number of adults in a classroom that impacts quality and job satisfaction. The quality of the classroom environment is found to improve with every additional adult in the room. When practitioners work together in a classroom, this provides opportunities for supervision, consultation and discussing work challenges (Goelman *et al.*, 2006). Clear roles and expectations must be defined to optimise teamwork in ECEC settings. Under current practice, the hiring of assistants has generally failed to compensate for larger groups and less contact with teachers (Chartier and Geneix, 2006; Finn and Pannozzo, 2004).

## Remunerations: wages and other benefits

Higher wages and better working conditions affect people's job satisfaction, work motivation and, indirectly, the quality of their teaching, caring and interactions with children (Huntsman, 2008; Moon and Burbank, 2004).

### Low wages leading to less process quality for child development

Research has indicated that where there are very low wages in ECEC, it "impacts quality primarily by preventing qualified and committed individuals from considering working in child care or early education in the first place" (Manlove and Guzell, 1997). Low wages are, as mentioned above, related to high staff turnover rates (Moon and Burbank, 2004), which influence children's language and socio-emotional development as well as the relationships they form with practitioners (Whitebook 2002; Torquati 2007). Low wages are also correlated with the perception that working in the ECEC sector is not a high-status profession (Ackerman, 2006).

Although pay in ECEC-related professions in most OECD countries is not very high (OECD, 2006), this is not the case in all OECD countries. In Scandinavian countries, for instance, where a bachelor's degree is needed to work as an ECEC teacher, staff receive better pay, and their job has a higher status than in countries with lower pay. Countries with split systems often have lower education requirements and lower wages for practitioners working with very young children (up to three or four years of age) and higher educational requirements and better pay (and better status) for those working with children ages three or four to primary school age.

### Non-financial incentives leading to better job satisfaction and better process quality

The number of vacation days and the compensation that ECEC practitioners receive for additional work hours are also found to have a positive effect on job satisfaction. This, in turn, is related to the quality of teacher-child interactions (Doherty et al., 2000).

### Social status and professional identity

Even when preschool teachers experience higher status within the sector, they do not necessarily experience improved recognition from the outside world, something seen in Denmark and Sweden (Berntsson, 2006). In order to raise the value attributed to the profession and counter gender stereotypes, it is suggested that the "professional identity" of the ECEC workforce must change (OECD, 2006).

## Turnover rate

Stability in care has been found to be strongly and consistently positively related to child outcomes (Loeb et al., 2004). High staff turnover is pronounced across studies of child care in various countries, somewhere between 30% and 50% annually (Huntsman, 2008; Moon and Burbank, 2004).

High staff turnover is associated with lower quality service and poorer child outcomes. Centres with low staff turnover rates have staff that engage in more appropriate and attentive interactions with children. High turnover rates disrupt the continuity of care. Moon and Burbank (2004) argue that when turnover rates are high, children spend less time being engaged in meaningful activities.

## Workload

Heavy workloads are associated with stressed staff. Workload refers to the number of working hours, indicating the extent to which staff's schedules are compatible with family life and the physical demands of the job. Large group sizes, low staff-child ratios and a heavy workload are potential stressors for ECEC practitioners. In general, stressed staff perform less well. Some research findings show the effects of workload on ECEC quality, indicating that practitioners with a heavy workload perform less well than colleagues with lighter schedules (De Schipper et al., 2007).

## Physical aspects of the setting

A rich playing and learning environment is found to be of importance. More space is considered beneficial for child development, although the full impact or effects of physical aspects remain unclear. The United States National Institute of Child Health and Human Development (NICHD, 2002) found a significant link between positive care giving behaviour and the physical characteristics of their environment, e.g., the space requirements in more general terms and the instruments and materials available within the setting. Children were found to be less easily distracted in settings where they had more space available to them. Also, in these circumstances, staff provided more age-appropriate practices and behaviour.

Cross-cultural studies of ECEC quality highlight the fact that differences in physical space and staff-child ratio create different opportunities for staff. With more space, staff are better able to organise children into smaller groups, which, in turn, creates better learning conditions and opportunities for children to play, relax and learn in a variety of ways (Sheridan and Shuster, 2001; Sheridan et al., 2009). Research appears to provide little or no guidance regarding the appropriateness of space requirement regulations (Huntsman, 2008), and further research on the importance of space for child development is needed.

## Role of the manager in supporting professional development

Managers are important in facilitating conducive working conditions and supporting professional development. Although part of working conditions are subject to regulation, another part is centre-specific. ECEC providers who provide better working conditions are observed to provide better care and education (Litjens and Taguma, 2010; Diamond and Powell, 2011). The role of managers of ECEC centres is important in this, as they are the key factor in providing favourable working conditions for their staff.

Evidence shows that ECEC practitioners who experience little professional support from the centre's management have lower job satisfaction and perform their teaching and care-giving tasks less well than those that are professionally supported (Ackerman, 2006). Professional support usually means that the centre supports, stimulates and subsidises professional development, there are regular staff meetings with the management of the centre, and there is encouragement and consultation by colleagues (Ackerman, 2006). The importance of ongoing professional development in making sure that practitioners stay up-to-date with evidence-based practices (staff meetings, conferences and workshops, supervised practices, etc.) has been found in various studies (Litjens and Taguma, 2010; see also "Research Brief: Qualifications, Education and Training Matter").

## What are the policy implications?

### Investing in ECEC to improve working conditions

Research findings indicate that staff who are happy in their job provide better care and are better practitioners. Group size and staff-child ratios are important quality factors in facilitating good working conditions as well as staff having enough time and attention to spend on the children under their supervision. Smaller groups and higher staff-child ratios can facilitate this. Time for staff to plan, document, analyse and reflect – individually and collectively – on their work with children is seen to improve quality. However, increasing staff-child ratios and reducing group size is expensive. For example, reducing the average class size from 15 to 10 requires a 50% increase in the number of teachers and, thus, total teacher salaries paid. Plus there is little clarity on exactly which group sizes or staff-child ratios are most favourable or optimal (Chetty *et al.*, 2011).

In order to enhance the status and quality of early childhood work, governments may wish to consider introducing equal working conditions (salaries, benefits and professional development opportunities) for equivalent qualifications across the early childhood and primary education fields. Care should be taken that in-service training is linked to career progression and to obtaining further qualification (OECD, 2006).

### Giving financial and non-financial incentives to keep well-trained staff

Compensation is one important factor in facilitating good working conditions. Increased salaries will most likely reduce staff turnover rates and attract better qualified staff. Additionally, it increases job satisfaction. Providing non-financial support and incentives for practitioners is also likely to improve staff well-being and encourage ongoing professional development.

Turnover should only be welcomed if the lowest-quality ECEC staff are leaving the profession; this practice opens the door to more high-quality staff. New research suggests that the "forcing out" of low-quality ECEC staff may dramatically improve student outcomes (Hanushek, 2010).

### Raising awareness of ECEC centre managers

Going beyond the regulations, centre managers can be seen to play an important role in providing good working conditions for their staff, facilitating professional development and further training of staff. Raising awareness among managers on the importance of ensuring favourable working conditions and how they can actually facilitate these are important in raising ECEC quality (OECD, 2006).

## What is still unknown?

### Relationship between working conditions and child development

The research evidence for the impact of working conditions on child outcomes is not yet very strong. Working conditions have not often been at the heart of studies. Researchers have linked certain workplace characteristics (staff-child ratios and staff compensation) to differences in programme quality and/or to staff turnover and less often to measures of child development (Whitebook, 2009). Research on how working conditions affect ECEC quality and child outcomes could shed new light on the importance of working conditions.

### More research on which aspects of working conditions matter most for which children

Staff-child ratios are found to be important for all young children, but there is evidence that infants and toddlers especially benefit from high staff-child ratios (De Schipper, 2006). The exact role of space in facilitating better working environments and enhancing child development also remains largely unknown, and the role of multiple adults in ECEC settings is not sufficiently defined to maximise the impact on child outcomes. Additionally, no studies have specifically investigated whether working conditions (and which aspects of working conditions) have different effects on different groups of children, e.g., migrant children or children at risk.

## REFERENCES

Ackerman, D. (2006), "The costs of being a child care teacher: Revisiting the problem of low wages". *Educational Policy*, Vol. 20, No. 1, pp. 85-112.

Berntsson, P. (2006), Lärarförbundet, förskollärare och statushöjande strategier: Ett könsperspektiv på professionalisering, Göteborg: Department of Sociology, Göteborg University.

Burchinal, M., D. Cryer and R. Clifford (2002), "Caregiver training and classroom quality in child care centers", *Applied Developmental Science*, Vol. 6, No. 1, pp. 2-11.

Canadian Council on Learning (CCL) (2006), "Why is High-Quality Child Care Essential? The link between Quality Child Care and Early Learning", *Lessons in Learning*, CCL, Ottawa.

Chartier, A.-M. and N. Geneix (2006), "Pedagogical Approaches to Early Childhood Education", paper commissioned for the EFA Global Monitoring Report 2007, Strong Foundations: Early Childhood Care and Education, Paris.

Chetty, R., J. N. Friedman, N. Hilger, E. Saez, D. Schanzenbach and D. Yagan (2011), "How does your kindergarten classroom affect your earnings? Evidence from project STAR", *Quarterly Journal of Economics* (forthcoming).

Clarke-Stewart, K. A., D. Lowe Vandell, M. Burchinal, M. O'Brien and K. McCartney (2002), "Do regulable features of child-care homes affect children's development?", *Early Childhood Research Quarterly*, Vol. 17, pp. 52-86.

De Schipper, E., M. Van IJzendoorn and L. Tavecchio (2004), "Stability in Center Day Care: Relations with children's well-being and problem behavior in day care", *Social Development*, Vol. 13, No. 4, pp. 531-550.

De Schipper, E. J., M. J. Riksen-Walraven and S. A. Geurts (2007), "Multiple determinants of caregiver behavior in child care centers", *Early Childhood Research Quarterly*, Vol. 22, pp, 312-326.

De Schipper, E. J., M. J. Riksen-Walraven and S.A. Geurts (2006), "Effects of Child–Caregiver Ratio on the Interactions Between Caregivers and Children in Child-Care Centers: An Experimental Study", *Child Development*, Vol. 77, pp. 861-874.

Diamond, K. E. and D. R. Powell (2011), "An Iterative Approach to the Development of a Professional Development Intervention for Head Start Teachers", *Journal of Early Intervention*, Vol. 33, No. 1, pp. 75-93.

Doherty, G., D. S. Lero, Donna S., H. Goelman, A. LaGrange and J. Tougas (2000), *You bet I care!: A Canada-wide study on wages, working conditions, and practices in child care centres*, University of Guelph; Centre for Families, Work and Well-Being Canada, Ontario.

European Commission (2009), *Early Childhood Education and Care - key lessons from research for policy makers*, NESSE Report to the European Commission, European Commission, Brussels, Belgium.

Finn, J. and G. Pannozzo (2004), "Classroom Organization and Student Behavior in Kindergarten", *The Journal of Education Research*, Heldref Publications.

Goelman, H., B. Forer, G. Doherty, D. S. Lero and A. LaGrange (2006), "Towards a predictive model of quality in Canadian child care centers", *Early Childhood Research Quarterly*, Vo. 21, No. 3, pp. 280-295.

Hanushek, E. (2010), "The Economic Value of Higher Teacher Quality", NBER Working Paper, No. 16606.

Huntsman, L. (2008), *Determinants of quality in child care: A review of the research evidence,* Centre for Parenting and Research, NSW Department of Community Services.

Litjens, I. and M. Taguma (2010), "Literature overview for the 7th meeting of the OECD Network on Early Childhood Education and Care", OECD, Paris.

Loeb, S., B. Fuller, S. L. Kagan and B. Carroll (2004), "Child Care in Poor Communities: Early Learning Effects of Type, Quality, and Stability", *Child Development*, Vol. 75, No. 1, pp.47-65.

Manlove, E. E., and J. R. Guzell (1997), "Intention to leave, anticipated reasons for leaving, and 12 Month turnover of child care centre staff", *Early Childhood Research Quarterly*, Vol. 12, No. 2, pp. 145-167.

Moon, J. and J. Burbank (2004), "The early childhood education and wage ladder; a model for improving quality in early learning and care programs", *Policy Brief*, Economic opportunity Institute, Seattle WA.

NICHD Early Child Care Research Network (2002), "Child Care Structure> Process>Outcome: Direct and indirect effects of caregiving quality on young children's development", *Psychological Science*, Vol. 13, pp. 199-206.

Rao, N., J. McHale and E. Pearson (2003), "Links between socialization goals and child rearing practices in Chinese and Indian mothers", *Infant and Child development*, Vol. 12, No. 5, pp. 475-492.

Sammons, P. (2010) "The EPPE Research Design: an educational effectiveness focus" in: Sylva *et al.* (eds.), *Early Childhood Matters: Evidence from the Effective Pre-school and Primary Education project,* Routledge, London/New York.

Sheridan, S., and K.-M. Schuster (2001), "Evaluations of Pedagogical Quality in Early Childhood Education - A cross-national perspective", Department of Education, University of Gothenburg, Sweden, *Journal of Research in Childhood Education, Fall/Winter 2001*, Vol. 16, No. 1, pp, 109-124.

Sheridan, S., J. Giota, Y. M. Han and J. Y. Kwon (2009), "A cross-cultural study of preschool quality in South Korea and Sweden: ECERS evaluations", *The Early Childhood Research Quarterly*, Vol. 24, pp. 142-156.

Shonkoff, J. P. and D. A. Phillips (2000), *From Neurons to Neighborhoods: The Science of Early Childhood Development,* National Academy Press, Washington DC.

Sylva, K. *et al.* (2004), *The Effective Provision of Pre-School Education (EPPE) Project: Final Report*, London: DfES and Institute of Education, University of London.

Torquati, J., H. Raikes and C. Huddleston-Casas (2007), "Teacher education, motivation, compensation, workplace support, and links to quality of center-based child care and teachers' intention to stay in the early childhood profession", *Early Childhood Research Quarterly*, Vol. 22, No. 2, pp. 261-275.

Whitebook, M. (2002), *Working for worthy wages: The child care compensation movement 1970-2001*, Center for the Study of Childcare Employment, Institute for Research on Labor and Employment, UC Berkeley.

Whitebook, M., D. S. Gomby, D. Bellm, L. Sakai and F. Kipnis (2009), *Effective teacher preparation in early care and education: Toward a comprehensive research agenda*, Center for the Study of Child Care Employment, Berkeley, CA.

# ACTION AREA 2 – BROADENING PERSPECTIVES THROUGH INTERNATIONAL COMPARISON

This section contains international comparisons of:

- Job titles, qualifications and requirements
- Professional development
- Staff working conditions

## JOB TITLES, QUALIFICATIONS AND REQUIREMENTS

### Findings

#### Job titles and qualifications

- Five job types are commonly used for staff working in the ECEC sector across OECD countries (Table 3.2).
    - Child care worker
    - Pre-primary teacher; primary teacher; kindergarten teacher; preschool teacher
    - Family and day care worker
    - Pedagogue
    - Auxiliary staff
- A wide range of qualifications are given to staff working in ECEC (by ISCED levels)[4] (Figure 3.1).
    - In "split" system countries, different qualifications exist for kindergarten/preschool teachers and child care workers.
- Kindergarten and preschool teachers generally have higher initial education requirements than care centre staff; the majority of countries responded for the former with ISCED Level 5; and for the latter, with Level 3.

- Exceptions include Portugal and Japan where the same qualification level is required for child care workers/nursery teachers and kindergarten/pre-primary teachers (at ISCED level 5).

- Countries aiming to deliver "integrated" ECEC services tend to have higher qualification requirements for staff working with children ages zero to three.

- Some countries have a unified qualification for staff working with children from age zero up to compulsory schooling; in some cases, there are overlaps. Countries take different approaches to arranging this. For example, in New Zealand, both play centres and kindergartens can host children age zero to compulsory schooling age. However, the qualification requirements to work in these centres are different: a qualification for "kindergarten teacher" for ages zero to six is set at ISCED Level 5B, while a "play centre leader" for ages zero to six requires a qualification at Level 3.

### *Initial education arrangement*

- A majority of countries reported that they provide full-time, as well as part-time, provision of initial education for kindergarten or preschool staff; fewer countries reported such programmes for child care and family or domestic care staff (Table 3.3).

- Initial education is more commonly provided by public institutions than private institutions; this is especially the case for kindergarten or preschool staff (Table 3.4).

- Initial education programmes are typically aligned with qualification arrangements, *i.e.*, different education programmes are in place for child care staff and pre-primary/kindergarten teachers and for primary and pre-primary/kindergarten teachers when the education requirements are different.

- However, in some countries, initial education for staff in child care and early education is integrated or co-ordinated (Table 3.5). Students follow the same education programme, but they can select a specialisation in either child care or pre-primary education within the programme.

- In a few countries, initial education for pre-primary teachers is integrated with that for primary teachers (Table 3.6). For example, teachers in the Netherlands are trained to work with children from ages four to twelve, and they follow the same initial education. Some other countries, such as Australia, prepare the same foundation education for primary and pre-primary teachers, but a specialisation is to be selected for one of the two qualifications.

### *Workforce characteristics*

- A highly uneven gender balance is found in the ECEC workforce (Figure 3.2).

  - In most countries, the median proportions for female pre-primary staff, child care workers and pedagogues are 95% or higher.

  - For pre-primary staff, Mexico is an exception, with males making up 17% of staff, the largest among the observed countries.

- Across respondents, pre-primary staff are around 40 years old, while child care staff is slightly younger (around 38 years old) (Figure 3.3).

    - The average for pre-primary staff is age 40, ranging from 32 in Korea to 48 in Chile.

    - The average for child care workers is age 38.3, with a range from 29.4 in Saxony-Anhalt (Germany) to 45.6 in Hesse (Germany).

    - The average for auxiliary staff is age 34, with a range from 26.5 in Mexico to age 48 in Chile.

    - The average for pedagogues is age 41.8, with a range from 34 in the Netherlands to 48 in Chile.

### *Licensing*

- ECEC practitioners most often need a licence to work in the ECEC sector. Licensing can be obtained by demonstrating the abilities to practice the profession or duties in ECEC.

- Whether the licence requires renewal after a certain period of time differs greatly among respondents (Table 3.7).

    - More countries require licensing renewal for kindergarten/preschool teachers than for child care workers or family day care staff.

    - Manitoba's (Canada) requirement for family day care services is found to be the strictest with a condition of "every year"; while, in Germany, it only needs to be renewed every five years. In, for example, Finland, no renewal is required.

    - Child care staff needs to renew their licence every three years in New Zealand; while, in Scotland (United Kingdom) this is every five years.

    - Preschool teachers need to renew their licence after over five years in the Flemish Community (Belgium) and Japan (every ten years); while, in New Zealand, this is done every three years.

    - Finland and Italy do not require licensing renewal for any staff working in ECEC.

For more detail, see the Survey Response Tables on "Provision of Initial Education and Licensing of Qualifications", "Contents of Initial Education" and "Structure and Content of Initial Staff Education" (Excel™ files) in the online Quality Toolbox at **www.oecd.org/edu/earlychildhood/toolbox**.

**Table 3.2. Job types for ECEC workers**

| | |
|---|---|
| **Child care workers** | The qualifications of child care workers differ greatly from country to country and from service to service. In most countries, child care workers have a vocational-level diploma, generally at a children's nurse level (upper secondary, vocational level); although many countries will also have specialist staff trained to secondary-level graduation, plus a one-to-two-year tertiary-level vocational diploma. |
| **Pre-primary teacher and/or primary teacher** (or kindergarten/ preschool teachers) | Pre-primary teachers are generally trained at the same level and in the same training institutions as primary school teachers. This profile is found in Australia, Canada, France, Ireland, the Netherlands, the United Kingdom and the United States. In some of these countries, *e.g.*, the Netherlands, the pre-primary teacher is trained both for the preschool and primary sectors. In federal countries, variation exists across different states or provinces, but the predominant type of training is in primary school-oriented pedagogy (readiness-for-school is a primary aim of early education). |
| **Family and domestic care workers** | Family and domestic care workers are caregivers working in a family day care provision or home-based care setting. These are traditionally provided in a home setting. This can be at the childminder's home or at the child's own home where a qualified or registered childminder looks after the child. This type of care is most common for children prior to preschool, *i.e.*, those up to three years old. |
| **Pedagogues** | In Nordic and central European countries, many pedagogues have been trained (upper-secondary or tertiary education) with a focus on early childhood services rather than primary teaching. Pedagogues may also have received training in other settings, *e.g.*, youth work or elderly care. In some countries, pedagogues are the main staff members responsible for the care and education of children. |
| **Auxiliary staff** | There are many types of auxiliary staff working in centres that have been trained at different levels. On one end of the scale is auxiliary staff who do not need a formal qualification in the area, while auxiliaries in the preschool service sector in Nordic countries have often gone through a couple years of upper secondary vocational training. |

*Source*: OECD Network on Early Childhood Education and Care's "Survey for the Quality Toolbox and ECEC Portal", June 2011; OECD Family Database, 2010.

### Figure 3.1. Required ISCED levels for different types of ECEC staff

Staff titles with minimum required ISCED level in brackets

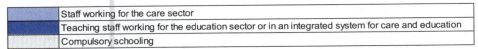

| Staff working for the care sector |
| Teaching staff working for the education sector or in an integrated system for care and education |
| Compulsory schooling |

| Country | Age 0 | 1 | 2 | 3 | 4 | 5 | 6 | 7 |
|---|---|---|---|---|---|---|---|---|
| Australia | Child care Worker (4) / Child care Manager (5) | | | | | | | |
| | Preschool/Kindergarten Teacher (5A) | | | | | | | |
| Austria | Kindergarten Pedagogue (4A) | | | | | | | |
| Belgium (Flemish Community) | Child care Worker in the care sector (3) | | | | | | | |
| | | | 2.5y | Child care Worker in the education sector (3) | | | | |
| | | | 2.5y | Kindergarten teacher / Pedagogue (5B) | | | | |
| Belgium (French Community) | | | Child care Worker (3) | | | | | |
| | | | 2.5y | Pre-Primary Teacher (5) | | | | |
| Canada (British Columbia) | Early childhood educator (3) | | | | | Kindergarten teacher (5A) | | |
| Canada (Manitoba) | Early Childhood Educator (5B) | | | | | | | |
| | | | | | Kindergarten teacher (5) | | | |
| Canada (Prince Edward Island) | Family Day Carer (3) / Child carer in centre-based care (4) | | | | | | | |
| | | | | Kindergarten teacher (4) | | | | |
| Czech Republic | Child care Worker (3) | | | Pedagogue (3) | | | | |
| Denmark | Pedagogue (5) | | | | | | | |
| Estonia | 1.5y | Preschool pedagogue (5) | | | | | | |
| Finland | Child care worker in kindergarten (2/3 of staff should have at least level 3) | | | | | | | |
| | Kindergarten Teacher (5B) | | | | | | Pre-primary Teacher (5B) | |
| Germany | Child care worker (3) | | | | | | | |
| | Pedagogue (4A) | | | | | | | |
| | Pedagogue for childhood or social pedagogue (5) | | | | | | | |
| Hungary | Child care Worker (3) | | | Pedagogue (5) | | | | |
| Ireland | | | | Pre-primary Teacher (5) | | | | |
| Israel | Child care Teacher (5) | | | | | | | |
| | | | | Pre-Premary Teacher (5) | | | | |
| Italy | Educator (child care centres) (5B) | | | Pre-primary teacher (6) | | | | |
| Japan | Nursery Teacher (5B) | | | | | | | |
| | | | | Kindergarten Teacher (5B) | | | | |
| Korea | Child care Worker (3) | | | | | | | |
| | | | | Pre-Primary Teacher (5) | | | | |
| Luxembourg | | | Pre-Primary Teacher (Instituteur) / Educator (5B) | | | | | |
| Mexico | Indigenous ECEC Teacher (3) | | Indigenous preschool Teacher (3) | | | | | |
| | ECE/Preschool Teacher (5) | | | | | | | |
| Netherlands | Child carer (centred child care) / Official Childminder (3) | | | | | | | |
| | | | Playgroup Leader (3) | | Kindergarten/ primary school teacher (4) | | until 12 y | |
| New Zealand | Playcentre Leader (3) | | | | | | | |
| | Qualified Education and Care Teacher / Kindergarten Teacher (5B) | | | | | | | |
| | Teacher for pacific/indiginous children (Kaiako) (5B) | | | | | | | |
| Norway | Child/Youth Worker (3) | | | | | | | |
| | Pedagogical Leader (Kindergarten & Family Kindergarten) / Head Teacher (5A) | | | | | | | |
| Poland | Child care Worker (3) | | | Kindergarten teacher (5) | | | | |
| Portugal | Preschool Teacher (5A) | | | | | | | |
| Slovak Republic | Nursery School Worker (3B) | | | Kindergarten Teacher (3) | | | | |
| Slovenia | Family Day Carer (3) | | | | | | | |
| | Preschool teacher (5B) | | | | | | | |
| Spain | Early education teacher (5B) | | | Preschool teacher (5A) | | | | |
| Sweden | Child minder (3) | | | | | | | |
| | Preschool teacher (5A) | | | | | | | |
| Turkey | Pre-Primary Teacher (5A) | | | | | | | |
| United Kingdom (Scotland) | Child care practitioners (5) | | | | | | | |
| | Preschool Teacher (5) | | | | | | | |
| United States (Georgia, Massachusetts, North Carolina, Oklahoma) | Preschool Teacher (5) | | | | | | | |

*Source*: OECD Network on Early Childhood Education and Care's "Survey for the Quality Toolbox and ECEC Portal", June 2011.

### Table 3.3. Provision of initial education across different types of staff

| | Kindergarten or preschool staff | Child care staff | Family day care staff |
|---|---|---|---|
| **Full time** | Australia, Austria, British Columbia (CAN), Czech republic, Denmark, Estonia, Finland, Flemish Community (BEL), French Community (BEL), , Germany, Hungary, Italy Japan, Korea, Luxembourg, Manitoba (CAN), Netherlands, New Zealand, Norway, Poland, Prince Edward Island (CAN), Scotland (UKM), Slovenia, South Australia (AUS), Spain, Sweden, Turkey | Australia, British Columbia (CAN), Denmark, Flemish Community (BEL), Finland, French Community (BEL), Germany, Hungary, Italy, Japan, Korea, Manitoba (CAN), Netherlands, New Zealand, Poland, Prince Edward Island (CAN), Scotland (UKM), Spain | Australia, Finland, Germany, Manitoba(CAN), Netherlands, Poland, Portugal, Prince Edward Island (CAN), Sweden |
| **Part time[5]** | Australia, Austria, Czech Republic, Denmark, Estonia, Finland, Flemish Community (BEL), Germany, Italy, Japan, Korea, Manitoba (CAN), New Zealand, Norway, Poland, Prince Edward Island (CAN), Scotland (UKM), Slovenia, Spain, Sweden. | Australia, British Columbia (CAN), Denmark, Finland, Flemish Community (BEL), French Community (BEL), Germany, Italy, Japan, Korea, Manitoba (CAN), Netherlands, New Zealand, Poland, Prince Edward Island (CAN), Scotland (UKM), Spain | Australia, Denmark, Finland, Germany, Manitoba (CAN), Netherlands, Poland, Portugal, Prince Edward Island (CAN) |

*Source*: OECD Network on Early Childhood Education and Care's "Survey for the Quality Toolbox and ECEC Portal", June 2011.

### Table 3.4. Public and private provision of initial education

| | Kindergarten or preschool staff | Child care staff | Family day care staff |
|---|---|---|---|
| **Public** | Australia, Austria, British Columbia (CAN), Denmark, Estonia, Finland, Flemish Community (BEL), French Community (BEL), Georgia (USA), Germany, Hungary, Ireland, Italy, Japan, Korea, Luxembourg, Manitoba (CAN), Massachusetts (USA), Mexico, Netherlands, New Zealand, North Carolina (USA), Norway, Oklahoma (USA), Poland, Portugal, Prince Edward Island (CAN), Scotland (UKM), Slovak Republic, Slovenia, Spain, Sweden, Turkey | Australia, British Columbia (CAN), Denmark, Finland, Flemish Community (BEL), French Community (BEL), Germany, Hungary, Japan, Italy, Korea, Manitoba (CAN), Mexico, Netherlands, Norway, Poland, Portugal, Prince Edward Island (CAN), Scotland (UKM), Spain, Sweden | Australia, Austria, Denmark, Finland, Germany, Manitoba (CAN), Poland, Portugal, Prince Edward Island (CAN) |
| **Private** | Austria, British Columbia (CAN), Estonia, Finland, Flemish Community (BEL), Georgia (USA), Germany, Italy, Korea, Massachusetts (USA), New Zealand*,North Carolina (USA), Norway, Oklahoma (USA), Poland, Portugal, Prince Edward Island (CAN), Scotland (UKM), Slovak Republic, Spain | Australia, British Columbia (CAN), Finland, French Community (BEL), Germany, Italy, Japan, Korea, New Zealand*, Norway, Poland, Portugal, Prince Edward Island (CAN), Scotland (UKM), Spain | Australia, Austria, Finland, Germany, Italy, Manitoba (CAN), Netherlands, Poland, Portugal, Prince Edward Island (CAN) |

* New Zealand: regarding kindergarten/preschool – private provision: data refers only to initial education provision for *kaiako* (teacher for indigenous/pacific children) and not for kindergarten teachers. Regarding child care – private provision: data refers only to the initial education provision for playgroup leaders.

*Source*: OECD Network on Early Childhood Education and Care's "Survey for the Quality Toolbox and ECEC Portal", June 2011.

### Table 3.5. Provision of initial education for child care and pre-primary staff[6]

| Integrated | Split |
|---|---|
| Czech Republic*, Denmark, Finland, Israel*, Italy*, New Zealand**, Slovak Republic*, Sweden** | Australia, Belgium, British Columbia (CAN), Germany, Hungary, Korea, Manitoba (CAN), Netherlands, Norway**, Poland, Prince Edward Island (CAN), Slovenia, Scotland (UKM) |

\* Students follow the same education programme, but a specialisation in either child care or pre-primary education is added to the initial education programme.

\*\* Data on New Zealand refers to Education and Care teachers only, excluding play centre leaders. Data on Norway refers to child/youth workers and pedagogical leaders who have a different initial education. Data on Sweden refers to preschool teachers only who work with one-to-seven-year-olds.

Note: Belgium refers to the Flemish Community and French Community of Belgium.

*Source*: OECD Network on Early Childhood Education and Care's "Survey for the Quality Toolbox and ECEC Portal", June 2011.

### Table 3.6. Provision of initial education for pre-primary and primary teaching staff[7]

| Integrated | Split |
|---|---|
| Australia*, Austria, British Columbia (CAN), Denmark, England (UKM), France, Ireland, Netherlands, Poland | Flemish Community (BEL), Japan, Korea, Norway, Sweden |

\* Students follow the same education programme, but a specialisation in either pre-primary education or primary education is added to the initial education programme.

*Source*: OECD Network on Early Childhood Education and Care's "Survey for the Quality Toolbox and ECEC Portal", June 2011 and www.inca.org.uk.

### Figure 3.2. Teacher (or pedagogue) staff profiles

#### Panel A. Pre-primary education

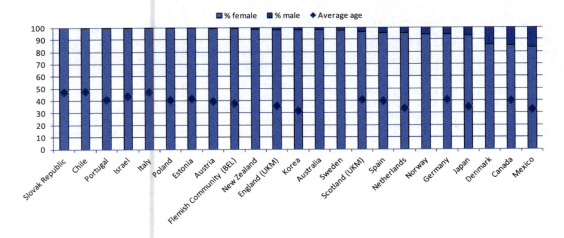

Panel B. Centre-based care

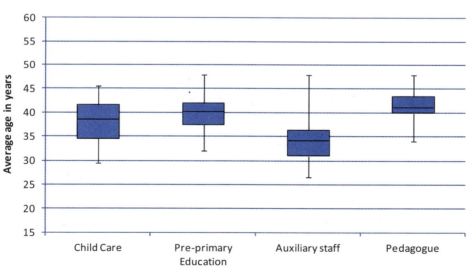

*Source*: OECD Network on Early Childhood Education and Care's "Survey for the Quality Toolbox and ECEC Portal", June 2011.

### Figure 3.3. Average age of staff per staff type

Black horizontal lines mark the median value; black vertical lines show the range

Note: Data series are responding countries and regions given averages for each type of staff. The blue boxes show the range between the first and third quartile with the median represented by the intersecting black line. The black bars show the minimum and maximum observations for each staff type. Based on data for the following countries and regions: Australia, Austria, Canada, Chile, Denmark, England (UKM), Estonia, Flemish Community (BEL), Germany, Israel, Italy, Japan, Korea, Mexico, Netherlands, Poland, Portugal, Scotland (UKM), Slovak Republic and Spain.

*Source*: OECD Network on Early Childhood Education and Care's "Survey for the Quality Toolbox and ECEC Portal", June 2011.

**Table 3.7. Renewal of licences of practitioners in ECEC by staff type**

|  | Kindergarten or preschool teacher | Child care staff | Family or domestic child carer |
|---|---|---|---|
| **More than every 5 years** | Flemish Community (BEL), Japan | | |
| **Every 5 years** | British Columbia (CAN), Georgia (USA), Massachusetts (USA), North Carolina (USA), Oklahoma (USA) | British Columbia (CAN), Scotland (UKM) | Germany |
| **Every 3 years** | New Zealand | New Zealand | Prince Edward Island (CAN) |
| **Every year** | | | Manitoba (CAN) |
| **No renewal required** | Finland, Germany, Italy, Korea, Manitoba (CAN), Mexico, Norway, Poland, Slovenia | Finland, Germany, Italy, Japan, Korea, Manitoba (CAN), Mexico, Poland | Finland, Italy, Poland |

Source: OECD Network on Early Childhood Education and Care's "Survey for the Quality Toolbox and ECEC Portal", June 2011.

The findings presented here are based on data from the OECD Network on ECEC's "Survey for the Quality Toolbox and ECEC Portal" (2011) and on the OECD's desk-based research. For each graph and table, the countries or regions for which data is used are listed.

## PROFESSIONAL DEVELOPMENT

### Findings

#### *Opportunities and financing*

- Professional development is more frequently mandatory for kindergarten or preschool staff than for care centre staff (Figure 3.4, Panels A and B).

- Six financing models are observed for professional development for child care workers (Figure 3.4, Panel A).

  1. Co-funded by government, employer and individual (e.g., Australia and Sweden)

  2. Co-funded by government and employer (*e.g.*, New Zealand and Norway)

3. Co-funded by employer and individual (*e.g.*, Italy)

4. Solely funded by government (*e.g.*, Flemish and French Communities in Belgium)

5. Solely funded by employer (*e.g.*, Czech Republic)

6. Solely funded by individuals (*e.g.*, Israel)

- Five financing models are observed for professional development for preschool or kindergarten teachers (Figure 3.4, Panel B).

    1. Co-funded by government, employer and individual (*e.g.*, Finland and Japan)

    2. Co-funded by government and employer (*e.g.*, Norway and Georgia [United States])

    3. Co-funded by government and individual (*e.g.*, Hungary and Turkey)

    4. Solely funded by government (*e.g.*, Ireland)

    5. Solely funded by individual (*e.g.*, Israel)

- Very few countries reported professional development opportunities for family day care staff (Figure 3.4, Panel C). Finland and the Flemish Community of Belgium both reported that it is mandatory for family day care staff to complete in-service training. In Finland and Belgium, the government pays for the training costs; while, in Italy, the costs are co-shared by the employers and individuals.

## *Providers and incentives*

- Many countries (*e.g.*, Austria, Japan, Portugal) have a wide range of providers of professional development, including government, employers, university/colleges and non-governmental institutions.

- For kindergarten/preschool staff, professional development is most often provided by universities or colleges; while, for child care staff, professional development is mostly offered by non-government-related providers (Figure 3.5).

- Various incentive types are found to encourage individuals to take up professional development (Table 3.8). Commonly found among countries include:

    - Financial support to cover the training costs

    - Financial support to cover the partial foregone salary

    - Opportunities leading to higher qualifications

    - Study leave

    - Linking it to higher salary

- Commonly used incentives for better take up of professional development in both preschools and child care centres (or ECEC centres) include financial support to cover their training costs, followed by pathways to obtain a higher qualification, and study leave to workers participating in professional development. More incentive types are given to kindergarten or preschool teachers than to child care or family day care staff.

– Recognition of prior learning (RPL) is used by a number of countries as a tool to recognise professional development or any skills and knowledge acquired through informal and non-formal learning (Table 3.9). Countries using RPL see it as a tool to up-skill the workforce, recruit and qualify the unqualified. In child care, qualifying the unqualified is more common than in preschool/kindergarten. RPL is used in the family day care sector as well, although only in a few countries.

### *Contents and format of professional development*

– In general, professional development opportunities are more commonly offered for kindergarten or preschool staff than for care centre staff (Figure 3.6).

– While the focus or content of professional development is on "new or revised curriculum" in preschools, it is on "methods and practice" in child care. Planning and management is a popular subject in training as well as monitoring, assessment and evaluation

– Special needs is the least frequently cited topic of professional development in both preschool and child care. Educational transitions are only offered to preschool staff often working with older children who are closer to the primary schooling age.

– Different forms are used for professional development for both preschool teachers and child care workers (Table 3.10):

  – Seminar or workshop

  – Onsite mentoring

  – Online training

  – Formal training course

– More countries use the face-to-face approach (*e.g.*, seminars, workshops, onsite mentoring, formal training options in an educational institution) than online training; however, they are not mutually exclusive but complementary.

For more detail, see the Survey Response Tables on "Provision of Professional Development" and "Structure and Content of Professional Development" (Excel™ files) in the online Quality Toolbox at **www.oecd.org/edu/earlychildhood/toolbox**.

### Figure 3.4. Who funds professional development?

#### Panel A. For preschool/kindergarten staff

| | Government | Employer | Individual |
|---|:---:|:---:|:---:|
| Australia | X | X | X |
| Austria* | X | X | X |
| Belgium (Flemish and French) | X | | |
| Czech Republic** | X | X | X |
| England (UKM) | X | | |
| Estonia* | X | X | X |
| Finland* | X | X | X |
| Georgia* (USA) | X | X | |
| Hungary* | X | | X |
| Ireland | X | | |
| Israel | | | X |
| Italy | X | X | X |
| Japan* | X | X | X |
| Korea | X | X | X |
| Manitoba (CAN)* | X | X | X |
| Massachusetts (USA) | X | X | |
| Mexico* | X | | |
| Netherlands | X | X | X |
| New Zealand | X | X | |
| North Carolina* (USA) | X | X | X |
| Norway | X | X | |
| Oklahoma* (USA) | X | | |
| Poland | X | X | X |
| Portugal | X | X | X |
| Prince Edward Island (CAN)* | X | X | X |
| Slovak Republic* | X | X | X |
| Slovenia* | X | X | X |
| Spain* | X | X | X |
| Sweden | X | X | X |
| Turkey | X | | X |

#### Panel B. For child care staff

| | Government | Employer | Individual |
|---|:---:|:---:|:---:|
| Australia | X | X | X |
| Austria* | X | X | X |
| Belgium (Flemish and French) | X | | |
| British Columbia* (CAN) | X | X | X |
| Czech Republic | | X | |
| England (UKM) | X | | |
| Finland* | X | X | X |
| Hungary* | X | | |
| Ireland | | | X |
| Israel | | | X |
| Italy | | X | X |
| Japan | X | X | X |
| Korea* | X | X | X |
| Manitoba (CAN) | X | X | X |
| Mexico* | X | | |
| Netherlands | X | X | X |
| New Zealand | X | X | |
| Norway** | X | X | |
| Poland | X | X | X |
| Prince Edward Island (CAN)* | X | X | X |
| Scotland (UKM) | X | X | X |
| Spain* | X | X | X |
| Sweden** | X | X | X |

#### Panel C. For domestic day care staff

| | Government | Employer | Individual |
|---|:---:|:---:|:---:|
| Finland* | X | | |
| Flemish Community (BEL)* | X | | |
| French Community (BEL) | X | | |
| Italy | | X | X |

\* Staff uptake of professional education is compulsory at the individual level. In countries without *, uptake of professional development by staff is voluntary.

\*\* For Czech Republic, training is only mandatory for directors of preschools/kindergartens. For Norway, data regarding child care refers to child/youth workers. For Sweden, data regarding child care refers to childminders.

*Source*: OECD Network on Early Childhood Education and Care's "Survey for the Quality Toolbox and ECEC Portal", June 2011.

## Figure 3.5. Providers of professional development

### Panel A. For kindergarten or preschool staff

| | Government | Employer | University / college | Non-government |
|---|---|---|---|---|
| Australia | | X | | X |
| Austria | X | X | X | X |
| British Columbia (CAN) | X | X | X | X |
| Czech Republic | X | X | X | X |
| Denmark | | | X | |
| England (UKM) | X | | X | X |
| Estonia | X | X | X | X |
| Finland | X | | X | X |
| Flemish Community (BEL) | | X | X | X |
| French Community (BEL) | | X | | |
| Georgia (USA) | X | X | | |
| Hungary | X | | X | |
| Ireland | X | | | |
| Israel | X | | X | |
| Italy | X | X | X | X |
| Japan | X | X | X | X |
| Korea | X | X | X | X |
| Manitoba (CAN) | X | X | X | X |
| Massachusetts | X | X | X | X |
| Mexico | X | | | |
| Netherlands | | X | X | X |
| New Zealand | | | X | X |
| North Carolina (USA) | X | X | | |
| Norway | X | X | X | X |
| Oklahoma (USA) | X | X | | |
| Poland | X | X | X | X |
| Portugal | X | X | X | X |
| Prince Edward Island (CAN) | X | X | X | X |
| Scotland (UKM) | | X | X | X |
| Slovak Republic | X | X | X | X |
| Slovenia | X | X | X | X |
| Spain | X | X | X | X |
| Sweden | | X | X | X |
| Turkey | X | | X | X |

### Panel B. For child care staff

| | Government | Employer | University / college | Non-government |
|---|---|---|---|---|
| Australia | | X | | X |
| Austria | X | X | X | X |
| British Columbia (CAN) | X | X | X | X |
| Czech Republic | | X | | |
| Denmark | X | | | |
| England (UKM) | X | | X | X |
| Finland | X | | X | X |
| Flemish Community (BEL) | | | X | X |
| French Community BEL) | | | | X |
| Georgia (USA) | X | | X | X |
| Hungary | X | | X | |
| Israel | X | | X | X |
| Italy | X | | | X |
| Japan | | X | X | X |
| Korea | X | X | X | X |
| Massachusetts (USA) | | X | X | X |
| Manitoba (CAN) | X | X | X | X |
| Mexico | X | X | | X |
| Netherlands | | X | X | X |
| New Zealand | | | X | X |
| Norway* | X | X | X | X |
| Poland | | X | X | X |
| Prince Edward Island (CAN) | X | X | X | X |
| Scotland (UKM) | X | X | X | X |
| Spain | X | X | X | X |
| Sweden* | | X | X | X |

\* For Norway, data regarding child care refers to child/youth workers. For Sweden, data regarding child care refers to childminders.

*Source*: OECD Network on Early Childhood Education and Care's "Survey for the Quality Toolbox and ECEC Portal", June 2011.

**Table 3.8. Incentives for ECEC workers to take up professional development**

By type of provision

| | Financial support for training costs | | Financial support to cover partial salary | | Path to higher qualification[1] | | Study leave[2] | | Higher salary/ promotion | |
|---|---|---|---|---|---|---|---|---|---|---|
| | Child care | Pre-school | Child care | Pre-school | Child care | Pre-school | Child care | Pre-school | Child care | Pre-school |
| Australia | X | X | | | | | | | | |
| Austria | X | X | | | | | X | X | | |
| British Columbia (CAN)* | X | X | X | | | | X | X | X | X |
| Czech Republic | X | X | | | | X | | X | | |
| Denmark | | | | | | X | | X | | X |
| England (UKM) | X | X | | | X | X | | | | |
| Estonia | | X | | | | | | X | | X |
| Finland | X | X | X | X | X | X | X | X | | |
| Flemish Community (BEL) | | X | | | | X | | X | | |
| French Community (BEL) | X | X | | X | X | | | X | | |
| Georgia (USA) | | X | | | X | | | | | |
| Germany | | | | | | | X | X | X | X |
| Hungary | X | X | | | | | | | | |
| Italy | | | | | | | X | X | | |
| Japan | X | X | | X | | X | | X | | |
| Korea | X | X | | | | | | | | X |
| Manitoba (CAN) | X | X | X | | X | X | X | | X | X |
| Massachusetts (USA) | | X | | | | | X | | | |
| Mexico | X | X | | | | | | | | X |
| Netherlands | X | X | X | X | X | X | X | X | X | X |
| New Zealand | X | X | | | X | X | | | | |
| North Carolina (USA) | | X | | | | | | | | |
| Norway* | X | X | | | X | X | | | | |
| Oklahoma (USA) | | | | | | | | | | |
| Poland | X | X | | | X | X | X | X | X | X |
| Portugal | | X | | X | | X | | X | | X |
| Prince Edward Island (CAN)* | | X | | | | X | | | | X |
| Scotland (UKM) | | | | | X | | | | | |
| Slovak Republic | | | | X | | X | | | | X |
| Slovenia | X | X | X | X | X | X | X | X | X | X |
| Spain | X | X | | | X | X | X | X | X | X |
| Sweden* | X | X | X | X | X | X | X | X | | |
| Turkey | | | | | | X | | | | X |

* For British Columbia (CAN), incentives for take-up of professional development can differ per employer. For Norway, data regarding child care refers to child/youth workers. For Prince Edward Island (CAN), data refers to entry-level ECEC staff. For Sweden, data regarding child care refers to childminders.

Note 1: "Path to higher qualification" refers to the availability of higher qualification through professional development. In some countries, higher qualifications are not available for the ECEC workforce; whereas in other countries, higher qualification is available and may be obtained through professional development.

Note 2: "Study leave" includes permitted time off from work to pursue professional development and replacement of an employee with a substitute.

*Source*: OECD Network on Early Childhood Education and Care's "Survey for the Quality Toolbox and ECEC Portal", June 2011.

## Table 3.9. Incentives for RPL (Recognition of prior learning)

| | Upskill | | | Recruitment | | | Qualify the unqualified | | |
|---|---|---|---|---|---|---|---|---|---|
| | Child care | Pre-school | Family day care | Child care | Pre-school | Family day care | Child care | Pre-school | Family day care |
| **Australia** | X | | X | | | | X | | X |
| **British Columbia (CAN)** | | | | X | X | | | | |
| **Denmark** | | | | | | | | X | |
| **England (UKM)** | | | | | | | X | | |
| **Finland** | | | | | | | | | X |
| **Flemish Community (BEL)** | X | X | | | | | X* | | |
| **Germany** | X | X | X | | | | | | |
| **Israel** | | | | X | X | | | | |
| **Italy** | X | X | X | | | | | | |
| **Korea** | X | X | | | | | | | X |
| **Manitoba (CAN)** | X | X | X | X | X | | | | |
| **Massachusetts (USA)** | | | | | | | X | | |
| **Netherlands** | | | | | | | X | | X |
| **New Zealand** | | | | X | X | | | | |
| **Scotland (UKM)** | | | | | | | X | | |
| **Slovenia** | | | | | | | X | | |
| **Spain** | | | | | | | X | | |
| **Turkey** | | X | | | X | | | X | |

Note: For the Flemish Community (BEL), data refers only to subsidised child care provisions.

*Source*: OECD Network on Early Childhood Education and Care's "Survey for the Quality Toolbox and ECEC Portal", June 2011.

## Figure 3.6. Content of professional development[8]

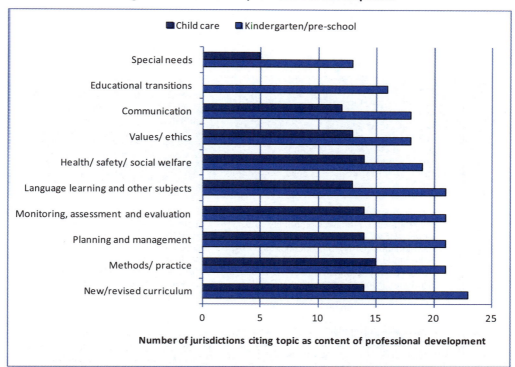

Note 1: Countries were given a range of topics to select from, including the possibility to list topics not mentioned in the selection. Answers indicating "other" without specifying which topic was referred to with "other" are not included in this figure.

Note 2: Countries with an integrated ECEC system who indicated that the subjects of professional development were similar for the whole ECEC sector/ECEC age range: responses have been included in both "child care" and "kindergarten/preschool" since the content of professional development refers to the whole ECEC age range, including ECEC workers with younger children (herein referred to as "child care").

*Source*: OECD Network on Early Childhood Education and Care's "Survey for the Quality Toolbox and ECEC Portal", June 2011.

**Table 3.10. Forms and structures of professional development opportunities**

| | | Staff type | |
| --- | --- | --- | --- |
| | | Kindergarten or preschool staff | Child care staff |
| **Training programme form and structure** | Seminar or Workshop | Australia, Austria, Czech Republic, Denmark, Estonia, Finland, Flemish Community (BEL), French Community (BEL), Israel, Italy, Japan, Korea, Massachusetts (USA), Manitoba (CAN), Mexico, Netherlands, New Zealand, North Carolina (USA), Norway, Oklahoma (USA), Poland, Portugal, Prince Edward Island (CAN), Scotland (UKM), Slovak Republic, Slovenia, Spain and Turkey | Australia, Austria, British Columbia (CAN), Czech Republic, Finland, Flemish Community (BEL), French Community (BEL), Israel, Italy, Japan, Korea, Manitoba (CAN), Massachusetts (USA), Mexico, Netherlands, New Zealand, Norway*, Oklahoma (USA), Poland, Prince Edward Island (CAN), Scotland (UKM) and Spain |
| | Onsite Mentoring | Australia, Austria, Czech Republic, Denmark, Estonia, Finland, Flemish Community (BEL), Georgia (USA), Ireland, Israel, Italy, Japan, Korea, Manitoba (CAN), Massachusetts (USA), Netherlands, New Zealand, North Carolina (USA), Norway, Oklahoma (USA), Poland, Portugal, Prince Edward Island (CAN), Scotland (UKM), Slovak Republic, Slovenia and Spain | Australia, Austria, British Columbia (CAN), Czech Republic, Denmark, Finland, Flemish Community (BEL), Georgia (USA), Israel, Italy, Japan, Manitoba (CAN), Massachusetts (USA), Netherlands, New Zealand, Norway*, Oklahoma (USA), Poland, Prince Edward Island (CAN), Scotland (UKM) and Spain |
| | Online Training | Australia, Czech Republic, Denmark, Estonia, Georgia (USA), Ireland, Israel, Italy, Japan, Korea, Manitoba (CAN), Massachusetts (USA), Netherlands, New Zealand, North Carolina (USA), Norway, Poland, Portugal, Prince Edward Island (CAN), Slovak Republic and Spain | Australia, British Columbia (CAN), Czech Republic, Georgia (USA), Israel, Italy, Korea, Manitoba (CAN), Massachusetts (USA), Netherlands, New Zealand, Norway*, Oklahoma (USA), Poland, Prince Edward Island (CAN), Scotland (UKM) and Spain |
| | Formal Training Course | Australia, Austria, Czech Republic, Denmark, England (UKM), Estonia, Finland, Flemish Community (BEL), French Community (BEL), Georgia (USA), Israel, Italy, Japan, Korea, Manitoba (CAN), Massachusetts (USA), Mexico, Netherlands, North Carolina (USA), Norway, Poland, Portugal, Prince Edward Island (CAN), Scotland (UKM), Slovenia and Sweden | Australia, Austria, British Columbia (CAN), Czech Republic, England (UKM), Finland, Flemish Community (BEL), Georgia (USA), Israel, Italy, Manitoba (CAN), Massachusetts (USA), Mexico, Netherlands, Norway*, Oklahoma (USA), Poland, Prince Edward Island (CAN), Scotland (UKM) and Sweden* |

* For Norway, data regarding child care refers to child/youth workers. For Sweden, data regarding child care refers to childminders.

*Source*: OECD Network on Early Childhood Education and Care's "Survey for the Quality Toolbox and ECEC Portal", June 2011.

## Definitions and methodologies

– **Professional development** refers to knowledge, skills and competencies attained for professional advancement. **Professional development opportunities** are aimed at improving the performance of ECEC staff in already assigned positions. Professional development opportunities are often referred to as "in-service training" and "continuous education/training". The contents indicate which subject areas and topics these training programmes seek to address and improve upon. Countries could choose from the following:

- *Language learning and other subjects*: includes language learning, languages, arts, math, sciences, information and communication technologies, etc.

- *New curriculum*: includes new and updated curriculum, reform in curriculum, etc.

- *Methods/practice*: includes teaching methodologies, teaching strategies and practices, such as Reggio Emilia or inclusive education.

- *Values/ethics*: includes ethics, anti-discrimination, equal opportunity, citizenship, etc.

- *Planning and management*: includes planning of activities and the curriculum, programming, management, leadership, etc.

- *Communication*: includes communication with parents, communication with other staff for team teaching/caring, use of information and communication technologies, etc.

- *Monitoring, assessment and evaluation*: includes monitoring, assessment (*i.e.*, of targets/goals/etc.) of child outcomes, evaluation of development, programme quality and staff performance, etc.

- *Health, safety and social welfare*: includes health, safety, well-being, social welfare, etc.

- *Special needs and educational transitions:* these two subjects were not included in the list to choose from as separate topics, but countries could indicate in a box named "other" whether they were addressing these subjects in professional development.

- **Recognition of prior learning** refers to a process used by governments, accreditation organisations, employers or universities or colleges to evaluate learning acquired outside the classroom and often formally recognised as academic credits, certificates, salary increase, etc.

The findings presented here are based on data from the OECD Network on ECEC's "Survey for the Quality Toolbox and ECEC Portal" (2011), and on the OECD's desk-based research. For each graph and table, the countries or regions for which data is used are listed (if not presented in the graph).

## STAFF WORKING CONDITIONS

### Findings

- All ECEC staff earn above the minimum wage set for their countries. But there is a significant wage range across countries. While the salary for kindergarten/preschool teachers is less than double the minimum wage in countries such as New Zealand and Chile, it is more than four times in British Columbia (Canada) and Portugal (Figure 3.7, Panel A).

- In general, kindergarten or preschool staff receive higher salaries than other ECEC staff. The exception is Spain, where kindergarten/preschool staff and child care workers are equally paid.

- In many countries, pre-primary and primary teaching staff are paid at the same rate, such as in Portugal and Manitoba (Canada); but primary teachers are paid higher than pre-primary teachers in countries such as Chile England (United Kingdom), Mexico, Poland, and Slovenia (Figure 3.7, Panel B).

- Turn-over rates are high in both child care and preschool/kindergarten. On average, the turn-over rate in kindergarten is 17.7%; while it is slightly lower in child care with 15.4% (Figure 3.8).

- Large differences are observed among countries for the rate for kindergarten staff: it is more than 30% in Denmark and the United States; while it is less than 5% in the Flemish Community of Belgium, Estonia and England (United Kingdom).

- For child care staff, the ratio is 35% in the United States; and the lowest is the Netherlands with 8.9%.

**Figure 3.7. Remuneration of ECEC staff**

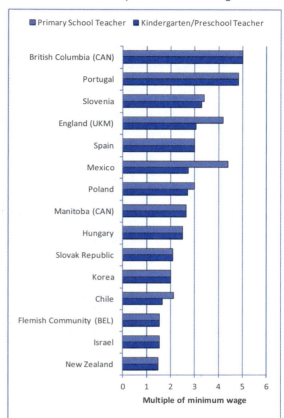

**Panel A: ECEC staff across different types of ECEC provision**

Given as multiple of minimum wage

**Panel B: Kindergarten/ preschool and primary school teaching staff**

Given as multiple of minimum wage

\* In Korea, remuneration for child care centre staff ranges between 1.3 and 1.5 times the minimum wage and refers to the average starting salary of child care staff in public institutions.

\*\* For North Carolina, assistance preschool teacher is used for the figure on assistant / auxiliary staff.

Note: "Assistant/Auxiliary Staff" typically require lower qualifications and work with primary staff in the specific ECEC setting.

*Source*: OECD Network on Early Childhood Education and Care's "Survey for the Quality Toolbox and ECEC Portal", June 2011.

**Figure 3.3. Staff turnover rates per different types of ECEC staff**

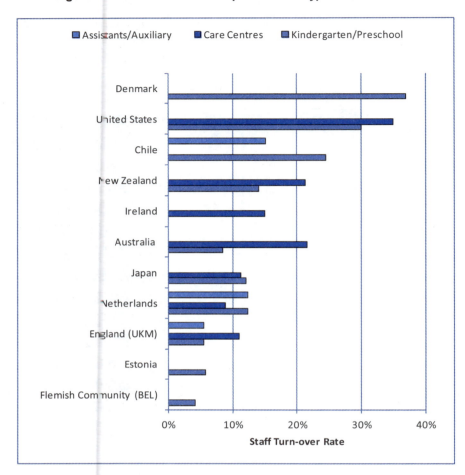

Note: "Assistant/Auxiliary Staff" cut across different types of services and will typically require lower qualifications and work with primary staff in the specific ECEC setting.

*Source*: OECD Network on Early Childhood Education and Care's "Survey for the Quality Toolbox and ECEC Portal", June 2011.

For more detail, see the Survey Response Table on "Working Conditions" (Excel™ file) in the online Quality Toolbox at **www.oecd.org/edu/earlychildhood/toolbox**.

## Definitions and methodologies

- **Working conditions** in ECEC refer to the characteristics of work and the workplace that can influence the ability and motivation of professionals to do their work well. They also relate to ECEC staff satisfaction with the workplace, work tasks and the nature of the job. Indicators to describe working conditions often include salaries and staff turn-over rate but also non-financial benefits, such as the possibility to participate in training (see International Comparison on "Professional development") and staff-child ratio (see International Comparison on "Minimum standards").

- **Staff turnover rate** is based on the number of workers that had to be replaced over a given period of time, calculated as the number of employee departures divided by staff members and multiplied by a hundred[9].

- Working conditions are compared among staff working in different settings (see the OECD Family Database):

  - **Centre-based day care**: encompasses all child care that is provided outside the home in licensed centres. The services provided can be full- or part-time and are most commonly referred to as nurseries, day care centres, *crèches*, playschools and parent-run groups.

  - **Preschool early education programmes (Kindergartens)**: includes centre- or school-based programmes designed to meet the needs of children preparing to enter primary education. In most countries, these programmes include at least 50% educational content and are supervised by qualified staff. Among respondents, it is common to enrol an older age bracket from circa age three in kindergartens or preschools.

The findings presented here are based on data from the OECD Network on ECEC's "Survey for the Quality Toolbox and ECEC Portal" (2011), and on the OECD's desk-based research. For each graph and table, the countries or regions for which data is used are listed (if not presented in the graph).

# ACTION AREA 3 – SELECTING A STRATEGY OPTION

This section contains a list of strategy options to tackle the following challenge:

- Improving workforce development and working conditions

## IMPROVING WORKFORCE DEVELOPMENT AND WORKING CONDITIONS

### Challenge 1: Improving staff qualifications

Qualifications for ECEC staff often overlap and are not transparent among child care workers and early education teachers. Different qualifications leading to different job titles/profiles do not always clearly communicate to staff or parents about what knowledge, skills and competencies staff have.

Different sectors – within ECEC – have different goals and visions for staff education and training. Revising or unifying ECEC staff qualifications poses a challenge especially in countries with a "split system" or fragmented services over child care and early education. Improving qualifications evenly across the country is also a challenge due to local control over the contents of the education programmes.

*Revising initial education programmes and requirements*

- **British Columbia (Canada)** revised the Child Care Licensing Regulation so that Early Childhood Educator (ECE) Assistants and other adults working in licensed facilities must fulfil specific course requirements. Prior to this change, ECE Assistants were only required to complete any ECE or related training. The requirements became more specific in an effort to increase the quality of the training. The change was made as a result of information received from the field consultations during the revision process. It responds to the implementation of two labour mobility agreements, which intend to facilitate the mobility of workers between provinces in Canada. Rather than creating an entirely new programme or course for ECE Assistants, the government used courses already designed and available through existing ECE programmes. The changes have not impacted content, duration, fees or modes of delivery.

- In **New Zealand**, in 1986, child care services were transferred from the Department of Social Welfare to the Department of Education. A year after integrating the child care and education sectors, the government established the Diploma of Education (Early Childhood Education) as the benchmark teaching qualification for the newly centralised system. In 1988, the first three-year teacher training programme with cultural training components began to be phased in. In the early 1990s, the focus of the sector was on quality, training and funding.

- In 2009-10, **Korea** embarked on upgrading the initial education of the ECEC workforce. For kindergarten teachers, the government set the qualification level at a four-year bachelor's degree and intends to gradually reduce the number of students at teacher training colleges in order to strike a better balance between demand and supply of the kindergarten workforce. For child care teachers, the government set a higher level by increasing the required credits from 35 to 51 credits (*i.e.*, 12 to 17 courses) at a college level and, furthermore, strengthened the training programme with a third level qualification (*i.e.*, one year of training after high school graduation), requiring a total of 1 105 hours including four weeks of field practicum. From March 2013, child care practice will take place only at accredited facilities with a minimum of 15 children.

- In **Flanders** (**Belgium**), the government agency, *Kind en Gezin* (Child and Family), worked with key stakeholders in the child care sector, as well as experts, to come up with a definition of a vocational qualification for a vocational bachelor's degree in child rearing and education of young children. It also consulted with the child care sector, educational organisations and the adult education sector to design the concept for a child-minding academy.

- In **Finland**, the education for practical nurses started in the 1990s. At that time, there was a call from the labour market for more flexible movement from one task to another. Formerly, there were several different examinations (childminder, day care nurse, rehabilitation nurse, nurse for the disabled, etc.), which are now merged into one broader examination with different sub lines to choose from.

- **Portugal** changed qualification requirements so that preschool teachers must obtain a four-year master's degree, which is the same qualification that must be obtained by primary and secondary school teachers. Up until 1998, the qualification required for this job profile was a three-year bachelor's degree. The Ministry of Education and the Ministry of Science and Higher Education worked with universities and polytechnics to establish the preschool teacher degree programme.

- In **Germany**, more bachelor degree-level ECEC programmes are emerging at the university level. The development started with universities like the Alice-Salomon-Hochschule in Berlin and the Evangelische Hochschule Freiburg in 2004. In 2011, the Ministers of Youth from German *Länder* agreed on a resolution about a common title (approved pedagogue for early childhood) and common contents for these degree programmes.

- In, **Slovak Republic**, ECEC teachers currently enter the profession with varying levels of training. Although ISCED level 3B is acceptable, the government is considering making it mandatory that teachers pursue higher initial education at ISCED levels 5A or 5B.

- In the **Czech Republic**, new requirements concerning the education and qualification of pedagogical staff went into effect in 2005. In addition to ISCED level 3 training, universities now offer ECEC study programmes at ISCED levels 4 and 5. The Ministry of Education, Youth and Sport is promoting university-level qualifications in an effort to improve the quality of ECEC services.

- **Slovenia** has made the following revisions to initial education:

  - In 1994, a new three-year higher professional study programme in preschool education was established. Prior to this, preschool education studies consisted of a two-year programme established in 1987 that was offered by teacher training colleges.

  - Students pursuing the new three-year programme have the possibility of continuing onto a master-level programme.

  - As of 1996, preschool teachers' assistants must hold an upper secondary technical qualification or an upper secondary general school with an additional qualification in preschool education.

- In **Sweden**, in 2010, the government proposed that current degrees in education be replaced by four new professional degrees: preschool education, primary school education, subject education and vocational education. The new degrees will lead to greater clarity regarding the components of teacher education; and the preschool education programme will have a more specific direction to secure the supply of well-educated teachers. The government introduced in 2011 a new initial training programme to increase the supply of well-educated preschool teachers. The following decisions have been made:

  - regulate preschool teachers as other teachers are regulated;

  - clarify teacher qualifications;

  - create a teacher certification process; and

  - design a state authorisation system (senior subject teachers) to strengthen incentives for preschool teachers to advance the quality of activities and to pursue continuous education.

- **Prince Edward Island**'s (**Canada**) Preschool Excellence Initiative (2010) requires all staff working in Early Years Centres to be provincially certified at either an Entry Level, Program Staff or Supervisor Level certification. The Entry Level certification requires uncertified staff in the system to participate in a training consisting of three courses: growth and development, developmentally appropriate practice, and guidance. The Department of Education and Early Childhood Development worked with staff at local colleges to design an appropriate entry level course. The Program Staff and Supervisor Level certifications require educators to have a two-year diploma in ECEC.

- **Scotland (United Kingdom)** is currently undertaking a review and discussion on what skills, knowledge and understanding ECEC staff should encompass. A Common Skills Working group has been established to identify what should be included in initial ECEC staff education programmes. Stakeholders are invited to comment on the identified skills and knowledge areas for ECEC staff. After receiving the comments, the plan will be revised. An implementation plan for the revision of initial ECEC education programmes will be drafted at the end of 2011. The goal of this initiative is to strengthen the workforce knowledge and improve quality ECEC delivery.

– **England** (**United Kingdom**) has launched an independent review of existing early education and child care qualifications and training. The review will look at the ways in which qualifications can be strengthened and pathways to support career progression in the sector improved to the benefit of young children, their families and those who work in the early childhood sector.

– **Spain** set out a new bachelor's degree in Pre-Primary Education, which requires four academic years, that is, one year longer than the previous programme. The total workload is 240 credits, 50 of which are devoted to practicum; whereas the previous diploma only required 320 hours. Furthermore, foreign languages have gained relevance, and students must demonstrate a certain level of competence in a foreign language at the end of the degree programme. Students also now have the possibility to enrol in specialised courses to meet the specific needs of early education, for example, organisation and optimisation of school libraries, innovation through ICT, school organisation and management, promoting joint action between school and its environment, etc. The syllabi of the general training module include new course proposals such as "Society, family and school", "Childhood, health and nutrition" and "Systematic observation and context analysis".

– In **Germany**, the federal government started the Action Programme Family Day Care (*Aktionsprogramm Kindertagespflege*) to foster a minimum qualification of 160 hours for all day care mothers and fathers. Training institutions have to apply for a seal of quality. Additionally, subsidies are given to day care workers who take part in a part-time qualification to become a pedagogue or a child care worker.

*Aligning qualifications between pre-primary and primary teachers*

– **Flanders** (**Belgium**) aims to merge kindergarten teachers and primary teachers into a single career profile with the same set of required competences.

– The **French Community** of **Belgium** has revised the initial education level of preschool teachers so that it is equivalent to the level of primary school teachers.

– **Finland** raised the level of education for kindergarten teachers and connected it more closely to the level for primary school teachers. In 1995, kindergarten teacher education was moved to the university level, as classroom teacher training and other teacher training had already been established in universities. This change created greater synergy and interaction between training for ECEC professionals and training for primary school teachers to better support children's development and learning and foster co-operation between teachers during children's transition from kindergarten to primary school.

- In **Portugal**, preschool and primary teachers follow the same programme in the first three years then specialise in either preschool or primary for the fourth year. Teachers can study for a fifth year if they wish to obtain certification for both levels.

*Promoting mobility/collaboration among preschool teachers, child care workers and other workers*

- **Slovenia** allows teachers and other graduates in the fields of education, arts, humanities, social sciences and social work to work as preschool teachers once they have acquired an additional qualification in preschool education.

- In **Australia**, the government is creating additional early childhood education university places; and tertiary education providers offer preschool teaching degrees tailored to the needs of diploma-qualified child care workers as a response to the need to increase integration of early education and child care. Articulation pathways have been created between the Vocation and Education Training sector and the Higher Education sector to support students through new training opportunities.

- In **Flanders** (**Belgium**), the education sector is considering extending certificates of competence to facilitate the mobility between primary teacher and nursery teacher. They are also considering whether other qualifications can be taken into account for the job of pre-primary teacher. This is still in a preparatory phase.

- In **Belgium**'s **French Community**, children's nurses have had rights and obligations in the academic domain as well as the care domain since 2004. In 2006, the government established a law by which children's nurses may be appointed to work in *maternelle* in collaboration with preschool teachers; and from 2007-09, slightly more than 25% of children's nurses were appointed to do so.

- **Japan** encourages ECEC staff to obtain both kindergarten and day care qualifications to promote co-operation between these facilities. Most college credits for both qualifications are already aligned, and around 80% of staff in ECEC facilities hold both qualifications.

- In **Korea**, kindergarten teachers studying early childhood education can be also qualified as child care teachers if they complete the required credits for child care. Child care practitioners can now also work at full-day kindergarten programmes, although there are still some limitations and barriers in this due to the dual training system and salary differences. Three municipal territories in Korea have therefore implemented an ECEC collaboration project called the *Yeong Cha* Project. These projects are partially funded by the local authorities and stimulate interaction and co-operation among different ECEC practitioners (child care and kindergarten). Within these projects, kindergarten and child care professionals plan activities together, care for infants co-operatively, etc.

*Setting or revising training outcome standards or curriculum for initial education*

- **Australia** has introduced ECEC vocational educational standards (training packages), which are nationally consistent and coherent; responsive to individual, industry and community needs; and provide quality outcomes. Developed by Industry Skills Councils or enterprises, each package is a set of nationally-endorsed standards, qualifications and guidelines used to recognise and assess the skills and knowledge people need to perform effectively in the workplace. The packages prescribe outcomes required by the workplace, not training or education. They are generally reviewed and resubmitted for endorsement every three years; however, within the three years, changes may occur under a continuous improvement process. Additionally, in the ECEC sector, national training packages have been developed for Certificate III, Diploma and Advanced Diploma in Children's Services through the Community Services and Health Industry Skills Council. The packages are regularly reviewed through consultation with the industry sector ensuring that the courses remain both relevant and effective.

- In **Korea**, initial training for kindergarten teachers requires specific academic credits and courses for the major (at least seven mandatory courses) as well as for the teaching profession (Article 19 of Teachers' Qualification Decree, 2008). In 2009, the National Standardization Projects for Child Care Teacher Qualification and Training were implemented, resulting in the provision of Standard Teacher Training Subject List and Field Practicum Guidelines, and the Standard In-service Training Curriculum. The implementation of these, which will be enforced by law, is expected to occur in 2013.

- **Japan** revised its *National Curriculum of Day Care Center Works* in March 2008, clarifying the enhancement of staff quality and the expertise of all staff. Due to the changes in the living environments of children and in the ways of child rearing by parents, the expectations for the role and quality of nursery centres increased. The Action Program to Improve the Quality of Nursery Centres was designed to address the following needs: 1) improvement and enhancement of child care practices; 2) assurance of the health and safety of children; 3) enhancement of the quality and expertise of nursery teachers; and 4) reinforcement of the foundation to support child care.

- In **Finland**, the national curriculum for practical nurse training has been reformed. In this reform, the view points of ECEC have been taken into consideration more profoundly than in the former curriculum. Also, the national curriculum for family child minders has been reformed.

- **New Zealand** has Graduating Teaching Standards in place, which were set by the New Zealand Teachers Council (NZTC) in 2007 under the Education Act 139AE. Minimum standards of teacher education are ensured by the accreditation and approval of all teacher education programmes by the NZTC. All teacher education providers with programmes approved by the NZTC must demonstrate how they enable students to reach the Graduating Teacher Standards. Providers guarantee that students have met these standards and are "fit to be a teacher" when they graduate from the programme.

*Mapping and assessing initial education programmes*

- **Australia** is undertaking a mapping exercise of all early childhood education courses to analyse the content of the subjects to ensure the quality of initial staff education at the tertiary level. This research will likely inform future policy development aimed at improving the quality and consistency of initial staff education across all institutions, including identifying gaps in the curriculum that may need to be addressed and steps that need to be taken to ensure consistency in the education delivered across all institutions. It is also expected that two national bodies – the new Australian Children's Education and Care Quality Authority and the Australian Institute for Teaching and School Leadership – will have roles in assessing and accrediting initial early childhood education courses, providing an opportunity to ensure quality and relevance.

- **Norway** established the Norwegian Agency for Quality Assurance in Education (*NOKUT*) in 2002. In 2008, *NOKUT* was tasked to evaluate the education of preschool teachers. The purpose was to develop knowledge and information on the current status of the quality of pre-primary teacher education in relation to the framework and regulations on higher education. The report was delivered in 2010 and concluded that: the preschool education programme has low status within the universities and the society; the sector does not recruit the best students, and its students do not put enough time/effort into the study; the focus is too much on children over three years of age and does not meet the needs of those under three years; and the programme needs to strengthen the staff competences of multiculturalism. Additionally, the evaluation pointed to the fact that today's preschool teacher training does not offer sufficient possibilities of in-depth studies of pedagogy for children with special needs. A new regulation for preschool teacher education is now being prepared. The government has appointed a commission to deliver a framework plan that will modernise preschool teacher education, which is relevant and of high quality.

## Challenge 2: Workforce supply

Securing a high-quality workforce supply is a major challenge in many OECD countries. Chronic shortages of ECEC staff are observed, especially in remote and disadvantaged areas. Furthermore, lower qualification levels of the workforce, especially in the child care sector, often raise concerns among parents and policy makers about the quality of services. Additionally, there are often insufficient incentives for people to work in the sector. The main reasons for the shortages are often cited as: low wages, low social status, heavy workload and lack of career progression paths, which make the profession unattractive and can cause or contribute to the challenge of recruiting staff.

The workforce is homogeneous, composed of mostly female, young workers and from the majority ethnic group.

*Funding students and professionals*

- In **Australia**, the removal of Technical and Further Education fees for diplomas and advanced diplomas in child care helps lessen the financial burden on students. Additionally, the Higher Education Contribution Scheme-Higher Education Loan Program provides debt relief for early childhood education teachers working in areas of high disadvantage.

- In **New Zealand**, student grants and scholarships are provided for hard-to-staff professions, including ECEC, to help students and services meet the costs of pursuing an ECE qualification. A number of scholarships are available to students undertaking a programme of study to prepare them for teaching in Pasifika or Māori immersion services. Additionally, the government funded expert assistance for initial teacher education providers who started developing programmes for preparing teachers to work in Pasifika and Māori immersion services: the assistance went to developing and implementing these programmes.

- In **England**, government funding is provided to local authorities to increase and sustain the number of graduates employed and to provide other types of pedagogical training for staff. This also extends to the recruitment and deployment of graduate leaders and investment in qualifications.

- When **Prince Edward Island** (**Canada**) implemented the Preschool Excellence Initiative's Entry Level certification programme, the Department of Innovation and Advanced Learning funded the cost of the tuition and books for all previously uncertified staff that were required to participate in the training. If participants did not meet the qualifications upon completion of the training, they could work with Workplace Prince Edward Island to upgrade their academic skills. This education was provided at no cost to the participant and was intended to prepare them for participating a second time in the Entry Level programme.

*Funding education and training programmes*

- In **Japan**, prefectures receive government funds to train nursery teachers, including people who do not have experience working in a centre. The government plans to increase the number of children accepted by day care centres from 20-38% during 2007-17 and, therefore, to increase the workforce supply in order to accommodate the demands.

- In **Norway**, the state budget was increased by NOK 25 in 2011, amounting to 130 million to:

  - recruit and educate enough preschool teachers to meet the demand;

  - provide education at the secondary level as well as further education for childminders; and

  - provide further education for preschool teachers (both pedagogical and head teachers).

  This was a response to a need to provide a sufficient and quality workforce to accommodate a large increase in the number of kindergarten places over a short period of time. Norway has also provided eight university colleges/universities with means to develop practices that support the follow-through and completion of teacher training for bilingual students. The implemented measures include providing help during the application process, providing support in Norwegian language, incorporating multicultural aspects into the curriculum and providing individual support to students throughout the duration of preschool teacher education in co-operation with ten university colleges/universities.

– In **Korea**, in-service kindergarten teacher training by local Offices of Education is subsidised with Financial Grants for Local Education. The budget for in-service child care teacher training was KRW 1 248 million for 2011; the National Office for Child Care Staff Qualification is administered by KRW 640 million; and Childcare Information Centers (a total of 18 centres in charge of in-service teacher training) by KRW 4 040 million. Diverse pathways to fund in-service teacher training and professional development exist in child care sector.

– **Spain**'s Ministry of Education and regional governments are jointly financing an increase in the provision of higher vocational training leading to a "certificate of technician in pre-primary education". The Ministry's Action Plan 2010-11 stresses the need to increase the number of places in the first cycle of pre-primary education and to transform other types of early child care into pre-primary provision for children under three. To attain these goals, the Ministry collaborates with regional governments in designing the Territorial Cooperation Programme, *Educa3*. One of the programme objectives is to improve the qualification and training of teachers and specialised staff. To help ensure that schools have enough adequately trained staff, the national and regional governments are financing the increase in training for the "certificate of technician in pre-primary education".

### Raising the status of ECEC professionals

– In **Slovak Republic**, kindergartens had not been always been a part of the school system, as children's attendance in kindergarten is not mandatory. The government took a systematic step to improve the status of kindergarten programmes and teachers by making kindergartens a part of the school system. As a result, kindergarten teachers are now able to pursue bachelor's, master's and doctoral degrees at the university level; whereas they once only had the opportunity to obtain an education at the secondary vocational level.

– **Manitoba**'s **(Canada)** Healthy Child Advisory Committee facilitates collaboration between government departments working to support children and their families as well as with non-government organisations, businesses and the general public. The Committee's efforts include public education on the importance of the early years. Additionally, the Educaring Subcommittee of the Advisory Council has made significant progress in advancing understanding and respect for and between the early years and the education sectors.

– **Spain** has been working towards raising the social status of the ECEC profession. Education authorities have launched public awareness campaigns to promote the advantages of schooling children under three, focusing on the professional status of teaching staff and, by doing so, improving their social image.

### Stimulating demand for a qualified workforce through employers and parents

- **England** (**United Kingdom**) seeks to encourage employers to have qualified staff and stimulate demand by encouraging parents to seek centres with qualified staff to build trust among key stakeholders. Early Years Professional Status (EYPS) was introduced in response to evidence on graduate leadership from the Effective Provision of Pre-School Education project. EYPs are graduate-level staff who have demonstrated that they have met a set of national professional standards and have been awarded EYP status.

### Diversifying the workforce

- **British Columbia** (**Canada**) has programmes targeted at increasing the number of Aboriginal staff. A number of universities and colleges offer training with an Aboriginal perspective. One university ran a programme entirely for Aboriginal participants, and another college offers an Aboriginal specialty for post-basic training (for working with infants and toddlers or children with special needs).

- **Slovenia** recruits Roma assistants who serve as a bridge between the Roma community and the educational institution. They help children in preschool institutions and primary schools to understand the Slovenian language and to confront prejudice, and they help them with their learning and school work. They also co-operate with parents of Roma children. Roma assistants are trained in the Roma language, history and culture. The government's initiative has led to higher attendance of Roma children in educational institutions; co-operation between Roma parents and educational institutions; and increased awareness among parents of the importance of learning and education. The project also helps fight racism and xenophobia and promotes better intercultural understanding.

- **England** (**United Kingdom**) continues work to attract and support the use of graduates in early education and child care settings; to attract career changers to consider the profession as a career option; and to improve recruitment among under-represented groups, *i.e.*, men, black and other minority ethnic groups. They also continue to invest in and encourage the development of the early education and child care workforce by supporting graduate training, including through the Early Years Professional Status and New Leaders in Early Years programmes.

- **Australia** established the Indigenous Remote Service Delivery Traineeships programme to support young Aboriginal and Torres Strait Islander trainees in eligible schools and Indigenous child care services in remote areas. The traineeships were developed in recognition of the barriers to employment and training in remote communities.

- **Germany** is working to raise the number of male pedagogues in early childhood education through a programme funded by the European Social Fund called *Mehr Männer in Kitas* (Men in early childhood education). The programme encompasses 1 300 preschool institutions. At the same time,

Germany is looking to create new paths into the profession for – particularly male – career changers.

- In **Korea**, child care staff with immigrant backgrounds are trained and often employed at ECEC services where a large proportion of children have multi-cultural backgrounds.

*Validating existing competencies to allow easier entry into the profession*

- In establishing graduate-level status for the early years sector, **England (United Kingdom)** has developed a "validation pathway", which allows graduates who have experience in the sector to demonstrate their competence against professional standards and be awarded the Early Years Professional Status.

- In **Australia**, the government has introduced a recognition of prior learning (RPL) initiative that will make it easier for experienced early childhood workers to obtain or upgrade their qualifications through a national assessment process. The initiative includes: development of a new national assessment tool for Certificate III, Diploma and Advanced Diploma's in Children's Services, funding for 600 existing RPL assessors to be trained in the use of this tool and grants of up to AUD 1 125 for rural and remote early childhood workers to contribute to the costs associated with accessing RPL.

- Since 2002, **Germany** has made efforts to stimulate and simplify transition between different ECEC education qualification levels. Colleges, technical schools and professional academies providing ECEC-related studies are obliged to recognise coursework completed by students at institutions other than their own, including studies carried out in other *Länder*. Institutions should, when suitable, give students exemption from passing certain courses when the required knowledge has already been obtained elsewhere. The aim of this is to stimulate students to obtain higher ECEC qualifications and make the transition from one level of education to another simpler and more attractive.

- **Chile** is undertaking a pilot project to certify school and work experience to validate existing competencies of ECEC staff. The project also includes the possibility of recognising secondary school courses in Technical Training. The continuity of the project will be determined upon its evaluation.

- The **Netherlands** uses validation and recognition of non-formal and informal learning on the basis of a collective agreement with the professional body, and there is an established validation procedure.

- **Poland** takes prior learning or work experiences into account when issuing teachers' qualifications on the basis of the minimum requirements for promotion, *i.e.*, from beginning teacher to contracted teacher, nominated teacher or certified teacher.

- **New Zealand** recognises prior learning (RPL), and people can convert prior learning experiences into credits towards a recognised ECE qualification. The government has funded the use of RPL to help increase the supply of qualified and registered teachers.

- **Spain** aims to increase the number of qualified staff in pre-primary education and, thus, uses recognition of training through work experience and of non-formal knowledge for those pursuing higher vocational training to become certified as a technician in pre-primary education. They have also implemented an extension and increase of specific in-class and distance training initiatives.

*Promoting workforce mobility across different regions and different countries*

- **British Columbia** (**Canada**) allows Early Childhood Educators (ECEs) trained outside of Canada to work in British Columbia if they meet all requirements to work in the sector. They are eligible for employment provided they complete a credential evaluation along with necessary paperwork prepared by the hiring institution. Additionally, ECEs trained outside of British Columbia who meet all requirements to work in the sector are eligible for employment provided they submit an official transcript along with the necessary paperwork prepared by the hiring institution.

- **New Zealand** assesses foreign qualifications and offers a diploma in ECEC if it is comparable to New Zealand's benchmark qualification, the Diploma of Education, required for early childhood teachers. New Zealand also offers relocation grants and return to teaching allowances to assist qualified staff to move to areas where there is a shortage of staff, such as remote areas.

## Challenge 3: Workforce retention

Many countries experience difficulties with retaining the workforce, with particularly high staff turnover rates in the child care sector. The factors that keep people from working in the ECEC sector are often the same factors that discourage people from pursuing a career in the ECEC sector: low wages; low social status; heavy workload; and lack of career progression paths.

*Improving salaries, minimum wage and benefits*

- **Manitoba** (**Canada**) introduced a wage adjustment grant, so that those with an Early Childhood Educator II classification would earn at last CAD 15.50 an hour, and Child Care Assistants in training would earn at least CAD 12.25 an hour. Furthermore, Manitoba increased operating grants to facilities by 3% in 2008 and by 3% again in 2009 to bolster staff wages. In 2010, the province launched funding for pensions and retirement supports for the child care workforce. When implementing the pension plans and retirement supports, consultations were required to ensure compliance with existing provincial and federal legislation. Additionally, those nearer to retirement were less able to take full advantage of the new pension plans, so Manitoba also introduced a lump-sum retirement benefit at the same time, in recognition of the contributions made by long-term child care workers.

- In **New Zealand**, **Portugal** and **Slovak Republic**, kindergarten teachers have been given pay parity with primary and secondary school teachers. New Zealand has a funding system for ECEC services in place that provides incentives for services to employ more qualified, registered teachers. This resulted in more services being able to afford paying better salaries and significantly increased the number of registered teachers in the ECEC workforce.

- In the **Czech Republic**, the Ministry of Education, Youth and Sport has approved an increase in the salaries of ECEC teachers with a university diploma in an effort to establish pay parity with primary school teachers; however, the government foresees a lack of financial resources, which would make it difficult to achieve pay parity.

- **Prince Edward Island** (**Canada**) set out to acknowledge and support the valued role played by early childhood educators by increasing wages for those who are certified. To do so, the government developed a policy framework, the Preschool Excellence Initiative, which addressed the need for a salary grid that would increase wages. Along with the Early Childhood Development Association, the government engaged stakeholders who would be effected by the wage grid changes and staffing requirement. Together, they reached a favourable agreement on the policy framework, which made it possible to implement this improvement of working conditions for ECEC staff.

- **Korea** will increase the wages for child care teachers working with the *Nuri Curriculum* by USD 300 per month in 2012 to close the wage gaps between child care and kindergarten teachers. Besides this, child care staff can receive additional allowances, such as extra remuneration for working in rural areas. Additionally, ECEC centres are obliged, from 2012 on, to pay for overtime working hours (staff working more than 40 hours per week), and evening shifts or weekend shifts will have additional pay.

- In **Japan**, public kindergarten teachers can receive adjusted allowances for overtime working hours.

*Inviting innovations from stakeholders through awards system*

- **Australia** has introduced the *Fair Work Act 2009*, which incorporated new National Employment Standards and required the introduction of modern industrial awards. The new early childhood awards were established by the Australian Industrial Relations Committee after hearing submissions from all parties; and the final awards establish consistent minimum rates of pay for early childhood settings with teachers in primary and secondary schools.

- In **Ireland**, the Early Years Education Policy Unit of the Department of Education and Skills led the creation of a Workforce Development Plan for the ECEC sector. An Interdepartmental Working Group was established comprising representatives from relevant government departments and state agencies. Additionally, a sectoral standards working group was set up to address the development of occupational role profiles and national award standards: this group was comprised of government representatives, education and training providers, national awarding bodies and workforce representatives. Occupational role profiles were agreed upon and associated with National Award Standards on the National Framework for Qualifications in Ireland. The Workforce Development Plan was published in December 2010; and Common Award Standards for staff was published in March 2011.

### *Assisting in bargaining or negotiating for working conditions in the ECEC sector*

- **Australia** has adopted a "multi-employer bargaining stream for low paid jobs" to assist both employers and low-paid employees in sectors like child care to reach agreements to improve wages and working conditions.

- In **New Zealand**, working conditions are negotiated between the teachers and their employers, except for kindergarten teachers where the Ministry of Education negotiates their terms and conditions on behalf of kindergarten associations.

- In **Slovenia**, preschool teachers and assistants are civil servants, so working conditions are generally determined by national regulations and are negotiated by the government and representative trade unions. Preschool staff have the possibility to use at least five days per year or 15 days every three years for professional training.

### *Targeting experienced workers or returning staff*

- In **Flanders** (**Belgium**), the government has introduced additional holidays for qualified, experienced, older employees working in approved day care centres with the aim to retain them.

- **British Columbia** (**Canada**) had the Early Childhood Educator (ECE) Incentive Grant Program in 2008, which recruited ECEs who had left the licensed child care sector to return to work in a licensed facility. ECEs who had not worked at a licensed setting for at least two years were eligible to receive up to CAD 5 000 over a two-year period. Uptake for this programme was not very high, so it was discontinued after 15 months.

- **New Zealand** offers relocation grants and return to teaching allowances to assist qualified staff to get back into the profession and to move to areas where there is a high shortage of ECEC staff.

### *Offering status, benefits or social values equal to other professions in education*

- In **Flanders** (**Belgium**), the government plans to regulate the child care sector and grant full employee status to family day carers affiliated with a service (*i.e.*, not independent providers). Currently, affiliated day carers have an ambiguous social status (in between volunteer and employee): they receive an allowance, a payment when children do not attend, a sickness payment and accrual of pension rights; but they do not receive holiday pay, a termination payment or unemployment benefits.

- In **Korea**, the government equalises the wages among ECEC teachers working with the new *Nuri Curriculum*. Additionally, the term "teacher" rather than "ECEC worker" will be used for both kindergarten and child care staff, indicating that staff in both sectors have equal status.

- In **Belgium**'s **French Community**, family day carers had no benefits and little incentive to remain in the profession until 2002 when the government created a minimum social protection for this job profile. They also changed the job title from *gardiennes encadrées* (trained guardian) to *accueillantes d'enfant conventionnées* (registered child carer).

- **Finland** issued the Day Care Act in 1973, regulating family day care and legitimising this form of service as equal to other forms of ECEC services. Family childminders became employees of the local authority, as was the case with centre-based ECEC staff, and now had their own working contract as part of the general working contract for employees at the municipality. Prior to the act, family childminders worked privately. The act established them as part of the municipal ECEC services and permitted them participate in service training and common events. Family childminders also follow the National Curriculum Guidelines for ECEC.

*Providing career opportunities for promotion and mobility*

- **Flanders** (**Belgium**) is planning a new Flemish qualification structure, calibrated to the European Qualification Framework, that promotes multi-directional mobility, such as from family day carer to kindergarten teacher (horizontal) and from staff to manager (vertical). This will be made possible by permitting the comparison of diplomas, certificates of training courses and recognition of prior learning certifications.

- In **Italy**, pre-primary teachers are eligible for an increase in basic compensation after fixed periods of time or competitive examinations. They also have the opportunity to be promoted to school manager or technical manager. Currently, they do not have opportunities for advancement within their job profile; but the Ministry of Education is considering proposals seeking to grant higher qualifications to pre-primary teachers based on the quality of their teaching.

- In **Korea**, experienced and high-quality kindergarten teachers are rewarded with a monthly grant of USD 400 within the Master Teacher System, and experienced teachers also have the opportunity to become a director of a kindergarten.

- **Norway** allows ECEC teachers to become school managers, municipal administrators and further education instructors for ECEC.

- In **Slovenia**, preschool teachers have an opportunity to be promoted, and participation in in-service training is taken into account when the promotion is being considered.

- In **Sweden**, preschool teachers have the opportunity to be promoted as senior subject teachers after pursuing research studies to have a licentiate or doctoral degree. Preschool teachers can also work as preschool heads, school managers and municipal administrators.

*Offering adequate support for new staff*

- **Italy** requires a one-year trial period for teachers with guidance and support from a tutor along with participation in an e-learning blended model training organised by the National Agency for the Development of School Autonomy.

- In **New Zealand**, following verification of the qualification of graduated ECEC students and a police vetting, beginning staff gain provisional teacher registration and then embark on a two-year teacher induction process with a mentor teacher to oversee their programme. They must demonstrate to their mentor teacher through evidence of their teaching that they are able to meet the Satisfactory Teacher Dimensions. At the end of the two years, the mentor may recommend the teacher to the professional leader of the early childhood service as meeting the Satisfactory Teacher Dimensions. The professional leader then recommends the teacher to the New Zealand Teacher Council for full registration. There is Ministry of Education funding support for the first two years of the induction and mentoring programme. Once a teacher is fully registered, the registration needs to be renewed every three years.

− In **Flanders (Belgium)**, new kindergarten teachers are entitled to an induction programme with a mentor during their first year. In a large classroom, child care workers can assist kindergarten teachers to reduce workload and establish a better staff-child ratio.

− **Norway** implemented a preschool teacher recruitment strategy for 2007-11, which includes establishing guidance for educated preschool teachers in their first year of work. The government has also increased the capacity of preschool teacher education and established work-place-based preschool teacher education for assistants in kindergartens in co-operation with Oslo University College and the University of Stavanger.

### Monitoring working conditions

− **Chile** has launched Work Environment Improvement Projects to monitor working conditions of staff working in the ECEC sector and aims to implement a Quality Care Assurance Model. The model involves a self-diagnosis to assess each preschool's educational plans, which are then validated by an external professional. The results are used to prepare improvement plans to tackle detected shortcomings.

## Challenge 4: Workforce development

Many countries offer some form of professional development opportunities for ECEC staff. However, the take-up rates are often found to be low. First and foremost, information about training opportunities may not be well known, or the benefits of participating may not be clearly articulated, especially among low-qualified ECEC workers. Second, continuous training and professional development might be disconnected from what they wish to learn, and, therefore, may not be motivated.

Even when staff are informed of such opportunities and are motivated to take up training, their manager may be reluctant to send them to professional development courses. It is often argued that, when the training leads to the possibility of a higher level of qualification, staff may subsequently wish for a pay raise or leave for a higher paying job elsewhere.

Another challenge is observed in aligning the contents of professional development, those of initial education and the implementation of a curriculum.

### Focusing on professional development for quality enhancement

− In **Norway**, continuous training is not mandatory. Employers are responsible for continuous training. As the government considers competent staff the most important factor concerning quality, a strategic plan was designed for a competence development initiative spanning 2007-10. The strategy prescribed NOK 60 million per year and prioritised pedagogical leadership, children's participation, language/ language stimulation and transition from kindergarten to school. The strategy led to increased activity among municipalities, encompassing all kindergartens public and private.

- **Belgium**'s **French Community** sees a need to improve initial education in order to improve the quality of ECEC services; however, a lack of funding currently prevents making modifications to improve initial education for staff. The government has focused on the importance of continuous education to ensure that staff are adequately trained to provide quality ECEC services.

- **Japan** commissioned a report in 2002 "Improvement in the Quality of Kindergarten Teachers – for the Purpose of Self-Study by Kindergarten Teachers", which was intended to encourage both current and potential teachers to strive to improve the quality of their services throughout employment.

- In the **Netherlands**, training is free for staff working in ECEC institutions. A source book was created to help training institutions include ECEC in their education programmes; and research is being done on whether institutions can offer a programme focusing solely on young children.

- In **Germany**, the federal government is investing EUR 400 million over four years towards professional development for specialist staff and systematic human resources development on the part of providers. There is emphasis on language and integration support in early childhood. Additionally, as part of the Qualification Initiative for Germany, the federal and *Länder* governments resolved, in 2008, to train more nurses and day care staff. These initiatives are in preparation for 2013, when every child from the age of one year will have a legal entitlement to child care in an institution or day care facility.

## Making continuous training a job requirement

- All early years practitioners in **England** (**United Kingdom**) are required to continually update professionally. This includes undertaking first aid training every three years and attending training provided by the local authority on safe guarding children.

- In **Finland**, the annual amount of in-service training for employees in social welfare (including day care staff) should be three to ten days depending on the employee's basic education, the qualifications required for the job and the job description. This is laid down in the Act on amending the Social Welfare Act (50/2005). This Act also obligates local authorities to ensure and offer an adequate level of continuous training to ECEC staff. The goal of the obligation to continuous training is to maintain and renew the professional skills of the staff.

## Raising awareness of the importance of continuous training among staff and their employers

- **England** (**United Kingdom**) has been working on, through an awareness-raising campaign, convincing employers and practitioners of the need for and the value of high-level qualifications.

- In **Germany**, in 2009, the Federal Ministry of Education and Research, the Robert Bosch Foundation and the German Youth Institute launched the project "*WiFF* – Advancing Further Education of Early Childhood Professionals". The project sets out to analyse, initiate and promote professional development of early childhood professionals. The project provides careful empirical analyses of the various actors, decision makers and institutions involved in this field. In collaboration with the field, *WiFF* has developed standards of good practice for the professional training of early childhood staff and promotes consistent use of these standards. Four sets of background materials for training have been compiled, enabling trainers to prepare for the following topics: working with children under the age of three, collaborating with parents, fostering language development in children, and the role of early childhood professionals in supporting early learning processes. The materials, along with related publications, are available free of charge and can be ordered on the project's website. *WiFF* actively supports lifelong learning and aims to ease the transition from vocational training or professional practice to academic studies. *WiFF* employs a team of fourteen social scientists from various disciplines and is sponsored by the European Social Fund.

## Designing demands-driven training

- **Norway** foresees a need for increasing the number of preschool teachers and raising the competence of staff through targeted measures. Efforts will have to be made by getting educated preschool teachers to choose to work in kindergartens and providing professional development for all staff. A national forum for kindergarten has been created to develop dialogue among stakeholders, which will, among other things, discuss the question of competence and quality in the sector. The government also uses the forum to discuss challenges and solutions with relevant stakeholders.

- In **Finland**, municipalities are responsible for determining the content of social welfare training; however, municipalities do not always maintain diversified know-how about the needs of the social welfare sector. Therefore, the government created centres of excellence on social welfare in 2002 to convey expertise to municipalities on this topic and ensure that training content is consistent and relevant. These centres of excellence work in close connection with universities and other education institutions. For example, at the University of Tampere (Finland), continuous training is carried out in co-operation with the city of Tampere and the kindergarten staff (especially the leaders of the kindergartens and the day care centres) as custom-made training. Identifying the demands and need for training derive from the staff and leaders.

- **Finland** and **Mexico** aim to cover a wide range of skills, such as communication with parents, orientation of activities' contents and materials, and teaching strategies and upbringing practices with a child-centred focus (*e.g.*, how children move, play, experience art, explore, etc.).

- **Portugal** and **Sweden** focus on language development, mathematics, experimental sciences and child assessment of learning and well-being. Following a recent evaluation of continuous training programmes, Sweden mostly focuses on children's linguistic and mathematical development as well as evaluation of preschool activities.

- **Korea** has diversified the training possibilities ECEC staff can participate in so as to meet the diverse needs of staff. Since time limits are often a barrier for staff to participate in training opportunities, on-line trainings are currently being offered as well.

### Offering diversity training

- **Flanders** (**Belgium**) recognised a need to diversify the workforce and adapt the pedagogy of child care centres to the multicultural society. In 1995, *Kind en Gezin* supported a large-scale action research project on respect for diversity in child care. Numerous narratives were collected from ethnic minority and majority trainees and showed how the project confronted practitioners with a paradigm shift. Trainees testified about the difficulties of addressing diversity issues and of constructing an inclusive professionalism.

- **Finland** recognised a need to develop inclusive education and multicultural working methods for ECEC staff. From 2007-11, they have participated in the European Commission's project INCLUD-ED, which analyses educational strategies that contribute to overcoming inequalities and promoting social cohesion, as well as educational strategies, that generate social exclusion, particularly focusing on vulnerable and marginalised groups.

- **Australia** funds the Inclusion and Professional Support Program, which funds Professional Support Coordinators and Indigenous Professional Support Units in each state and territory. These co-ordinators/units provide professional development, advice and resources to assist child care services to provide quality care and to be inclusive of children from diverse backgrounds.

- **Korea** developed a 60-hour training programme and a teaching manual for teachers working with children from multicultural family backgrounds in 2010. Teachers can register voluntarily for the training course, and when they do so, they receive full financial support.

### Offering training for curriculum implementation

- **New Zealand** focuses on the implementation of *Te Whāriki*, the Early Childhood Curriculum, and provides training to improve learning outcomes for all young children, especially those at risk. Teachers are expected to strengthen their teaching practices. The government also provides training to support the implementations of *Kei Tua o te Pae*, Assessment for Learning. Teachers are expected to develop effective assessment practices that meet the aspirations of the curriculum.

- **Prince Edward Island** (**Canada**) provided developmental and implementation funding to allow for entry-level training of all uncertified staff working within

Early Years Centres so they could be educated as an Early Years educator and learn about the new Learning Framework. The province also provides in-service training to early childhood directors and educators already working in the centres on the newly established Early Learning Framework, a curriculum document for the early childhood sector focusing on children from birth to school entry.

- **Mexico** is providing training courses and workshops to support teachers as they implement new curriculum and adapt to revised pedagogical orientations. The government has also consulted educational promoters to inform the development of materials on how to improve their work through self-evaluation and reflection on practice. A web page has been established to help all educational figures find materials on this topic and exchange pedagogical practices and advice. Additionally, the government is working on providing safety strategies to all child care workers, focusing not only on care but also on education elements. New professional development plans are being proposed for child care workers, which introduce more pedagogical orientations to training that was focused on care.

- In **England** (**United Kingdom**), local authorities are responsible for providing training and support on implementing the *Early Years Foundation Stage*.

- The National Agency for Education in **Sweden** has, in co-operation with Swedish Television, made short films to give inspiration on how to implement and stimulate different curriculum subjects, such as mathematics and natural science, in preschool. Additionally, training in the curriculum subject of language development is very common in Sweden.

- In **Korea**, 20 000 ECEC professionals were trained in 2011 to implement the new *Nuri Curriculum* in 2012. Training sessions focused on the differences between the *Nuri Curriculum* and the existing kindergarten and child care curricula, including basic principles, areas of learning and development, and teaching methods.

- The early years sector in **England** (**United Kingdom**) has recently introduced a new curriculum of learning for zero-to-five-year-olds: the *Early Years Foundation Stage* (EYFS). Training has been developed on delivering the new curriculum. Ordinarily, the key areas for training/updating are: anti-discriminatory practice; equality of opportunity; child protection; health and safety; curriculum planning and early learning goals.

- In **Finland**, regarding continuous training and development, municipalities (the providers of training) focus on the centre's child-specific ECEC plans, which are based on the national ECEC plan. They focus especially on the processes of drawing up the ECEC plans and the contents of the ECEC plans, such as parental engagement, interaction between the child and the adult, the environment, the child's ways of acting (how the child moves, plays, experiences art, explores, etc.), leadership and special needs of children.

*Supporting employers for staff replacement*

- **Manitoba** (**Canada**) has established a replacement grant to pay for staff members' salaries when they are attending workplace training.

- **Japan** remunerates staff pursuing training and substitutes staff with staff members who are hired to replace individuals away on training.

*Financing training costs*

- To strengthen staff competence, **Sweden** has allocated SEK 600 million on continuing education for preschool teachers and childminders for a three-year period running from 2009-11 under the programme "The boost for preschool". The training is primarily directed at advancing pedagogical competence for preschool staff. The programme gives some thousands of preschool teachers and childminders the chance to take further education courses – at the university level (for preschool teachers) and at the upper secondary/high school level (for childminders). Teachers and childminders keep 80% of their salary during the study period, co-funded by the government and the preschool principal organisers. The courses focus on children's linguistic and mathematical development and evaluation of preschool activities. There is also an opportunity for preschool teachers to take research studies to have a licentiate degree. The purpose is to increase the number of post-graduated preschool teachers in preschool.

- Every year, **Slovenia** offers "Study help for school fees for further education of pedagogical workers". The grant helps employed teachers and other pedagogical staff to reach a higher level of education or qualification. Candidates can apply if they meet the certain criteria (*e.g.*, they must be employed; they must enrol in programmes for further education with which they will meet the level of education required by law).

- **Finland** provides state-funded in-service training and Continuous Professional Development (CPD) for teachers and other education personnel. Since 2010, the Ministry of Education and Culture has nearly doubled its funding for the (CPD) and in-service training of teachers and education personnel, including ECEC staff. Currently, a total of EUR 21 million is spent annually for this purpose. Additionally, the in-service training for employees in social welfare (including day care staff) receives about 33% of its funding from the state. This training amounts to three to ten days per year depending on the employee's basic education, the qualifications required for the job and the job description. The state funding helps ensure that local authorities offer an adequate level of continuous training that maintains and renews the professional skills of ECEC staff.

- In **England (United Kingdom)**, funding for training for ECEC staff is available through local authority training budgets and other sources. Pathways to support the attainment of qualifications up to Level 6 are available with funding support.

- **Manitoba (Canada)** introduced training grants to support the child care workforce and assist facilities in meeting trained staff requirements. The grants include funding for students to study full-time as well as a workplace grant for those who study part-time while remaining employed. The province also has a grant for facilities to cover the cost of replacing a staff member who is enrolled in a workplace training programme.

– **Spain**'s Ministry of Education finances the Territorial Cooperation Programme "Teacher professional development". The programme has been jointly developed by the Ministry and regional governments and aims at: agreeing on priority teacher professional development areas; increasing provision of teacher training programmes; guaranteeing attention to minorities; opening up new channels for collaboration and exchanges of experience among teachers; and fostering continuity of joint actions to share and spread good practices that may lead to successful educational projects. While the Ministry finances this programme, it is implemented by regional governments. Additionally, the Territorial Cooperation Programme, *Educa3*, includes among its measures the organisation of professional development provision for teachers of pre-primary education, especially of zero-to-three-year-olds. This is co-financed by the Ministry and regional governments.

*Funding institutions that provide continuous training*

– **British Columbia** (**Canada**) funded the following professional development initiatives:

  – Grant funding was provided over two years (2005-07) to a post-secondary institution that designed and offered professional development that built on reflective practice capacity to improve quality within child care facilities. The training focused on building capacity and bringing innovation to the field in direct work with children. The number of rural and remote communities coupled with the geographic and cultural diversity of the province make it difficult to ensure professional development opportunities are available and accessible to all. The post-secondary institution worked with a broad group of Early Childhood Education (ECE) staff from a variety of settings within the South Coast area of the province, including Aboriginal, multicultural, rural, urban, part-time preschool, full-time day care and family child care.

  – Grant funding of CAD 2 million was provided to a professional association in 2006-07 to develop leadership capacity in ECE across the province, looking beyond direct child care to increasing the understanding and stature of ECE within communities as a whole. The association focused on constructing a culture of ECE leadership, recognising the unique and significant leadership capacity within the sector and developing ways that work to take knowing and being to the broader community. The association worked with the South Coast area, as well as the North and Interior areas, with staff from the following groups: Aboriginal, multicultural, rural, urban, part-time preschool, full-time day care and family child care. Fiscal realities did not allow for ongoing funding of this nature.

  – Grant funding of CAD 20 million was given to a provincial agency in 2006-07 to provide training directly to child care providers to increase the quality within their programmes. A portion of the funding was for learning materials, supplies and equipment that contribute to quality child care and enhancing the development growth of children; some of the funding was intended for minor capital enhancements and/or facility repairs or renovations; and the remainder of the funding was to be directed towards professional development and training opportunities. Fiscal realities did not allow for ongoing funding of this nature.

- In **Japan**, the government provides funding to prefectures for training beginner teachers as well as teachers with ten years of experience. Teacher training is mainly paid for by the training providers.

- In **New Zealand**, the Ministry of Education developed a new programme for centrally funded professional development. The change was in response to a reduction in available funding, which provided an impetus for targeting professional development to ECEC services catering to children from the government's priority groups: Māori, Pasifika and low-socio-economic communities. Centrally-funded professional development contracts are for a three-year period. Providers are required to go into targeted communities, carry out a needs analysis and plan a programme that best meets the needs of particular communities. This new approach to central funding for providers intends to decrease the competitive environment for providers and give way to a more collaborative approach to providing professional development.

## Challenge 5: Private provision

A challenge in many countries is the role of private provision, particularly how policy challenges are addressed where much of the delivery is private. In countries where provision is largely public, changes can be initiated through direct government action; whereas when the private market delivers a significant proportion of ECEC services, action may need to be taken through regulation or incentives.

Private, community or voluntary services are often under-funded and, therefore, may not be able to respect basic structural standards, such as providing regular in-service training or requiring a certain level of staff certification. As a result, the quality of the workforce in private provision may be considerably lower than in public services. Governments can face difficulties improving the quality when private provision is not substantially subsidised, as it less malleable by regulations and policies.

### *Regulating private provision as rigorously as the public sector*

- **England (United Kingdom)** aimed to develop a single qualification and pay structure for all services. Inspections were integrated under one office, the Office for Standards in Education, which was made responsible for standards across all types of services within the sector; and a statutory responsibility was placed on local authorities to secure adequate, affordable ECEC for all families who need it. These changes were intended to establish consistent standards affecting the quality across various providers. For example, a single qualification ensures that staff in private and public sectors alike enter the profession with the same level of training.

- Licensing of children's services in the **French Community** of **Belgium** is strict and closely supervised; and the ECEC system is made up of a mix of public and private provision. In the care sector, public services are licensed, supervised and continually evaluated; and private services are licensed and supervised. In the education sector, three main organisations provide free education that is open to enrolment from all sections of the public, and they function in accordance with the laws governing public services.

- Legislation in **Finland**, though decentralised, sets out strong and clear requirements for staff qualification and staff-child ratios, which apply to both public and private service providers.

- To prevent family day carers from operating privately without any external supervision, **Flanders** (**Belgium**) denies tax breaks and child care subsidies to parents who do not use licensed day carers. This ensures that self-employed family day carers are licensed and operate under the regulation of public authorities.

# ACTION AREA 4 – MANAGING RISKS: LEARNING FROM OTHER COUNTRIES' POLICY EXPERIENCES

This section summarises country experiences as lessons learned from:

- Improving qualifications, training and working conditions

It aims to be a quick read about challenges and risks to consider when implementing policy initiatives.

## IMPROVING QUALIFICATIONS, TRAINING AND WORKING CONDITIONS

### Lesson 1: Consider cost implications and be cautious in setting numeric targets for the percentage of qualified workforce

In **New Zealand**, the shift towards a qualified workforce occurred at the same time as a strong increase in demand for ECEC and a rapid expansion of the workforce. When the government established the Diploma of Education (Early Childhood Education) as the benchmark teaching qualification for the newly centralised system, targets were set for the percentage of the workforce that was qualified. The government found that the targets were difficult to achieve due to the increase in the total number of teachers employed. Furthermore, the increased demand for qualified teachers had a strong impact on their salaries. Pay parity for kindergarten teachers with primary and secondary teachers was introduced; and the government policy was to provide funding to meet the cost of quality improvements so that the cost to parents would not increase. New Zealand found that this policy led to a significant increase in the cost of ECEC funding for the government. As a result, the government reduced its target of 100% registered teachers in the sector to 80%, deciding that achieving a minimum level of 80% registered teachers by 2012 will maintain sufficiently high standards across the sector.

### Lesson 2: Plan sufficient time for the implementation of the revised qualifications

When **British Columbia (Canada)** revised licensing regulations, the province found that immediate implementation of the revised requirements led to many people not being in compliance. Staff needed considerable time and exemptions to come into compliance with the new standards. British Columbia notes the importance of ensuring that those most impacted by the revisions have time to make the necessary changes to meet new requirements.

### Lesson 3: When changing qualification requirements, ensure that the changes are introduced in pre-service education as well as in-service training

Upon changing qualification requirements so that preschool teachers must obtain a four-year masters' degree, **Portugal** has found that it is important to foster the career of preschool professionals from the start of their first degree programmes through to in-service training. While the qualification requirements have been raised, teachers will still require continuous support after obtaining their degree, as changes occur in educational practices.

An evaluation on the quality of pre-primary teacher education in **Norway** has led the government to acknowledge the need for improving initial training. Norway finds that the importance, complexity and size of the kindergarten sector combined with the demands for ECEC require the government to discuss the findings of the evaluation. Strengthening the education of educators, pedagogical leaders and administrative leaders in ECEC needs to be a priority if children are to have high-quality ECEC. This requires allocation of resources to preschool teacher education, and there must be a continuous effort to provide training combining theory and practice.

### Lesson 4: When changing curriculum, prepare staff for the change, and ensure that staff training is embedded in the implementation plan

As **Mexico** trains teachers to implement new curriculum and revised pedagogical orientations, the government has learnt that before establishing new policies, it is necessary to make educators sensitive to the need for change. It is equally important to follow up on the training by monitoring teachers' practice and observing whether they are implementing the changes.

A key lesson learned from **Sweden** is that staff competence is decisive for quality in preschool. The education and skills of preschool teachers are one of the most important factors ensuring a successful preschool system. To work in accordance with the curriculum, staff must have good knowledge of young children's development and learning.

Through long-endeavoured processes towards the integration of ECEC, **Korea** developed the *Nuri Curriculum for Age 5* in 2011 and set up nationwide in-service training for 20 000 kindergarten and child care teachers working with five-year-olds to prepare them for the new curriculum content and pedagogy. About 150 teacher trainers from education and care sectors will be trained together for the first time in December 2011, and local education and care authorities will collaborate in organising and arranging teacher training.

### Lesson 5: Consider whether training with a holistic approach or an individual needs-based approach would better suit your country's context

**Belgium**'s **French Community** emphasises that ECEC services must be carried by a strong and pertinent care project, or the effects of continuous training will be reduced. Additionally, the training programme should be holistic and not determined on an individual basis, or it will lack direction, which could negatively impact the quality of ECEC provision.

**Portugal** stresses the importance of making sure that continuous training is provided in context so as to meet the needs of teachers, children and families. **Mexico** also stresses the need to ensure the effectiveness of professional development courses and the quality of course content. The government values asking teachers which training courses they would find useful.

While pre-service training in **Korea** tends to focus on universal contents required for prospective teachers, in-service training takes into account the needs and competence levels of individual teachers and is designed according to the developmental phases of their teaching profession (*e.g.*, beginning, experienced and managerial status). Korea increasingly emphasises the provision of diversified in-service training contents and methods, which are tailored to individual teachers and their working circumstances (*e.g.*, rural areas and class sizes).

### Lesson 6: Consider whether a universal or targeted approach would better suit your country's context

**New Zealand**'s experience has been that allowing ECEC services to self-select for participation in professional development activities can mean that some services over participate in professional development while other services do not participate at all. Learning from this lesson, the government pursued a new approach to funding professional development, which requires providers to go into targeted communities and determine training programmes that best meet the needs of those communities.

### Lesson 7: Mainstream the ECEC workforce into the recognised teaching profession, while recognising cost implications

**Finland** raised the level of education for kindergarten teachers, connecting it more closely to education for primary school teachers. One of the main lessons learned is that when kindergarten and primary teachers are trained in connection to one another, they can better support children's development and learning by knowing how to co-operate during children's transition from pre-primary to primary school.

In **Slovak Republic**, importance is placed on improving the status of kindergarten programmes and teachers so as to secure a high quality workforce supply. The government supports the following improvements: kindergarten teachers should pursue the same level of education as primary and secondary teachers; remuneration should be equal across all levels of teaching; and kindergarten teachers should have the same obligation and right to pursue continuous training as other teachers.

## Lesson 8: Ensure stakeholder engagement through a regular consultation/review process

**Australia** has found that consultation with the ECEC sector is critical to the success of workforce reform. For instance, sector engagement has been critical in developing a national training package for ECEC vocational education which meets the needs of the industry, the community and delivers high quality outcomes. Australia has learnt that a regular consultation/review process involving the sector is critical to maintaining the relevance of the training to ensure that the training remains current to the industry. The government notes the importance of seeking broad agreement on the principles and aims of initiatives and then tailoring specific implementation requirements to accommodate existing systems and processes. To support the development of its National Quality Agenda, Australia undertook extensive consultation in the development phase and is currently undertaking consultations to support the introduction of reforms to the sector.

**British Columbia** (**Canada**) finds that it may be helpful to engage stakeholders to assist in planning opportunities that will meet the variety of needs in the sector, especially given the potential for great diversity in geographic, cultural and interest areas.

## Lesson 9: Mainstream diversity in the workforce

For **Norway**, training for minority-language assistants and recruitment of minority students to preschool teacher education has led to an increase in the proportion of staff with minority background, including the number of preschool teachers coming from an immigrant background.

In the context of diversifying the workforce, **Flanders** (**Belgium**) finds that diversity may be more about accepting that differences are difficult to understand than about trying to understand something based on an individual's frame of reference. This requires openness and flexibility and recognition of multiple perspectives and paradigms. Dealing with diversity presents practitioners with complex issues that cannot be solved with a technical body of knowledge. Practitioners in Flanders expressed a need for interpreting professionalism based on continuous reflection upon practice as well as a need to move beyond reflection and develop the ability to be reflexive.

## Lesson 10: Create centres of excellence to communicate the sector's needs and facilitate networks

In **Finland**, where social welfare training is mandatory for all staff, centres of excellence on social welfare were created to inform municipalities about the needs of the social welfare sector and ensure the relevance of training content. Finland has found that the creation of the centres has succeeded in networking regional social actors; and as the ECEC sector is closely linked to the social sector, the ECEC sector benefits from the centres as well.

## Lesson 11: Support the salaries of workers in private institutions

**Korea** has recognised that the enhancement of ECEC service quality should be accompanied by a balanced provision of work as well as an increase in salary. As the private sector of Korean ECEC outweighs the public sector, it has become important on Korea's policy agenda to make the rewards parallel/equivalent between teachers of the public and private sectors. Local authorities currently provide various types of teacher allowances and subsidies in addition to a basic salary as a way of encouraging monitoring and ensuring the quality of private ECEC services.

# ACTION AREA 5 – REFLECTING ON THE CURRENT STATE OF PLAY

This sheet has been prepared based on international trends and is designed to facilitate reflection on where your country stands regarding:

- Workforce

The aim is to raise awareness about new issues and identify areas where changes could be made; the aim is not to give marks on practices. Please reflect on the current state of play by circling a number on the scale from 1-5.

## WORKFORCE

| Qualifications | Not at all | | | | Very well |
|---|---|---|---|---|---|
| 1. ECEC job profiles and qualifications reflect relevant skills for today's ECEC settings. | 1 | 2 | 3 | 4 | 5 |
| 2. ECEC job profiles and qualifications are transparent and easily understood by prospective candidates, staff and parents. | 1 | 2 | 3 | 4 | 5 |
| 3. ECEC staff qualifications are aligned appropriately with those of primary teachers, especially those teaching children in the early years of primary schooling. | 1 | 2 | 3 | 4 | 5 |
| 4. The contents of initial education are reviewed periodically to improve quality and increase relevance of the qualifications. | 1 | 2 | 3 | 4 | 5 |
| 5. The qualifications are of equal quality across different ECEC qualification programmes while allowing institution-specific approaches. | 1 | 2 | 3 | 4 | 5 |
| 6. Qualifications to work with infants and toddlers (0-3 years) and young children (3-6 years) can be obtained in a streamlined process without unnecessary repetition or duplication regardless of the qualification system (dual or integrated for child care and early education). | 1 | 2 | 3 | 4 | 5 |

| | | | | | |
|---|---|---|---|---|---|
| 7. There is no stigma or parity in social status associated with different job titles and qualifications for preschool teachers, child care workers and other workers in ECEC. | 1 | 2 | 3 | 4 | 5 |
| 8. ECEC qualifications are portable across different regions and different countries. | 1 | 2 | 3 | 4 | 5 |
| **Workforce supply and retention** | Not at all | | | | Very well |
| 9. There is a monitoring system for workforce supply and demand. | 1 | 2 | 3 | 4 | 5 |
| 10. There is sufficient diversity in the workforce (*e.g.*, male workers, immigrants, different ethnic groups). | 1 | 2 | 3 | 4 | 5 |
| 11. There is a monitoring system on working conditions (*e.g.*, raising the salary level, providing non-financial benefits, increasing the staff-child ratio). | 1 | 2 | 3 | 4 | 5 |
| 12. There is a comprehensive recruitment strategy for ECEC staff (*e.g.*, prospective students, new graduates, job changers, under-represented groups, staffing in remote or disadvantaged areas). | 1 | 2 | 3 | 4 | 5 |
| 13. There are appropriate types of support and incentives given to students and graduates to work in the sector, especially in hard-to-staff settings and locations. | 1 | 2 | 3 | 4 | 5 |
| 14. Validating existing competencies has been explored to determine whether there are possibilities for easier entry to the profession. | 1 | 2 | 3 | 4 | 5 |
| 15. Specific initiatives have been taken to retain experienced workers in the sector and reduce turnover rates within centres to improve staff-child attachment and child development. | 1 | 2 | 3 | 4 | 5 |
| 16. Sufficient opportunities for career development, progression and mobility are available to ECEC staff. | 1 | 2 | 3 | 4 | 5 |
| 17. ECEC staff are supported on-site to develop the skills needed for working in a more integrated way across the broader early childhood development sector. | 1 | 2 | 3 | 4 | 5 |

| | | | | | |
|---|---|---|---|---|---|
| 18. In-service support is provided to staff, especially new staff, such as through mentoring programmes by experienced staff. | 1 | 2 | 3 | 4 | 5 |
| **Professional development** | Not at all | | | | Very well |
| 19. The importance of continuous professional development is well understood by staff and their employers. | 1 | 2 | 3 | 4 | 5 |
| 20. Professional development is driven by demands and provided with a variety of content and access options. | 1 | 2 | 3 | 4 | 5 |
| 21. Information about professional development opportunities is easily accessible. | 1 | 2 | 3 | 4 | 5 |
| 22. Professional development is available at a reasonable cost and at flexible times and locations for working professionals. | 1 | 2 | 3 | 4 | 5 |
| 23. Evaluations have been carried out to assess the quality and relevance of the professional development courses being taken up by ECEC staff. | 1 | 2 | 3 | 4 | 5 |
| 24. Take-up rates for professional development courses have been monitored, and the results have been used to examine how to improve the rates. | 1 | 2 | 3 | 4 | 5 |

# NOTES

1  In the literature, "staff" is the term that is usually used to refer to those who work directly with children in the ECEC field. They are also referred to as "professionals", "teachers", "caregivers" or "practitioners".

2  "Process quality" refers to what children actually experience in their programmes: that which happens within a setting. "Content quality" specifically refers to the substance of what is being learned (*e.g.*, curriculum).

3  "Ongoing professional development" refers to in-service education and training. Litjens and Taguma (2010) give a clear definition of in-service education. This "includes all planned programmes of learning opportunities for staff members of ECEC providers for the purpose of improving the performance of individuals in already assigned positions".

4  The international ISCED classification system is often used to facilitate international comparisons, four of which are relevant to the OECD survey responses: Level 2: Lower secondary school – normally considered the end of basic education; Level 3: Upper secondary school – normally the end of compulsory education; Level 4: Post-secondary non-tertiary education (*e.g.*, short vocational programs; pre-university courses); Level 5: First stage tertiary education (*e.g.*, first university degree); Level 6: Second stage of tertiary education (leading to an advanced research qualification).

5  Part time means that an education or training course takes up less time than a full-time job over a given period of time.

6  Integrated initial education: initial education for child care and pre-primary staff is integrated; students follow the same education, *i.e.*, students are being educated for working in child care and the early education sector (although a further specialisation for either child care or early education might exist within the programme). Split initial education: initial education for child care and pre-primary staff is split: they do not follow the same education and are trained separately. Data refers to centre-based ECEC workers only (excluding family day care workers).

7  Integrated initial teaching education: initial education for pre-primary and primary teaching staff is integrated; students follow the same education, *i.e.*, students are being educated for teaching in pre-primary and primary schooling (although a further specialisation for either pre-primary or primary might exist within the programme). Split initial teaching education: initial education for pre-primary and primary teaching staff is split: they do not follow the same education and are trained separately.

8  For kindergarten/preschool, based on data from: Australia, Austria, British Columbia (CAN), Czech Republic, England (UKM), Estonia, Finland, Ireland, Israel, Italy, Japan, Manitoba (CAN), Mexico, Netherlands, New Zealand, Norway, Poland, Portugal, Prince Edward Island (CAN), Scotland (UKM), Slovak Republic, Slovenia, Spain, Sweden and Turkey. For child care, based on data from: Australia, Austria, British Columbia (CAN), Czech Republic, Finland, Israel, Italy, Japan, Manitoba (CAN), Mexico, Netherlands, New Zealand, Norway, Prince Edward Island (CAN), Scotland (UKM), Spain and Sweden.

9  Capko, J. (2001), "Identifying the Causes of Staff Turnover", *Family Practice Management*, Vol. 8, No. 4.

# POLICY LEVER 4

# ENGAGING FAMILIES AND COMMUNITIES

*Parental engagement is increasingly seen as an important policy lever to enhance healthy child development and learning. There is recognition that it is a fundamental right and obligation for parents to be involved in their children's education. And parental partnership is critical in enhancing ECEC staff knowledge about their children. Furthermore, research has shown that parental engagement – especially in ensuring high-quality children's learning at home and communicating with ECEC staff – is strongly associated with children's later academic success, high school completion, socio-emotional development and adaptation in society.*

*Community engagement is also increasingly highlighted as an important policy lever. It can act as a "connector" between families and ECEC services as well as other services for children; a "social network" to support parents in reducing stress and making smart choices, especially for disadvantaged families; an "environment" to promote social cohesion and public order; and a "source of resources".*

# ACTION AREA 1 – USING RESEARCH TO INFORM POLICY AND THE PUBLIC

This section contains the following research brief:

- Parental and Community Engagement Matters

## PARENTAL AND COMMUNITY ENGAGEMENT MATTERS

### What is parental and community engagement?

Parental engagement refers to the formal and informal relations that parents have with ECEC services. The engagement can take a variety of forms and meanings, depending on the education stage of the child concerned (*e.g.*, early child care or preschool) and the perspective taken on the issue (*e.g.*, early years practitioner, teacher, parent, researcher). Literature often uses the terms "family-school partnership", "parental involvement", "family involvement" and "parental engagement" interchangeably.

Community engagement refers to the connections between the ECEC services and all forms of input and contribution by community services to ECEC (Litjens and Taguma, 2010). Community can be defined as "people from the same neighbourhood" in a narrow sense or "the whole community, including NGOs, etc." in a broader sense.

The most common and widely used parent and community engagement strategies (Oakes and Lipton, 2007; Epstein, 1995) can be summarised into six categories of constructive engagement.

**Table 4.1. Types of parental and community engagement**

| Child-focussed | |
| --- | --- |
| *Communicating* | Design effective forms of centre-to-home and home-to-centre communications about programmes and children's progress. |
| *Parenting* | Help all families establish home environments to support children as learners (*e.g.*, parenting classes). |
| *Stimulating development at home* | Provide information and ideas to families about how to help children at home with stimulating children's development and other curriculum-related activities, decisions and planning. |
| **Centre-oriented** | |
| *Volunteering* | Recruit and organise parent/communities help and support (*e.g.*, helping to plan and run centre events and fundraising activities, accompanying trips, donating their time to improve facilities, or assisting in the centre and sharing their skills and expertise). |
| *Decision making* | Include parents/communities in centre decisions, develop parent councils and parent-staff organisations. |
| *Collaborating with community* | Identify and integrate resources and services from the community to strengthen programmes, family practices and children's learning and development. |

*Source*: Adapted from Epstein *et al.*, 1995.

## What is at stake?

Children spend the larger, if not largest, part of their young life in their direct home environment, interacting with their parents[1], siblings, other family members and neighbours. Over the last decades, however, the amount of time children spend with their families and neighbours, as well as the types of interactions with them, have changed due to factors, such as changing family structures, increasing maternal employment and increasing immigration, in many OECD countries (OECD, 2006).

Parents' willingness to delegate part of the care for their children to ECEC services does not mean that the importance of the parent's role has diminished. It is still widely acknowledged that parental behaviour in the child's first five years is critical for the development of important academic and social skills and abilities. The current challenge for ECEC services is to embrace the crucial role of parents in young children's development and involve them in the services as much as possible (OECD, 2006).

The continuity of children's experience across environments is greatly enhanced when parents and staff members exchange information regularly and adopt consistent approaches to socialisation, daily routines, child development and learning. When done well, it can improve the quality of the centre, parenting at home, and the home-learning environment. Families with low socio-economic status (SES) could particularly struggle to provide appropriate care and enrichment for children due to lack of resources to do so (Barbarin *et al.*, 2008; Boyce *et al.*, 2010; Ermisch, 2008; Feinstein *et al.*, 2007, 2008; Hauser-Cram *et al.*, 2003).

Young children's development is not exclusively dependent on the input of parents and ECEC centres (day care, early education). Children grow up in a neighbourhood and are part of a community. Therefore, it is important that different services – formal ECEC services, day care, health services, out-of-school services – work together and create a "continuum of services" that is reassuring for parents and can meet the needs of young children. Community involvement in ECEC is important not only for providing expanded services and referrals where necessary, but also as a space for partnership and the participation of parents.

Patterns of parental, family and community engagement in ECEC differ from country to country. Several formal and informal mechanisms are used to foster full participatory and managerial engagement. Some of the challenges to active engagement of parents include cultural, attitudinal and linguistic barriers. It is particularly difficult to ensure equitable representation and participation across families from diverse backgrounds (OECD, 2006).

## Why does it matter?

### Parental engagement

The involvement of parents in young children's education is a fundamental right and obligation. Both the OECD (2006) and UNICEF (2008a) argue that ECEC services should recognise mothers' and fathers' right to be informed, comment on and participate in key decisions concerning their child. Research shows that there is a substantial need and demand for a parental component in ECEC services (Desforges and Abouchaar, 2003). Research also demonstrates that parental engagement in ECEC services enhances children's achievements and adaption (Blok et al., 2005; Desforges and Abouchaar, 2003; Edwards et al., 2008; Harris and Goodall, 2006; Powel et al., 2010; Sylva et al., 2004; Weiss et al., 2008).

Examples of successful ECEC services that promote parental engagement (e.g., Early Headstart, the Perry Preschool and the Chicago Parent Centers from the United States) offer evidence that parental engagement matters (UNICEF, 2008b). The federally funded Chicago Parent Center's programme in the United States has been cited as evidence that parent participation has a major impact on children's academic success and social development, and that it is an effective strategy for reducing the dropout rate. Each year parents took part in the programme increased the chances – by 16% – that their child would complete high school. For students whose parents were involved for the whole six years of the project, more than 80% graduated from high school, compared with 38% of students whose parents did not participate (Reynolds and Clements, 2005).

### Community engagement

The involvement of wider community services (e.g., health or social services and sport organisations) or community members in ECEC plays an important role in the development of young children. Community support of the early development process is considered as one of the characteristics common to high-quality ECEC centres (Henderson et al., 2002). The earlier the role of the community in the lives of young children is recognised, the better the chances children have of achieving at school and in life in general (Cotton, 2000). If the connection between schools and communities is strong, it is easier for children to develop the skills needed to be successful socially and emotionally, physically and academically (Edwards *et al.*, 2008, Oakes and Lipton, 2007; OECD, 2006).

Families with different socio-economic backgrounds (defined by factors such as parental education, income and occupation) have different capacities to provide their children with a nutritious and healthy lifestyle, provide for quality child care and invest in other learning resources, *e.g.*, books and visits to libraries and museums (Bradley *et al.*, 1989). Family's socio-economic background is, therefore, powerfully associated with children's educational development (Duncan *et al.*, 1998).

A study of children adopted between the ages of four and six into families that vary widely in socio-economic backgrounds highlights the impact of the environment children grow up in (Duyme *et al.*, 1999). Adopted children (without any genetic links with their adoptive parents) have shown that non-genetic parents' SES factors can impact the cognitive development of a child. The IQ of these children was measured before adoption, and all children, whether adopted by low- or high-SES families, had higher IQ's after adoption. But children adopted by higher-SES families had significantly larger gains in IQ than children adopted in lower-SES families because they were raised in richer, more stimulating environments. ECEC services, in collaboration with other services that can mitigate the negative effects of family backgrounds, are especially important for children with socio-economically disadvantaged backgrounds.

In the child's environment (the family, the neighbourhood), risk factors have a negative effect on the child's development of intellectual skills, school achievement, social-emotional competence, social adjustment and health (Van Tuijl and Leseman, in press) even to the extent that poverty leads to irreversible effects on brain functioning (Hackman and Farrah, 2009). Edin and Lein (1997) show that, in poor families, child care and medical care arrangements are unstable or of low quality. Additionally, their economic hardship often results in chronic stress. This is more prevalent among low-income populations because they have fewer resources to mitigate these events (McLeod and Kessler, 1990; Shonkoff and Philips, 2000). The connection between economic status and mental health is important because poor mental health is related to harsh, inconsistent, less involved parenting and less caring interactions. In turn, this has been associated with behavioural problems, for example, children are more often involved in fights and less capable of collaborating with peers; and it can cause severe attention issues leading to decreasing school performance (Shonkoff and Philips, 2000). A strong community can act as a social network that supports parents to reduce stress and maintain positive emotions, and gives them tools for raising their child.

If the quality of the social network is low, it may lead to low emotional involvement and cohesion (Van Tuijl and Leseman, in press). Community engagement means a higher level of social cohesion (mutual trust between neighbours and common values) and (informal) social control and collective efficacy (Shonkoff and Phillips, 2000). Collective efficacy relates to neighbourhood levels of violence, personal victimisation, homicide, etc.

Moreover, a continuum between ECEC services, parents, neighbours and other civil society stakeholders can enhance co-operation between different services leading to a comprehensive services approach. Comprehensive services are more responsive to what children actually need in terms of their overall development and to what parents need for child care, health care and other opportunities. A strong comprehensive system of community and formal ECEC services empowers disadvantaged families to cope with their specific poverty-related problems (Van Tuijl and Leseman, in press, Weiss et al., 2008).

A precondition is that ECEC programmes and communities – as well as parents – design and implement common standards and foster similar goals, because standards reflect the values of people who set them (Bodrova et al. 2004). ECEC services engaging families and communities is especially important in low income, minority communities where differences in socio-economic background and cultural values about child rearing and education are likely to negatively affect child development (Larner, 1996).

## What aspects matter most?

It has been argued that evaluating outcomes of parent or community engagement on children's performances and development is difficult due to varying definitions of what constitutes engagement and disagreement on how best to measure such engagement (Marcon, 1999). However, a few studies have compared different effects of parent or community engagement.

### Home learning environment (HLE)

#### Parent-infant interactions within the HLE

Children of parents who were least involved in the HLE at ages 10 to 36 months scored less well on cognitive skills test (e.g., in mathematics) later in life than children who experienced positive parent-child interactions in the HLE (Figure 4.1). The same effects were shown in research by Sylva et al. (2004), and these outcomes were still continuing at age seven plus.

### Figure 4.1. Impact of home learning environment (HLE) on student outcomes

English and Mathematics attainment at age 11

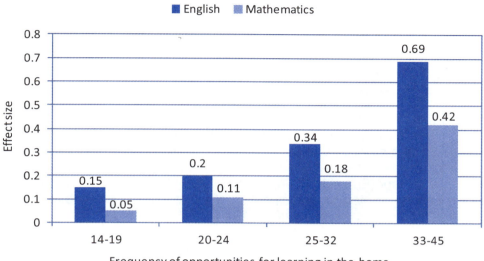

Source: Melhuish, 2010.

## *Programme guiding parents and providing materials*

Reviews by Deforges and Abouchaar (2003) and Harris and Goodall (2006) indicate that the most effective approach to boost children's later achievement and adjustment is support for parents to actively engage in children's learning activities at home. The HLE is one of the most powerful influences upon children's development (Belsky *et al.*, 2007; Melhuish, 2010). It includes such activities as reading to children, singing songs and nursery rhymes, going to the library and playing with numbers.

The Effective Provision of Pre-School Education (EPPE) study of England (United Kingdom) has shown the importance of parent-child activities in contributing to the quality of children's HLE. The research results indicate that programmes which directly promote activities for parents and children to engage in together are likely to be most beneficial for young children (Sylva *et al.*, 2004).

The quality of the HLE is also found to be strongly associated with the child's "at risk" status. A poorer quality HLE in the early years has been put forward as one of the possible reasons for the lower attainment levels observed at the start of compulsory education in "at risk" children. There are several ways in which ECEC services can help enhance the HLE, including providing activities and materials for parents and children to do together, offering parents tips on reading aloud to children and offering literacy learning kits. ECEC staff can also encourage parental engagement in early learning by providing them with resources and activities that further the work that is being addressed within the classroom. This helps families feel more connected to their child as well as to the programme (Halgunseth and Peterson, 2009).

## Home curriculum

ECEC services can inspire parents to offer their children all kinds of learning situations at home, both informal and explicit. Henderson and Mapp (2002) stress the importance of seizing learning opportunities during informal interactions. Parents can involve children in daily routines (*e.g.*, meals, phone calls, making grocery lists, getting dressed), enrich these routines with stimulating discussions, and trigger their children's curiosity and exploration urge. This kind of "home curriculum" boosts children's language development, cognitive development and academic achievement (Foster *et al.*, 2005; Weigel *et al.*, 2006).

Scandinavian research reveals that existing social, cultural and religious practices in the home provide children with a variety of written activities (Hjort *et al.*, 2009). A more effective home curriculum also includes more explicit learning activities, such as shared book reading. This activity has a major impact on children's cognitive and language development (Ermisch, 2008; Leung *et al.*, 2010). There is strong evidence that parents can be trained to participate in book reading in ways that boost this development effectively (Huebner *et al.*, 2010).

Support for parents to foster their children's learning is especially needed in low income families and dysfunctional families. Parents with limited education and low social status tend be less capable of engaging their children in learning activities (Ermisch, 2008; Feinstein *et al.*, 2007, 2008). ECEC services can effectively support these parents to realise a successful curriculum at home (Boyce *et al.*, 2010).

## Reading stories at an early age at home

A popular form of parental engagement seems to be helping with children's reading development: this has been well researched, and clear benefits have been found (Keating and Taylorson, 1996). Research undertaken in the United States with three- and four-year-olds has shown that early learning activities at home make a difference: children who are frequently read to and told stories are more likely to recognise all letters of the alphabet, count to 20 or higher, write their own names and read. In addition, children who are taught letters, words or numbers and are taken to the library regularly are more likely to show signs of emerging literacy (Nord *et al.*, 1999).

The PIRLS study[2], undertaken across 40 countries, has also shown a positive relationship between engaging in early literacy activities at home prior to compulsory education and reading performance at the age of ten. The study recorded the following parent-child activities: reading books, telling stories, singing songs, playing with alphabet toys (*e.g.*, blocks with letters of the alphabet), playing word games and reading aloud signs and labels. Findings show that the reading performance of children in the highest frequency of parent-child activities (*i.e.*, on a daily regular basis) is well ahead of that of their peers with lower frequencies of parent-child activities (Mullis *et al.*, 2003; 2007).

## Volunteering and participating in decision-making processes

Other types of parental engagement – such as volunteering and participation in parent councils or parent-teacher organisations, while recognising its importance for parental satisfaction and staff support – have been found to have little or no impact on children's achievement (Deforges and Abouchaar, 2003; Harris and Goodall, 2006).

### *Knowledge about parenting and child development*

Reviews show that parenting programmes affect both parents and children positively. The OECD found that children whose parents often read to them show markedly higher scores in PISA 2009 than students whose parents read with them infrequently or not at all, regardless of their family's socio-economic background (OECD, 2011). The Harvard Family Research Project found that about one-third to one-half of the variation in school outcomes between poor and not poor children can be accounted for by differences in parenting (Brooks-Gunn and Markman, *2005*). Parents strongly influence child outcomes and children's cognitive and linguistic development. Parental attributes found to be important are education, training and employment. Aspects of parenting that are found to matter for child development include the interactions with children, the HLE and parental understanding or knowledge of child development (Yoshikawa, 1995).

The overall findings from parenting programmes indicate that:

- parents feel more secure in interactions with their children, boost their sense of well-being and benefit their children (Diamond and Hyde, 2000; Scott, 2003; Sylva *et al.*, 2004);

- parents increase self-confidence in good parenting, particularly for poor families (Epstein, 2001);

- parents better understand appropriate educational practices and improve children's educational outcomes, especially in literacy (Cooter *et al.*, 1999; Bryant *et al.*, 2000);

- parents are more likely to talk directly with the practitioner and be better able to help their children at home with learning and homework (Corter *et al.*, 2006);

- participants reduce their reliance on public assistance, find employment, earn college credit or degrees, and own homes after their experience with the programme (Halgunseth and Peterson, 2009); and

- access points provided at ECEC centres or through home visits have been reported as key in empowering parents to engage in their children's learning (Sime *et al.*, 2009).

Gains in parenting skills and knowledge of child development and learning were found through participation in education courses and engagement in the ECEC service (Mitchell *et al.*, 2008). Furthermore, training parents of preschoolers to help their children's learning at home has been found to have positive results on later school achievements, regardless of family background or income (Graue *et al.*, 2004). Early Head Start parents participating in programmes offering child development services with parenting education through home visits were found to be more supportive of their children during play, more likely to read to their children every day, and less likely to smack their children than parents who did not participate (Love *et al.*, 2005).

### Strategic partnership between parents, communities and ECEC services

#### Frequent communication

*Starting Strong II* pointed out that the frequency of parent-staff relationships is linked positively with the quality of care provided in centres (OECD 2006), although a High/Scope study suggests that much depends on the content of the contact (Schweinhart and Weikart, 1997). Drop-off and pickup meetings, for example, can remain routine and focus only on immediate concerns. For this reason, it was emphasised in *Starting Strong II* that if these encounters do not provide opportunities for mutual learning, they should be supplemented by focused parent-staff meetings, newsletters and home visits (OECD, 2006).

A survey on parental needs shows that parents in Korea mainly utilise media and the on-line community to obtain and share information about child rearing and early childhood education. In contrast, parents in Japan regard neighbourhoods and grandparents as main sources for child-relevant information. Japanese parents frequently use child welfare centres to meet other parents and also visit local public health centres to consult issues on child care and support (Hwang, Nam and Suh, 2010).

#### Shared goals

It is important for ECEC staff to communicate with parents about programme goals and the best way to achieve them since parents can have misconceptions, such as school readiness (Bodrova *et al.*, 2004). They conceive readiness largely in terms of the ability to name objects, letters or numbers, without recognising the importance of inferential skills. Parental views and expectations of ECEC may, however, vary among countries and even regions. In Sweden, for instance, parents are found to demand that ECEC focus on both play and learning-oriented activities (Sheridan *et al.* 2009).

The EPPE study found ECEC settings that produced good socio-cognitive outcomes for children had "strong parental involvement, especially in terms of shared educational goals with parents" and provided "regular reporting and discussion with parents about their child's progress" (Siraj-Blatchford *et al.*, 2003). There is also evidence that a combined home and centre-based ECEC approach has a positive impact on children's development (Blok *et al.*, 2005; Brooks-Gunn and Markman, 2005; Sylva *et al.*, 2004). However, real partnerships and complementary practices are essential to achieving the best results (Bodrova *et al.*, 2004; Van Tuijl and Leseman, in press).

The Early Authors Programme is a United States-based 12-month early literacy intervention implemented in child care centres in ethnically and linguistically diverse, urban low-income communities.[3] The programme approaches literacy skills by emphasising highly meaningful language interactions and positive attitudes through empowering activities involving children and families (Bernhard *et al.*, 2008).

#### Parental aspirations

Some see parents mainly as supporters of the ECEC facility, assisting as volunteers; others see them merely as users or clients of ECEC services. Some view them as partners in a joint enterprise (Bloomer and Cohen, 2008; Moss, 2007); parents and professionals strive for the same educational aims at home and at the centre and harmonise their activities to achieve the best possible results for children. For this joint effort, it is critical that professionals communicate with parents about their aspirations for their children's achievements and their expectations about the best educational practice.

ECEC facilities should inspire parents to have *high hopes* for their children because parental aspirations and expectations are strongly related to children's achievement (Fan and Chen, 2001). It is especially important to raise the aspirations of low-income parents. Research suggests that children from low-income families enter a path of diminished expectations (Hauser-Cram *et al.*, 2003)

### Home visits

Home visits are associated with greater confidence in parents' interactions with children's education programmes and greater knowledge in children's development. Children who receive home visits from ECEC practitioners have been found to have greater engagement in literacy activities and are more likely to choose to participate in group activities. Staff also benefit, as they gain positive relationships with children and families and better understand how the child's home environment might affect school performance (Halgunseth and Peterson, 2009).

There is wider evidence on the benefits of targeted home visitation programmes, such as HIPPY[4]. HIPPY is a home-based programme that centres on the role of parents as home educators. It focuses on pre-literacy and pre-numeracy and is provided for two years, starting when the child is four. The HIPPY evaluation in New Zealand showed that children who have participated in HIPPY have scored higher in a variety of school achievements (literacy, reading, word recognition, numeracy), adjust better in class and show less disturbing behaviour (less fighting with peers and more active participation). In particular, HIPPY children have been found to be less likely to become in need of targeted support for literacy skills development (BarHava-Monteith *et al.*, 1999).

The High/Scope Perry Preschool programme[5] provides preschool education and home visits to disadvantaged children during their preschool years (from age three). The Perry Study stemming from the programme follows participants from ages three through to 40. The programme lasts two years and consists of two-and-a-half hours a day of preschool in addition to weekly home visits by preschool teachers. Findings show that the impact of the programme varies by gender and with age. The programme appeared to have a significant effect on males' criminal activity, later life income, and employment at age 27 and 40; whereas it had more effect on education and early employment for females ages 19 and 27. The general pattern is one of strong early results for females and later results for males (Heckman *et al.*, 2010).

### Strategic partnership with the wider community

### Tapping into community resources

Research cites family and community engagement as key to children's motivation for learning and development (Barton, 2003). In Canada, engagement with local organisations offering information to ECEC providers and the use of community-based resources (toy lending libraries, telephone support, etc.) positively correlates with more sensitive care giving and children's early social development (Doherty et al., 2000).

## Supporting harder-to-reach families

In Ireland, partnerships between ECEC programmes and community services have been found to be effective in approaching and supporting harder-to-reach families, such as Roma and travelling families. Specialists offer those families tailored services designed with respect to their cultural context, which improve children's skills as well as those of parents. The development of distance learning materials in collaboration with community members and consultants specialised in travelling education has enhanced the likelihood of achieving improved child outcomes on literacy rates and math skills. Specialists understand how to design effective learning materials for children within their communities, and parents learned how to implement different learning approaches for young children (Robinson and Martin, 2008).

## Targeting families and neighbourhoods

Neighbourhood conditions matter more for disadvantaged than advantaged children (Cook et al. 1998). In 1994, five Head Start programmes developed model substance abuse prevention projects with a goal to strengthen families and neighbourhoods of economically disadvantaged preschool children. The initiative, named Free to Grow, targeted families and neighbourhoods of Head Start children in an effort to protect them from substance abuse and its associated problems. It included a strong focus on community-based strategies in the form of coalitions, implementation of "safe space" task forces that ensured safe and substance abuse-free spaces for young children, and training in substance abuse prevention. Different community services were included in the implementation, e.g., local police forces, youth organisations, churches and numerous grassroots organisations. Outcomes included increased parental engagement in ECEC, cleaner and safer schools and neighbourhoods, improved relationships among residents and between ECEC practitioners, parents and community members, and stronger community norms against drug and alcohol use (Harrington, 2001).

## Combination of different approaches

A programme or centre does not need to limit itself to one approach. Several forms of parental and community engagement can be used simultaneously and complement each other. Since ECEC settings provide services for a range of people with different backgrounds, not every strategy or type of engagement meets all needs or is suitable for each child, family or community. Therefore, implementing plural approaches may encourage parent and wider community engagement. An example of combining different engagement approaches is the REAL project, explained below.

## The REAL project (Realising Equality and Achievement for Learners)

Hannon and Nutbrown (2001) have reported on the REAL project, where ten preschool centres in areas of high deprivation in Sheffield (England) took part. Eighty-eight families participated in the 12-18 month programme. The programme included a combination of five components, including home visits by the preschool teachers; provision of literacy resources; centre-based group activities; special events (*e.g.*, group library visits); and postal communication. Adult education for the parents was also incorporated into the programme through an accredited course on REAL along with information, advice and support for accessing other providers' courses. Each preschool teacher was funded to work one half-day per week with eight families.

The evaluation provided strong evidence of the benefits of the programme to the children, parents and teachers. Parents' experiences were reported as "extraordinarily positive". Preschool teachers greatly valued the opportunity to work closely with parents and found it changed their thinking, although they felt that other responsibilities in the school made their work on the project difficult. Parents and teachers noted "global benefits", as well as specific literacy benefits, for the children. Results showed the programme group was ahead of the control group in terms of literacy development and letter recognition (Hannon and Nutbrown, 2001).

## What are the policy implications?

### Including parental engagement as a benchmark for quality ECEC services

One suggestion is the use of a "quality report.card" based on a list of dimensions and critical components by which any non-formal, informal or formal activity can be evaluated. This should include support for the sharing of educational aims and regular communication about the child's progress (Jualla and Van Oudenhoven, 2010).

### Engaging parents and wider communities as strategic partners for integrated ECEC services

This means that national authorities involve regional and local authorities, NGOs, private businesses and community groups in policy and decision making and recognise them as partners in the ECEC coalition. This helps ensure broad public support and a multi-perspective contribution to decision-making. A key success factor is the availability of substantial funding, for example, to pay parents and community members who are the main implementers of the programme. Funding can also be used to encourage and implement co-operation.

### Concentrating efforts on improving the HLE in the early years

Early literacy projects for children, as well as parenting and empowerment activities for parents, can be delivered through ECEC services and in close partnership with parents. The focus should be on "home curriculum", especially shared book reading at home as well as home visits. Focusing on socio-economically disadvantaged families and children is of particular importance. Awareness should be raised about the importance of good HLEs and the possibilities available in local communities to engage in ECEC. This can be done through public relations campaigns, parental education, etc.

### Training staff on parental and community engagement

ECEC centre's attitudes and actions toward parent involvement are largely influenced by administrators and practitioners. Because leadership is critical in family and community engagement (OECD, 2006), administrators and practitioners may need special training to help them develop the skills needed to promote family-centre partnerships and community involvement (Siraj-Blatchford *et al.*, 2003; Sime *et al.*, 2009).

Practitioners' training programmes can include general information on the benefits of and barriers to parental and community involvement; information on awareness of different family backgrounds and lifestyles; techniques for improving two-way communication between home/community and the centre; information on ways to involve parents in helping their children learn in school and outside; and ways that centres can help meet families and communities' social, educational and social service needs (Litjens and Taguma, 2010; OECD, 2006).

## What is still unknown?

### Research from non-Anglo-Saxon countries

While there is a general recognition of the importance of parental and community engagement in improving children's learning outcomes, determining what precisely constitutes successful parental or community engagement in ECEC services is much harder. A number of long-term child outcomes could be measured to test the effectiveness of involving parents or communities in different ways; but for robust data to be gathered and sound conclusions to be made about "what works", significant investments would be required to undertake well-designed experimental longitudinal research. Most large-scale and technically sound studies on the impact of parental engagement were conducted in the United States and the United Kingdom (Desforges and Abouchaar, 2003; Harris and Goodall, 2006; OECD, 2006). Sound research in other countries and cultures is needed. Parental engagement in children's schooling may have different meanings in different cultures (Huntsinger and Jose, 2009). Little is known about how these differences affect the outcome of parental engagement.

### Research on effects of different communication strategies

Although there is a growing body of research that points to the importance of communication between parents and ECEC staff, there is no strong evidence as to which particular strategy works best.

### Effects on hard-to-reach groups

Relatively little is known about effective ways of increasing parental engagement in hard-to-reach groups (Harris and Goodall, 2006). More research is needed on targeted strategies to involve parents of ethnic minority children and parents who are not interested in being active ECEC participants.

## *Evaluation of community initiatives*

There is hardly any literature describing the difference in impact between community initiatives with the aim to strengthen educational programmes and community initiatives with a more autonomous goal. A challenge is the evaluation of the quality of non-formal/informal community-based activities because they are heterogeneous and, therefore, hard to compare. Elaborate research on the effects of non-formal activities remains necessary.

## *Neighbourhood effects*

Although there is a large body of literature suggesting that neighbourhood conditions influence development and behaviour, it seems hard to define "precise, robust and unbiased" estimates of neighbourhood effects (Duncan and Raudenbusch, 1999; Shonkoff and Phillips, 2000).

# REFERENCES

Barbarin, O. A. *et al.* (2008), "Parental Conceptions of School Readiness: Relation to Ethnicity, Socioeconomic Status and Children's Skill's", *Early Education and Development*, Vol. 19, No. 5, pp. 671-701.

BarHava-Monteith, G. *et al.* (1999), "Hippy New Zealand: An Evaluation Overview", *New Zealand Journal of Social Policy*, Vol. 12.

Barton, P. E. (2003), *Parsing the Achievement Gap: Baseline for Tracking Progress*, Princeton, NJ, Educational Testing Service.

Belsky, J. *et al.* (2007), "Are there Long-Term Effects of Early Child Care?", *Child Development*, Centre of Excellence for Early Childhood Development and Strategic Knowledge Cluster on Early Child Development, Montreal.

Bernhard, J. K. *et al.* (2008), "Read My Story! Using the Early Authors Program to Promote Early Literacy among Diverse", *Journal of Education for Students Placed at Risk*, Vol. 13, No. 1.

Blok, H. *et al.* (2005), "The Relevance of the Delivery Mode and Other Program Characteristics for the Effectiveness of Early Childhood Interventions with Disadvantaged Children", *International Journal of Behavioural Development*, Vol. 29, pp. 36-37.

Bloomer, K. and B. Cohen (2008), Young Children in Charge, Children in Scotland, Edinburgh.

Bodrova, E., D. Leong and R. Shore (2004), Child outcome in Per-K Programs: What are standards: What is needed to make them work?, New Brunswick NJ, NIEER.

Boyce, L. *et al.* (2010), "Telling Stories and Making Books: Evidence for an intervention to help parents in migrant Head Start families support their children's language and literacy", *Early Education and Development*, Vol. 21, No. 3, pp. 343-371.

Bradley, R. H. *et al.* (1989), "Home Environment and Cognitive Development in the First Three Years of Life: A Collaborative Study involving Six Sites and Three Ethnic Groups in North America", *Developmental Psychology*, Vol. 25, pp. 217-235.

Brooks-Gunn, J. and L. B. Markman (2005), "The Contribution of Parenting to Ethnic and Racial Gaps in School Readiness", *Future of Children*, Vol. 15, No. 1, pp. 139-165.

Bryant, D. *et al.* (2000), *Head Start parents' roles in the educational lives of their children*, paper presented at the Annual Conference of the American Educational Research Association, New Orleans.

Cook, T., J. R. Kim, W. S. Chan and R. Settersten (1998), "How do neighborhoods matter?" in Furtenberg, F., Jr., T. Cook, J. Eccles, G. Elder and A. Sameroff (eds.), *Managing to make it: Urban Families in high risk neighborhoods*, Chicago, University of Chicago Press.

Cooter, R. B. *et al.* (1999), "Family and Community Involvement: The Bedrock of Reading Success", *Reading Teacher*, pp. 52-58.

Cotton, K. (2000), *The Schooling Practices that Matter Most*, Portland: Northwest Regional Educational Laboratory.

Corter *et al.* (2006), "Toronto First Duty Phase 1 Summary Report: Evidence-based understanding of integrated foundations for early childhood", Toronto.

Desforges, C. and A. Abouchaar (2003),"The Impact of Parental Involvement, Parental Support and Family Education on Pupil Achievement and Adjustment: A Literature Review", Research Report No. 433, Department for Education and Skills, London.

Diamond, C. and C. Hyde (2000), Parent education programmes for children's behaviour problems: Medium to long term effectiveness, West Midlands Development and Education Service, Birmingham.

Doherty, G. *et al.* (2000), "Caring and Learning Environments: Quality in Regulated Family Child Care Across Canada", Centre for Families, Work and Well-being, University of Guelph, Ontario.

Duncan, G. J. and S. W. Raudenbush (1999), "Assessing the Effects of Context in Studies of Child and Youth Development," *Educational Psychologist*, Vol. 34, No. 1, pp. 29-41.

Duncan, G. J. *et al.* (1998), "How much does childhood poverty affect the life chances of children?", *American Sociological Review*, Vol. 63, No.3.

Duyme, M. *et al.* (1999), "How best can we boost IQ's of 'dull children'?: A late adoption study", *Proceedings of the National Academy of Sciences*, Vol. 96, No. 15.

Edin, K. and L. Lein (1997), Making Ends Meet: How Single Mothers Survive Welfare and Low Wage Work, Russell Sage Foundation, New York.

Edwards, C. P., S. M. Sheridan and L. Knoche (2008), *Parent Engagement and School Readiness: Parent-Child Relationships in Early Learning*, Lincoln, NE: University of Nebraska, available at: http://digitalcommons.unl.edu/famconfacpub/60.

Epstein, J. L. (2001), School, Family and Community Partnerships: Preparing Educators and Improving Schools, Westview Press, Colorado.

Epstein, J. L. (1995), "School/Family/Community Partnerships: Caring for the Children We Share", *Phi Delta Kappan*, Vol.76, No. 9, 701-712.

Ermisch, J. (2008), "Origins of Social Immobility and Inequality: Parenting and Early Child Development", *National Institute Economic Review*, Vol. 205, No. 1, pp. 62-71.

Fan, X. and M. Chen (2001), "Parental Involvement and Student's Academic Achievement: A Meta-Analysis", *Educational Psychology Review*, Vol. 13, No. 1, pp. 1-22.

Feinstein, L. *et al.* (2008), Education and the Family: Passing Success Across the Generations, Routledge, London.

Feinstein, L. *et al.* (2007), Reducing Inequalities: Realizing the Talent of All, NCB, London.

Foster, M. *et al.* (2005), "A model of home learning environment and social risk factors in relation to children's emergent literacy and social outcomes", *Early Childhood Research Quarterly*, Vol. 20, No. 4, pp. 13-36.

Graue, E. *et al.* (2004), "More than Teacher Directed or Child Initiated: Preschool Curriculum Type, Parent Involvement, and Children's Outcomes in the Child-Parent Centres", *Education Policy Analysis Archives*, Vol. 12, No. 72.

Hackman D. A. and M. J. Farrah (2009), "Socioeconomic status and the developing brain", *Trends in Cognitive Sciences*, Vol.13, No. 2, pp. 65-73.

Harris, A. and J. Goodall (2006), *Parental Involvement in Education: An overview of the Literature*, University of Warwick, Coventry.

Halgunseth, L. C. and A. Peterson (2009), "Family Engagement, Diverse Families, and Early Childhood Education Programs: An Integrated Review of the Literature", *Young Children,* Vol. 64, No. 5.

Hannon, P. and C. Nutbrown (2001), "Outcomes for Children and Parents of an Early Literacy Education Parental Involvement Programme", Paper presented at the Annual Conference of the British Educational Research Association, Leeds.

Harrington, M. (2001), Evaluation of Free to Grow, Phase II: Detailed Profile of the Free to Grow Project in California. Final Report, Robert Wood Johnson Foundation, New Jersey.

Hauser-Cram, P. *et al.* (2003), "When Teacher's and Parent's Values Differ: Teacher's Ratings of Academic Competence in Children from Low-Income Families", *Journal of Educational Psychology*, Vol. 95, No. 4, pp. 813-820.

Heckman, J. et al. (2010), A Reanalysis of the High/Scope Perry Preschool Program, University of Chicago, Chicago.

Henderson, A. and K. Mapp (2002), *A new wave of evidence: The impact of schools, family and community connections on student achievement*, National center for family and community connections with schools, Austin TX.

Henderson, L. *et al.* (2002), *The report of the findings from the early childhood study: 2001-2002*, Atlanta: Andrew Young School of Policy Studies, Georgia State University.

Hjort *et al.* (2009), "Research Mapping and Research Assessment of Scandinavian Research in the year 2007 into pre-school institutions for children aged 0-6 years", Danish Clearinghouse for Educational Research: Copenhagen.

Huebner, C. E. and K. Payne (2010), "Home support for emergent literacy: Follow-up of a community-based implementation of dialogic reading", *Journal of Applied Developmental Psychology*, Vol. 31, No. 3, pp. 195-201.

Huntsinger, C. S. and P. E. Jose (2009), "Parental involvement in children's schooling: Different meanings in different countries", *Early Childhood Research Quarterly*, Vol. 24, No. 4, pp. 398-410.

Hwang, S., M. Nam and H. Suh (2010), "Comparison between Korean and Japanese pre-school parents' awareness and the actual condition of childcare and child support", *Journal of Eco Early Childhood Education Research*, Vol. 9, No. 2, pp. 105-124.

Jualla R., and N. van Oudenhoven (2010), "Community-based Early Years Services: the Golden Triangle of Informal, Nonformal and Formal Approaches", *Psychological Science and Education*, Vol. 3, pp. 22-31.

Keating, I. and D. Taylorson (1996), "The other mums' army: Issues of parental involvement in early education", *Early Years*, Vol. 17, No. 1.

Larner, M. (1996), "Parents' perspectives on quality in early care and education", in: S.L. Kagan and N.E. Cohen (eds.), *Reinventing early care and education: A vision for a quality system*, Jossey-Bass, San Francisco.

Leung, C. *et al.* (2010), "Evaluation of a Program to Educate Disadvantaged Parents to Enhance Child Learning", *Research on Social Work Practice*, Vol. 20, pp. 591-599.

Litjens, I. and M. Taguma (2010), "Revised Literature Overview for the 7th Meeting of the Network on Early Childhood Education and Care", Paris: OECD.

Love, J. M. *et al.* (2005), "The effectiveness of early head start for 3-year-old children and their parents: lessons for policy and programs", *Developmental Psychology,* Vol. 41, No. 6.

Marcon, A. (1999), "Positive Relationships Between Parent School Involvement and Public School Inner-City Preschoolers' Development and Academic performance", *School Psychology Review,* Vol. 28, No. 3, 1999.

McLeod, J. D. and R. Kessler (1990), "Socioeconomic status differences in vulnerability to undesirable life events", *Journal of health and social behaviour,* Vol. 31, 1990.

Melhuish, E. (2010), "Why children, parents and home learning are important", in Sylva *et al.* (eds.), *Early Childhood Matters: Evidence from the Effective Pre-school and Primary Education Project*, pp. 44-70, Routledge, London/New York.

Mitchell, L. *et al.* (2008), "Outcomes of early childhood education: Literature review", Report to the Ministry of Education, Ministry of Education, Wellington.

Moss, P. (2007), "Bringing politics into the nursery: early childhood education as a democratic practice", *European Childhood Education Research Journal*, Vol. 15, No. 1, pp. 5-20.

Mullis, I. V. S., M. O. Martin, A. M. Kennedy and P. Foy (2007), *PIRLS 2006 International Report: IEA's Progress in International Reading Literacy Study in Primary Schools in 40 Countries*, TIMMS and PIRLS International Study Center, Lynch School of Education, Boston College, Chestnut Hill, MA..

Mullis, I. V. S., M. O. Martin, E. J. Gonzales and A. M. Kennedy (2003), PIRLS 2001 International Report: IEA's Study of Reading Literacy Achievement in Primary Schools, Chestnut Hill, MA.

Nord, C., J. Lennon, B. Liu and K. Chandler (1999), *Home Literacy Activities and Signs of Children's Emerging Literacy, 1993 and 1999*, United States Department of Education, Washington DC.

Oakes, J. and M. Lipton (2007), *Teaching to Change the World*, New York: McGraw-Hill.

OECD (2011), PISA in Focus Nr. 10: What can parents do to help their children succeed in school?, OECD, Paris.

OECD (2006), Starting Strong II: Early Childhood and Care, OECD, Paris.

Powell, D. R. *et al.* (2010), "Parent-school relationships and children's academic and social outcomes in public pre-kindergarten", *Journal of School Psychology*, Vol. 48, pp. 269-292.

Reynolds, A. and M. Clements (2005), "Parental Involvement and Children's School Success", in: *School-Family Partnerships: Promoting the Social, Emotional, and Academic Growth of Children*, Teachers College Press, New York.

Robinson, M. and K. Martin (2008), Approaches to Working with Children, Young People and Families for Traveller, Irish Traveller, Gypsy, Roma and Show People Communities: a Literature Review Report for the Children's Workforce Development Council, Leeds.

Schweinhart, L. J. and D. P. Weikart (1997), *The High/Scope pre-school Curriculum Comparison Study*, High/ Scope Press, Ypsilanti, Michigan.

Scott, S. (2003), "Parenting Programmes: What works? Some UK evidence", Paper presented to DfES discussion group, Department for Education and Skills, London.

Shonkoff, J. P. and D. A. Phillips (2000), *From Neurons to Neighborhoods: The Science of Early Childhood Development*, Washington, D.C.: National Academy Press.

Sime, D. *et al.* (2009), "A report for Save the Children and West Dunbartonshire Council – Improving outcomes for children in poverty through home-school partnerships in the early years – Summary report", Save the Children, Strathclyde.

Siraj-Blatchford, I. *et al.* (2003), "Technical Paper 10: The Effective Provision of Pre-School Education (EPPE) Project: Intensive Case Studies of Practice across the Foundation Stage", DfES, London

Sheridan, S., J. Giota, Y. M. Han and J. Y. Kwon (2009), "A Cross-Cultural Study of Preschool Quality in South Korea and Sweden: ECERS Evaluations", *The Early Childhood Research Quarterly*, Vol. 24, pp. 142-156.

Sylva, K. *et al.* (2004), "The Effective Provision of Preschool Education (EPPE) Project: Final Report", Report No. SSU/FR/2004/01, Department for Education and Skills, Nottingham.

UNICEF (2008a), "The Child Care Transition", Innocenti Report Card 8, UNICEF Innocenti Research Centre, Florence.

UNICEF (2008b), Innocenti Working Paper 2008-01, available at: www.unicef-irs.org.

Van Tuijl, C. and P. P. M. Leseman (in press), "School or Home? Where early education of Young immigrant children work best" in E.L. Grigorenko (ed.), *Handbook of US Immigration and Education*, New York: Springer.

Weigel, D. J. *et al.* (2006), "Contribution of the home literacy environment to preschool-aged children's emergent literacy and language skills", *Early Child Development and Care*, Vol. 176, pp. 357-378.

Weiss, H., M. Caspe and M. E. Lopez (2008), "Family Involvement Promotes Success for Young Children: A Review of Recent Research" in M.M. Cornish (ed.), *Promising Practices for Partnering with Families in the Early Years*, Plymouth: Information Age Publishing.

Yoshikawa, H. (1995), "Long-term effects of early childhood programs on social outcomes and delinquency", *The Future of Children*, Vol. 5, No. 3.

# ACTION AREA 2 – BROADENING PERSPECTIVES THROUGH INTERNATIONAL COMPARISON

This section contains an international comparison of:

- Parental and community engagement

## PARENTAL AND COMMUNITY ENGAGEMENT

### Findings

- The most commonly used approaches for family and community engagement include: 1) making it a legal obligation, and 2) involving parents or communities in decision-making bodies (Table 4.2).

- While a majority of countries make it an "obligation" for ECEC services to engage parents in their activities, a few countries (e.g., Slovenia and Sweden) also make it a parent's "right".

- In several countries (e.g., the Flemish and French communities of Belgium, Germany, the Netherlands and New Zealand), parents and community members can run an ECEC centre and receive public subsidies for such activities if following a certain set of standards or quality framework.

- Some countries involve parents in the evaluation of ECEC services. When parents are part of the monitoring process, they are rarely the sole agent but tend to be included together with ECEC staff and often also with managers (Table 4.3). Finland is unique in a sense that children are also regarded as part of the evaluation agents along with ECEC staff and parents; Japan is also unique in a sense that it involves local stakeholders as part of the evaluation agents along with parents.

- When parents are involved in the evaluation exercise, typically used evaluation methods include observations, evaluation forms, surveys, checklists, portfolios and questionnaires

- Several countries reported administering parental satisfaction surveys. They are administered by local authorities (e.g., Denmark and Sweden), evaluation institutes (Spain), or ECEC centres themselves (e.g., Norway and Slovenia) (Table 4.4).

For more detail, see the Survey Response Tables on "Parental and Community Engagement" and "Monitoring" (Excel™ files) in the online Quality Toolbox at **www.oecd.org/edu/earlychildhood/toolbox**.

**Table 4.2. Preferred approaches to engaging families and communities**

Panel A. Parental engagement

| Making it a legal obligation[6] | Making it a parental right | Putting it in a policy paper | Involving parents in decision making | Allowing parents to be providers |
|---|---|---|---|---|
| Australia, Belgium, Czech Republic, Estonia, Finland, Germany, Japan*, Netherlands*, New Zealand, Poland, Portugal*, Prince Edward Island (CAN), Slovak Republic, Slovenia, Spain, Sweden, Turkey | Czech Republic, Norway, Poland, Prince Edward Island (CAN), Slovenia, Spain, Sweden | New Zealand, Norway, Slovak Republic | Australia, Belgium, British Columbia (CAN), Czech Republic, Denmark, Estonia, Finland, Germany, Ireland, Japan, Manitoba (CAN), Mexico, Netherlands, New Zealand, Norway, Poland, Portugal, Prince Edward Island (CAN), Slovak Republic, Slovenia, Spain, Sweden, Turkey | Belgium, Germany, Manitoba (CAN), Netherlands, New Zealand, Norway, Poland, Slovak Republic, Sweden |

* Only regarding kindergartens/preschools for Japan and Portugal; only regarding child care for the Netherlands.

Panel B. Community engagement

| Making it a legal obligation[7] | Putting it in a policy paper | Involving community members in decision making | Allowing community members to be providers |
|---|---|---|---|
| Australia, Belgium, Finland, Japan*, Mexico, Norway, Portugal*, Slovenia, Spain, Turkey | Norway, Slovenia, Spain | Australia, Belgium, Finland, Ireland, Japan, Mexico, Netherlands, New Zealand, Norway, Portugal, Slovak Republic, Slovenia, Spain, Sweden, Turkey | Belgium, Finland, Ireland, Japan, Mexico, Netherlands, New Zealand, Norway |

* Only regarding kindergartens/preschools for Japan and Portugal.

Note: Belgium refers to both the Flemish and French Communities of Belgium.

*Source*: OECD Network on Early Childhood Education and Care's "Survey for the Quality Toolbox and ECEC Portal", June 2011.

Table 4.3. Inclusion of parents in evaluation of ECEC services

| Country or region | Institutions under evaluation | Parents in conjunction with… | Type of evaluation |
|---|---|---|---|
| Denmark | Child care centres, Pre-primary education (Kindergarten) | ECEC staff | Survey |
| England (UKM) | Care centres, Pre-primary Education | ECEC staff, Management | Observations |
| Finland | Child care , Family care, Pre-primary education | ECEC staff, Children | Questionnaires, Portfolios |
| Flemish Community (BEL) | Care centres | missing | Survey |
| Italy | Care centres, Preschool | ECEC staff, Management | Survey, Observations, Portfolios |
| Japan | Kindergarten, Care centres | Local stakeholders | Evaluation forms, Consultation |
| Norway | Kindergarten | ECEC staff | Observation, Questionnaires |
| Poland | Kindergarten | ECEC staff, Management, Local stakeholders | Questionnaires, Interviews |
| Slovak Republic | Preschool | ECEC staff | Checklist |
| Slovenia | Preschool | ECEC staff, Management | Evaluation forms, Questionnaires |
| Sweden | Preschool | ECEC staff, Management | Evaluation forms |

*Source*: OECD Network on Early Childhood Education and Care's "Survey for the Quality Toolbox and ECEC Portal", June 2011.

Table 4.4. Parental satisfaction surveys on provision of ECEC services

| Types of provisions | Administrator of the survey | Frequency | Country |
|---|---|---|---|
| Kindergarten/ Preschool | ECEC centre | every 3 years | Korea |
| | | missing | Norway, Slovenia |
| | | 1 to 2 times per year | Sweden |
| | Local authority | every 2 years | Denmark |
| | | missing | Prince Edward Island (CAN) |
| | Institute of evaluation | missing | Spain |
| Child care centres | ECEC centre | every year | Italy |
| | | at least once during the child's participation in child care | Flemish Community (BEL) |
| | | missing | Norway, Slovenia |
| | | 1 to 2 times per year | Sweden |
| | Local authority | every 2 years | Denmark |
| | | missing | Prince Edward Island (CAN) |

Note: Countries with an integrated ECEC system are listed under both "kindergarten" and "child care" since their ECEC system integrated care and early education.

*Source*: OECD Network on Early Childhood Education and Care's "Survey for the Quality Toolbox and ECEC Portal", June 2011.

## Definitions and methodologies

Parental and community engagement refers to the formal and informal relations between parents or community members with ECEC services. The scope of community includes, for example, neighbourhoods, NGOs, faith organisations, private foundations and services focusing on child development, such as social and health services.

The findings presented here are based on data from the OECD Network on ECEC's "Survey for the Quality Toolbox and ECEC Portal" (2011) and the OECD's desk-based research.

# ACTION AREA 3 – SELECTING A STRATEGY OPTION

This section contains lists of strategy options to tackle the following challenges:

- Engaging families in ECEC
- Engaging communities in ECEC

## ENGAGING FAMILIES IN ECEC

### Challenge 1: Lack of awareness and motivation

Motivating parents to engage in the ECEC of their children and encouraging centres to involve families is challenging due to a lack of awareness among parents, staff and centre management about the importance of parental involvement. In addition, there are insufficient incentives stimulating parents to become involved.

#### *Making family engagement a policy priority, an obligation or right*

- In **Finland**, parental engagement is included in different legislations. According to the Day Care Act, the objectives of day care are to support parents in raising their children and to promote children's personal and balanced development together with their parents. The Basic Education Act, Section 3.1, mentions that "those providing education (including pre-primary education) shall co-operate with children's parents". In the *Core Curriculum for Pre-primary Education* for six-year-olds, co-operation with parents is stated in Section 5.2 as an element of the curriculum which should be implemented in preschool. Parental engagement and partnership with parents are also highly raised issues in the *Finnish National Guidelines for Early Childhood Education and Care* (2005).

- In **Korea**, the Early Childhood Education Act (Article 5) and the Childcare Act (Article 6 through 11) stipulate parental involvement in the central and local ECEC policy committees and indicate that parents should be involved in these committees. Collaborating and communicating with parents are manifested as an important part of the quality assurance systems as well as pre- and in-service ECEC teacher trainings.

- In **Spain**, the participation of parents in schools and preschools is regulated by the Spanish Constitution of 1978 (Article 27.7). The Education Act 8 of

1985 also stipulates the right of parents to be involved in the planning of education of their children and in decision-making bodies. Preschools and schools are obliged to accept the involvement of parents in these activities. Additionally, the Act on Education of 2006 urges preschools and schools to promote participation of parents and staff in ECEC and education. The core curriculum for the second cycle of ECEC (pre-primary education for three-to-six-year-olds) also highlights the importance of parental engagement.

- The Child Care Act in the **Netherlands** requires all child care provisions to have a parent board. The board supports and monitors the quality in the provisions.

- In **Slovenia**, the Preschool Institutions Act states that preschools should implement parental involvement activities. It also defines the principals of parental involvement. Parents have the right to participate in planning the activities of preschool institutions and to participate actively in the centre's educational activities. Parents also have a right to continuous information exchange with staff on the development of their child.

- Regulations in **Flanders** (**Belgium**) obligate child care facilities to have a policy in place that promotes parental participation. The regulations are less strict for independent (not subsidised) provisions than for publically subsidised centres. The new Child Care Decree (in development) will also make it compulsory for ECEC centres to provide parents the possibility to evaluate ECEC services.

- ECEC centres in the **French Community** of **Belgium** are legally obliged to give parents the opportunity to share their opinions and views on the centre's care and educational provision. The board of directors of early childhood centres are also legally obliged to have parents and community members on the board. Moreover, the educational programme for child care providers emphasises the importance of engaging parents in ECEC.

- In **Sweden** and the state of **North-Rhine Westphalia** (**Germany**), parents of children in preschools have a right to a minimum of one "development dialogue" per year in which ECEC staff discuss the development of the child with the parents. Parental engagement is also included as an aspect in Sweden's *Curriculum for the Preschool*, which is a binding document.

- In **Norway**, to ensure opportunities for engagement and co-operation between kindergarten staff and parents, both the former 1975 and 1995 Kindergarten Acts and the current 2005 Kindergarten Act state that every kindergarten must have a parent council comprised of parent/guardians of all children in kindergarten and a parent-staff co-ordinating committee comprised of representatives of parents/guardians and staff so that each group is equally represented. The owner of the kindergarten can also be part of the committee. Parental engagement is integrated in the legislation through the purpose clause and the Framework Plan for the Content and Tasks of Kindergartens.

- **Australia** included parental engagement in their *National Quality Standard Framework*, obliging ECEC services to "form collaborative partnerships with parents and communities".

- In **Manitoba** (**Canada**), under Manitoba Regulation 62/86, a child care centre is only eligible for grant funding if at least 20% of the membership on the board of directors is made up of parents or guardians of children in attendance at the centre. Therefore, publically funded child care centres are obliged by law to accept parents on the board of directors of their centre.

- **Prince Edward Island** (**Canada**) has made Parent Advisory Committees mandatory in all Early Years Centres. These committees provide direct input into the programmes and services being provided to their child and their family. Besides this, the holistic Early Learning Framework recognises parents as key in the overall health and well-being of their child.

- **Czech Republic** made family engagement part of their curriculum framework (*FEP*). The *FEP* states that the relationship between the school and the family should be based on mutual respect, understanding, helpfulness and co-operation. Teachers, therefore, should observe concrete needs of children and families and try to meet these needs. Besides this, parents have a legal right to be engaged in ECEC in the Czech Republic. Parents have a right to participate in school activities and be informed about them, and they have a right to be informed about the development of their child. Preschools also offer families advice on stimulation of child development.

- *Síolta*, the National Quality Framework for Early Childhood Education in **Ireland**, includes "Parents and Families". The framework states that parents and families should be engaged in the early education of their children and that "valuing and involving parents and families requires a proactive partnership approach evidenced by a range of clearly stated, accessible and implemented processes, policies and procedures".

- In Poland, various regulations ensure family engagement in preschool **education**. According to the School Education Act, parents in kindergartens may form a Parents Board, which shall be involved in a variety of decision making and consultation processes connected to, among others, the budget and education programmes and selection of the director of the institution (a representative of the Parents Board participates in the election commission). The Parents Board has a right to give proposals and share its views on all issues relating to kindergarten with the authorities of kindergartens as well as with local municipalities. Parents may also participate in a Kindergarten Board. Additionally, according to the Core Curriculum, teachers are obliged to inform parents about the kindergarten's activities, curricula, children's development and ways to stimulate children's development. Teachers shall engage parents in educational processes and encourage them to take part in decision-making processes in kindergarten and to actively participate in the work of the facility.

*Providing public financial resources to involved parents*

- **Mexico** provides parent associations with public financial resources, which they can spend on quality improvement measures in ECEC centres, such as building an extra room or buying better study supplies. This improves the quality level of the services and strengthens the role of the parent associations in the community.

- **Japan** provides financial remuneration to stimulate the participation of members in the education management council of community schools. The council consists of parents and other community members.

- In **Australia**, community playgroups are generally initiated by parents or caregivers and are supported by state/territory playgroup associations, funded by the Australian government. The government also funds supported, locational and intensive playgroups for children and families from disadvantaged groups. The government's Parental and Community Engagement Program also supports Aboriginal and Torres Strait families and communities to reach into schools and education providers and develop partnerships to enhance children's educational outcomes. Australia also remunerates parents who work as tutors in the Home Interaction Program for Parents and Youngsters. Parents currently participating in the home-based intervention programme are given financial incentives to become future tutors.

- In the **United States**, parents and community members participating in substance abuse prevention projects were paid a monthly remuneration for their efforts and work. In 1994, five Head Start programmes developed model substance abuse prevention projects with a goal to strengthen families and neighbourhoods of economically disadvantaged preschool children. The initiative, named Free to Grow, targeted families and neighbourhoods of Head Start children in an effort to protect them from substance abuse and its associated problems. A key success factor of these programmes was the substantial amount of funding, which made it possible to pay a monthly remuneration (USD 100) to parents and community members who were the main implementers of the programme.

- In **Korea**, parents working as members of the Early Childhood Education Policy Committee or Childcare Policy Committee at the central and/or local government levels are remunerated USD 100 per committee meeting attended. This stimulates participation and ensures their professional commitment.

*Providing public financial resources to ECEC programmes*

- **Japan** earmarked financial resources for nursery centres to promote the exchange of information on parenting and provided funding to pay for professionals providing advice on parenting.

- **British Columbia** (**Canada**) provides funding to Child Care Resource and Referral Centres, which provide support, resource and referral programmes for parents and child care providers on care and early education. They provide information to parents about available child care providers and ECEC centres in their community and assist parents in choosing quality child care arrangements. The provincial government has also provided funding to the BC Association of Family Resource Programs to support professional development and advocacy for approximately 270 Family Resource Programmes (FRPs). FRPs support parents' engagement with their families and work with ECEC programmes to ensure best practices and consistency in family development, play-based learning, early literacy and learning, parent education and learning and information exchange.

*Engaging parents as providers or support to providers*

- Parents in the **French Community** of **Belgium** can set up and run child care provisions. Parents in **Flanders** (**Belgium**) can be involved in centres' activities like story-telling groups, organising a school party, participating in extra-curricular activities, such as field trips.

- In **New Zealand**, parents can run play centres as parent co-operatives. Parents are then closely involved in both running the centre and working with the children during session times. Typically they are open for one to five sessions each week to provide play, social and learning opportunities for children. These play centres are often less formal than other Early Childhood Education (ECE) services in New Zealand. All early childhood education services, including parent-led play centres, can receive an ECE Funding Subsidy. They are eligible for up to six hours each day and 30 hours each week of ECE Funding Subsidy for each licensed child place. This funding offsets the cost of providing ECEC, so that parents do not need to pay the full amount. The services receive this funding directly from the Ministry of Education.

- In **Korea**, parents can set up and run a parent co-op child care by forming a union of 15 parents or more (Enforcement Rules of the Childcare Act, Article 9). Such a facility is managed in the same way as other child care centres. Based on the policy for facilitating parental engagement, which has been implemented at city, provincial and local education offices since 1997, parents running a co-op child care facility receive training on the features of child development and learning activities. After completing this training, parents are eligible to serve as volunteer assistants at kindergartens. The purpose of this training is to utilise parents as assistants in overpopulated classrooms, and at the same time, foster well-balanced personality development in children and provide them with safe education. The classroom teachers also receive similar training so that the teachers and parents can provide pedagogical activities in a consistent manner.

- In **Norway** and **Sweden**, many parents establish and run kindergartens. They receive earmarked funding for this as well as guidance material. In 2005, 14% of all Norwegian kindergartens were run by parents. The number of parents running kindergartens has gone down to 11.6% since the right to a kindergarten place was introduced in 2009. In Sweden, parents can run preschools as "parent-co-operatives". In 1983, the government made state grants available to parental co-operatives. In 2009, Sweden had just over 900 preschools with 21 000 children run by parent co-operatives (4.6% of all children in preschool).

- In **Germany**, parents can set up and run their own child care centres. They also receive public funding for their institutions. In 2010, 4 423 of the 50 849 kindergartens, which is 8.7%, were driven by parents.

- Parents in the **United Kingdom** can start a registered child care service at their home. These childminders provide child care in their own home, looking after small groups of children (up to six at a time).

- In **Ireland**, parents can either run their own playgroup (private playgroup), or they can co-operate in a parent committee and run a playgroup together (community playgroup). A private playgroup is run by an individual, often in a private home. On the other hand, a community playgroup is organised and run by a committee of parents. In the latter, parents other than the manager can be actively involved in the planning of such playgroups and provide support to and participate in the activities. The emphasis in a playgroup is on the total development of the child by providing him/her with an environment with ample opportunity for exploration and discovery. There is no formal teaching of academic skills. Ireland gives both public and private providers of playgroups the opportunity to receive public funding for starting up a playgroup. The level of funding will be determined by the number of places the group proposes to provide, whether there is a need for such facilities in the area and several criteria set locally, which differ per region or municipality.

- **Japan** offers a "day in the life of a nursery teacher" experience to parents. Parents can voluntarily do an "internship" for one day in an ECEC centre and work as a nursery teacher to better understand the profession and be involved in the education of their own children. This also promotes trust between the nursery centre and parents.

- **Mexico** offers parents the possibility to volunteer in the ECEC centre. A popular activity is parents giving a "class" on what their profession is about and what kind of work they do and demonstrating the work to the young children – making it an interactive event.

- In **Slovenia**, parents can participate in the planning and preparation of preschool activities, such as sports days and cultural events. It increases mutual understanding and respect between staff and parents regarding each others' views on child development.

### *Engaging parents in an advisory or management body for ECEC policies and services*

- **Norway** has established a national advisory board of parents for ECEC called *FUB*. The board makes parents' voices heard in contemporary ECEC policies and secures parents' perspectives in the development of ECEC. The board also provides the Ministry with advice on the co-operation between kindergarten and family homes. Each ECEC provision is required to have a parent council. This council has the right to express an opinion on all matters of importance relating to parental relationships with the kindergarten.

- In **Germany**, ECEC facilities provide assemblies where parents and staff meet. These serve to inform parents concerning organisational and ECEC issues. Parents also typically elect advisory boards that represent all parents and thereby allow them to participate in important matters. In most states, parental councils with advisory functions are established at the municipal and state levels.

- In **Portugal**, the National Confederation of Parents Associations has been established, comprised of not-for-profit parent associations. Their goal is to congregate, co-ordinate, stimulate, argue for and represent the local and regional associative movements of parents at the national level. Furthermore, it acts as a social partner for governing bodies, local authorities and institutions to enable and facilitate the execution of parental rights and duties with regard to kindergartens and schools. Portuguese parent associations are also represented in Municipal Education Councils: bodies that promote the co-ordination of education policies within the municipality in co-operation with education agents and social organisations.

- **Flanders (Belgium)** has set up Local Consultative Forums for child care and out-of-school care, and these include professionals, centre managers, parents, local administration servants and other stakeholders. Within the Forums, stakeholders can share their opinions, ideas and concerns regarding child care. The Forums function as a municipal advisory body and give advice on child care to the local administration/ authority. There are currently 301 Forums in Flanders. Besides this, parents can become a member in the school board, school council and parent council of pre-primary schools and be involved in decision-making processes. Parents can also participate in a parent association, which is a more informal form of involvement.

- In **Japan**, a system of school management councils (community schools) was introduced in 2004. Parents and local residents have the opportunity to participate in the management of preschools and are assigned certain tasks and responsibilities regarding the management of the centres.

- In **Korea**, the Early Childhood Education Policy Committee and Child Care Policy Committee at the central and local government levels are obliged to involve parent representatives in decision-making processes of policy planning and execution. In addition, child care centres with at least 40 children are required to have a child care centre management committee to advise and deliberate the issues related to service operations. Starting from 2012, as a follow-up of the *Plan for the Advancement of Early Childhood Education*, individual kindergartens are also legally obliged to have a management committee consisting of five to nine representatives of parents and teachers. Representatives review issues concerning regulation revisions, budget, curriculum implementation, meals, etc. They are expected to elicit more parental engagement and promote transparency in the operation of private kindergartens as well as contribute to the development of more tailored services that better meet local needs.

- **Portugal** has a strategic governing body named *Conselho Geral* (General Council). The Council is represented by early education teaching staff, parents, local authorities and the local community. This governing body approves, by voting procedures, the internal school rules and regulations and strategic and planning decisions. ECEC staff, parents and community members choose which individuals or community organisations will be a member in the General Council.

- Early Year Centres in **Prince Edward Island (Canada)** are to institute Parent Advisory Committees in their centres. These Parent Advisory Committees are to help centres make decisions around centres' communication with parents and any non-regulated decisions that are to be made around the Early Years Centres.

- Parents in **Slovenia** can participate in two different councils related to preschool institutions: the preschool institution council and the council of parents. Preschool institution councils are composed of staff, parents and the municipality. The duties of the preschool institution council include the appointment and dismissal of the head of the preschool institution; adoption of the annual programme of the preschool institution and the annual work plan; and discussing complaints from parents. The councils of parents were formed to represent parental needs. Parent councils can share their opinions on proposed development plans and annual programmes of work, discuss educational problems, discuss parents' complaints and elect representatives for the councils of preschool institutions.

- Educational institutions, including pre-primary schools, in the **French Community of Belgium** are obliged to have a Participation Council in which educational staff, parents and members of the civil society can participate. All parents have the right to become a member of the council and the parental members are being elected by other parents for two years. Within the Council, the educational project of the institution can be discussed and changes can be proposed. The Council is an advisory organisation and has no decision-making rights.

### *Engaging parents in setting the curriculum*

- **Finland**'s *Core Curriculum for Pre-primary Education* (2010) states that it is important to provide parents and guardians with opportunities to participate in setting objectives for, planning and evaluating the educational work within pre-primary education. Parents in Finland are involved in the development of the educational plan of their child. Parents set the objectives of the educational plan of their child in co-operation with ECEC staff. Also, parents and ECEC staff work together to plan on how to achieve these objectives. This stimulates engagement of parents and encourages further involvement since they are familiar with the curricular plan of their child. Staff also inform parents about the curriculum in the centre and provide parents with advice on how they can implement elements of the curriculum at home.

- In **Korea**, the national kindergarten curriculum review committee includes parent representatives as its members.

- In **Spain**, parents are directly involved in setting the teaching-learning processes as part of the curriculum staff are using in preschools. Parents are also involved in setting the educational plan, in collaboration with teachers, for their children.

- **Japan** included parental engagement in their kindergarten curriculum (*Course of Study for Kindergartens*). The curriculum states that kindergartens should give consideration to "deepening the understanding of parents of the importance of early childhood education by creating opportunities for information exchange with parents, and developing activities for both the parents and children".

- Parents in **Norway** are actively involved in establishing the annual plan for pedagogical activities in Norwegian kindergartens. The co-ordinating committee of each kindergarten draws up this annual plan and includes parents as its members.

### Supporting and training staff to engage parents

- In **Norway**, the former Ministry of Children and Family Affairs established the parental guidance programme (1995-98). In 2006, the Norwegian Directorate for Education and Training created the handbook "Children in Multilingual Families", which provides parents with answers to frequently asked questions about children's bilingual or multilingual development. In addition to offering advice to parents, it also helps staff in day care centres respond to parents' questions and reflections on the bilingual development of their children. It includes examples and articles on how to involve parents actively in language stimulation.

- Information material on involving parents in preschools in **Sweden** has been developed by the National Agency for Education and distributed to ECEC centres, *e.g.*, a booklet focusing on resources in language stimulation presents examples and articles on how to actively engage parents in language stimulation both in and outside preschools.

- The **Netherlands** is upgrading the training level of staff in child care to a minimum qualification level instead of having unqualified staff working in child care next to qualified staff. The training includes an aspect on parent engagement, and it is expected that this stimulates staff to encourage parental engagement and increases the quality level. The training upgrade started in 2007 and runs until 2014, costing EUR 55 million. Additionally, in 2009, the Ministry of Education, Culture and Science requested the *ITS* (Dutch research institute) to design a brochure called "Action Plan to optimise parental involvement in Early Childhood Education (ECE)". With this brochure, ECE centres can set up plans to increase parental engagement.

- In **Germany**, the Federal Ministry of Family Affairs, Senior Citizens, Women and Youth established a programme promoting specialised child care centres for language and integration. The government is providing a total of EUR 400 million to subsidise as many as 4 000 child care facilities throughout Germany. With these funds, selected facilities can hire additional child care staff who devote their time to activities and special services that promote language learning. Activities include providing individual children and groups with language-learning support as well as monitoring and documenting the children's language development. The activities also include advising the child care team on language-learning issues and emphasise working with parents. Therefore, additional staff are enabled to actively engage parents in daily issues of speech and language development.

- The initial training curriculum for ECEC teachers in **Korea** includes parent involvement and family and community co-operation courses as selective courses (three credits each). In addition, practitioners enrolled in qualification level advancement training for kindergarten teachers (grade one), directors and assistant directors are mandated to take a "Parent Training and Counselling" course as part of their education programme. The family and communication co-operation course includes information on parent involvement programmes; parent counselling; and theory and practice of parent-teacher communication.

- **Portugal** and **Finland** developed training opportunities dedicated to how staff can encourage and improve communication with parents of children. In both countries, this is included in the initial education of ECEC workers and in continuous on-the-job training as well.

## Providing support materials to parents

- **Slovak Republic** provides families with counselling by ECEC staff on how to implement home learning activities and gives them curriculum materials to ensure parents carry out the activities correctly.

- The **Netherlands** hands out materials to parents, such as story books and CDs, to encourage parents to organise activities with their children at home that stimulate language development.

- Under the strategy of **Spain**'s *Educa3* programme, which includes enhancing the number of ECEC places for zero-to-three-year-olds and stimulating quality in ECEC, a website is being developed, which will provide parents with learning resources and materials as well as advice from experts on issues regarding early childhood education and development.

- Parents with children in preschools in **Czech Republic** receive advice and counselling from preschool staff on how to be more engaged in the early education of their child and how they can stimulate early child development. Additionally, preschools provide various advisory documents on parenting and stimulation of learning to parents, including methodological materials and lending them children's books.

- In the **French Community** of **Belgium**, the website www.parentalité.be provides information to parents on various aspects of child development. It was created by the Observatory for Children, Youth and Youth Assistance with the aim of supporting parents in the upbringing of young children. The website is now administered by the *ONE* (Department for Birth and Childhood).

- **Norway** and the **United States** provide parents with materials to stimulate them in implementing qualitative home learning activities: giving parents story books to read from, CDs with children songs and online curriculum material, such as *Curious George* in the United States, which is based on the animated television series of *Curious George* and provides examples of home activities that play and early development. The *Curious George* initiative is partially funded with public federal funding. Additionally, the American website of *Sesame Street* lists a range of activities and resources parents can use in their home environment to stimulate early child development. The activities and resources are often accompanied by a video or linked to an episode which provides play-based learning opportunities for children. The site was set up with partial funding from the United States federal government and still receives federal funding. Several longitudinal studies on the effects of watching educational programmes, including *Sesame Street*, on child development have been conducted during the last forty years. These studies found that early viewing of educational children's television, and *Sesame Street* in particular, appeared to contribute to children's school readiness. Children performed significantly better than their peers on age-appropriate standardised achievement tests of letter-word knowledge, mathematics skills and vocabulary size.

- The **United Kingdom** launched *CBeebies* in 2002. *CBeebies* is a television channel produced by the BBC, a British public service broadcaster, aimed at children age six and under. The channel launched a website with activities (such as games, songs and print-outs) related to the programmes, which parents can implement with their children at home. In 2011, the BBC launched a new micro site called *CBeebies Grown-ups*, full of advice and help for parents in bringing up children and toddlers. The BBC, *CBeebies* included, is funded publicly through charging homes a television licence fee, which is set by the national government.

- Parents in **India** whose children attend child care are given age-appropriate toys and booklets with information and example activities to enhance early development at home.

### *Engaging parents in evaluating ECEC provisions*

- **Japan** introduced school evaluation in 2007. Evaluation councils are made up of persons related to the kindergarten, such as parents and local residents. They evaluate the results of the self-evaluation assessments as implemented by the kindergarten staff and decide whether they agree with the self-evaluation exercises or not. This is done through observing the kindergarten's daily activities and analysing the information exchanged with parents and community.

- In **Korea**, a Parent Monitoring Group has been managed by local governments since 2005. This group aims to improve the public service function in operating child care centres, and it evaluates relevant projects/programmes and policies. Parents working as members of this group visit the child care centres in question, observe/monitor their activities and provide child care policy recommendations to the government. Such monitoring takes place at least once a quarter, and the term of group membership is two years.

- In **Finland**, the National Curriculum Guidelines on ECEC states that parents and children must be involved in the evaluation of curricular activities. Parents are expected to monitor and evaluate the attainment of the goals set in the curriculum.

- The new Child Care Decree (in development) of **Flanders** (**Belgium**) will make it compulsory for ECEC centres to provide parents the opportunity to evaluate ECEC services. In addition to the external evaluations by an authorised organisation, each child care facility will have to send out an evaluation and satisfaction survey to parents. The parental survey is part of centre's self-assessment assignment with the goal to improve quality provision. The facilities will also have to implement a procedure on how to accept and process complaints.

- **Norway**'s Framework Plan for the Content and Tasks of Kindergartens states that parents have to be actively encouraged to take part in quality monitoring and reviewing the kindergarten activities. The most common methods of parents reviewing kindergartens are through meetings organised by kindergarten staff and sending out surveys. Eighty-five percent of Norwegian kindergartens make use of the surveys.

- Every parent in **Slovak Republic** is invited to evaluate the quality of the ECEC provision either directly by sharing opinions with staff, or indirectly, through surveys and questionnaires. Parents can also express their opinions on the quality of ECEC provision through the School Council in which parents have representatives as well.

### Assessing and evaluating family engagement

- In **Australia**, as part of assessment and rating against the National Quality Standards, long day care, family day care, preschool and out-of-school hours care services will be assessed from 2012 onwards on how well they maintain collaborative partnerships with families and communities. Additionally, an evaluation of the Home Interaction Program for Parents and Youngsters programme is currently being conducted. A report on the evaluation findings is due at the end of 2011.

- **British Columbia** (**Canada**) has evaluated its StrongStart Early Learning Programmes. The evaluations show that parents highly value their involvement and see a significant effect on their children and an increase in their own sense of ability to support their children's development and learning. British Columbia plans to continue monitoring parent satisfaction over time.

- In **Korea**, parental involvement is one of the quality indicators for both kindergarten evaluation and child care accreditation. Indicators include the links between ECEC institutions and families and communities, the various available parent education services and forms of communication with families. In addition, kindergartens are required to conduct a questionnaire regarding parents' satisfaction with the quality of the service.

- Within the inspection framework of Early Childhood Institutions in the **Netherlands**, aspects regarding parental involvement and informing parents about the development of their child are included. The Dutch Education Inspectorate assesses whether these institutions involve parents sufficiently.

- The Institute of Evaluation in **Spain** carried out a pilot evaluation of family engagement in preschool and school to analyse which forms of parental involvement parents are most satisfied with. It was found that parents are most happy with the parent-teacher meetings of the preschools and schools to discuss child development. The evaluation also found that, although 87% of preschools and schools have parent associations, only 8.5% of parents participate. This evaluation provided insights as to how parental engagement can be stimulated and what aspects of parental involvement could be improved.

*Encouraging private foundations to support parental engagement*

- In **Japan**, Sony established the Sony Foundation for Education. Its Early Development Activity Centre conducts an extensive programme of activities in its quest to make science widely known among the public, to foster well-balanced personality development in young individuals, and to educate the general public about the importance of building a healthy relationship between parents and children. The achievements of the various programmes and the lessons learned about child rearing are shared in various ways with parents, the community and child care workers. The Foundation started Photo Contests for parents with an aim to stimulate their interest in child rearing and their engagement in children learning science.

## Challenge 2: Communication and outreach

Many countries experience challenges in informing parents about how they can get involved. There is insufficient awareness and knowledge among parents about how they can participate or where they can find this information. A lack of communication channels between the national government, local governments, ECEC staff and parents is one of the key outreach challenges.

In countries where ECEC services are provided with a market-oriented approach, it is important that parents have all necessary information for them to make informed decision about their choice of ECEC services.

*Using written forms of dissemination*

- In **Australia**, the Office on Early Childhood Education and Child Care provides comprehensive information for parents about ECEC on websites. The office is part of the Department of Education, Employment and Workplace Relations and is responsible for delivering the government's key commitments to ECEC, guiding major policy reforms at a national level and informing the public about this on-line. Additionally, the government developed a website for parents, which gives information on different types of child care and how to get assistance with the cost of child care. The Raising Children Website and DVD's through the Raising Children Network deliver consistent, scientifically proven information to parents on early childhood development.

- **Japan** has contact memos and notices hanging in all ECEC centres. These inform parents about the latest developments, possibilities to be engaged, data of meetings and other ECEC-related information.

- Parents in **Slovenia** receive a brochure each year containing basic information on the preschool. Additionally, the Regional Institutes of Public Health in Slovenia prepared a variety of written information materials on parenting and educating in the form of pamphlets or leaflets. These inform parents about preventive activities and appropriate child care. The leaflets and pamphlets are available to parents in the preschool free of charge.

- A mail shot was sent out in **Ireland** after the introduction of universal preschool provision. A physical letter was sent to each household with a child eligible for preschool. The mail shot has proven to be effective since the take-up rate within the eligible age cohort increased to 94% within less than two years.

- ECEC provisions in **Korea** send out newsletters and weekly curriculum reports to parents to inform them of upcoming events, classroom educational activities, child rearing related policies, field trips, etc. The weekly curriculum update informs parents of the fact that learning at early childhood settings is not merely based on textbooks but on a variety of educational activities.

- In the **French Community of Belgium**, the *ONE* (Department for Birth and Childhood) published a series of brochures for parents, which include information about child care for zero-to-three-year-olds and (early) education for three-to-twelve-year-olds. Some of these brochures are designed with pictures and images so as to ensure that language is not an obstacle in understanding them.

- Kindergarten teachers in **British Columbia (Canada)** communicate with parents a minimum of five times a year about children's progress. Three formal written letters and two informal reports are sent to them each year.

- ECEC centres in **Slovak Republic** provide information about the centre and activities through messages posted on notice boards, bulletin boards, e-mails and centres' websites.

- ECEC centres in the **Netherlands**, **Norway** and **Sweden** often have their own website to inform parents about the services they offer, costs and parental engagement opportunities.

- In the *Länder* of **Berlin**, **North-Rhine Westphalia** and **Schleswig-Holstein (Germany)**, information letters and brochures are sent to parents, which provide information about child rearing and child development and give examples of good practices and how to stimulate early child development. At the national level, the Federal Ministry of Family Affairs, Senior Citizens, Women and Youth runs a website to inform and engage stakeholders, such as parents, ECEC staff, youth welfare services, business organisations and other partners within the ECEC field. Information is provided on a wide range of relevant ECEC issues, such as programmes, child care facility options, qualification and professional development. The website provides ECEC news, reports, expertise, interviews and papers for practical use as well as a collection of relevant internet links. Additionally, the website offers surveys and online commenting options to ensure the participation of relevant stakeholders.

- **Manitoba (Canada)** produces materials and resources for parents seeking child care options, including a parent guide to child care, which is currently under revision. All parents in Manitoba receive print and on-line information about parenting resources, referrals to parenting programmes and supports, and opportunities to take part in decision making. Furthermore, Manitoba recently launched a website called ManitobaParentZone.ca, which provides parents with parenting and child development information that reflects current best practices in health and child and adolescent development and includes important links to Manitoba-based public education and public health campaigns. The new Online Child Care Registry has been a key tool in providing timely information about child care spaces to both parents and facilities.

### *Creating a central information contact point*

– The government of **Australia** set up a free telephone hotline that provides information on ECEC to callers. The hotline was developed to provide on-demand information to parents, families and community members about ECEC services in the country and can also be used to file complaints about ECEC services.

– In the **French Community** of **Belgium**, multi-service structures have been developed in cities and neighbourhoods. In addition to providing care services for zero-to-three-year-olds, these services provide parental advice and support parents in their upbringing skills. These multi-service structures are also open to discuss and debate child development and answer questions parents may have related to day care and child development.

– In **Korea**, 61 Childcare Information Centres have been established since 1993 to help parents, providing information on: child care, child care centres and child care services for disadvantaged children, such as special needs children and multi-cultural children. The centres also offer child care consultation services. To enhance the efficiency of child care centre operations, the information centres also provide child care teaching materials, offer child care accreditation assistance programmes, and carry out various projects related to the education and management of substitute teaching when needed.

– In **Germany**, family offices are established throughout the country. Different social services are bundled in this office, and families can ask for information or consult the family offices for anything related to family life and child development, including information about ECEC provisions. Learning arrears are being detected at these offices, which also provide and inform about services that can help children in overcoming these arrears. Additionally, the Federal Ministry of Family Affairs offers a central online service that can be consulted for information on ECEC. For family day care workers, there is an additional online and phone service with experts supplying specific information, e.g., on law-related issues.

– **Slovenia** has counselling centres in its major cities for children and families. These centres provide support to families and children on parenting and education.

### *Organising meetings and activities*

– In **Mexico**, all school principals meet with parents in the first 15 days following the start of a school cycle. These meetings are organised to inform parents about parental involvement possibilities and parent associations; to explore who has an interest in participating in what; and to choose the board of the parent association. Mexico also organises information sessions in ECEC centres on educating and upbringing children. The focus is on upbringing skills and information exchange on early education. These sessions are held twice per week and target parents with a low socio-economic or educational background, although all parents are free to participate in them.

- ECEC centres in the **Netherlands** organise at least one open visiting day per year. On this day, ECEC centres open their doors to parents, families, community members and others who have an interest in the ECEC centre. Information about the centre is provided as well as an explanation of what activities the centre undertakes and how staff contribute to early development.

- In **Slovenia**, preschool teachers hold regular meetings with parents to discuss the principles of early childhood education, the management policies and the activities of the centre. These meetings are also used as an opportunity to listen to the needs of families and share their concerns. By exchanging ideas in the meetings, preschool teachers can build a positive relationship with parents. Parents can also meet with the preschool teacher for individual meetings, where the preschool teacher explains in detail to parents about their child's activities and development. This process helps the preschool teacher learn about new aspects of the child's home life. Preschool institutions also organise "open-door" days, where parents can attend the centre and receive additional information on the provision and early development.

- In **Paraguay**, monthly meetings are organised in schools or community centres. Parents with children ages zero to five are informed about child development and encouraged to promote early development through play. They are also informed about health and nutrition, ECEC participation possibilities and other early intervention services.

- Preschools in **Spain** organise meetings for parents to inform them about general preschool issues and the preschool system. Besides this, meetings are held to inform parents of preschool curriculum and courses; and conferences are organised for parents and teachers, where they can discuss any other preschool-related issues and the development of their child. Spain is launching an awareness campaign, which will inform parents on how they can be involved in ECEC and contribute to their child's development.

- Municipalities in **Finland** organise multi-professional prenatal training for parents expecting their first child that incorporates peer group activities. The goal is to support expecting parents during pregnancy and in their care and upbringing tasks (during the child's first year). Prenatal training focuses on available ECEC services but also parenthood, intimate partner relationships, pregnancy and childbirth, child care and breastfeeding, family benefits and the postnatal period.

- **Turkey** has developed the Basic Education Programme for Families (*AİTEP*) in co-operation with UNICEF. It was a Childhood Care and Teaching Programme in which UNICEF and ECEC staff co-operated on providing different informative sessions to the community and parents. The programme lasted for six weeks. Learning subjects included understanding the behaviour of children, positive discipline methods and the impact of play on development.

- In **Korea**, parent-teacher conferences are held once every semester (twice per year), providing an opportunity for parents and staff to discuss children's overall development and learning and any problems a child may have.

- **Sweden** organises at least one development dialogue per year. This is a meeting with ECEC staff and parents of the child to discuss the development and learning of their child. In addition, preschools hold regular meetings with parents to provide them with opportunities to exercise influence over how the goals can be turned into concrete pedagogical activities. Furthermore, parents are involved in the evaluation of preschool activities and have opportunities to participate in work on quality improvement.

- In **Germany**, ECEC facilities provide assemblies where parents and staff meet, which serve to inform parents concerning organisational and ECEC issues. Parents also typically elect advisory boards that represent all parents and thereby allow them to participate in important matters. In most states, parental councils with advisory functions are established on the municipal and state levels.

*Developing contact books*

- Some child care centres in **Flanders** (**Belgium**) use the *Heen en Weer Boekje* (Take Home Booklet). It is a booklet in which staff write about what the child did at the centre each day: if the child ate well, what the child ate, if she/he slept well, what they did as daily activity, such as playing and drawing. Due to the booklet, parents are well informed about the development of their child and feel more engaged.

- **Japan** developed Contact Books in which daily progress is described by ECEC staff. This enables parents to be informed about the behaviour and growth of their children in daily life and is found to be effective in engaging parents in early education and care.

*Ensuring that parents can make informed choices in market-oriented services*

- The government of **Australia** developed *Mychild*, and online child care portal that provides families with information on different types of child care and how to get assistance with the cost of child care. *Mychild* provides information on child care provisions in the neighbourhood of parents, the costs of these provisions and contact information to ensure that parents can make well-informed choices. It also explains how parents can receive financial aid in covering the costs for child care by guiding parents in how to apply for subsidies. For more information on the *Mychild* website, visit www.mychild.gov.au.

- **Iowa** (**United States**) has a website that provides free online information for parents about ECEC in their state. The information provided is primarily for families with children ages zero to five. The website informs parents objectively about early child development and education and provides information about which services can be contacted for which purpose. The page directs parents to the service(s) needed for stimulation of early child development, *e.g.*, early education or health services. The Iowa Child Care Resource and Referral website provides information to parents about which licensed child care centres are available in their neighbourhood.

- In the **United Kingdom**, Family Information Services (FIS) are available in many districts and cities. The services act as a central information point, which support parents and carers who need child care and information about education. Each FIS has close links with child care provisions, preschools, schools, youth clubs and libraries and can inform parents about any of these services so that parents can choose which service best suits their needs.

- The Citizens Information website of **Ireland** provides information about all public services in the country, including information on child care and early education. The website gives a list of tips on choosing a day care centre or preschool and a list of questions parents should keep in mind when choosing a service. The website also gives information about the different care and preschool services available, which standards they should meet, and what the programme teaches children so that parents are better able to make a good decision about which school or centre they want their children to attend.

## Challenge 3: Time constraints

Involving parents who work or study full-time, work non-standard hours or those getting back into employment poses a great challenge. The magnitude of the challenge is increasing as family structures, circumstances and lifestyles are changing.

### Changing the operational hours

- **Norway** adapted the opening hours and provision of ECEC services to changing parental needs during the 1990s. This resulted in longer and more flexible opening hours of kindergartens. Additionally, meetings with parents can be planned in the evenings for parents who work and/or study.

- In **Korea**, late-night child care services have been operating in major cities since March 2010 to meet parental needs, especially for dual-earning families. After attending full-day kindergartens, which finish at 19:00, children can attend the late-night service to receive care until 22:00. At present, a total of 173 facilities – one in each *gu* (district) – are operating as part of a pilot programme. The late-night child care kindergartens are required to have 15 to 20 children per group, and the central government financially supports these services (USD 250 per class each month). After implementing the late-night child care service, the level of parental satisfaction increased from 58% in 2009 to 97% in 2010. In addition, there are all-day care classrooms available that operate from 6:30 to 22:00, which have been operating on a trial basis since March 2011 in a total of 1 000 institutions across the country. The central government has operated the classrooms in diverse service forms, tailored to local needs. For example, there are classrooms operating in both kindergartens and primary schools in a certain region where there are large parental demands for providing care service through partnership between kindergartens and primary schools. These all-day care classrooms receive financial support from the central government (USD 50 000). The services are also expected to create job opportunities for women who left their job in the past due to family duties and who hold a teaching licence: they are given priority in the recruitment process of ECEC practitioners.

*Guiding ECEC centres in setting more flexible times for contacts and communication*

- ECEC staff in **Japan** attempt to speak briefly to parents every day when they drop off or pick up their child since many parents do not have time for long meetings. They speak about what the child will do, or has done, and how the child is developing in general. It is an important information source for parents but also for staff since they have the chance to ask parents a few questions about their child. Additionally, informative meetings with ECEC staff are organised in the evenings for parents who cannot attend parent-teacher meetings during daytime.

- Pre-primary education schools (preschools) in **Spain** are stimulated to open early in the morning and/or later afternoon, during general school holidays, and to offer additional services, such as meals, transport and extra-curricular activities. This is to suit parental needs regarding extension of ECEC provisions. Such additional services and opening hours increase the chance that staff can communicate with parents.

- ECEC centres in **Thuringia (Germany)** are open for at least ten hours per day, which is a full day of day care and early education. Centres are allowed and encouraged by law to be open longer than these ten hours per day, and some also open during weekends and holidays. This gives parents greater flexibility in organising their professional and work lives.

- Several countries, including **Flanders (Belgium)**, the **Netherlands** and **Finland**, organise informational meetings for parents conducted by ECEC staff or parent umbrella organisations and debates about ECEC services at times more convenient for working parents. Meetings and debates are organised in the (late) evening to stimulate their engagement, since they are unable to participate in activities during regular work hours.

## Challenge 4: Increasing inequity

Growing inequity in economic, social and cultural backgrounds of children in ECEC centres is becoming a challenge in many OECD countries. It is often reported that deprived families, despite the fact that their children need high-quality ECEC the most, often have lower interest, lack of knowledge and lack of time to be engaged in ECEC.

Increasing diversity can also be a challenge for getting parents engaged in ECEC services. Often reported barriers include different cultural needs, views or languages.

Uneven parental engagement with different socio-economic backgrounds can result in greater inequity. It is therefore particularly important that real efforts are made to reach out to the most deprived families. Collaboration with parents is especially important in low income, minority families where differences in socio-economic background and cultural values about child rearing and education are likely to affect the home learning environment.

*Prioritising participation of children with an immigrant or low-educational background*

- **Flanders** (**Belgium**) gives priority access to child care to children of single parents and/or parents with a low income (below a certain threshold) and who are unable to care for their children during the day due to their work or study or for whom child care is an important factor facilitating their socio-economic integration and participation. Flanders also gives priority access to children for whom it is believed to be important that they receive out-of-home guidance and care, *e.g.*, children with a risk of learning arrears. This regulation enables parents to learn the Flemish language, to study or work or look for a job, which increases their socio-economic development.

- **Slovenia** gives preference to children from economically disadvantaged families when admitting children to a preschool institution. To be eligible for this, parents and welfare centres have to provide proof of low income.

*Providing free ECEC services to families in need*

- **Norway** offers free part-time kindergarten to children in areas with a high proportion of migrant families. The measure is universal within these areas to avoid stigma. Participation in kindergarten stimulates the child's social and language development and helps prevent children-at-risk from falling behind their peers. Kindergartens also hope that this stimulates parents' interest in ECEC.

- Several child care provisions in the **French Community** of **Belgium** offer voluntarily free day care or care at a highly reduced cost for families with low incomes (EUR 2.19 per day for the lowest income families). Centres with a large proportion of children from a low-income background are further subsidised by the government to cover all their costs.

*Developing targeted interventions*

- **Australia** has implemented the Home Interaction Program for Parents and Youngsters in 50 disadvantaged communities nationally and supports around 3 000 families free of cost for parents. It is a two-year home-based parenting and early childhood enrichment programme that empowers parents and carers to be their child's first teacher. The programme builds the confidence and skills of parents and carers to create a positive learning environment to prepare their child for school. Home tutors are available to help disadvantaged families implement the programme at home, and role-play activities are organised to demonstrate to parents how they should implement the programme activities.

- In 1994, five Head Start programmes in the **United States** developed model substance abuse prevention projects with a goal to strengthen families and neighbourhoods of economically disadvantaged preschool children. The initiative, named Free to Grow, targeted families and neighbourhoods of Head Start children in an effort to protect them from substance abuse and its associated problems. It included a strong focus on community-based strategies in the form of coalitions, implementation of "safe space" task forces that ensured safe and substance abuse-free spaces for young children and training in substance abuse prevention. Different community services were included in the implementation, *e.g.*, local police forces, youth organisations, churches and numerous grassroots organisations. Outcomes included increased parental involvement in ECEC, cleaner and safer schools and neighbourhoods, improved relationships among residents and between ECEC practitioners, parents and community members, and stronger community norms against drug and alcohol use.

- The **French Community** of **Belgium** uses the "baby bus" in areas where there is a shortage of child care provisions. The bus is run by two nursery professionals and contains age-appropriate pedagogical materials and care materials for young children. These children are brought to temporary child care facilities in, for example, sport halls, and costs are EUR 7 per day per child. A budget of EUR 1.5 million has been dedicated by the region of Wallonia, the province and local partners for the extension of this network with 10 extra baby buses by 2015. Additionally, for migrant children, "bridging classes" have been created. Upon arrival in the French Community, children can attend these classes for up to six months to learn the French language and get used to the Belgian educational system before attending regular ECEC or education services.

- **British Columbia** (**Canada**) offers the Parent-Child Mother Goose programmes, which are available across the province to families with infants and toddlers. The programme provides a secure environment in which interactive singing and storytelling between parent and child strengthens the family bond, while simultaneously supporting language and pre-literacy development. The programme also focuses on enhancing confidence and self-esteem and developing social skills in children.

- The Manukau Family Literacy Programme (MFLP) in **New Zealand** offers learning opportunities to parents of children in ECEC. The MFLP is targeted at low-decile communities. Enrolment is sought from family members in the child's household who have low or no educational qualifications. The programme is delivered over the regular early childhood centre week using an integrated approach consisting of 20 hours per week for the parent. It has four components: 1) an adult education component designed to extend basic education skills of participants and help them acquire successful interpersonal skills; 2) children's education to promote growth and development of young children and engage parents in their child's learning; 3) exercising Parent and Child Together Time involving shared learning experiences between child and parent; and 4) parent learning of parenting skills and other family and parenting issues. Currently, 80 families are taking part in this programme.

- **England** (**United Kingdom**) has contracted the National Academy of Parenting Research on a five year contract until March 2012 to conduct a programme of parenting and family research, examining and evaluating innovative parenting interventions that work with vulnerable families. Part of this includes a project on the Commissioning Toolkit, which describes many of the parenting programmes offered in England and highlights the programmes which are most effective.

## Providing home visits

- For children with learning arrears, the **Netherlands** and **Slovak Republic** have implemented home-based early childhood education programmes, which require great parental involvement and include regular home visits by early education professionals. The programmes also focus on improving the home learning environment.

- The Parent-Child Home Programme in the **United States** is an early childhood literacy, parenting and school readiness programme. The programme uses trained professionals to work with families with a low-educational background and aims to strengthen families and child development through home visits. Home Visitors help parents realise their role as their children's first and most important teacher, generating enthusiasm for learning and verbal interaction through the use of engaging books and stimulating toys during regular visits of half-an-hour, twice per week. Families participate in the two-year programme when their children are two and three years old, completing the programme as they turn four and transition into pre-kindergarten or Head Start. A child can, however, enter the programme as young as 16 months, and some sites serve families with children up through four years of age if there are no other preschool services available in the community.

- In **Baden-Württemberg** and **Berlin** (**Germany**) there exist so-called "family visitors" or "welcome visitors". These people either work on a full-time or voluntary basis and are well trained and informed about all local social services, including ECEC services, available for families and children. The family or welcome visitors visit families at home and inform them about the services available in their neighbourhood. When needed, they provide information in a non-German language. Their goal is to motivate parents to use these services, such as child care, for the benefit of the family and stimulate them to become highly interested and aware of the development of their child.

- **Prince Edward Island** (**Canada**) provides a home-visiting programme called Best Start to support families and assist high-risk parents with information on parenting, child growth and child development.

- For children in low-income families, **Korea** has implemented home visit programmes. These programmes aim at educating and informing parents about child development, parenting, community and social services. The home visit is carried out by a welfare co-ordinator and a kindergarten teacher. It helps practitioners increase their awareness and knowledge about the family environment of children in their class and improves parental knowledge about their children's development.

## Assisting parents to provide qualitative home learning environments

- In **Brazil**, ECEC centres organise workshops for disadvantaged mothers. The workshops consist of demonstrations of best practices that improve interactions with children and home learning through play. In each workshop, a maximum of eight mothers participate to maximise learning.

- In **New Zealand**, the Early Reading Together initiative has been implemented. It is a programme which helps parents of young children (babies to six-year-olds) to support their children's language and literacy development at home and is specifically designed to support children and parents from diverse language/literacy, cultural, educational and socio-economic backgrounds. It is implemented on a voluntary basis by junior school teachers, early childhood educators and librarians, and includes three workshops of one hour and fifteen minutes each, spread over three weeks. Therefore, the time commitment is low. Its results include increased competence of parents on assisting their children at home with reading.

- In **Australia**, the national project Engaging Families in the Early Childhood Development Story has developed a set of key messages for parents about the importance of early learning and development, based on neuroscience research. The project hopes to establish a parenting tool kit, which will assist in the delivery of parenting programmes.

### *Providing training for parents*

- **Norway** combines Norwegian language training for immigrant parents with open access to kindergartens. Parents can take up language training while their children are being taken care of in kindergartens. The objective is to stimulate immigrant parents to learn the language and stimulate participation of immigrant children in ECEC. When immigrant parents learn the native language, there is also a chance that their involvement and interest in the early education of their children increases.

- ECEC centres in **Flanders** (**Belgium**) give Dutch language courses to parents of immigrant children in nursery education. Community-based centres also provide official training to immigrant and low-educated parents on ECEC. The training results in an official qualification and stimulates their labour market participation.

- In **Baden-Württemberg** (**Germany**), the programme *STÄRKE* (POWER) has been implemented in 2008. It aims at empowering parents to care properly for their children by giving them professional advice and ideas to organise family life. All families received a voucher/gift certificate valuing EUR 40 to pay for selected training courses for parents during the first year of their child's life. Families that experience difficulties in child care, such as single, very young or immigrant parents, can receive another kind of support through this programme: the initiative provides training to parents at home and advice on how parents can deal with their specific situation. The aim is to prevent disregard of the children's interests in terms of care and education.

- In **Bayern** and **North-Rhine Westphalia** (**Germany**), training courses are offered to parents of young children (ages zero to three). The aim of this training is to strengthen the knowledge of parents regarding child rearing and deepen the relationships between parents and their children. During the course, it is also explained how children develop and how parents can stimulate the development of their babies and infants.

- In **Rheinland-Pfalz** (**Germany**), the parenting skills programme "In the beginning, it matters! – A course for young parents" aims to strengthen parental skills regarding partnership, parenting and financial management. The programme targets all young families and parents and, particularly, low-income families. The programme received funding for a minimum of five years and is a popular programme among families in Rheinland-Pfalz with many families wishing to participate.

- In **Mexico**, the Ministry of Education requested that the Centre of Investigations and Top Studies in Social Anthropology (*CIESAS*) evaluate an ECEC programme that offers initial education to parents and childminders in rural and indigenous areas. This ECEC programme requires families and childminders to attend a meeting to reflect on and improve their nurturing practices. The results of the evaluation show that parents who participated in the programme have improved their nurturing skills compared to the control group. The main difference is improvement in autonomy, communication and social development. Parents indicated that initial education, as well as self-diagnosis and its strategies, are beneficial to develop their nurturing skills.

## Providing support in different languages

- The **Netherlands**, **Norway** and **Sweden** have developed informational material in multiple languages about how to stimulate early development in the home environment, available ECEC services, the importance of ECEC, and how parents can be involved in the education of their young children. For example, Norway has developed a booklet focusing on resources in language stimulation for minority speaking children. The booklets can be used by professionals with parents or handed out to parents for individual use.

- Language translation services are available for families in **British Columbia** (**Canada**) seeking to apply for ECEC services or child care subsidies.

- Regional governments in **Spain** provide translation and interpretation services to immigrant families when having meetings in schools.

- **Korea** published a guidebook for parents about early childhood education, *What every mother and father should know*, and has translated it into eight different languages. The guidebook intends to raise awareness of the importance of early childhood education and current relevant policies and informs parents of their role in promoting child development and learning (*e.g.*, brain development, literacy, creativity, peer relationships, artistic appreciations, and health and nutrition) and how to select and engage in a kindergarten.

- In many *Länder* in **Germany**, all new parents receive several information sheets in different languages about how to educate and raise young children, and how to stimulate their development. They also receive information in different languages about the associations or boards they can be involved in as parents, such as school boards of preschools.

## ENGAGING COMMUNITIES IN ECEC

### Challenge 1: Lack of awareness and motivation

Motivating the community to engage in ECEC and encouraging centres to involve the community have not been major policy objectives in many OECD countries. The notion of "community" varies across countries and across centres within a country: it is thought of as a neighbourhood where children grow up as well as wider community partners, including public services for young children, education services, libraries and museums, NGOs, private foundations and faith organisations.

There is a lack of awareness among staff, centre managers and parents about the potential resources within communities. There is also lack of knowledge among community organisations about how they can work with ECEC centres.

*Making community engagement a policy priority, an obligation or right*

- **Finland** made it a legal obligation for municipalities to set up a plan for arranging and developing child welfare services (Child Welfare Act 2007/147). The plan should include arrangements for co-operation between the different public authorities and the organisations and institutions that provide services for young children. Additionally, Finland's *Core Curriculum for Pre-primary Education* (2010) states that every effort must be made to involve as many people as possible in implementing education to ensure commitment to and compliance with it.

- In **Norway**, the Kindergarten Act (sections 8, 21 and 22) defines the responsibility of the municipalities to co-operate with social and child welfare services, kindergartens, schools and special education assistance and share information among the various services. Chapter 5 of the Framework Plan for the Content and Tasks of Kindergartens describes the co-operation with other institutions and services in more detail. Additionally, the Ministry of Education stressed the importance of community involvement in early education in the draft of White Paper No. 28 (2007-08) on language learning and development.

- In **Spain**, the participation of communities in schools and preschools is regulated by the Spanish Constitution of 1978 (Article 27.7). The Education Act 8 of 1985 also stipulates the right of communities to be involved in decision-making bodies. Additionally, the Act on Education of 2006 urges preschools and schools to promote participation of communities and staff in ECEC and education. The core curriculum for the second cycle of ECEC (pre-primary education for three-to-six-year-olds) also highlights the importance of community engagement.

- In **Turkey**, Law No. 22 on Primary Education, which includes preschool programmes, states that preschools and primary schools "should co-operate with the community". The country's National Action Plan for Education also emphasises the importance of community engagement.

- The Ministry of Education in **British Columbia** (**Canada**) emphasises the importance of family and community connections in its Kindergarten Guidelines in section 5 on "Kindergarten, Family, and Community".

- In **Manitoba** (**Canada**), under section 22 of the Healthy Child Manitoba Act, Parent Child Coalitions, have been enshrined in legislation. Parent Child Coalitions bring together parents, early childhood educators, educators, health care professionals and other community organisations to plan and work collaboratively to support the healthy development of children ages zero to six. Parent Child Coalitions support existing community programmes for families with young children and develop new initiatives that reflect each community's diversity and strengths. There are currently 26 funded parent child coalitions province-wide.

- **Australia** included community engagement in their *National Quality Standard Framework*, obliging ECEC services to "form collaborative partnerships with parents and communities".

- **Prince Edward Island** (**Canada**) Children's Secretariat is comprised of government and community members working together on behalf of children and families. Under the leadership of the provincial government, it is stated that the community should be a key stakeholder in the work and function of the Secretariat.

- **Korea** included community engagement as one of the indicators in the national evaluation of kindergarten and child care centre accreditation. This indicator focuses on how closely these institutions co-operate with community and how to exchange and utilise human and material resources of the community. Community involvement is also emphasised in pre- and in-service ECEC teacher training.

- **Ireland** included community involvement as one of its 16 standards in *Síolta*, the National Quality Framework for Early Childhood Education, stating that "promoting community involvement requires the establishment of networks and connections evidenced by policies, procedures and actions which extend and support all adults' and children's engagement with the wider community *i.e.*, it requires a proactive partnership approach evidenced by a range of clearly stated, accessible and implemented processes, policies and procedures".

- **Japan** included community engagement in its *Course of Study for Kindergartens*. The curriculum states that kindergartens should give consideration to "deepening the understanding of community members of the importance of early childhood education by creating opportunities for information exchange with the community".

### *Providing public financial resources to engaged communities*

- **Japan** provides financial remunerations to stimulate the participation of members in the education management council of community schools. The council consists of parents and other community members.

- **Australia** gives financial incentives to community members who wish to work as tutors in the Home Intervention Program for Parents and Youngsters: tutors receive remuneration to encourage their interest in the work.

- In the **United States**, community members participating in substance abuse prevention projects were paid a monthly remuneration for their involvement. Five Head Start programmes developed model substance abuse prevention projects in 1994. The goal was to strengthen families and neighbourhoods of economically disadvantaged preschool children, and the initiative was called Free to Grow. Families and neighbourhoods of Head Start children were targeted in an effort to protect them from substance abuse and its associated problems. Due to the large public funding available for these projects, a monthly remuneration (USD 100) could be paid to parents and community members who were the main implementers of the programme.

- In 2006-08, the government of **British Columbia** (**Canada**) provided funding to community members (local residents) to create official child care spaces in their own homes. This increased the number of child care spaces in the province. The provincial government also provided funding to a community service organisation focusing on strengthening and supporting families. The funding was allocated to develop a post-secondary certification programme that was offered to individuals working in community programmes providing support to families.

- Municipalities in the **French Community of Belgium** can, on a voluntary basis, set up advisory committees regarding child care and receive subsidies from the French Community to hire a co-ordinator for the advisory committee to ensure that the committee is well-structured and co-ordinated. Additionally, the 2006 decree *Culture-école* stimulates preschools and schools to co-operate with cultural institutions to broaden children's cultural experiences and knowledge. To enhance these co-operations, funding from the French Community is available.

*Engaging the community in an advisory or management body for ECEC policies and services*

- **Flanders** (**Belgium**) has set up the Local Consultative Forums for child care and out-of-school care, which include ECEC professionals, ECEC managers, parents, local administration servants, community members, integration centres, immigrant representative organisations and other stakeholders. Within the Forums, stakeholders can share their opinions, ideas and concerns regarding ECEC. The Forums function as a municipal advisory body and give advice on child care or nursery education to the local administration/authority. There are currently 301 Forums for nursery education.

- In **Japan**, a system of school management councils (community schools) was introduced in 2004. Parents and local residents have the opportunity to participate in the management of the preschools and are assigned certain tasks and responsibilities regarding the management of the centres. The councils discuss the curriculum and methods of co-operating with the community to ensure that the views of the parents and local residents are reflected in the curriculum and engagement initiatives.

- **Portugal** has a strategic governing body named *Conselho Geral* (General Council). The council is represented by early education teaching staff, parents, local authorities and the local community. This governing body approves, by voting procedures, the internal school rules and regulations and strategic and planning decisions. ECEC staff, parents and community members choose which individuals or community organisations will be members of the council. With regard to community organisations, this can be health centres, foundations, conservatories, enterprises, etc.

- In **British Columbia (Canada)**, a member of the business community can become a member of the Provincial Child Care Council, which is a statutory body that provides advice and recommendations to the Minister of Children and Family Development on issues related to child care. This engages the business community on child care issues and provides an avenue to explore closer connections between business and child care services.

- In **Korea**, a representative of the community is obliged to participate in the Early Childhood Education Policy Committee or Child Care Policy Committee in co-operation with local governments.

## Engaging communities as providers of ECEC

- In **Norway**, there is a large variety in ownership of kindergartens. NGOs, churches, parents, business communities, private owners and companies can open and run kindergartens as long as the kindergarten meets legal requirements and has been approved by the local authorities. In a period when kindergarten places were lacking, the business community was engaged in both running and providing ECEC services as well as co-operation with ECEC services. The motivation for businesses to engage in ECEC has been to ensure that their employees have care and education places for their children and to stimulate continuous parental employment.

- In **Turkey**, private businesses and civil society organisations can run ECEC services, as well as co-operate on the organisation of ECEC activities, such as field trips or giving young children "classes" on their field of expertise, *e.g.*, nature or healthy living.

## Engaging communities as volunteers to the centre

- **Japan** offers a "day in the life of a nursery teacher" experience to community members. Local residents can voluntarily do an "internship" for one day in an ECEC centre and work as a nursery teacher to better understand the profession. This promotes trust between the nursery centre and the community.

- **Mexico** offers community members the possibility to volunteer in the ECEC centre. A popular activity is parents giving a "class" on what their profession is about, what kind of work they do and demonstrating the work to the young children – making it an interactive event.

- Most schools in **British Columbia (Canada)** welcome community volunteers to take part in kindergarten and school activities. Typically, volunteers are involved in reading with or to children, doing art and sport activities and offering other support to the kindergarten staff. Members of the aboriginal community often provide children with cultural experiences and information about their culture to enhance mutual respect and understanding.

### *Encouraging private foundations to support the ECEC centres*

– The *Haus der kleinen Forscher* (Little Scientist's House) association in **Germany** promotes nationwide early childhood education in the areas of the natural sciences and technology. Its goal is to promote interest in natural phenomena among three-to-six-year-olds. The foundation develops workshops and teaching materials for educators, hosts annual promotion days and provides comprehensive background information and experiments on the internet. To offer workshops throughout Germany, the foundation established local networks.

– In **Japan**, Sony established the Sony Foundation for Education. Its Early Development Activity Centre conducts an extensive programme of activities in its quest to make science widely known among the public, to foster well-balanced personality development in young individuals and to educate the general public about the importance of building a healthy relationship between parents and children. The achievements of the various programmes and the lessons learned about child rearing are shared in various ways with parents, the community and child care workers. The Foundation gives awards to ECEC centres to stimulate excellent practices and support teachers by providing materials, such as booklets and posting information, experiences and lessons learned on the internet. The Foundation also actively promotes science in early education through its Science Education Programme.

### *Offering qualifications and employment opportunities for local communities*

– To stimulate local development of very low-educated people, community child care centres in **Flanders** (**Belgium**) provide training and employment opportunities for these people within the centre. The training results in an official qualification and can be retrieved while being employed at the care centre.

### *Embedding community engagement in a wider evaluation process*

– **Japan** introduced school evaluation in 2007. Evaluation councils are made up of persons related to the kindergarten, such as parents and local residents. They evaluate the results of the self-evaluation assessments as implemented by the kindergarten staff and decide whether they agree with the self-evaluation exercises or not. This is done through observing the kindergarten's daily activities and analysing the information exchanged with parents and the community.

– In **Australia**, as part of assessment and rating against the National Quality Standards, long day care, family day care, preschool and out-of-school-hours care services will be assessed from 2012 onwards on how well they maintain collaborative partnerships with families and communities.

– In **Norway**, the early development project *Språkløftet* (Language Promotion), which stimulates participation in the ECEC of children in need of language stimulation through co-operation with health services, will be subject to an evaluation in 2012.

## Challenge 2: Communication and outreach

Many countries experience challenges in informing the community about engagement possibilities. There is insufficient awareness and knowledge among community members and organisations about the relevance of co-operating with ECEC, in what ways they can be involved or co-operate, or where they can find information on engagement possibilities. A lack of established communication channels between the national government, local governments, ECEC staff and the community is one of the key factors explaining the dissemination challenges.

### Training staff on how to engage communities

- The **Netherlands** is upgrading the training level of staff in child care to a minimum qualification level instead of having unqualified staff working next to qualified staff. The training includes an aspect on community engagement: how to communicate and co-operate with other social and health services on learning and development arrears.

- **Finland**, **Korea** and **Portugal** developed training opportunities dedicated to how staff can improve communication and co-operation with community services. In these countries, this is included in the initial education of ECEC workers.

### Using written forms of dissemination

- In **Australia**, the Office on Early Childhood Education and Child Care provides comprehensive information for parents about ECEC on websites. The office is part of the Department of Education, Employment and Workplace Relations and is responsible for delivering the government's key commitments to ECEC, guiding major policy reforms at a national level and informing the public about this on-line.

### Having one central information system or contact point

- In **Korea**, the Ministry of Health and Welfare established the *I-Sarang* (Child-Loving) *Child Care Portal* in 2008 (formerly *e-Childcare system*) to ensure that parents and communities have access to practical information on individual child care centres, such as the staff-child ratio, costs, meals and environments. Additionally, the *Early Childhood Education Comprehensive Information System* (*e-Kindergarten System*) was created in 2010 to provide parents and communities with information on child rearing and early childhood education in kindergarten.

- The government of **Australia** set up a free telephone hotline that provides information on ECEC to callers. The hotline was developed to provide on-demand information to parents, families and community members about ECEC services in the country and can also be used to file complaints about ECEC services or raise concerns.

*Organising meetings*

- ECEC centres in the **Netherlands** and **Berlin** (**Germany**) organise at least one open visiting day per year. On this day, ECEC centres open their doors to parents, families, community members and others who have an interest in the ECEC centre. Information about the centre is provided as well as an explanation of what activities the centre undertakes and how staff contributes to early development.

## Challenge 3: Dysfunctional communities

Communities can play a role of a social network to support parents to reduce stress, as well as to provide resources for children, adding value to the ECEC centres. However, when communities are dysfunctional or lacking social cohesion, (informal) social control and collective efficacy, extra efforts are required to reach out to families at risk.

*Reinforcing co-operation between ECEC and other social services*

- In **Norway**, co-operation with health services was established in the project *Språkløftet* (Language Promotion) in finding and guiding children with a need for language stimulation to participate in ECEC. In Groruddalen (in Oslo), the project offers 20 hours per week of free time in kindergarten for all children ages four and five. Co-operation between the services has meant an increase in participation for all children, but especially for minority language children.

- Immigrant Settlement and Service Agencies in **British Columbia** (**Canada**) provide a variety of services for recent immigrants, including providing information about ECEC-related services to stimulate participation.

- In **Germany**, in many municipalities, parent-child centres have been established that co-operate with different social services to stimulate early child development and detect early learning arrears. The services co-operate on a regular basis with other institutions related to family life, (early) education and family or parent counselling. The centres also provide health information to families with (young) children and co-operate with health services on this.

- In co-operation with local hospitals and public health centres, **Korean** children enrolled in kindergartens and child care centres receive a free medical examination annually or when necessary. ECEC institutions having disadvantaged children with an immigrant or low-income background collaborate with Multicultural Family Support Centres, Healthy Families Support Centres and Dream Start Centres so that they can provide comprehensive and integrated support services to these children and families regarding health, nutrition, care and education.

*Developing community child care centres in target areas*

- **Flanders** (**Belgium**) has developed community care centres in low socio-economic areas. These operate differently than regular care centres since they specifically promote use of child care by vulnerable families. The key to this special approach is that it is embedded in a neighbourhood, and the target group is very much involved. The centres recruit staff directly from the community; and staff work directly with children and offer them equal opportunities in the organisation. The workforce is, therefore, a representation of the neighbourhood, which encourages community engagement. The goal is to stimulate the development of children within the centre, as well as community members, through training.

### Targeting low socio-economic neighbourhoods

- In 1994, five Head Start programmes in the **United States** developed model substance abuse prevention projects, named Free to Grow, with a goal to strengthen families and neighbourhoods of economically disadvantaged preschool children. The projects targeted families and neighbourhoods of Head Start children in an effort to protect them from substance abuse and its associated problems. It included a strong focus on community-based strategies in the form of coalitions, implementation of "safe space" task forces that ensured safe and substance abuse-free spaces for young children, and training in substance abuse prevention. Different community services were included in the implementation, *e.g.*, local police forces, youth organisations, churches and numerous grassroots organisations. Outcomes included increased community involvement in ECEC, cleaner and safer schools and neighbourhoods, improved relationships among residents and between ECEC practitioners, parents and community members, and stronger community norms against drug and alcohol use.

- In **Bavaria (Germany)**, child protection and development services co-operate together in a network (*Koordinierende Kinderschutzstellen [KoKi]*). *KoKi*'s are part of the Youth Welfare Offices (with subsidies from the Ministry for Youth) and target socio-economic disadvantaged families and families experiencing large amounts of stress. These families are given specialised support from actors within the network, including professional child, youth and health services. The work from the network prevents families from experiencing unfavourable family situations, decreases stress among family members, improves parenting skills and promotes early child development and learning.

- In **Baden-Württemberg (Germany)**, about 50 mothers' centres and family centres, organised as Mothers' Forum Baden-Wüttermberg and networking within, contribute to integrating families in their local community. This influence can improve the general situation of families. The activities of the mothers' centres and family centres focus on the social learning of children and aim at contacts with and exchanges of life experiences among parents. Mothers, the main target group of the activities, can deepen and enlarge their social competences in mothers' centres. Single parents get the opportunity to develop sustainable perspectives for their future. Developments leading to a crisis in the family can be discovered, attenuated and averted. Many child care institutions have gone through a process of development to family centres. By this, they achieve contact with parents and empower their capacities to care for their children.

## Challenge 4: Co-operation with other services and other levels of education

Many countries experience challenges in promoting co-operation across different services for children although such co-operation is critically important for holistic and continuous child development. This is often due to the fact that these services are managed and administered by different authorities.

This is also due to ECEC staff and managers having insufficient knowledge about what kinds of other services have been offered to or made available for the children and families who use their centres.

*Integrating child care and early education at the municipality level for more coherent services*

- In **Sano City**, **Tochigi** (**Japan**), the administration for child care and early education has been integrated at the municipality, where private kindergartens are encouraged to become integrated child centres (*Kodomo-en*). The *Komodo-en* serve as contact points for community members regarding family life and child up-bringing in the city. It is often reported that they have been able to ensure better child development and stimulate community development. At the moment, not all private kindergartens have been turned into integrated child centres, although Sano City is currently working on turning several private kindergartens into *Komodo-en*. To achieve this, staff are being trained to be able to work in integrated child centres.

*Encouraging co-operation between ECEC and primary school for smooth transition*

- In **Slovenia**, preschools can be organised within the primary school. The preschool and primary school share a common headmaster, counselling service and other aspects, such as corridors and kitchens. Within such an integrated system, preschool and primary school children, have the opportunity to meet frequently and co-operate. Each educational institution has its own pedagogical staff responsible for the pedagogical work and contents of work in their field. Due to this integrated system, some approaches, ways and methods of work used by preschool teachers become more frequently used in the first grade of compulsory schooling. This eases the transition from preschool to primary school. When ECEC provisions and primary schools in Slovenia are divided, primary school children often visit preschool children and prepare various activities for them, for example, puppet shows or dancing. They also jointly organise celebrations and share common rooms and areas (playground). These initiatives are established to facilitate the transition from preschool to primary school.

- In **British Columbia** (**Canada**), the number of funded licensed child care spaces on primary school grounds has grown rapidly. In 2009/10, approximately 800 facilities with 27 000 child care spaces were located on school grounds. This co-operation between school boards and child care provisions decreases the transitions children have between school and child care.

- In **Germany**, to smooth the transition for children from preschool to primary school, the two different provisions co-operate frequently. Both institutions share their curriculum activities and pedagogical methods and try to ensure that they match on most relevant subjects and topics. Besides this, the development of children is discussed across services, and parents are involved by staff members from both preschool and primary school about the transition and what will change for the child. This to ensure continuity in the child's learning and development process and to prepare schools for children and children for school.

## Bridging between ECEC centres and different community services

- In **Norway**, the project *BOKTRAS* is based on co-operation between public libraries and kindergartens, with the aim of introducing young children to literature. It is a three-year project, which consists of setting up branch libraries in kindergartens. The libraries involved reach out to more families than those who already know about and make use of library services. In this way, family access to children's books is no longer restricted by pressures of time, distance to the nearest library or opening hours. The libraries use the kindergarten as an arena for the active promotion of literature, thereby helping to develop children's language and social skills.

- The **China** Development Research Foundation (CDRF) implemented early child development projects focusing on health and early education in Early Education Centres. As part of their contributions to the health development of young children, free nutritional supplements and health checks were provided to pregnant women. Besides this, township hospital medical staff provide nutritional training classes to pregnant women and mothers of children under two years on nutrition and complementary feeding. They also distribute sachets (dietary supplements) for infants over six-months-old (up until the age of 24 months).

- In the **Netherlands**, educational and welfare services are more regularly being integrated into broad-based schools. There are many different types of broad-based schools, but all are based on the idea of service integration. Educational facilities, recreational facilities, child care services, child health services, etc., are integrated in an area-based network or even in one multifunctional building.

- In **Australia**, ECEC centres invite community services, such as health services, to attend parent group meetings to inform participants about their services. This strengthens the knowledge of the parents, as well as the ECEC staff, about the community services and stimulates co-operation between education providers and social services.

- **Prince Edward Island**'s (**Canada**) Department of Education and Early Childhood Development has a division for Early Childhood Development that co-operates with other school divisions, government departments, and services and the community to collaborate in areas of mutual involvement and mandate regarding early development.

- Kindergartens in **British Columbia** (**Canada**) increasingly co-operate with health services on hearing and vision screening, safety planning for children with health disorders, and child-specific training or nursing support for children who need medical intervention in kindergarten. Speech therapy, physical therapy and occupational therapy are also provided for children with special needs who may require interventions in order to participate in kindergarten. When children have been removed from their parents' care, ECEC centres also co-operate with child welfare services.

–   In April 2011, **Manitoba (Canada)** established the Early Childhood Education Unit in Manitoba Education to strengthen the connection between early learning and care and the provincial kindergarten to grade 12 education system. The work of the unit involves enhanced cross-sectoral collaboration through partnerships with school divisions, other government departments (provincial, federal), the early learning and child care sectors, educational stakeholder groups and parents to promote developmentally appropriate programming and services that help to prepare children for successful school entry and optimal learning in the early years. Besides this, some child care facilities are co-located with other community and social welfare services. These centres allow community members to gain easier access to services and can better address the needs of the community.

–   In **Slovenia**, the ongoing project The Healthy Preschool, set up by the Regional Institutes of Public Health, has been implemented in a large number of preschools. The project includes different activities to encourage children, parents and professional staff to make healthy everyday choices in all areas which affect people's health, *e.g.*, transport (walking) and food (fruit). To ascertain that all children in Slovenia have healthy lives, preschools employ health and hygiene experts. They are responsible for assembling quality, nutritious menus and advising and monitoring the hygiene and safety of the centre. Special menus are provided to children who, due to various health problems, need a special diet. Before enrolling their children into preschool, parents are obliged to bring a certificate given by the child's paediatrician regarding the child's vaccinations and health condition as well as information on the child's potential health problems. This to ensure that staff and management are well informed about the health of all children.

–   **Germany** supports the establishment of 600 local initiatives aiming at enhancing ECEC. Support includes facilitation, moderation, capacity building and communication in public. In these networks, ECEC centres and other local actors join a process of analysis and local agenda setting. Networks include the local authorities and the local independent sector so as to ensure the development of locally adaptable concepts. The programme works nationwide; local initiatives are given the opportunity to meet at regional and national levels and to share their experiences. The overarching aims of the programme are 1) enhancing the quality and quantity of ECEC; 2) stimulating public debate and involving decision makers at local and national levels; and 3) creating synergies between the different federal, state and local initiatives in the field of ECEC. This programme, called *Anschwung* (Push), is a joint initiative of the federal government, Ministry of Family, Senior Citizens, Women and Youth, and the German Children and Youth Foundation.

–   Preschools in **Spain** often seek co-operation with local community services and corporations in financing extra-curricular activities and to help or support them in setting up teaching and learning activities. Besides this, local health services or other community services can come to preschools and schools to teach children about hygiene, health, etc.

*Developing a network to promote early child development and well-being*

- The European Network Cities for Children was initiated by the **City of Stuttgart** (**Germany**) with the support of the Robert Bosch Stiftung in 2007. The Network offers European cities the possibility to exchange and develop progressive concepts across national borders on how to promote the well-being of children, young persons and parents in the urban environment. It has been created in the view of the demographic situation in Europe, which constitutes an enormous challenge for the long-term viability of European cities. In 2008, the City of Stuttgart, the Network Cities for Children, the Robert Bosch Stiftung, the Congress of Local and Regional Authorities of the Council of Europe, and the Council of European Municipalities and Regions initiated the European Award of Excellence "City for Children" for a city which excels in promoting the well-being of children and parents. The award is presented annually as an incentive for cities to exchange initiatives and best practices in the field of child and family friendliness.

- The government of **Prince Edward Island** (PEI) (**Canada**) affirmed its commitment to children and families through the establishment of the Children's Secretariat in 2000. The PEI Children's Secretariat is a group of community and government representatives working across sectors, communities and departments as a collective voice to improve outcomes for children to age eight. In essence, the Secretariat is a "network of networks" that links with other existing networks and coalitions who are working on behalf of young children and their families. The focus is on profiling healthy child development, promoting knowledge exchange and public education, inspiring action, and influencing policy. The PEI Children's Secretariat membership includes representatives from seven government departments and 12 community networks.

# ACTION AREA 4 – MANAGING RISKS: LEARNING FROM OTHER COUNTRIES' POLICY EXPERIENCES

This section summarises country experiences as lessons learned from:

- Improving family and community engagement

It aims to be a quick read about challenges and risks to consider when implementing policy initiatives.

## IMPROVING FAMILY AND COMMUNITY ENGAGEMENT

### Lesson 1: Overcome administrative boundaries and recognise that family and community engagement concerns both social policy and education policy

The **Flemish** and **French Communities** of **Belgium**, **British Columbia** (**Canada**), **Japan**, **Korea**, **Mexico**, the **Netherlands**, **Norway** and **Slovenia** recognise that fostering good relationships and facilitating open communication with other services (*e.g.* social or health services) is important. The main reason for this is that it increases early detection of learning arrears; but it also improves awareness of parents whose children are not participating in ECEC about possibilities for participation. Japan learnt that by working with relevant social and development agencies, child-rearing can be carried out by society as a whole; and nursery centres learnt from other services how to improve the learning environment of young children. Korea learnt through its *Dream Start* project for disadvantaged children and families that multi-sectoral collaboration is essential to providing comprehensive services, including health, nutrition, care and education. They found that sectors can contract people from other sectors to help integrate contents (*e.g.*, the education sector can contract a person from the medical sector to incorporate health-related information into family support programmes and vice versa).

**New Zealand** learnt that parental engagement can be integrated not only into ECEC policies but also into social policies for families, which was found to support development of a stable home environment and children's early development at the same time. Services in New Zealand either add parental development activities into a pre-existing early childhood education centre or blend early childhood education into a suite of services delivered by a social service agency. Either way, parents are largely involved in the activities and implementation of the programme. These initiatives are most often implemented in areas with a large number of disadvantaged families.

The Early Head Start programme in the **United States** integrates early education policies and social policies into their approach. It is clear that the integration of different policies and co-operation with social services better meets the needs of families, and families are more engaged and interested in the education of their children. Early Head Start helps families access necessary services either directly or through referrals to community resources. The services help families with emergency or crisis assistance, such as food, housing, clothing and transportation; nutrition education; mental health education; family literacy services; and prenatal and postpartum care and health education for pregnant women in Early Head Start programmes.

### Lesson 2: Clarify the purpose of family and community engagement, and make sure that governments, ECEC managers and staff know how to communicate with and engage families and communities

**Australia**, the **Flemish** and **French Communities** of **Belgium**, **Finland**, **Mexico**, the **Netherlands**, **Norway**, **Japan**, **Slovenia**, **Sweden** and **Turkey** find that systems of informing parents and community members of the possibilities for engagement should be in place at both the centre and policy levels. Countries have learnt that continuous, honest and open two-way communication with educators assists families to feel connected with their children's experience in education and care and helps them develop trust and confidence in the service. Regarding this, it was found useful to make information on different participation possibilities publicly available, for example, through the internet. Countries also pointed out that explaining the aims and goals of parental and community involvement to the public contributes to achieving widespread awareness of the goals of each type of involvement.

**British Columbia** (**Canada**), the **Netherlands**, **Norway**, **Portugal**, **Slovak Republic**, **Sweden** and **Turkey** agree that stimulation and encouragement to implement involvement activities from management level to practitioner level is crucial. When support is lacking at the management level, countries found that there is less family and community involvement in centres.

In **Japan**, kindergarten teachers and child care workers proactively talk to parents on a daily basis when they are picking up their children from the centre. This has been found to stimulate parental interest in their child's development as well as in the work of the centre. **Finland** and **Slovenia** stated that there needs to be a good understanding of parent-practitioner relationships where all stakeholders are considered equally important for a child's development. The objective of these relationships should be early child welfare, since this is the ultimate goal of the relationships. **Norway** also indicated that these engagement relationships should suit a multi-cultural society since families often have different cultural and linguistic backgrounds.

## Lesson 3: Diversify communication channels and methods according to different family backgrounds and needs (*e.g.*, language, time schedule and message delivery means)

**Norway** learnt that having parents with different backgrounds, including minority or low-educated parents, participate in Norway's parental advisory board for kindergartens promotes co-operation between kindergartens and the children's homes. The co-operation contributes to levelling social inequalities. To get parents engaged, linguistic and cultural diversity needs to be taken into account. The **Netherlands** points to the importance of providing clear and easy-to-read written guidance in multiple languages about the possibilities for involvement. This stimulates interest in involvement activities from lower socio-economic families as well as ethnic minority families. **Korea** strives to develop multiple ways to communicate with multicultural families, as children ages zero to five years made up almost 60% of under-18-year-olds in multicultural families in 2010. Various information materials are developed based on the findings from interviews and a translated questionnaire survey for multicultural families regarding their knowledge level of the daily routines and programmes of ECEC institutions, the information needed most in child-rearing, etc. Additionally, a parent guidebook has been translated into eight languages; helpers have been dispatched to support child-rearing at home; translation services and a counselling hotline were made available; etc.

**Australia** indicated that the Home Interaction Programme for Parents and Youngsters was very useful in engaging minority and socially disadvantaged families through home visits. Parents reported that the programme had a positive effect on their relationship with their child and their child's achievements at school, and it heightened their interest in early intervention programmes. Both the child and parent were found to have improved their sense of identity and self esteem. For some parents, their participation in the programme also opened opportunities to undertake further education and/or employment. The country learnt that continuous, open, two-way communication makes parents feel connected with the centre or programme and helps parents in developing trust and confidence in the service and educators.

**Ireland** finds that the proactive provision of information to parents and community members is highly important and stimulates engagement. Although internet is widely used in Ireland, eligible households received physical letters regarding the introduction of universal preschool provision. The distribution of these letters was seen to increase the number of families that registered their children for ECEC.

**Korea** learnt that meeting parental needs regarding opening hours of ECEC facilities greatly contributes to parental satisfaction levels of service provision. Since the availability of late-night care services in kindergartens, parental satisfaction level on full-day kindergartens increased from 58% in 2009 to 97% in 2010, while the effects of longer care services on child development are unclear. It is expected that higher parental satisfaction will lead to boosting female employment.

**Flanders (Belgium), British Columbia (Canada), Japan, Mexico**, the **Netherlands, Norway Portugal, Slovak Republic, Slovenia** and **Sweden** find it effective to offer opportunities for working parents to get involved outside of normal working hours (*i.e.*, not only during daytime when most people work). This increases parental involvement, especially in meetings about children's development.

## Lesson 4: Make a case for long-term outcomes, and show that early engagement begets later engagement in children's learning

In **British Columbia** (**Canada**), with respect to the StrongStart BC early learning programmes, evaluations have shown that parents highly value their involvement and see a significant effect on their children and an increase in their own sense of ability to support their children's development and learning. British Columbia learnt that parents who are engaged in the ECEC programme are more likely to remain engaged in their children's learning in later stages of schooling, which positively influences their success in school.

# ACTION AREA 5 – REFLECTING ON THE CURRENT STATE OF PLAY

This sheet has been prepared based on international trends and is designed to facilitate reflection on where your country stands regarding:

- Family and community engagement

The aim is to raise awareness about new issues and identify areas where changes could be made; the aim is not to give marks on practices. Please reflect on the current state of play by circling a number on the scale from 1-5.

## FAMILY AND COMMUNITY ENGAGEMENT

| Family engagement | Not at all | | | | Very well |
|---|---|---|---|---|---|
| 1. A comprehensive family and child policy is shared across different social and education services with an aim to engage families in ECEC services. | 1 | 2 | 3 | 4 | 5 |
| 2. Sufficient communication and co-operation is facilitated and ensured between the national government and local authorities on strategies for parental engagement. | 1 | 2 | 3 | 4 | 5 |
| 3. Policy makers and ECEC providers are aware of the importance of "Home Curriculum", *i.e.*, daily routines, stimulating discussions with children, reading at home, etc. | 1 | 2 | 3 | 4 | 5 |
| 4. There have been efforts to help parents ensure good home learning environments for effective child development, such as through staff training, curriculum and a public relations campaign. | 1 | 2 | 3 | 4 | 5 |

| | | | | | |
|---|---|---|---|---|---|
| 5. ECEC staff are trained to support parents, such as through guidelines and training. | 1 | 2 | 3 | 4 | 5 |
| 6. Parenting skills programmes or other support programmes are used by those who need them the most and are relevant to their needs. | 1 | 2 | 3 | 4 | 5 |
| 7. Parents are engaged not only as "users" of ECEC services but in a variety of ways (*e.g.*, ECEC providers, volunteers, decision makers on a board, partners). | 1 | 2 | 3 | 4 | 5 |
| 8. The degree of parental involvement is monitored by ECEC services for quality enhancement. | 1 | 2 | 3 | 4 | 5 |
| 9. Home visits are arranged for those who need such programmes. | 1 | 2 | 3 | 4 | 5 |
| **Community engagement** | Not at all | | | | Very well |
| 10. There is co-ordination among ECEC services and other services (*e.g.*, health services, social workers) designed for families. | 1 | 2 | 3 | 4 | 5 |
| 11. Sufficient communication and co-operation is being facilitated and ensured between local authorities and ECEC services about strategies for community involvement. | 1 | 2 | 3 | 4 | 5 |
| 12. Resources that exist in communities (*e.g.*, libraries, museums, NGOs, businesses) are being explored and utilised. | 1 | 2 | 3 | 4 | 5 |
| 13. Community leaders have been involved in the planning and development of curriculum and materials to reflect the community values in the local adaptation of the curriculum. | 1 | 2 | 3 | 4 | 5 |
| 14. Children and their parents living in dysfunctional communities are being helped in co-operation with other target measures for the communities. | 1 | 2 | 3 | 4 | 5 |

# NOTES

1   For the purpose of this paper, the term "parents" refers to all carers holding prime responsibility for the upbringing and care of a child.

2   Progress in International Reading Literacy Study, http://pirls.org.

3   The intervention stresses the importance of active parental engagement and collaboration in ECEC. It contains five key aspects: a) involving literacy specialists working with preschool teachers; b) bringing technology and book-making equipment into the classrooms; c) children self-authoring books with the help of literacy specialists, educators and parents; d) parents coming in for on-site group parent/family meetings in which parents and other family members share family stories and, together, make books based on the stories and e) frequent reading, sharing, display and dissemination of the children's self-authored books in the classroom and the larger community. The intervention did not focus on teaching children literacy skills specifically but concentrated on children and families creating meaningful self-authored texts on the assumption that this approach would motivate children, teachers and families to engage in literacy activities. The evaluation included pre- and post-test assessments. Evaluation findings were found to be positive: the participating three- and four-year-olds' language and literacy developmental outcomes were found to be enhanced by the programme activities. The programme appeared to not only increase children's absolute language skills but also prevent children living in poverty from continuing to fall further behind in comparison with national age norms. There was also evidence of a qualitative change that took place in classrooms: teachers and literacy specialists noted that "the children became more verbal formed fuller sentences and saw the connections between writing and reading". Qualitative data indicated that the programme strengthened the children's identities and fostered their self-esteem (Bernhard *et al.*, 2008).

4   HIPPY is the Home Interaction Programme for Parents and Youngsters which originated in Israel in the late 1960s and has been implemented with positive results in a number of countries. More details are available at: www.hippy.org.il/.

5   The High/Scope Perry Preschool approach has its own curriculum (High/Scope curriculum) and is used in both public and private half- and full-day preschools, nursery schools, Head Start programmes, day care centers, home-based day care programmes, and programmes for children with special needs. Originally designed for low-income, "at-risk" children, the High/Scope Perry preschool approach is now used for the full range of children and has been successfully implemented in both urban and rural settings both in the United States and overseas.

6   Making it a legal obligation: ECEC provisions are obliged to provide opportunities for parents or community members to be engaged in ECEC, or they are obliged to accept the engagement of parents/communities.

7   Making it a legal obligation: ECEC provisions are obliged to provide opportunities for parents or community members to be engaged in ECEC, or they are obliged to accept the engagement of parents/communities.

# POLICY LEVER 5

# ADVANCING DATA COLLECTION, RESEARCH AND MONITORING

*Data and monitoring can be a powerful lever to encourage quality in ECEC by establishing facts, trends and evidence about whether children have equitable access to high-quality ECEC. They can be used to ensure accountability and/or support programme improvement. They can help analyse and determine appropriate policy responses with appropriate indicators. They can also help parents make informed decisions about their choice of services. Countries use various monitoring tools, such as interviews, observations, standardised testing, portfolios, quality rating and surveys, fit for the purpose.*

*Research can also be an influential tool to inform policy and practice. In ECEC, research has played a key role in explaining the success or failure of ECEC programmes; prioritising important areas for ECEC investment; and informing ECEC practices through evidence. Countries report challenges in advancing research, such as: i) a need for more evidence on the effects of ECEC and cost-benefit analysis; ii) under-researched areas or areas with newly growing interest; and iii) dissemination.*

# ACTION AREA 1 – USING RESEARCH TO INFORM POLICY AND THE PUBLIC

This section contains the following research briefs:

- Data Collection and Monitoring Matter
- Research in ECEC Matters

## DATA COLLECTION AND MONITORING MATTER

### What is data collection and monitoring?

Data collection in ECEC involves the collection of strategic information on ECEC services (*e.g.*, supply, utilisation of funds, unmet needs and teacher qualifications) to support national and local decision making (OECD, 2001).

Monitoring in ECEC refers to the ongoing evaluation of system performance, as well as rating programme quality, for accountability and/or for improvement purposes, highlighting trends in the ECEC sector and contributing to parental choice (OECD, 2006).

### What is at stake?

The recent global economic crisis and pressure on education funding emphasise the need for accountability and seeking "value for money" in the education sector, including ECEC, and for evidence-based policy development. To achieve evidence-based policy making, government administrations need to organise data collection in the ECEC field and cover important areas of ECEC policy, such as demand, supply and utilisation of ECEC places; the volume and allocation of public financing; the status of children (demographic, health, socio-economic, etc.) within and outside ECEC services; and the recruitment and training levels of staff (OECD, 2006).

In educational research, programmes funded by the same source or serving the same age group are often assumed to be equivalent in programme provision and level of quality[1] (Patton, 2008). Information relevant to early childhood policy is often derived from data sets created for other age groups and purposes. Such limitations lead to uncertain policy making at the national level and to a lack of reliable comparative data at the international level (OECD, 2006).

The coherence and co-ordination of data collection and monitoring regarding ECEC continue to pose challenges, although several OECD countries are modifying their information systems to include data on young children. As an example, the Data Quality Campaign in the United States encourages and supports state policy makers to improve the availability and use of high-quality data regarding ECEC and other levels of education. The campaign provides tools and resources that help states implement and use longitudinal data systems (Laird, 2008). Despite improved data collection and monitoring efforts, data on very young children (ages zero to three) remain hard to access (OECD, 2006). These gaps in knowledge about young children undermine policy making in the ECEC field, and have implications not only for international comparability but also for national issues, such as child protection (OECD, 2006).

## Why do data collection and monitoring matter?

### *Increased accountability and improved services*

Data collection and monitoring can help establish facts and evidence about the ECEC sector, for example, whether children have equitable access to high-quality ECEC; and it can ensure accountability on quality ECEC systems. For example, financial tracking and monitoring can help inform planning, contribute to more efficient resource allocation and increase cost-effectiveness (Bennett, 2002).

Several studies have found that the collection and monitoring of quality data can lead to increased programme quality, as reflected by the adoption of higher standards, improved classroom environment ratings and more credentialed teachers (Office of Child Development and Early Learning, 2010; RAND, 2008).[2]

### *Contribution to better child outcomes*

Improvements in programme quality can lead to important and meaningful impacts on child development (Pianta *et al.*, 2008). Monitoring practices and collection of data can provide feedback on what works and help identify areas of improvement. For example, in New Jersey, the introduction of a quality rating score allowed practitioners and management to improve their practices, and statistically significant effects were found on children's literacy skills (Figure 5.1) (Frede *et al.*, 2007, Frede *et al.*, 2011).

**Figure 5.1. New Jersey classroom change in literacy quality scores**

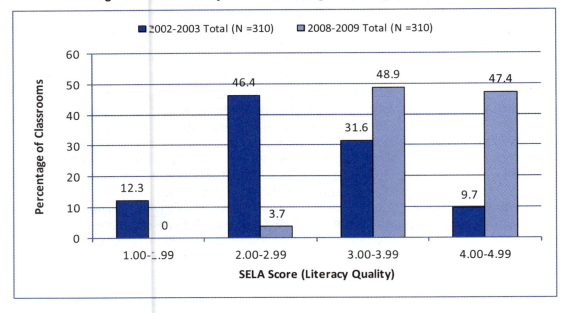

Note: The SELA (Supports for Early Literacy Assessment) is an observation-based assessment instrument designed to measure the quality of supports for young children's language and literacy development in center-based preschool settings (*e.g.*, child care, prekindergarten, Head Start).

*Source*: Frede *et al.* 2011.

## What aspect matters most?

### *Monitoring targets*

Data collection and monitoring can contribute to evidence-based policy making and improved pedagogical practices. It first needs to be determined what should be monitored or evaluated. Most often, minimum standards (regulations) or child outcomes are being monitored (the latter more frequently in Anglo-Saxon countries) (OECD, 2006). Monitoring minimum standards helps understand the current state of the ECEC sector. It can also help detect special learning needs, which plays a critical role in offering supplementary early intervention and support.

To better understand under what conditions ECEC staff are working, how different factors impact, for instance, turn-over rates, and whether work conditions meet regulations, it is important to collect data and monitor this over time. Monitoring curriculum implementation might give insights into what can be improved in curriculum and pedagogical practices, or training for curriculum, which can enhance quality and child outcomes. Furthermore, family satisfaction is often monitored through the use of, for instance, surveys. Monitoring such aspects of ECEC contributes to creating a greater understanding of what constitutes quality ECEC (OECD, 2006).

## Co-ordination of data collection

Data collection requires the capability to co-ordinate a strategic collection of data and maintain high standards of reliability over time across multiple data collectors and geographical regions (Zaslow *et al.*, 2009). It is challenging for countries to collect appropriate data on ECEC. A United States review of ECEC data systems reveals that, while states are collecting a lot of early education related data, their efforts are often uncoordinated. Most state data systems are not able to link individual child- or site-level data with workforce data (Figure 5.2). This makes it difficult for states to understand how its workforce policies or professional development investments are related to children's learning and development, despite the fact that a solid body of research indicates that workforce is a critical quality indicator for enhancing child development. Furthermore, almost all states are unable to determine which children are simultaneously enrolled in multiple ECEC programmes. When this cannot be determined, it can lead to duplication of services and present barriers for ECEC programmes to co-ordinate and build on each others' efforts when working with the same children (Early Childhood Data Collaborative, 2011).[3]

**Figure 5.2. Lack of co-ordination of data collection across ECEC programmes in the United States**

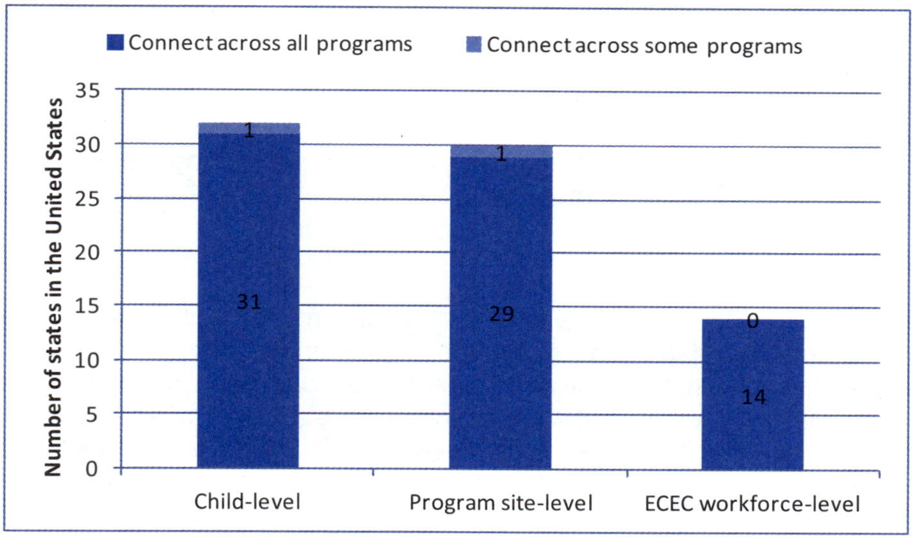

*Source*: Early Childhood Data Collaborative, 2011.

## Selection of indicators

A careful selection of indicators can help improve programmes and the workforce, increase access (especially in underserved communities), and improve practice and child outcomes (Early Childhood Data Collaborative, 2011). Information on structure and process indicators contributes to increased knowledge about the level of quality provision; while information on the demographic and background characteristics of children served can be included in data systems to determine programme effects on target groups and the current state of play of ECEC.

A comprehensive efficacy study should measure the programme components, as well as child outcomes, to inform stakeholders about the relationship of certain aspects or characteristics (*e.g.*, minimum standards or family income) and child development. Having this information allows researchers to draw clearer conclusions regarding who benefits and under what conditions. Research institutes in the United States have highlighted several indicators as "fundamental" for ECEC data collection and monitoring (Early Childhood Data Collaborative, 2011):

- Unique state-wide or region-wide child identifier, which allows governments to track ECEC participants over time if they change school or move to another city

- Child-level demographic and programme participation information, including family background characteristics

- Child- and group- level data on child development

- Ability to link child-level data with school and other key data systems

- Unique programme site identifier with the ability to link with children and the ECEC workforce

- Programme site data on structure, quality and the work environment (such as staff-child ratio)

- Unique ECEC workforce identifier with ability to link with programme sites and children

- Individual ECEC workforce demographics, including education and professional development information

### *Monitoring methods*

Even among ECEC programmes with objective and measurable goals, monitoring quality and measuring effectiveness can be a daunting challenge (OECD, 2006). Numerous systems of assessment and observation have been developed to judge ECEC quality. These include programme records, structural observation of child development and child learning outcomes. Tools, such as checklists and questionnaires to evaluate programme structure and implementation in local-level evaluations, are increasing in popularity, although they are still far less used than other monitoring methods. In the United States, for example, official programme records are the most commonly collected source of monitoring information (75%), while the use of a questionnaire is the least frequently used method with 18% (Figure 5.3) (Barnett *et al.*, 2010).

However, methods can have different purposes and should be chosen with careful consideration, since different methods can provide different information. The *Starting Strong* reports indicate that it is important for information and data collection to take a more consultative approach by involving parents in monitoring in addition to national/local administrations, ECEC centres and staff. In this approach, information on many variables can be collected, such as ease of access, convenient hours of opening, efficient administration and distribution of places, sensitivity to family background (socio-economic, cultural, religious, linguistic, etc.), parents' perception of the happiness and well-being of children, the provision of meals and normal healthcare to children, and relationships with teachers. Such information is also useful for parents in choosing the centre suitable for their child(ren) (OECD, 2001; 2006).

**Figure 5.3. Monitoring methods at state level in the United States**

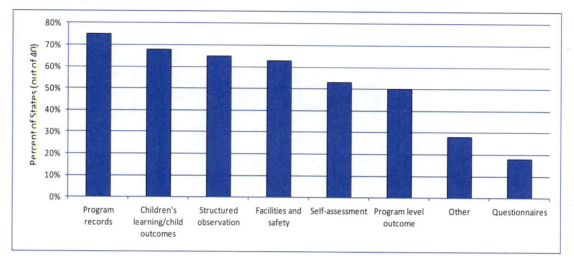

*Source*: Barnett *et al.*, 2010.

## *Use of the data*

The collected data in use varies across countries, and the purpose of data should be well-considered before collection and monitoring mechanisms are being implemented (OECD, 2006). The most common application of data is to provide technical assistance (83%), followed most closely by teacher professional development (80%), corrective actions or sanctions (73%) and changes to ECEC policy (38%). What is evident from Figure 5.4 is that data and monitoring are not frequently used to implement policy changes, while evidence-based policy making can contribute to greater policy effectiveness and efficiency (Barnett *et al.*, 2010).

**Figure 5.4. Uses of monitoring information at state level in the United States**

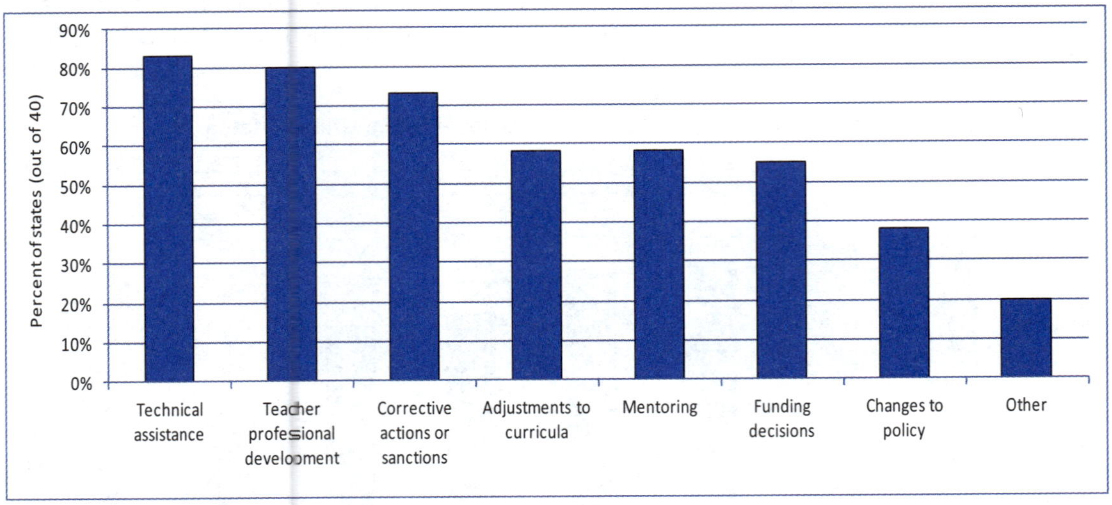

*Source*: Barnett *et al*., 2010.

## What are the policy implications?

### *Defining the purpose, scope and critical policy questions*

Without a clear understanding of why data are needed, governments run the risk of collecting data for purely compliance reasons instead of tapping into the potential of data to inform continuous improvement. Different purposes may require different data, collection methods, and rigorous attention to research design, what is measured and how it is measured. Defining the purpose and scope of data collection before starting data collection is, therefore, important (Patton, 2008).

Taking stock of existing data collection efforts to determine whether all current data collection activities are needed, and assessing where data gaps exist and what linkages among ECEC programmes are needed, will help answer agreed-upon policy questions. Policy questions determine the purpose of monitoring and consider potential uses for monitoring information. Examples include (Barnett *et al*., 2010):

- to identify needs that will guide teacher training or professional development
- to identify programmes for corrective action or sanctions
- to make funding decisions about programmes or guarantees
- to make adjustments to curricula
- to provide staff with technical assistance
- to provide staff with mentoring
- to make changes to preschool policy

The agreed purpose of monitoring will help define the scope of data collection, linking aspects depending on purpose. The most appropriate combination of indicators should be determined in accordance with the country's ECEC quality goals and its specific political, socio-cultural and financial contexts. The collection and monitoring of such data will require a high level of co-ordination and funding. Each country must balance the regulations of a programme with its resource constraints. The linkages among these three components are critical to understanding how policies that create changes in one area (*e.g.*, professional development) are related to another (*e.g.*, child development).

### Setting up a unified data system and quality monitoring at the national level

Data systems need to link data on children, programme characteristics and workforce across multiple programmes and governance structures in order for policy makers, providers and other stakeholders to acquire a holistic understanding of the system. Countries that adopt "dual" or "split" systems where different authorities are in charge of child care and early education, as well as countries that continue decentralised monitoring and accountability procedures, can find it increasingly difficult to make national comparisons and ensure that high-quality ECEC is available to all children as a universal measure. Setting up a unified data system and monitoring quality at the national level can be beneficial.

### Collecting and monitoring of financial data

Useful data would include: public and private expenditure on early education and child care services (in total and/or separate), parental leave and child allowance (cash benefits and tax credits). The information can help formulate government objectives and policies for children across various sectors and determine the appropriateness of a universal or targeted policy in the country-specific socio-economic and demographic contexts (OECD, 2001).

### Developing cross-national data on quality in ECEC

In an increasingly global economy, countries find more value than ever before in comparing progress across countries, sharing best practices and improving ECEC globally. A study exploring national adaptations of the same rating scale in South Korea and Sweden found that cross-cultural comparison of quality in preschools is both achievable and valuable (Sheridan *et al.*, 2009).

Parents and local administrators can be a valuable source of information. Parents can offer an important perspective on the perceived happiness of their children and raise concerns. Involving local administrators in the monitoring processes can encourage their efforts and is considered of particular relevance where responsibility for ECEC is delegated to the local level (OECD, 2006).

### What is still unknown?

#### Data on ECEC in general

Internationally, information is lacking across all areas of ECEC provision (Hustedt and Barnett, 2010), which makes research on the effects of implementing and maintaining well-designed data bases difficult to conduct. We know very little about who is being served across the various ECEC sectors, what resources are committed to the programmes, the characteristics of the staff, the structural characteristics of many programmes and the dynamic quality characteristics. Although extensive data on children and programmes will help answer questions about subgroups and programme effectiveness, governments and other funding agencies often do not conduct studies that are rigorous in their design and, thus, leave too many unanswered questions. In the United States, most evaluations of state preschool provision were found to be so flawed in their design that there were severe limitations in interpreting their results (Gilliam and Zigler, 2004). Thus, we not only need to develop and build extensive data bases that can connect information across ECEC sectors, but we must ensure that these are connected with rigorously designed research studies if we are to use the data to inform programme improvements leading to increasing the effectiveness of our early learning efforts globally.

### Data on quality, financing and costs in particular

It is too early to validate the theory of action behind ECEC data systems. Although there have been some one-time studies of the use of patterns and surveys of aspects of child care, in most countries, there is no permanent, regular source of information about the range of ECEC programmes, especially on financing and cost information (Cleveland *et al.*, 2003).

### Effects on child development and learning

Although there is some emerging evidence of the effects of some aspects of data collection and monitoring, such as quality rating, on increased programme and classroom quality, more research is still needed on how use of data and data systems can enhance children's learning and development.

### Insufficient knowledge for international comparative studies

A lack of coherent monitoring policies at the national levels makes it difficult for countries to obtain a full picture of the ECEC services provided and impedes international comparisons of programmes and their outcomes.

## REFERENCES

Barnett W. S., D. J. Epstein, M. E. Carolan, J. Fitzgerald, D. J. Ackerman and A. H. Friedman (2010), *The state of preschool 2010: State preschool yearbook*, National Institute for Early Education Research, New Brunswick.

Bennett, J. (2002), "Strengthening Early Childhood Programmes: A Policy Framework", *Education Policy Analysis,* OECD, Paris.

Cleveland, G., S. Colley, M. Friendly and D. S. Lero (2003), *The state of data on early childhood education and care in Canada*, Toronto: Childcare Resource and Research Unit, University of Toronto.

Early Childhood Data Collaborative (2011), "10 Fundamentals of Coordinated State Early Care and Education Data Systems", *Inaugural State Analysis*, Berkeley, available at: http://ecedata.org/files/DQC%20ECDC%20brochure%202011%20Mar21.pdf.

Frede, E. (2005), "Assessment in a continuous improvement cycle: New Jersey's Abbott preschool program", invited paper for the National Early Childhood Accountability Task Force with support from the Pew Charitable Trusts, the Foundation for Child Development and the Joyce Foundation, available at: http://nieer.org/docs/?DocID=192.

Frede, E. and W. S. Barnett (2011), "New Jersey's Abbott Pre-k Program: A model for the nation", in E. Zigler, W. Gilliam, and W. S. Barnett (eds.), *The pre-k debates: Current controversies & issues*, Baltimore, MD: Brookes Publishing.

Frede, E. C., G. S. Walter and L. J. Schweinhart (2011), "Assessing Accountability and Ensuring Continuous Program Improvement: Why, How and Who" in E. Zigler, W. Gilliam and W. S. Barnett (eds.), *The pre-K debates: Current Controversies & Issues*. Baltimore, MD: Brookes Publishing.

Frede, E., W. S. Barnett, K. Jung, C. E. Lamy and A. Figueras (2007), "The Abbott Preschool Program Longitudinal Effects Study (APPLES)", Interim Report, New Brunswick, NJ: National Institute for Early Education Research.

Gilliam, W. S. and E. F. Zigler (2004): "State Efforts to Evaluate the Effects of Prekindergarten: 1977 to 2003", Yale Univeristy Child Study Centeer, New Haven, available at: http://nieer.org/resources/research/StateEfforts.pdf.

Hustedt, J. T. and W.S. Barnett (2010), "Issues of Access and Program Quality" in P. Peterson, E. Baker and B. McGaw (eds.), *International Encyclopedia of Education*, Vol. 2, pp. 110-119, Oxford: Elsevier.

Laird, E. (2008): "Developing and Supporting P–20 Education Data Systems: Different States, Different Models", *National Center for Educational Achievement, Data Quality Campaign*, available at: http://dqcampaign.org/files/meetings-dqc_quarterly_issue_brief_011508.pdf.

Montie, J. E., Z. Xiang and L. J. Schweinhart (2006), "Preschool experience in 10 countries: Cognitive and language performance at age 7", *Early Childhood Research Quarterly*, Vol. 21, pp. 313-331.

OECD (2001), Starting Strong I: Early Childhood Education and Care, OECD, Paris.

OECD (2006), Starting Strong II: Early Childhood Education and Care, OECD, Paris.

Office of Child Development and Early Learning (2010), "Keystone Stars: Reaching Higher for Quality Early Education", *Program Report*, Pennsylvania Department of Public Welfare.

Patton, M. Q. (2008), "Utilization-Focused Evaluation - 4th Edititon", Saint Paul, Minnesota.

Perlman, M. and G. Zellman (2008), "Child-Care Quality Rating and Improvement Systems in Five Pioneer States: Implementation and Lessons Learned", RAND Corporation, Santa Monica.

Pianta, R. C., A. J. Mashburn, J. R. Downer, B. K. Hamre and L. Justice (2008), "Effects of web-mediated professional development resources on teacher-child interactions in pre-kindergarten classrooms", *Early Childhood Research Quarterly*, Vol. 23, pp. 431-451.

RAND (2008), "Assessing Child-Care Quality: How Well Does Colorado's Qualistar Quality Rating and Improvement System Work?", *Policy Brief*, RAND, Santa Monica.

Sheridan, S., J. Giota, Y. M. Han and J. Y. Kwon (2009), "A Cross-Cultural Study of Preschool Quality in South Korea and Sweden: ECERS Evaluations", *The Early Childhood Research Quarterly*, Vol. 24, pp. 142-156.

Zaslow, M., K. Tout, T. Halle and N. Forry (2009), "Multiple Purposes for Measuring Quality in Early Childhood Settings: Implications for Collecting and Communicating Information on Quality", *OPRE Issue Brief*, Washington, DC: Office of Planning, Research and Evaluation, Administration for Children and Families, U.S. Department of Health and Human Services.

## RESEARCH IN ECEC MATTERS

### What is research in ECEC?

Research in ECEC refers to studies and analyses on any issues related to the early education and development environment of children in ECEC centres. Both qualitative and quantitative research has been undertaken in the field of ECEC with different methodological approaches. A brief overview is given below, to be detailed in later sections.

### *Qualitative research*

Qualitative research provides an in-depth analysis of a topic in ECEC, often based on small samples since in-depth studies can be very time consuming. Different approaches in collecting data for qualitative studies include *case studies, narratives, ethnography*, etc., and most often include *interviews* or *observation techniques*. Within ECEC, the research focus is often placed on topics such as how child developments are facilitated; how staff and parents interact with children and how these different interactions are related to child development; how positive interactions can be facilitated for staff and parents; how staff job satisfaction or parental satisfaction is affected; etc.

### Quantitative research

Standardised measures and other measures that can be numerically coded, administered on a large scale and analysed statistically are used in quantitative research. Some examples of quantitative research methods include:

*Descriptive statistics* in ECEC. These can help us establish facts and report trends, such as the number of places, number of hours, spending on ECEC, and types of verbal communications that take place in different family types (social benefits, working class, professional families, etc.).

*Correlational studies* in ECEC can tell us about relationships, controlling for the effect of other factors to some extent. A research question in a correlational study can be as follows: if participation in ECEC has a positive correlation with child development regardless of children's family backgrounds, which of the quality indicators may have bigger effect sizes on child development? Correlations cannot prove a causal relationship, that is, what causes or has a proven direct effect/impact on child development.

*Experimental research* can most likely support strong conclusions on causal effects, controlling for certain factors or aspects which can influence the outcomes while holding other variables constant. For causal questions (*e.g.*, "Does this policy or programme improve child outcomes?"), large scale randomised trials or quasi-experiments with at least some longitudinal follow-up are usually preferred. However, the administration of research and analysis is costly and time consuming. *Cost-effectiveness and cost-benefit analyses* in particular, compare policies and programmes to evaluate their efficiency from an economic perspective. Sound economic analyses require strong underlying studies of programme impacts and cost studies, such as studies which calculate the return on investment in certain ECEC programme*s*.

### What is at stake?

Globally, ECEC enrolment rates have grown substantially since the 1960s. Simultaneously, expenditures on ECEC programmes have grown greatly to support this increase. As a consequence, there is a growing need for policy makers (and other stakeholders) to be informed of programme effectiveness.

ECEC policies are designed and implemented with certain goals in mind. Policy goals for ECEC can include: decreasing inequalities in learning and development between different groups of children (with particular concern for immigrant and other disadvantaged groups); tackling poverty; improving child development, educational achievement and attainment in general; supporting women's participation in the labour force; advancing work-life balance; and increasing fertility rates. The extent to which these goals are actually furthered by ECEC policy remains often unknown. There is also a growing need for practice to be informed by research, in order to ensure and enhance the quality of ECEC services for children, staff and parents (OECD, 2006). Research can provide insight into these issues. Without research, evidence-based policy making, which can lead to greater policy effectiveness and cost-efficiency, would be impossible; and little would be known about the effects of ECEC policies and programmes.

## Why does research in ECEC matter?

### *Evaluating ECEC programmes for improvement and accountability*

Research can provide insights into why some programmes succeed and others fail as well as what improvements might make them more effective. As the number of ECEC programmes grew over the last half century, evaluation research developed as a means to improve public policy and practice. One impetus for public investments in ECEC has been research on the short- and long-term benefits of ECEC for children, families and society.

### *Justifying ECEC investment in improving quality*

Political and public support for ECEC depends to some extent on research evidence that ECEC programmes produce desirable benefits on a large scale (OECD, 2006). In the past, ECEC policies have tended to be more focused on improving quantity than quality. More research is needed today to establish the value of quality and to identify the most productive investments in quality improvement so as to increase ECEC programme effectiveness and return on investment.

### *Improving ECEC practices through evidence*

Evidence-based practice is advancing in medicine, psychology, social work and education. These fields seek to have practice informed by the best current scientific evidence rather than relying on theories and beliefs. Practitioners' experiences, contexts and values play important roles in decisions about practice, but evidence-based practice relies more heavily on research findings to guide effectiveness (Slavin, 2002; Thomas and Pring, 2004).

## What types of research are commonly carried out in ECEC?

Countries such as Belgium, Finland, France, the Netherlands, Norway, Sweden, the United Kingdom and the United States have established well-co-ordinated research agendas, linked to data systems and government-university agreements. Although research in ECEC is growing rapidly, much advancement is needed (OECD, 2006). The following types of research are most usually undertaken – although the favoured research methodologies and themes can vary greatly from country to country.

### Country-specific policy research

Country-specific policy research investigates policy questions for national administrators. This type of research is often funded directly by governments and frequently focuses on programme or policy evaluations. In some countries, a number of university departments or private agencies engage in this type of research. There has been a growing interest in this type of research in ECEC, although some caution needs to be taken in applying findings from country-specific research to other countries or cultures (OECD, 2006).

### Large-scale programme evaluations

Programme evaluation is designed to assess the effectiveness of a programme. Its aims include: 1) programme improvement; 2) accountability; 3) assessment of value for money; and 4) assessment of the utility of particular aspects of a programme. Examples include the evaluations of Head Start (the United States), Sure Start, the Effective Provision of Pre-School Education (EPPE) project and the Neighbourhood Nursery Programme Evaluation (England, United Kingdom).

Experimentation and quasi-experimentation with random sampling are the strongest designs for assessing impact. However, critiques include: 1) technical (*i.e.*, selection of unbiased samples), ethical and political difficulties, that is, difficulties to set up a control group which does not take part in the programme through random sampling when the intervention is believed to have a positive impact on early development; 2) large amounts of resources required; 3) full implementation of the programme required; 4) lack of information on how the programme achieved its effects; and 5) focus on easily measurable results rather than important, less quantifiable goals (Meisels *et al.*, 1996; Wortham, 2004)

Results may or may not have a direct impact on decision making, depending on the interactions between research, politics and policy making. When followed up with a longitudinal approach, the confidence level – the level at which findings are statistically significant – improves, and the possibility of having an impact on decision making increases.

### Longitudinal studies

Longitudinal studies have been initiated in several OECD countries but are funded more frequently in the United States. Longitudinal studies involve repeated observations of the same sample over long periods of time and aim to investigate the effectiveness of ECEC programmes and long-term outcomes (OECD, 2006). Frequently cited studies include: the High/Scope Perry Preschool Study, the Chicago Parental Centre Programme, the North Carolina Abecedarian Programme, National Institute of Child Health and Human Development studies, and the Cost Quality and Child Outcomes Study of the United States; Competent Children/Learners of New Zealand; and the EPPE study of England (United Kingdom). These studies have contributed to clarifying, for example, quality indicators and their effects on child development, or the associations between family backgrounds and child outcomes (including educational, health or labour market and economic outcomes). The temporal aspect of longitudinal research allows time for both children and programmes to mature, showing how immediate outcomes from programmes may change over time (Chatterji, 2004).

## Comparative, cross-national research

Comparative, cross-national research identifies specific policies and practices from which people in other countries can draw inspiration. Its intention is not to identify "models" for imitation or to construct league tables, but to assist policy makers to think more broadly and critically about ECEC. It reveals important differences in management and practice, for example, the wide range of public funding or staff-child ratios practised across different OECD countries. The awareness of such differences can lead to a reassessment of domestic policy and provide an impetus for further research on important issues, such as funding patterns or the relative importance across countries of literacy and numeracy practices. Examples of comparative cross-national research include policy reviews such as the OECD thematic reviews, peer-learning efforts, such as the OECD Network on ECEC, or socio-cultural/socio-economic analyses. Socio-cultural and socio-economic analyses aim to understand the context of ECEC in different countries. Such analysis helps countries understand the policy environments of their ECEC systems as part of the larger socio-economic structures or current labour market organisation. An example of such an analysis is gender studies on maternal employment and gender equality in the ECEC workforce (OECD, 2006).

## Neuroscience and brain research

Over the past decades, the research focus on young children has shifted from what is fixed by genetics to what can be influenced by environments. Recent neuroscience research has indicated that the child development process is "experience dependent" and requires social interactions and structured experiences (OECD, 2006).

Some of the most relevant findings include (OECD, 2006):

- The capacity to learn is most sensitive during the first four years of life;
- Interactive environments enhance brain development;
- Learning is strongly connected to socio-emotional development; and
- Children continuously build understanding in interaction based on their prior experiences and new information.

## What research matters most to inform policy and practice?

### Furthering research on the effects of quality indicators on child outcomes

The impacts of structural factors should be sufficiently researched before implementation, since it can greatly contribute to evidence-based policy making and benefit child development. As explained in "Research Brief: Minimum Standards Matter", structural quality aspects, such as staff-child ratio, staff qualifications and minimum space (and others), affect children's learning outcomes as well as practitioner's effectiveness.

Although such quality indicators can impact child outcomes, studies show that ECEC effectiveness also depends largely on the competences of staff (see "Research Brief: Qualifications, Education and Training Matter") and the support of a curriculum (see "Research Brief: Curriculum Matters").

## Comparing different intervention types

There are multiple avenues for improving child development and outcomes. Comparison of different effect sizes by different intervention types could help make an informed policy choice and contribute to increased knowledge on the effects of different programmes. Table 5.1 compares effect sizes among different interventions: 1) nutrition services, 2) cash benefits and 3) ECEC. For cognitive and schooling outcomes, the effect size is the largest for ECEC, while nutrition services have the largest effects on social outcomes. To improve health outcomes, nutrition provision and cash benefits have larger effects than ECEC.

**Table 5.1. Effect magnitudes by type of early childhood development policy**

Percent of 1 standard deviation

|  | Nutrition | Cash Incentives | ECEC |
|---|---|---|---|
| Cognitive | .26 | .17 | .35 |
| Social | .46* | .21 | .27 |
| Schooling | .11 | --- | .41 |
| Health | .38 | .38 | .23 |

Note: *only one study in this category.

*Source*: Nores and Barnett (2010).

## Comparing different pedagogical strategies and programme approaches

Research projects like the European Commission supported INCLUDE-ED seek to promote better practice by facilitating knowledge exchange between practitioners and stakeholders more directly. Identifying well-performing institutions and interviewing practitioners can encourage rethinking about practices and broaden perspectives. This can be used to define quality in ways that guide practice. One approach is to provide a balance of teacher-directed and child-initiated activities (see "Research Brief: Curriculum Matters"). Another is to ensure a reasonably high ratio of staff to children and use of small groups to facilitate individualised interactions between staff and child (see "Research Brief: Quality Goals Matter").

Research on special needs education and early intervention can identify more responsive pedagogical approaches that can mitigate further disadvantages, and curricula that help tackle disabilities (OECD, 2006). Successful inclusion of children with special needs requires attention to the organisation and management of ECEC settings, in particular, the adaptation to the needs of children, the hiring or allocation of specialised staff, and more flexible organisation of group sizes and rooms to cater for specialised sessions. With intense early intervention, some adverse effects can be reversed or even prevented for much less than it costs to provide special services later.

### Furthering research on practice and process

Research on practice and process, sometimes referred to as "action" or "practitioner research", is a valuable mode of research in that it enables staff to reflect systematically on their own practice. Some researchers express reservations about this type of research, claiming that its methods are rudimentary and that it lacks rigour and reliability. However, if carried out by practitioners with the support of university research departments, methodology and reliability can be ensured. As a practice, it also models a major aim of ECEC: to encourage participants to build theories and to experiment and reflect on their environment in a democratic and mutually supportive way. Practitioner research has high value as a tool for professional development because of the clear methodological links to pedagogy, reflection and quality improvement processes. A possible weakness is that many of its valuable findings and insights remain at the local level and are not passed upward to ministries in a systematic way, unless ministries are proactive in keeping open lines of communication (OECD, 2006).

## What are the policy implications?

### Setting out research frameworks with sustained funding to support long-term policy goals

If research is to guide policy and practice, it is important to set out a long-term framework for ECEC policy research (OECD, 2001). Without a stable research infrastructure and long-term funding, it is difficult for research to inform policy and practice, especially by advancing national or international research on a large scale. This will require political will to invest in research and have policy and practice guided by research.

Furthermore, the potential for local research to inform practice also seems considerable. ECEC programmes have several strong traditions of practitioner research or inquiry, including Reggio Emilia, reflective practice and other forms of participatory self-evaluation. However, with a few exceptions, national support for practitioner research is weak (OECD, 2006). Effective use of research to inform practice needs to be combined with a planned research agenda; training opportunities for conducting ECEC research; development of evaluation instruments; and procedures sensitive to the country-specific contexts (OECD, 2001).

### Advancing quality in qualitative research

In qualitative research, the difficulty remains in the explicit justification (and consequences) of the choice in design and methodology. For example, case studies on children's interactions are so rich in example and detail that they provide the perfect basis for professional reflection and can support ECEC staff to better support a child's learning and development (Jensen *et al.*, 2007). However, the lack of co-ordination in research has resulted in literature that is often haphazard and contains so few randomised trials or other approaches capable of clearly identifying effects that we still know very little about the effects of different programme features or staff behaviour.

### Supporting rigorous quantitative research and meta-analyses

Decision making should rely on an entire body of research rather than the latest single evaluation or study. To ensure that there are enough studies for useful summaries, the number of rigorous studies supported must be increased. Research quality makes a difference: in some circumstances, poor quality studies seriously underestimate programme impacts; and other times, poor quality studies greatly exaggerate impacts (Camilli *et al.*, 2010; Nores and Barnett, 2010). Integrating research and practice will help greatly if the focus is on longitudinal studies with sufficient rigour and sample size (Jenson *et al.*, 2007). An important function of a good review is to evaluate the quality of the evidence and report the extent to which findings differ based on the methodology used.

Governments should create and support systematic research frameworks focused on key issues of policy and practice. Systematic programmes of research designed to build information over time on policies and programme features (particularly those that are costly) would be particularly useful. Such a programme would prioritise the study of policy or programme features that are readily manipulated by government and have some evidence already linking them to effectiveness. It may be more efficient to test coherent sets of policies or programme features rather than to examine each individually.

The ECEC field should integrate research and practice by adopting an experimental approach to policy and programme development where innovations are systematically tested in randomised trials before being adopted system wide. The information generated would be increased if these studies could be linked to existing large-scale data systems (birth cohort studies; education, social welfare and administrative tax records; and national surveys – see "Research Brief: Data Collection and Monitoring Matter"). Place-based randomised trials may sometimes be used when it is not desirable to randomise individual children and families. For example, at the national level, a new ECEC programme or approach could be rolled out in randomly selected communities before a decision is made to implement nationwide. At the local level, alternative curricula might be compared with neighbourhoods or local programmes randomly assigned to one or another before a decision is made to adopt one new approach throughout a city or region.

### Expanding research agendas to include disciplines and methods currently under-represented

*Starting Strong* (OECD, 2001) notes the dominance of concerns and methodologies derived from mere programme evaluations and developmental psychology in ECEC research. While this focus is deemed important for ECEC, a wider research perspective using other disciplines is also needed. Anthropology, sociology, public policy, gender studies and learning theory are cited as disciplinary bases to be researched from which pertinent policy and practice could be developed. Cross-country studies are also seen as useful for assessing the impact of different policy initiatives.

### Making research accessible to policy makers and practitioners

It is important to train policy makers, administrators and teachers in the interpretation of research and research summaries as well as to train researchers to be able to explain research results in non-technical language. The translation of research summaries and reports of study findings into forms more easily accessed by practitioners is of particular importance. It is also important that research be widely disseminated to improve the theoretical and methodological contributions of research through constructive criticism and feedback (Jensen *et al.*, 2007).

Up-to-date research findings can help guide practitioner behaviour if well understood and supported. High-quality ECEC services require a combination of structural aspects and competence of practitioners to use their own knowledge in order to support and stimulate children's development in different learning areas. Staff also need good content knowledge in a variety of areas, knowledge of how to direct a child's attention on a shared object for learning and communicate this with the child in a reflective way (Pramling and Pramling, in press; Sheridan 2001; Sheridan *et al.*, 2009).

### Advancing and disseminating research in international communities

International co-operation can greatly facilitate the production of useful research summaries to guide practice. The inclusion of common measures and the use of common reporting conventions would be particularly helpful. Also useful would be the translation of studies and research summaries into multiple languages.

## What is still unknown?

### Research on children's spaces and environments

An important indicator of quality is the level of investment in, and the appropriateness of, early childhood buildings and learning environments, both indoor and outdoor. This is generally admitted from a health and hygiene perspective but is not always understood from an educational perspective.

The study of children's spaces and environments is a growing area of research in both the United States and Europe (Finland, Italy, the Netherlands, Norway, the United Kingdom, etc.). Cross-country comparisons have been useful in calling attention to this issue, *e.g.*, questioning the assumption that "serious" learning and education of young children can only take place indoors, compared to the strong outdoors approach of the Nordic countries. The growing inclusion of children with disabilities has alerted school designers and architects to the fact that, in many countries, few buildings have access for disabled children and are often poorly designed for group work and children's activities (OECD, 2006).

## How to optimise ECEC effectiveness

To inform policy and practice, there must be a sufficient body of rigorous and relevant evidence. Much of the most rigorous research to date has focused on whether or not ECEC participation has positive effects rather than on quality and its impacts. It is unclear how much specific guidance research will be able to provide regarding quality. A great deal remains to be learned about how to optimise ECEC effectiveness.

## Effectiveness of universal vs. targeted interventions

Although immigrant and disadvantaged children appear to benefit more from ECEC than others, they also appear to benefit more when they attend ECEC with the general population. Whether targeted or universal programmes offer more benefits for their cost could be clarified by additional research.

## Research on effective interventions for children with diverse backgrounds

Increased patterns of migration can have profound consequences on the daily functioning of institutions (Jensen *et al.*, 2006). Research on the ways to integrate diverse populations is lacking, yet it is of utmost importance. A related issue that needs clarification is the best way to address language development with immigrant populations, in particular, how to provide dual language immersion cost-effectively. In general, there is relatively little information on the costs of policies and programmes and even less on the economic return on these expenditures outside of North America. Such information is vital for making sound policy choices at the national level and for programme design at the local level.

## REFERENCES

Camilli, G., S. Vargas, S. Ryan and W. S. Barnett (2010), "Meta-analysis of the effects of early education interventions on cognitive and social development", *Teachers College Record*

Chatterji, M. (2004), "Evidence on "What Works": An Argument for Extended-Term Mixed-Method (ETMM) Evaluation Designs", *Educatonal Researcher*, Vol. 33, No. 3, available at: http://edr.sagepub.com/content/33/9/3

Jensen, B. (2007), "Action Competencies in Social Pedagogical Work with Socially Endangered Children and Youths – Intervention and Effects (The ASP Project): an introduction to the daycare study", Paper Presented at the *Eurochild Conference: Policy and Practice for Social Inclusion of Children and Young People*, Berlin, Germany, 14-16 November, 2006.

Meisels *et al.* (1996), Assessment of Social Competence, Adaptive Behaviour and Approaches to Learning with Young Children, Washington, NCES.

Nores, M. and W. S. Barnett (2010), "Benefits of Early Childhood Interventions Across the World: (Under) Investing in the Very Young", *Economics of Education Review*, Vol. 29., pp. 271-282.

Pramling, N., and I. Pramling Samuelsson (in press), *Educational encounters: Nordic studies in early childhood didactics.* Dordrecht, The Netherlands: Springer, in press.

Sheridan, S. (2001), "Quality Evaluation and Quality Enhancement in Preschool – A Model of Competence Development", *Early Child Development and Care*, Vol. 166, pp. 7-27.

Sheridan, S., J. Giota, Y. M. Han and J. Y. Kwon (2009), "A cross-cultural study of preschool quality in South Korea and Sweden: ECERS evaluations", *The Early Childhood Research Quarterly*, Vol. 24, pp. 142-156.

Siraj-Blatchford, I., K. Sylva, S. Muttock, S. Gilden and D. Bell (2002), *Researching Effective Pedagogy in the Early Years*, University of London, London.

Slavin, R. E. (2002), "Evidence-based education policies: Transforming educational practice and research", *Educational Researcher,* Vol. 31(7), pp. 15-21.

Thomas, G. and R. Pring (2004), *Evidence-based practice in Education*, Open University Press, United Kingdom: McGraw-Hill Education.

Wortham, S. 2004, *Assessment in Early Childhood Education* (4th ed.), Prentice Hall.

## ACTION AREA 2 – BROADENING PERSPECTIVES THROUGH INTERNATIONAL COMPARISON

This section contains international comparisons of:

- Monitoring practices
- Longitudinal research

### MONITORING PRACTICES[4]

### Findings

- Based on country responses to the "Survey for the Quality Toolbox and ECEC Portal", monitoring practices can be categorised into seven types by the purpose/target of the exercise (Tables 5.2-5.8).

    1. Child development or outcomes
    2. Staff performance
    3. Level of service quality
    4. Regulation compliance
    5. Curriculum implementation
    6. Parent satisfaction
    7. Workforce supply and working conditions

- All topics listed above are monitored by all ECEC settings – kindergarten/preschools, child care centres and family day care – except that there are no reported monitoring practices in place for "curriculum implementation" and "workforce supply/workforce conditions" in family day care.

- Of the seven targets, widely practiced among countries are: "child development and outcomes"; "staff performance"; and "level of service quality".

### Child development or outcomes

- A great number of countries monitor child development or outcomes; more countries report monitoring practices for kindergarten/preschool than for child care centres. Very few countries – *i.e.*, Nordic countries, the Flemish Community of Belgium and Prince Edward Island (Canada) – monitor child development or outcomes for family day care.

- Most countries use either an internal evaluation or a mixture of external and internal evaluations. An external evaluation is hardly used alone; exceptions include Scotland (United Kingdom) and Ireland for monitoring child care centres.

- Commonly used monitoring tools include rating scales, checklists, observations and portfolios for internal evaluation; and inspections, checklists and questionnaires for external evaluation. Standardised testing is used as an internal evaluation tool in Ireland for kindergarten, while it is used as an external evaluation tool in Finland for child care centres.

### Staff performance

- More countries reported external evaluations for staff performance than for child development or outcomes.

- More countries reported a mixed use of external and internal evaluations in any of the ECEC settings – kindergarten/preschool, child care centre or family day care.

- Commonly used tools for external evaluations include inspections, survey and observations; and for internal evaluations, self-assessments and rating scales.

### Service quality

- A great number of countries monitor service quality across different ECEC settings; more countries reported external evaluation than internal evaluation for service quality, unlike child development or outcomes. Many others practice a mixture of external and internal evaluations.

- More countries monitor service quality of family day care than child development or staff performance of this type of service, but less than regulation compliance.

- A wide range of tools were reported to monitor service quality by external evaluation, including inspections, observations, surveys, questionnaires, rating scales and checklists. Tools reported for internal evaluation include rating scales, checklists, self-assessments, evaluation reports and portfolios.

### Regulation compliance

- Monitoring practices for compliance with set regulations are mostly implemented through external inspections by national authorities or an independent inspection agency.

- More countries reported monitoring regulation compliance for child care centres than for kindergarten/preschool on this aspect. In both cases, more external evaluations are reported than internal evaluations. For family day care, only external evaluation or a combination of external and internal evaluation is reported; no country reported internal evaluation only.

### Curriculum implementation

- More countries reported the use of a combination of external and internal evaluation for curriculum implementation for both kindergarten/preschool and child care centres.

- Commonly used tools to monitor curriculum implementation include: inspections and observations, exchange of opinion and rating scales for external evaluation; and self-assessments, rating scales and portfolios for internal evaluation. Japan's response, "exchange of opinions" as an external evaluation, can imply that evaluation can facilitate dialogue for improvement.

- No monitoring is reported for family day care. This may be a result of the non-existence of curricula or any other learning framework or standards for family day care in most countries.

### Parental satisfaction

- Several countries indicated they monitor parental satisfaction. It is administered by ECEC institutions.

- Denmark, Norway, Slovenia and Sweden reported that they monitor parental satisfaction for both kindergarten and child care centres

### Workforce supply/working conditions

- Only a few countries monitor workforce-related aspects. It is mostly done by external evaluation such as national or regional authorities or statistics agencies, such as in Finland, New Zealand and Norway; while Denmark uses internal evaluation by ECEC employers and managers. Slovak Republic uses a mixture of external monitoring by national and regional authorities and checklists by ECEC managers.

For more detail, see the Survey Response Table on "Monitoring" (Excel™ file) in the online Quality Toolbox at **www.oecd.org/edu/earlychildhood/toolbox**.

**Table 5.2. Monitoring practices for child development or outcomes**

Panel A. Kindergarten

| Type of evaluation | Monitoring method | Administrator / Evaluator | Frequency | Country |
|---|---|---|---|---|
| **Internal evaluation** | Rating scales, checklist, self-assessment | ECEC staff | every 6 weeks | Georgia (USA) |
| | | | 2 times per year | Massachusetts (USA) |
| | | | every 2 years | Manitoba (CAN) |
| | | | missing | France, Hungary |
| | Standardised testing, portfolios, checklist | ECEC staff | every year (standardised testing), ongoing (portfolios) and checklist (depends on institutions) | Ireland |
| | Observation, portfolios | ECEC staff and/or management | ongoing | Prince Edward Island (CAN), Ireland, Norway, Slovak Republic, Spain, Sweden, Norway |
| | | Local stakeholders | every year | Belgium (French Comm.), Portugal |
| | | National, regional and local authorities | 2 times per year | Massachusetts (USA) |
| | | HM Inspectorate of Education | 3 times per year | Israel |
| | Observation | Parents, ECEC staff and management | ongoing | England (UKM) |
| **Mixed use of external and internal evaluation** | Standardised testing, observation, checklist, portfolios | Local authorities (standardised testing, checklist, questionnaire) and parents and ECEC staff (portfolios) | ongoing | Finland |
| | | Certified preschool education expert (standardized testing), ECEC staff (observation and portfolios) | every 5 months to year | Turkey |
| | | National authorities, ECEC staff | missing | Netherlands |
| | Rating scales, checklist, portfolios | Local authorities and ECEC staff | every 2 years | Denmark |
| | | National authorities, ECEC staff and management | every 5 years (rating scales and checklist), 2 times per year (portfolio) | Slovak Republic |
| | | missing | every year | Italy |
| | Inspection and rating scales | National, regional, and local authorities (inspection) and ECEC staff (rating scales) | every 10 years (inspection); missing (rating scales) | Flemish Comm. (BEL) |
| | Inspection and portfolio | National, regional and local authorities (inspection) and ECEC staff and/or management (portfolio) | missing (inspection); every year (portfolio) | Estonia |
| | Inspection, survey, observation, rating scale | Regional, superintendents' office (inspection, survey, observation, rating scale), ECEC staff and management (observation, chosen methods of internal evaluation) | every year (internal); depends on institution (external) | Poland |

Panel B. Child care centre

| Type of evaluation | Monitoring method | Administrator / Evaluator | Frequency | Country |
|---|---|---|---|---|
| **External evaluation** | Inspection | Care Commission | missing | Scotland (UKM) |
| | missing | National, regional and local authorities | every 1 to 2 years | Ireland |
| **Internal evaluation** | Checklist | ECEC staff | ongoing | Prince Edward Island (CAN), Turkey |
| | | | depends on the *Länder* | Germany |
| | | | missing | Hungary |
| | Observations / portfolios | ECEC staff and/or management | ongoing | Prince Edward Island (CAN), Norway, Spain, Sweden |
| | | | every year | Netherlands, Turkey |
| | Self-assessment (SiCS) | ECEC staff | missing | Flemish Comm. (BEL) |
| | Rating Scales | Local authorities and ECEC staff | every 2 years | Denmark |
| **External and internal evaluation** | Portfolios | ECEC staff and management and parents | ongoing | England (UKM) |
| | Standardised testing, checklist, questionnaire, portfolios | Local authorities (standardised testing, checklist, questionnaire) and parents and ECEC staff (portfolios) | ongoing | Finland |
| | Inspection and observations/ portfolios | External body (inspection); ECEC staff and/or management (observations/ portfolios) | every 1 to 3 years (inspection); every year (observations/ portfolios) | Japan |

Panel C. Family day care

| Type of evaluation | Monitoring method | Administrator / Evaluator | Frequency | Country |
|---|---|---|---|---|
| **Internal evaluation** | Observations, portfolios, rating scales | Family day care staff/manager | ongoing | Prince Edward Island (CAN), Norway, Sweden |
| | Self-assessment (SiCS) | Family day care staff | missing | Flemish Comm. (BEL) |
| **Mixed use of external and internal evaluation** | Rating scales | Local authorities and ECEC staff | every 2 years | Denmark |
| | Standardised testing, checklist, questionnaire, portfolios | Local authorities (standardised testing, checklist, questionnaire) and parents and staff (portfolios) | ongoing | Finland |

*Note:* For England (UKM), at least once within the first three or four years of the implementation of the Early Years Foundation Stage. For Flemish Community (BEL), SiCS stands for "Self-evaluation Instrument for Care Settings". For Portugal, only non-profitable organisations conduct evaluation every year; for private organisations, every three years.

*Source:* OECD Network on Early Childhood Education and Care's "Survey for the Quality Toolbox and ECEC Portal", June 2011.

**Table 5.3. Monitoring practices for staff performance**

Panel A. Kindergarten

| Type of evaluation | Monitoring method | Administrator / Evaluator | Frequency | Country |
|---|---|---|---|---|
| **External evaluation** | Inspections | National, regional and local authorities | min. one time | England (UKM) |
| | | High inspectorate and Educational inspectorate | depends on communities | Spain |
| | Rating scales / checklist | External education inspectors | missing | Netherlands |
| | Survey | Parents | missing | Slovak Republic |
| | Self-assessment | ECEC staff and/or management | every year | Portugal |
| | | | missing | Netherlands |
| **Mixed use of external and internal evaluation** | Self-assessment and rating scales | ECEC staff (self-assessment) and management (rating scales) | every year | Finland |
| | External exchange of opinions and internal self-assessment | Parents and local stakeholders (external exchange of opinions); ECEC staff and/or management (self-assessment) | not regulated (external evaluation); every year (self-assessment) | Japan |
| | Observation | Regional and local authorities, ECEC staff | every 3 months/ every year | Mexico |
| | Observation and self-assessment | State/territory authority and ECEC staff and management | missing | Australia |
| | | External body (observation) and ECEC staff (self-assessment) | every 1-2 years for preschools; every 4-8 years for infant classes (external observations), depends on provisions (self-assessment) | Ireland |
| | Survey | ECEC staff and management and parents | 1 to 2 times per year | Sweden |
| | missing | National authorities, ECEC staff and management and parents | missing | Slovenia |
| | Inspection, survey, observation, rating scale, checklist | Regional, superintendents' office (inspection, survey, observation, rating scale, checklist), ECEC staff and management (chosen methods of internal evaluation) | every year (internal); depends on institution (external) | Poland |

Panel B. Child care centre

| Type of evaluation | Monitoring method | Administrator / Evaluator | Frequency | Country |
|---|---|---|---|---|
| **External evaluation** | Inspections | External body | every 1 to 3 years | Japan |
| | | National, regional and local authorities | min. one time | England (UKM) |
| | | High inspectorate and Educational inspectorate | depends on communities | Spain |
| | | Care Commission | missing | Scotland (UKM) |
| | Survey | National authority | every year | New Zealand |
| **Internal evaluation** | missing | National, regional and local authorities | every 1 to 2 years | Ireland |
| | Self-assessment | ECEC staff and/or management | every year | Japan |
| | Self-assessment and rating scales | ECEC staff (self-assessment) and management (rating scales) | every year | Finland |
| **Mixed use of external and internal evaluation** | Rating scales / checklist, self-assessment | External education inspectors (external evaluation); ECEC staff and/or management (self-assessment) | missing | Netherlands |
| | Observation and self-assessment | Regional and local authorities and ECEC staff | every 3 months/ every year | Mexico |
| | | National authority and ECEC staff and management | missing | Australia |
| | Survey | ECEC staff and management and parents | 1 to 2 times per year | Sweden |
| | missing | Parents, ECEC staff and management | ongoing | Norway |
| | | National authorities, ECEC staff and management and parents | missing | Slovenia |

Panel C. Family day care

| Type of evaluation | Monitoring method | Administrator / Evaluator | Frequency | Country |
|---|---|---|---|---|
| **External evaluation** | Inspections | National, regional and local authorities | min. one time | England (UKM) |
| | Rating scales, observation | Regional authorities | ongoing | Mexico |
| **Mixed use of external and internal evaluation** | Self-assessment and rating scales | Family day care staff (self-assessment) and management (rating scales) | every year | Finland |
| | Observation and self-assessment | National authority and family day care staff/management | missing | Australia |
| | missing | Parents, family day care staff and management | ongoing | Sweden |

Note: For Australia, the frequency of monitoring practices depends on previous monitoring results. For England (LKM), at least once within the first three or four years of the implementation of the Early Years Foundation Stage. For Portugal, only non-profitable organisations conduct evaluation every year; for private organisations, every three years.

Source: OECD Network on Early Childhood Education and Care's "Survey for the Quality Toolbox and ECEC Portal", June 2011.

**Table 5.4. Monitoring practices for level of quality of ECEC services**

Panel A. Kindergarten

| Type of evaluation | Monitoring method | Administrator / Evaluator | Frequency | Country |
|---|---|---|---|---|
| **External evaluation** | Inspections | National, regional and local authorities | every 4 years | Hungary |
| | | | every 10 years | Flemish Comm. (BEL) |
| | | | min. one time | England (UKM) |
| | | National authority | every 3 years | New Zealand |
| | | External body | on request | Italy |
| | | Inspectorate of Education | when needed | Scotland (UKM) |
| | | Regional and local authorities | missing | Norway |
| | | Regional authorities | depends on the *Länder* | Germany |
| | | Regional and local authorities | missing | North Carolina (USA) |
| | | External education inspectors | missing | Netherlands |
| | Questionnaire / survey | Institute for Evaluation | every year or every 2 years | Spain |
| **Internal evaluation** | Evaluation reports | ECEC staff and management | every year | Sweden |
| | Checklist, observation, portfolios | ECEC staff and management | ongoing | Sweden |
| | | | every year | Georgia (USA) |
| | | | every 2 years | Czech Republic |
| | | | every 3 years | Estonia |
| | | | missing | Hungary, Slovenia |
| **Mixed use of external and internal evaluation** | External evaluation, self-assessment, observation and portfolios | National, regional and local authorities (external); ECEC staff (self-assessment, observation and portfolios) | every 1-2 years for preschools and every 4-8 years for infant classes (external evaluations); self-assessment depends on provisions (ECEC staff) | Ireland |
| | Rating scales and self-assessment | National, regional and/or local authorities (rating scales) and ECE C staff and management (self-assessment) | every year | Portugal |
| | Questionnaire / survey | Local authorities and ECEC staff and parents | every 2 years | Denmark |
| | | National and local authorities, ECEC staff and management and parents | depending on the needs and resources | Finland |
| | Observation | Regional and local authorities, ECEC staff | every 3 months/ every year | Mexico |
| | | Parents, ECEC staff and management | missing | England (UKM), Italy |

Panel A. Kindergarten (continued)

| Type of evaluation | Monitoring method | Administrator / Evaluator | Frequency | Country |
|---|---|---|---|---|
| Mixed use of external and internal evaluation (continued) | Observation/ inspection and self-assessment/ survey | National authority (inspection) and ECEC staff (self-assessment) and parents (survey) | every year | Japan |
| | | National and local authorities (inspection) and ECEC staff and management (self-assessment) | every 3 years (inspection); ongoing (self-assessment) | Korea |
| | | External body (observation) and ECEC staff (self-assessment) | depends on provisions | Ireland |
| | | Czech School Inspectorate (inspection) and ECEC staff and management (self-assessment) | every 4 years (inspection); every 2 years (self-assessment) | Czech Republic |
| | | National authority (Inspection) and ECEC management (self-assessment); State/territory departments (Inspection) and ECEC staff and management (self-assessment) | every 5 years (inspection); 2 times per year (self-assessment) | Slovak Republic |
| | | | missing | Australia |
| | Self-assessment and survey | ECEC staff and/or management (self-assessment); parents (survey) | 1 to 2 times per year | Sweden |
| | Inspection, survey, observation, rating scale | Regional, superintendents' office (inspection, survey, observation, rating scale), ECEC staff and management (observation, chosen methods of internal evaluation) | every year (internal); depends on institution (external) | Poland |

Panel B. Child care centre

| Type of evaluation | Monitoring method | Administrator / Evaluator | Frequency | Country |
|---|---|---|---|---|
| External evaluation | Inspection | National authority | every year | New Zealand |
| | | External body | every year | Italy |
| | | Independent agency | every 5 years for subsidised settings, every 18 months for independent provisions | Flemish Comm. (BEL) |
| | | Local authorities | every 1-3 years | Portugal |
| | | National, regional and local authorities | min. one time | England (UKM) |
| | | Care Commission | missing | Scotland (UKM) |
| | Rating scales / Checklist | National, regional and local authorities | every 2 years | Manitoba (CAN) |
| | | | depends on the *Länder* | Germany |
| | | | missing | Czech Republic |
| | | Local authorities | every 1-3 years | Portugal |
| | | | missing | Prince Edward Island (CAN) |
| | | External education inspectors | missing | Netherlands |

Panel B. Child care centre (continued)

| Type of evaluation | Monitoring method | Administrator / Evaluator | Frequency | Country |
|---|---|---|---|---|
| **External evaluation (continued)** | Questionnaire / survey | Institute for Evaluation | every year or every 2 years | Spain |
| | Rating scales / checklist, questionnaire / survey | National, regional and local authorities | missing | Slovak Republic |
| | missing | National, regional and local authorities | every 1-2 years | Ireland |
| **Internal evaluation** | Evaluation reports portfolio | ECEC staff and management (evaluation reports); ECEC Staff (Portfolios) | every year (evaluation reports); ongoing (portfolio) | Sweden |
| | Inspection and self-assessment | External body (inspection); ECEC staff and management (self-assessment) | every 1 to 3 years (inspection); every year (self-assessment) | Japan |
| | Observation | National, regional and local authorities; ECEC staff | every 3 months/ every year | Mexico |
| | | ECEC staff and parents | every year | Norway |
| **Mixed use of external and internal evaluation** | Questionnaire / survey | Local authorities and ECEC staff and parents | every 2 years | Denmark |
| | | National and local authorities, ECEC staff and management and parents | depending on the needs and resources | Finland |
| | Observation/ inspection and self-assessment | National authority (observation) and ECEC staff and management (self-assessment) | missing | Australia |
| | | National and regional authority (inspection) and ECEC staff and management (self-assessment) | every 3 years (inspection) and ongoing (self-assessment) | Korea |
| | | National, regional and local authorities (inspection) and ECEC staff/management (self-assessment) | every 4 years for inspection | Hungary |
| | Self-assessment and survey | ECEC staff and/or management and parents (survey) | 1 to 2 times per year | Sweden |

Panel C. Family day care

| Type of evaluation | Monitoring method | Administrator / Evaluator | Frequency | Country |
|---|---|---|---|---|
| **External evaluation** | Inspection / rating scales / checklist | Local authorities | missing | Netherlands |
| | | | | Norway |
| | | National, regional and local authorities | every 18 months | Flemish Comm. (BEL) |
| | | | min. one time | England (UKM) |
| | Observation | Regional and local authorities | every 3 months/every year | Mexico |
| | | | every 1-3 years | Portugal |
| **Internal evaluation** | Rating scales / checklist | ECEC staff and management | voluntary | Manitoba (CAN) |
| | Self-assessment sheet | ECEC staff and management | missing | Slovenia |
| **External and internal evaluation** | Questionnaire / survey | Local authorities and ECEC staff | every 2 years | Denmark |
| | | National and local authorities, ECEC staff and management, and parents | depending on the needs and resources | Finland |
| | Observation and self-evaluation | National authority (observation) and ECEC staff and management (self-evaluation) | missing | Australia |

Note: For Australia, the frequency of monitoring practices depends on previous monitoring results. For England (UKM), at least once within the first three or four years of the implementation of the Early Years Foundation Stage. For Portugal, only non-profitable organisations conduct evaluation every year; for private organisations, monitoring practices are conducted every three years.

*Source*: OECD Network on Early Childhood Education and Care's "Survey for the Quality Toolbox and ECEC Portal", June 2011.

**Table 5.5. Monitoring practices for regulation compliance**

Panel A. Kindergarten

| Type of evaluation | Monitoring method | Administrator / Evaluator | Frequency | Country |
|---|---|---|---|---|
| **External evaluation** | Inspection | National authority | every 3 years | New Zealand |
| | | | every year | Italy |
| | | National regional and local authorities | every 4 years | Hungary |
| | | | min. one time | England (UKM) |
| | | High inspectorate and Educational inspectorate | depends on communities | Spain |
| | | Education Inspectorate | missing | Netherlands |
| **Internal evaluation** | Self-assessment sheet | ECEC staff and management | missing | Hungary |
| | Questionnaire / Survey | Local authorities and ECEC staff | every 2 years | Denmark |
| | | National authorities and ECEC staff | missing | Finland |
| | Rating scales and self-assessment | National, regional and/or local authorities (rating scales) and ECEC staff and management (self-assessment) | every year | Portugal |
| **Mixed use of external and internal evaluation** | Observation/ inspection and self-assessment | Czech School Inspectorate and ECEC staff and management | every 4 years for inspection and every 2 years for self-assessment | Czech Republic |
| | | State/territory education departments and ECEC staff and management | missing | Australia |
| | | National and regional authority (inspection) and ECEC staff and management (self-assessment) | every 3 years for inspection and ongoing for self-assessment | Korea |
| | | National authority (inspection) and ECEC management | every 5 years for inspection, self-assessment 2 times per year | Slovak Republic |
| | Inspection, checklist, interview and self-evaluation | Local authorities (inspection, checklist and interview), regional authorities (inspection), and ECEC management (self-evaluation) | depends on local level | Norway |
| | Inspection, survey, observation, rating scale | Regional, superintendents' office, local authorities (inspection, survey, observation, rating scale), ECEC staff and management (observation, chosen methods of internal evaluation) | every year (internal); depends on institution (external) | Poland |

Panel B. Child care centre

| Type of evaluation | Monitoring method | Administrator / Evaluator | Frequency | Country |
|---|---|---|---|---|
| **External evaluation** | Inspection | National authority | every 3 years | New Zealand |
| | | National, regional and local authorities | min. one time | England (UKM) |
| | | Local authorities | every year | British Columbia (CAN) |
| | | | missing | Prince Edward Island (CAN), Portugal |
| | | | depends on institution | Poland |
| | | High inspectorate and Educational inspectorate | depends on communities | Spain |
| | | County governor, Health board | missing | Estonia |
| | | Care Commission | missing | Scotland (UKM) |
| | | Independent agency | missing | Flemish Comm. (BEL) |
| | Rating scales / Checklist | National, regional and local authorities | missing | Czech Republic |
| | | Education inspectorate | missing | Netherlands |
| | Inspection and rating scales/chec klist | Regional authorities | every year for inspection and every 2 years for rating scales | Manitoba (CAN) |
| | | Local authorities | public provisions: every year and every 3 years for private provisions | Portugal |
| | Observation and survey | National, regional and local authorities | missing | Slovak Republic |
| | Questionnaire / survey | Local authorities and ECEC staff | every 2 years | Denmark |
| | Survey and self-assessment | National authorities and ECEC staff (survey); ECEC staff and management (self-assessment) | missing | Finland |
| **External and internal evaluation** | Observation / inspection and self-assessment | External body (inspection) ECEC staff and management (self-assessment) | every 1 to 3 years | Japan |
| | | National and regional authority (inspection) and ECEC staff and management (self-assessment) | every 3 years for inspection and ongoing for self-assessment | Korea |
| | | National authority and ECEC staff and management | missing | Australia |
| | Inspection, checklist, interview and self-evaluation | Local authorities (inspection, checklist and interview), regional authorities (inspection), and ECEC management (self-evaluation) | depends on local level | Norway |

Panel C. Family day care

| Type of evaluation | Monitoring method | Administrator / Evaluator | Frequency | Country |
|---|---|---|---|---|
| **External evaluation** | Inspection | Local authorities | missing | Prince Edward Island (CAN), Italy, Norway |
| | | | depends on institution | Poland |
| | | National, regional and local authorities | min. one time | England (UKM) |
| | | | every year | Manitoba (CAN) |
| | | National authority | every 3 years | New Zealand |
| | | County governor, Health Board | missing | Estonia |
| | Checklist | Local authorities (Municipal Health Services) | missing | Netherlands |
| | Observation | Local authorities | missing | Portugal |
| | Questionnaire / survey | Local authorities and family day care staff | every 2 years | Denmark |
| | | National authorities, family day care staff | missing | Finland |
| **External and internal evaluation** | Observation and self-assessment | National authority and family day care staff and management | missing | Australia |
| | Inspection and self-assessment (self-assessment only for subsidised family day care) | Inspectorate and family day care staff | every 18 months for inspection | Flemish Comm. (BEL) |

Note: For Australia, the frequency of monitoring practices depends on previous monitoring results. For British Columbia (CAN), additional inspections are conducted if compliance issues arise during the annual inspection. For England (UKM), at least once within the first three or four years of the implementation of the Early Years Foundation Stage. For Portugal, only non-profitable organisations implement an evaluation every year; for private organisations, monitoring practices are conducted every three years.

*Source*: OECD Network on Early Childhood Education and Care's "Survey for the Quality Toolbox and ECEC Portal", June 2011.

**Table 5.6. Monitoring practices for curriculum implementation**

| Types of provisions | Type of evaluation | Monitoring method | Administrator / Evaluator | Frequency | Country |
|---|---|---|---|---|---|
| Kindergarten | External evaluation | Inspection | National, regional and/or local authorities | missing | French Comm. (BEL) |
| | | | High inspectorate and Educational inspectorate | depends on communities | Spain |
| | Internal evaluation | Self-assessment | ECEC staff and Management | every 3 years | Estonia |
| | Mixed use of external and internal evaluation | Inspection and self-assessment | National, regional and/or local authorities (inspection); ECEC staff and Management (self-assessment) | every 3 years (inspection); ongoing (self-assessment) | Korea |
| | | External observations and rating scales, internal rating scales and portfolio | missing (external evaluation); ECEC staff (internal rating scale and portfolio) | missing (external evaluation); every 5 month (internal rating scale); every year (internal portfolio) | Turkey |
| | | Observations | National authorities, parents, ECEC staff | ongoing | Slovak Republic |
| | | | ECEC staff and parents | every year | Norway |
| | | External exchange of opinions and self-assessment | Local stakeholders and parents (external exchange of opinions); ECEC staff and management (self-assessment) | missing (external evaluation); every 1 to 3 years (self-assessment) | Japan |
| | | Inspection, survey, observation, rating scale | Regional, superintendents' office (inspection, survey, observation, rating scale), ECEC staff and management (observation, chosen methods of internal evaluation) | every year (internal); depends on institution (external) | Poland |
| | | missing | ECEC staff and parents | ongoing | Finland |
| Child care centres | External evaluation | Inspections | High inspectorate and Educational inspectorate | depends on communities | Spain |
| | Mixed use of external and internal evaluation | Inspection and self-assessment | External body (inspection); ECEC staff and management (self-assessment) | every 1-3 years (inspection); every year (self-assessment) | Japan |
| | | | National, regional and local authorities (inspection) and ECEC staff and management (self-assessment) | every 3 years for inspection, and ongoing for self-assessment | Korea |
| | | Observations | ECEC staff and parents | every year | Norway |
| | | | ECEC staff and parents | ongoing | Finland |

*Source*: OECD Network on Early Childhood Education and Care's "Survey for the Quality Toolbox and ECEC Portal", June 2011.

## Table 5.7. Monitoring practices for parent satisfaction

Surveys administered by ECEC centres

| Types of provisions | Frequency | Country |
|---|---|---|
| Kindergarten | 1 to 2 times per year | Sweden |
| | every 2 years | Denmark |
| | every 3 years | Korea |
| | missing | Norway, Slovenia |
| Child care centres | every year | Italy |
| | 1 to 2 times per year | Sweden |
| | every 2 years | Denmark |
| | at least once during a child's stay in the centre | Flemish Comm. (BEL) |
| | missing | Prince Edward Island (CAN), Norway, Slovenia |

*Source*: OECD Network on Early Childhood Education and Care's "Survey for the Quality Toolbox and ECEC Portal", June 2011.

## Table 5.8. Monitoring practices for workforce supply/workforce conditions

| Types of provisions | Type of evaluation | Monitoring method | Administrator / Evaluator | Frequency | Country |
|---|---|---|---|---|---|
| Kindergarten | External evaluation | Evaluation reports | National, regional and local authorities | ongoing | Finland |
| | | Survey | National authority | every year | New Zealand |
| | | Administrative records | Statistics Norway | every year | Norway |
| | Internal evaluation | Self-assessment | ECEC employers and managers | every 3 years | Denmark |
| | External and internal evaluation | Inspections, survey, checklist | National and regional authorities (inspections and survey) and ECEC management (check list) | ongoing for checklist | Slovak Republic |
| | | Self-assessment, administrative records | Educational Information System managed by national authority (administrative records), ECEC management (self-assessment) | every year | Poland |
| Child care centres | External evaluation | Evaluation reports | National, regional and local authorities | ongoing | Finland |
| | | Survey | National authority | every year | New Zealand |
| | | Administrative records | Statistics Norway | every year | Norway |
| | Internal evaluation | Self-assessment | ECEC employers and managers | every 3 years | Denmark |

*Source*: OECD Network on Early Childhood Education and Care's "Survey for the Quality Toolbox and ECEC Portal", June 2011.

## Definitions and methodologies

**Monitoring** refers to the ongoing evaluation of system performance for accountability as well as for rating programme quality, highlighting trends and informing parental choice. In ECEC, it can play a crucial role in promoting better ECEC services and child outcomes, assuring that standards and regulations are followed and that children receive appropriate care and education, keeping track of workforce supply and conditions or surveying parent satisfaction.

- **Standardised test** is a test administered and scored in a consistent or "standard manner". Standardised tests are designed in such a way that the questions, conditions for administering, scoring procedures and interpretations are consistent and are administered and scored in a predetermined, standard manner.

- **Inspection** is the process of assessing the quality and/or performance of institutions, services and programmes by those (inspectors) who are not directly involved in them and who are usually specially appointed to fulfil these responsibilities.

- **Rating scale** is a monitoring or assessment tool used to decide on a rating in a given scale. In ECEC, it is often used to rate the quality of ECEC services and/or the environments that children are in against a set of quality criteria.

- **Checklist** is a list of items, tasks or steps to be taken in a specific order to be checked or consulted. In ECEC, it can be used to assess or evaluate the developmental status of children, staff performance and the quality of ECEC services by observing the regulation compliance.

- **Observation** is a direct tool or a method of collecting data using scientific instruments or qualitative research methods in order to study the subject with an outsider's objective view. In ECEC, it can be used to collect data on child development and outcomes, staff competencies and their way of interacting with children, staff interactions among themselves, managers' interaction with their staff, etc.

- **Portfolio** is a collection of documents or documentations held by an individual – *e.g.*, child, staff member, etc. In ECEC, it can be used as an assessment, data collection or monitoring tool to examine the quality of ECEC services by observing what a child or a staff member has produced.

- **Questionnaire/Survey** is an instrument consisting of a series of questions and an efficient way to collect data from a potentially large number of respondents. In ECEC, it often can be used to gather information on the satisfaction of ECEC staff and parents.

- **Self-assessment** is the way a person views him/herself. It is the process of determining personal growth and progress. A self-assessment sheet is a paper the person has to fill in about themselves, reviewing their own knowledge, skills, performance or capabilities.

- **Evaluation report** is the process of publishing a report on a regular basis based on the results of monitoring and evaluation. It can be used to inform

ECEC staff, parents and relevant committees or associations about a wide range of ECEC data in practice, *e.g.*, supply of ECEC provisions, staff-to-child ratio, job profiles and qualifications, co-operation with other institutions.

The findings presented here are based on data from the OECD Network on ECEC's "Survey for the Quality Toolbox and ECEC Portal" (2011) and on the OECD's desk-based research. However, due to insufficient survey responses, it has not been possible to make international comparisons regarding the monitoring practices of family/domestic ECEC services.

## LONGITUDINAL RESEARCH

### Findings

– Since the last two decades, a growing number of countries have launched longitudinal studies (Table 5.9).

– The oldest longitudinal studies were launched in the United States. The first longitudinal study measuring the impact of participation in preschool on child outcomes dates back to the High/Scope Perry Preschool Project from the United States, which started in 1962. The sample size of this study was small, with only 123 children. Another long-standing frequently cited longitudinal study from the United States is the Abecedarian Programme, which was launched in the early 1970s.

– Increasingly, European and Asian countries, such as the United Kingdom, Korea, Norway and the Netherlands, as well as Australia and New Zealand, are conducting longitudinal studies on ECEC and its effects on child development. This provides further insights into the effects of different types of ECEC programmes worldwide as well as increased knowledge on country-specific ECEC provisions and policies

– Recent examples include the Canadian Longitudinal Survey of Children and Youth (1994-), the Danish Longitudinal Survey of Children (1995-), Competent Children: Competent Learners from New Zealand, the Effective Provision of Pre-school Education Project of England (United Kingdom) (1997-), the Cost, Quality and Outcomes Study of the United States (1993-), etc. These studies have started to reveal new findings regarding early child development or ECEC, or consolidate prior knowledge.

For more detail, see the Survey Response Table on "Research" (Excel™ file) in the online Quality Toolbox at **www.oecd.org/edu/earlychildhood/toolbox**.

### Table 5.9. List of longitudinal studies

| Country | Title | Period | Sample size (Cohort) | Administered by | Funded by |
|---------|-------|--------|---------------------|-----------------|-----------|
| **Australia** | Growing Up in Australia: Longitudinal study of Australian Children (LSAC) | 2004-2018 | 5 000 children for each (1, 2) cohort | Department of Families, Housing, Community Services and Indigenous Affairs, the Australian Institute of Family Studies and the Australian Bureau of Statistics, with advice provided by a consortium of leading researchers | Australian government Department of Families, Housing, Community Services and Indigenous Affairs |
| | Footprints in Time - The Longitudinal Study of Indigenous Children (LSIC) | Ongoing from 2008 | 1 687 Indigenous children at Wave 1 | Department of Families, Housing, Community Services and Indigenous Affairs | Australian government Department of Families, Housing, Community Services and Indigenous Affairs |
| **Belgium (Flemish Community)** | Policy Research Centre for 'Study and School Careers' (Steunpunt Studie- en Schoolloopbanen) | 2006-2012 | 6 000 children | missing | Ministry of Education and Training, Ministry of Economy, Science and Innovation |
| **Belgium (French Community)** | Grandir en l'an 2000 | 1989-2009 | 387 children | Recherche réalisée par l'Université de Liège | Ministère de la Communauté française de Belgique |
| **Canada** | National Longitudinal Survey of Children and Youth (NLSCY) | 1994 - cycle 8 is ongoing (every 2 years) | 6 685 children at cycle 8 | Statistics Canada and Human Resources and Skills Development Canada | Statistics Canada and Human Resources and Skills Development Canada |
| **Denmark** | Danish Longitudinal Survey of Children (DALSC) | 1995-ongoing | 5 000 children from all over the country, different social classes, and different cultural backgrounds (Danish, other ethnic backgrounds) | SFI – Danish National centre for Social Research | The Ministry of Social Affairs and Integration |
| **Germany** | Nubbek (National study on education and care in early childhood) | 2009-2012 | 2 006 children | Paedquis HU Berlin, DJI München, IFP München, Forschungsgruppe Verhaltenbiologie (research group on behaviour biology), Nubbek-Arbeitsgruppe (Nubbek work group) University of Bochum/Osnabrück | Federal Ministry for Family Affairs, The *Länder* of: Bavaria, North Rhine-Westphalia, Brandenburg, and Lower Saxony. The Jacobs Foundation, the Robert-Bosch-Stiftung. |
| | European Child Care and Education Study | 1993-1998 | About 400 German children of a total 1 244 children from Germany, Austria, Portugal and Spain. | Free University of Berlin, University of Lüneburg, University of Salzburg in Austria, University of Porto in Portugal) and the University of Sevilla in Spain. | *Länder* and the European Union |

**Table 5.9. List of longitudinal studies (continued)**

| Country | Title | Period | Sample size (Cohort) | Administered by | Funded by |
|---|---|---|---|---|---|
| **Germany (continued)** | KiDZ Kindergärten der Zukunft in Bayern (Kindergartens of the future in Bavaria) | 2004-2010 | 191 children | Otto-Friedrich-University of Bamberg | |
| | BiKS: Education processes, competence development and selection procedures in pre- and primary schooling age | 2005-2012 | 547 children for kindergarten cohort | Otto-Friedrich-University of Bamberg | DFG (German Research Foundation) |
| | NEPS (National education panel on early education and schooling) | 2011-ongoing | 3 000 children | Co-ordination University of Bamberg, 150 researchers from different institutions | Federal Ministry of Education and Research |
| **Ireland** | Growing up in Ireland | 2006-2012 | *Infant Cohort:* 11 100 *Child Cohort:* 8 500 | Department of Health and Children through office of the Minister of Children | Department of Health and Children through office of the Minister of Children |
| **Korea** | Panel Study of Korean Children (PSKC) | 2008-2020 | 2 078 households with newborn in 2008 | Korea Institute of Child Care and Education | Korean Ministry of Education, Science and Technology, Korean Ministry of Health and Welfare |
| **Netherlands** | Pre-COOL | 2009-2020 | about 2 000 children in 150 primary schools and 450 ECEC provisions from 50 municipalities | Dutch Organization of Academic Research | Ministry of Education, Culture and Science |
| **New Zealand** | Competent Children: Competent Learners | 1994 to 2009 | 500 children in their final year in ECE, in 1994 | missing | New Zealand Ministry of Education |
| | Growing Up In New Zealand | 2009-2014 | 7 000 children born between 2008 and 2010 | missing | New Zealand Ministry of Social Development is the lead agency, with funding contributed by a large number of other agencies. |
| **Norway** | The Norwegian Mother and Child Study | 1999-(ongoing) *ECEC part 2011-2016 | 108 599 births, children, mothers, and fathers | The Norwegian Institute of Public Health (MOBA) | The ECEC part is funded by the Ministry of Education and Research |
| | Behaviour Outlook Norwegian Development Study (BONDS) | 2006-ongoing (ECEC part 2008-2011) | 1 159 children, both parents, 135 child care centres | The Norwegian centre for Child Behavioral Development (BONDS) | The ECEC part is funded by The Norwegian Centre for Child Behavioral Development and The Ministry of Education and Research |

**Table 5.9. List of longitudinal studies (continued)**

| Country | Title | Period | Sample size (Cohort) | Administered by | Funded by |
|---|---|---|---|---|---|
| Poland | School effectiveness predictors – Longitudinal study of Polish Children II | 2012-2015 | 10 000 children (2nd cohort 6- and 7-year-olds included) | Educational Research Institute | Ministry of National Education |
| Slovenia | The effects of pre-school on child development and school achievement | 2001-2006 | 430 children | Agency for research in the Republic of Slovenia | Ministry of Education and Sport |
| Turkey | Lasting Effects of Early Intervention During Adulthood | 1982-2005 | 133 children | Mother-Child Training Foundation (AÇEV) | Mother-Child Training Foundation (AÇEV) |
| United Kingdom | National Child Development Study (NCDS) | 1958-ongoing | 17 634 children | National Children's Bureau, Social Statistics Research Unit (City University), Centre for Longitudinal Studies (Institute of Education) | National Birthday Trust Fund and various others |
| | 1970 British Cohort Study (BCS70) | 1970-ongoing | about 17 200 children | Department of Child Health, Bristol University, International Centre for Child Studies, Social Statistics Research Unit (City University), Centre for Longitudinal Studies (Institute of Education), National Centre for Social Research | National Birthday Trust Fund in association with the Royal College of Obstetricians and Gynaecologists |
| | Millennium Cohort Study (MCS) | 2000-ongoing | 19 000 children | Economic and Social Research Council | a consortium of Government departments and the Wellcome Trust |
| England | Effective Provision of Pre-School Education (EPPE) Project | 1997-2003 * 2008-2013 ongoing | 3 000 children | Institute of education, University of London | Department for Education |
| Scotland | Growing up in Scotland (GIS) Study | 2005-ongoing | Cohort 1: 8 000 children Cohort 2: 6 000 children | Scottish Centre for Social Research in collaboration with the Centre for Research on Families and Relationships at the University of Edinburgh and the MRC Social and Public Health Sciences Unit in Glasgow | Scottish Executive Education Department, Scottish Government |
| | Avon Longitudinal Study of Parents and Children (ALSPAC) | 1991-ongoing | Over 14,000 mothers | Department of Social Medicine, University of Bristol | University of Bristol, Wellcome Trust, Medical Research Council and various others |
| Northern Ireland | Effective Pre-School Provision in Northern Ireland (EPPNI) Project | 1998-2004 | Over 800 children | Statistics and research agency – Northern Ireland | Department for Education- Northern Ireland |

**Table 5.9. List of longitudinal studies (continued)**

| Country | Title | Period | Sample size (Cohort) | Conductor | Financer |
|---|---|---|---|---|---|
| United States | Abecedarian Programme | 1972-1985 | 107 children from low-income families | FPG Child Development Institute, University of North Carolina-Chapel Hill | Mental Retardation and Developmental Disabilities Branch of the National Institutes of Child Health and Human Development, Department of Human Resources of the State of North Carolina |
| | Chicago Child Parent Centres | 1986-ongoing | 1 539 children | Waisman Center | National Institute of Child Health and Human Development and the National Institute for the Education of At-Risk Students in the Office of Educational Research and Improvement, U. S. Department of Education |
| | Cost, Quality, and Outcomes Study | 1993-1997 | 826 children | National Center for Early Development and Learning | Carnegie Corporation of New York, William T. Grant Foundation, JFM Foundation, A. L. Mailman Family Foundation, David and Lucile Packard Foundation, Pew Charitable Trusts, USWEST Foundation, Smith Richardson Foundation, and Educational Research and Development Centers Programs as administered by the Office of Educational Research and Improvement, PR/Award Number R307A60004, U.S. Department of Education |
| | Early Childhood Longitudinal Studies - Birth cohort (ECLS-B) | 2006-ongoing | approximately 14 000 children | National Center for Education Statistics | U.S Department of Education Institute of Education Sciences |
| | Head Start Impact Study | 2002-2006 | 4 667 children | Westat ( a research corporation) | U.S Department of Health and Human Services, Administration for children and families, Office of planning, research and evaluation |

*Source*: OECD Network on Early Childhood Education and Care's "Survey for the Quality Toolbox and ECEC Portal", June 2011.

## Definitions and methodologies

A **longitudinal study** refers to a research study that involves repeated observations of the same variables during certain periods of time. Reiterative data, collected at different intervals on a representative national sample or on a population cohort of a certain type, that allow researchers to study – in depth and over time – important issues for children in contemporary society, such as quality parameters and their effects, or the relationship between family characteristics and children's health, educational or employment outcomes.

The findings presented here are based on data from the OECD Network on ECEC's "Survey for the Quality Toolbox and ECEC Portal" (2011) and on the OECD's desk-based research.

# ACTION AREA 3 – SELECTING A STRATEGY OPTION

This section contains lists of strategy options to tackle the following challenges:

- Data collection and monitoring
- Research

## DATA COLLECTION AND MONITORING

### Challenge 1: Lack of data on demand and supply of ECEC places

Access to reliable information about demand and supply of ECEC places is a challenge in many OECD countries. Without sufficient data in these areas, policy makers and providers fail to plan an adequate provision level for today and for the future. Without transparent information on supply, working parents will have difficulty finding ECEC services, and those who wish to resume working may not be motivated to seek employment.

Data collection at the national level can be a challenge if there is no consistent framework among local authorities and/or providers.

*Launching a unified ECEC data system aligned with national or regional goals*

- In **Australia**, under the National Partnership for Early Childhood Education, the government and state/territory authorities are committed to publish annual reports on the progress of implementation towards the National Partnership, aimed at achieving universal access to early childhood education by 2013. The development of a National Minimum Data Set will gather nationally consistent data on preschool participation across the ECEC sector.

- In **Germany**, the efforts at the federal, *Länder* and municipal levels to increase the number of child care spaces available for children under the age of three until 2013 are being evaluated and documented in an annual report. For the report, the Ministry of Youth inquires with parents, child care centres and youth welfare offices about their specific needs and expectations and to what extent progress can be observed.

*Launching a comprehensive, child-centred database*

- In **Flanders** (**Belgium**), *The Child in Flanders,* a comprehensive compendium of statistics on young children, has been published every year. It encompasses a broad spectrum of: demographic data (*e.g.*, birth rates, the number of children per age cohort, the number of ethnic minority children, the number of adopted children); data on family circumstances (*e.g.*, family composition, ethnicity, family income); data on the utilisation of child care and out-of school care; data on children with special support needs; and data on the health and physical development of young children.

- In **Norway**, all Norwegian kindergartens fill out an annual report through a web-based tool. The report includes comprehensive information about: the number of ECEC places and children (by age), including the number of minority language children and children with disabilities; attendance rates; the quality of ECEC provisions (*e.g.*, number of staff, staff positions, qualifications and gender); organisation of kindergarten (*e.g.*, ownership and opening hours); and parental fees, sibling discounts and reductions targeting low-income families.

- **Korea** produces *Annual Statistics on Child Care*, which are available both as a publication and online. The reports provide detailed information on children enrolled in child care services (*e.g.*, the number of children by age and sex, participation rates in different types of child care centres by regions, the estimated number of children in the future). Each child care centre is required to report and update their information through a web-based tool. The data are confirmed by individual local authorities to ensure reliability. The data on early childhood education are collected as part of the *Annual Statistics on Education*, which provide data on elementary and secondary school education. The reports are available online, prepared by the Ministry of Education, Science and Technology and the Korean Educational Development Institute.

*Taking stock of existing micro-surveys relevant to ECEC*

- In **Austria**, Statistics Austria has been conducting micro-censuses, including a special section entitled "Household management, Day Care and Nursing Care" in 1995 and 2002. The Federation of Austrian Parent-Toddler groups also has collected data using questionnaires filled out by the parent-toddler groups. It aims to determine how the different framework conditions impact ECEC provisions, legislation and funding compared across different provinces.

*Revising the legal framework to mandate national and regional systems to monitor ECEC status*

- In **Korea**, according to the Child Care Act, a *National Survey on Child Care* must be conducted every five years to obtain comprehensive data and information on the current status of child care services, such as the number of children, teachers and child care centres, costs and opening hours. In 2010, despite the high costs of conducting the national survey, the term for conducting the survey has been shortened to every three years so that more up-to-date information is available.

## Challenge 2: Lack of data on workforce quality and working conditions

Data on workforce quality and working conditions are not rigorously collected across OECD countries. This is mainly because workforce-related aspects have not been articulated as important components among policy makers as part of wider data collection efforts on ECEC.

It is also due to the lack of understanding on the need for collective data among different ECEC service providers; for example, preschools and kindergartens, child care centres, and family day care. The profiles, qualification levels and working conditions for ECEC staff vary across different ECEC services in all OECD countries. It is difficult both technically and politically to build consensus and understanding around the need to collect data on this issue.

*Setting up a system to monitor the ECEC workforce aligned with national quality goals*

- **Ireland** is in the process of establishing a system to monitor the qualification profiles of the ECEC workforce and the availability of education and training programmes: this system will be aligned with Ireland's Workforce Development Plan for the Early Childhood Care Education sector.

- In **Norway**, Statistics Norway collects data on employees in different sectors, among them the ECEC sector, on working conditions and workforce supply. In addition, the kindergartens annually report on the number of staff and their qualifications. Regular monitoring in these areas was able to identify the need for more qualified staff and, more specifically, which regions had difficulties in workforce supply. As a result, a general action plan for the recruitment of preschool teachers in targeted regions has been launched by the Ministry of Education and Research.

- In the **United Kingdom**, the Effective Provision of Pre-School Education project collected information on workforce and working conditions across various ECEC providers, including working hours, access to professional development opportunities, proportion of full-time and part-time staff and age. The results show that full-time staff has access to better development opportunities than part-time staff. More specifically, staff working in playgroups have fewer training opportunities, fewer training resources, less access to training materials and fewer opportunities to have their training paid for by their employers.

- **Korea** rolled out the Teacher Competence Evaluation for kindergarten teaching staff, reinforcing the practice of self-assessment. The evaluation assesses competences of teachers, including self-assessment by teachers, with an aim for teachers to improve their own teaching and interaction skills and, therefore, the overall quality of the provision. In addition, the Office for Childcare Teachers Certification under the Korea Childcare Promotion Institute created a database on child care teacher certification.

*Monitoring the quality of the ECEC workforce through renewal of certificates/licensing*

- In **New Zealand**, registered teachers need to renew their registration for a teacher practicing certificate (licence). They must provide evidence of meeting the requirements for full registration during the appraisal process every three years. This includes a vetting process conducted by the Licensing & Vetting Service Centre "to minimise the likelihood of the more vulnerable members of society (children, older people and those with special needs) being put at risk by individuals who may have displayed behaviour that could be detrimental to others' safety and wellbeing".

- In **Prince Edward Island (Canada)**, early childhood educators must submit to the licensing board a record of on-going training, which is required for staff to maintain their certification. This documentation must confirm the training that has been taken and is submitted every three years for re-certification. Through this, the quality of the workforce is being monitored.

## Challenge 3: Lack of data on financing and costs

The recent global economic crisis is putting increasing pressure on educational funding and calls for proven results and accountability. This involves the financial tracking and monitoring of outcomes. However, it is difficult to pull together one consolidated figure for public spending at the national level.

First, accumulating combined spending for early education and child care can be problematic in countries with "split" systems where financing is administered by different ministries. Second, ECEC costs are often shared among national and local governments. Financing from the national government is often included in local accounting, in which case adding all the figures may run the risk of counting the same sources twice at the local level. Third, financing is often co-financed with private sector, whether it is partially covered by ECEC providers or the employers of parents. This is often not taken into account in the figures.

*Collecting reliable data on spending on children and families*

- In **Australia**, the government has tracked their financial spending on ECEC funding. This funding has resulted in a marked increase in the number of children enrolled in child care services from 1 078 710 in 2006-07 to 1 158 690 in 2009-10. Also, substantial improvement in affordability has been observed after the implementation of government subsidies. In 2004, the out-of-pocket costs for a family with a single child in long day care if earning AUD 55 000 a year, was approximately 13% of their disposable income, but this proportion had decreased to around 7% in 2010.

*Evaluating a programme to explore the effects of increased funding*

- Under the direction of the current government, **Prince Edward Island (Canada)** saw the largest increase in public funding to early learning and child care in recent history. The Preschool Excellence Initiative was implemented in May 2010, and at the same time, an evaluation process was being developed by the Department of Education and Early Childhood Development in conjunction with two local academic institutions. This evaluation is to be completed by academic institutions in 2012, and it will inform the government of possible changes to the Preschool Excellence Initiative. It will also provide information about the programme's successes as well as the impact the increased funding has had on the early childhood system.

## Challenge 4: Lack of data on child development

Many countries have insufficient knowledge to define indicators and measure child development. There is tension between measuring child outcomes and recording child development processes. Contentions involve debates about ideology, privacy and ethics.

Proponents for measuring child outcomes would argue that it is difficult to measure the effectiveness of a set of policy or programme interventions without measuring progress made on child outcomes; evaluation is critically important to design evidence-based interventions. They would also argue that it is particularly important to help those children who need special support, by identifying their weaknesses at an early stage.

Proponents for monitoring child development and recording children's experiences would argue that it is not clear what types of child outcomes should be measured at a particular age. They would also argue that monitoring should serve other purposes than tracking child development.

What is measurable may not be necessarily the most important outcomes to consider for young children. They would also argue that it is too early to measure child outcomes and that, even as a diagnostic tool, assessing child outcomes can run the risk of stigmatising young learners.

### *Mandating national and/or regional systems*

- In the **United Kingdom**, the Children Act (2004) has made legal changes necessary to ensure central and shared data collection, which should reduce the burden on local individual service providers.

- In the **United States**, the National Center for Education Statistics, under the Institute of Education Sciences (IES), assists states in developing and implementing state-wide, longitudinal data systems. Through the American Recovery and Reinvestment Act of 2009, IES awarded grants to 20 states to link data across time and databases, from early childhood into career, including matching teachers to students.

### *Launching a longitudinal study*

- In **England** (**United Kingdom**), the Effective Provision of Pre-School Education project collected a wide range of information on over 3 000 children, their parents, their home environments and the preschool settings to investigate the effects of preschool education for three- and four-year olds. Settings were drawn from a range of providers, such as local authority day nursery, integrated centres, playgroups, private nurseries, maintained nursery schools and maintained nursery classes. As a result, good quality can be found across all types of early year settings. However, children tended to make better intellectual progress with higher overall quality in integrated settings and nursery schools.

– **Belgium**'s **French Community** found that children held in a non-obligatory third year of *école maternelle* and, thus, entering late into their first year of primary school did not experience a beneficial effect on the rest of their schooling. A study was initiated on this phenomenon. Since 2009, a longitudinal study of a cohort of children was launched to better understand educational paths and identify aspects to remedy in the education system.

*Developing monitoring instruments or tools*

– In **Australia**, the Australian Early Development Index (AEDI) is a population measure of children's development as they enter school. The AEDI measures five areas of early childhood development collected by teacher-completed checklists, based on the teacher's knowledge and observations of children in their class along with demographic information. The five developmental domains include: 1) physical health and well-being; 2) social competence; 3) emotional maturity; 4) language and cognitive skills (school-based services), and; 5) communication skills and general knowledge.

– **Flanders** (**Belgium**), for the care sector, a team based at the Research Centre for Experiential Education at Leuven University has developed a Self-evaluation Instrument for Care Settings (SICS), which serves as a tool for process-oriented staff self-assessment in care settings. It focuses on the child and his/her experience in the care environment and is designed to help create an awareness of the optimal conditions for child development. The procedure for self-evaluation contains three steps. First, the levels of child well-being and engagement are assessed. Second, observations are analysed. Third, actions to improve quality are identified and implemented. A manual is designed to help users to become familiar with SICs. For the education sector, a student monitoring system, *Leerlingvolgsysteem voor Vlaanderen*, is available for registered schools. It allows teachers to keep track of the development and progress of individual students through a sequence of tests. It also gives insight into a student's well-being and his/her involvement in school activities. The process consists of several tests to measure a student's achievements on language and numeracy in nursery school as well as spelling and technical reading in primary education.

– In **British Columbia** (**Canada**), the province provides funding to a research organisation that collects population-based information. The organisation measures the state of children's development at the onset of kindergarten using the Early Development Instrument (EDI), which is intended to measure children's school readiness at a group level – it is not an individual assessment tool. The EDI assesses children's development in five different areas: 1) physical health and well-being; 2) social competence; 3) emotional maturity; 4) language and cognitive development; and 5) communication skills. It reflects the strengths and needs of children's communities related to how they prepare children for school.

- **Manitoba (Canada)** also uses the Early Development Instrument (EDI), collecting data on a biennial basis within all of its 37 school divisions (and some independent schools). Kindergarten teachers complete the EDI questionnaire on each of their students, and it is collected later in the academic year, which allows teachers enough time to get to know each child. Parents are informed of the EDI collection and may request to withdraw their child from the EDI. The EDI alone cannot tell the whole story of childhood; other data must be used in companion with the EDI, such as asset mapping, school performance data, prenatal data, parent survey data and community-level census data.

- **Prince Edward Island (Canada)** transitioned kindergarten into the public school system in 2010 and decided to pilot a universal screen to assess children's development as they enter kindergarten. The government uses the Early Years Evaluation (EYE), both the Direct Assessment (DA) and the Teacher Observation, and has completed its second year of the EYE-DA with the second year of children entering kindergarten. The EYE-DA assesses four areas of development: 1) awareness of self and environment; 2) cognitive skills; 3) language and communication; and 4) gross and fine motor development. The government is looking at the results from the first and second years to see what information is produced by EYE and how best to use the information as well as the evaluation. Prince Edward Island is also considering using the Early Development Instrument beginning in February 2012 and repeating it every three years.

- In **Germany**, the *NUBBEK* Consortium, an affiliation of several institutes and individual researchers, has taken on the following tasks within the framework of a study: to make reliable, basic, empirical and practical knowledge available; to scientifically examine the existing and emerging conditions and problems; and to use this empirical knowledge to expand the basis for the design of good early childhood education, care and upbringing for children and to increase support for families with child-raising responsibilities. The research takes the form of a national study and is carried out in different locations in eight German states. The main data collection took place in the first half of 2010. Over 2 000 children between the ages of two and four and their families (one-third of whom have immigrant backgrounds) were included in the study.

- The test *Excale – Tercer año de preescolar* in **Mexico** evaluates child outcomes during the third year of preschool. In total, 10 300 pupils of 1 091 schools were tested in 2007 for the subjects of literacy and mathematical thinking. In addition to these achievement tests, questionnaires were administered to address other aspects of educational activities as well as to collect the opinion of pupils, parents, teachers and principals.

- In **Turkey**, the Ministry of National Education provides achievement assessment forms and progress reports to preschool education programmes. Achievement assessment forms cover four development areas: psychomotor, social-emotional, linguistic and cognitive development, and self-care skills for children ages 36 to 72 months. Progress reports are a series of summaries about children's performance, including a child's knowledge, abilities, behaviours and habits.

- **New Zealand** implemented *Kei Tua o te Pae*, Assessment for Learning, in which teachers are expected to develop effective assessment practices that meet the aspirations of the *Te Whāriki* curriculum. The national government offers training on this assessment practice to ECEC staff. The curriculum programme is also evaluated in terms of its capacity to provide activities and relationships that stimulate early development. Children and parents can help in deciding what should be included in the process of assessing the programme and the curriculum.

## Challenge 5: Lack of data and information on the quality of ECEC services

Many countries report major challenges in monitoring the quality of ECEC services and its compliance with regulations, especially concerning independent providers. First, there is no consensus among stakeholders and parents on what indicators should be collected on quality, although there is a growing understanding on what constitutes quality in ECEC services. Second, collecting data on quality itself would not be politically and financially feasible. It will need to be developed drawing on existing data systems. Aligning the collection of quality information with existing ECEC data systems will require strategic thinking, political and financial support, and stakeholder buy-in.

### *Aligning data collection on structural quality indicators with national quality goals*

- In **British Columbia** (**Canada**), kindergarten class size was integrated into legislation in 2001. Education boards must ensure that the average class size for kindergarten across school districts is no greater than 19 and that no single class is larger than 22 students. These standards are monitored every year for compliance. In 2010, the average kindergarten class in British Columbia was smaller than 18.

- In the **United States**, the goals or standards for public programmes in different states derive essentially from the National Education Goals Panel, Head Start Child Development and Early Learning Framework or the National Association of the Education of Young Children developmentally appropriate practice, which are broad in scope. The domains include language and literacy development, cognition and general knowledge (including early mathematics and early scientific development), approaches toward learning, physical well-being and motor development (including adaptive skills), and social and emotional development. Many states also use programme standards to ensure that adequate pedagogy can be implemented; for example, the focus may be on staff-child ratios, staff qualifications, space per child and/or the learning materials to meet the needs of young children. The work of inspectors is to ensure that standards are met in all centres and that each of them strives for high-quality pedagogical work.

- In **Sweden**, a national evaluation of preschools, carried out by the National Agency for Education in 2003, provides policy makers at central and local levels with many valuable insights into how the national preschool curriculum is understood and implemented in practice. The evaluation also reported significant disparities in preschool quality (*e.g.*, class size) across municipalities. The evaluation shows that the lack of support in terms of financial resources and management appears to affect preschools in low-resource catchment areas. A second national evaluation was made in 2008 and shows that, ten years after it was introduced, the curriculum has gained increasingly larger significance. The results show that extensive evaluations are carried out both at the municipal level and at the preschool level. A broad spectrum of different evaluation models is used, including self-evaluation, colleague evaluation, parental surveys and evaluations involving children.

- The **French Community** of **Belgium**'s decree of March 2002 on the running of the education system tasks a Commission with providing a coherent system of education indicators. Each year, a report presents a set of objective and structured information, which, given the available statistical data, contributes to a rich and coherent reflection on the education system.

### *Publishing quality reports on a regular basis and communicating quality*

- In **Australia**, the National Childcare Accreditation Council produced a Quality Trends Report every six months to keep families, funders and services well informed of progress and key developments. The National Childcare Accreditation Council is being wound down on 31 December 2011. From 1 January 2012, the Australian Children's Education and Care Quality Authority (ACECQA) will be responsible for guiding the implementation of the National Quality Framework for Early Childhood Education and Care at the national level and for ensuring consistency in its delivery. ACECQA will report to and advise the Ministerial Council on Education, Early Childhood Development and Youth Affairs on the National Quality Framework.

- In **Korea**, the Ministry of Education, Science and Technology has commissioned the Korea Institute of Child Care and Education to publish *The Annual Report on Early Childhood Education* since 2009. The report is the "Korean Early Childhood Education at a Glance" and provides information on the current status of early childhood education across cities and provinces. It also includes information on quality indicators, such as, staff-child ratio, group size, the proportion of full-day operating kindergartens, the proportion of teaching staff holding a bachelor's degree, and the number of supervisors specialised in early childhood education in the Provincial Offices of Education, as well as outcome indicators, such as, participation rates in different kinds of kindergartens. The report gives information about trends on certain indicators as well as comparative information on quality. It is distributed to the Provincial Offices of Education.

- In the **United States**, the National Institute of Early Education Research (NIEER) has been publishing *The State of Pre-School* annually since 2003. These yearbooks show the extent of state investment in preschool, enrolment rates, group sizes and child-staff ratios, the qualification of teachers, and data on other important quality indicators. In addition, NIEER works with state and national policy makers and other organisations to develop research and communication strategies to fill gaps in knowledge and to effectively apply scientific knowledge to early education policy.

–  The **French Community** of **Belgium** requires care co-ordinators of out-of-school and free time care to draft overview reports (*états des lieux*), which provide a snapshot of the sector and identify focus points on which to act. The Observatory for Children, Youth and Youth Assistance is responsible for carrying out a synthesis of these reports every five years. The first synthesis was published in 2004, and the second will come out in 2012.

–  In **Spain**, the Ministry of Education carried out a pilot evaluation research of pre-primary education in 2007, focusing on the following issues: child learning outcomes, parental satisfaction with school management, degree of consensus within school organisation, service level supplementary services, the different types of programmes and beneficiaries, teaching staff profiles and staff evaluation. The Ministry shares the results of such evaluation research, showing the status of ECEC. In addition, the National School Board issues an annual report in which the most important outcomes and challenges of pre-primary education are being addressed, and it proposes areas for action or attention to the different regional education authorities.

*Launching a parent satisfaction survey*

–  In **Finland**, the National Institute for Health and Welfare carried out an online survey for parents' views on the quality of ECEC services. The results revealed that most parents are satisfied with ECEC services and trust the professional competences of staff but also feel the need for a more sufficient workforce supply.

–  The **Swedish** authorities, in addition to collecting statistical data, sponsored a network of centres (including parents) to collect qualitative information on the specific needs of children and families.

–  **Denmark**, **Norway** and the **United Kingdom** undertake surveys on parents' opinions and consult these stakeholders on a regular basis about their difficulties and wishes regarding ECEC services. This procedure plays a critical role in maintaining quality, affordability and transparency in the spending of budgets. National surveys and parent consultations reveal information on the ease of access, hours of operation, administration and distribution of places, family background, quality standards, parents' perception of the well-being of children, and the provision of meals and healthcare for children.

–  Kindergartens in **Korea** are required to conduct a questionnaire each year regarding parents' satisfaction with the level of quality of the service as part of the kindergarten evaluation scheme. The survey includes information on educational activities and child development, quality of meals, parental education provided by kindergartens and teacher quality and performance. Parents are randomly selected to participate in the survey.

*Establishing a framework for inspection and providing materials for inspection*

- In **Flanders** (**Belgium**), under the CIPO (Context, Input, Processes and Output) Framework, the Inspectorate of Education carries out inspections in non-compulsory nursery education settings for ages two-and-a-half to six. This comprehensive Framework consists of context, input, process and output. The context includes the identification, situational location, history and regulatory framework. The input covers characteristics of staff and students, while processes comprise four components: general policies, personnel, logistics and educational policies. The output component encompasses student performance, school careers and satisfaction.

- In **Finland**, according to the Basic Education Act Chapter 5 Section 21, every education provider should evaluate their education services and its impacts. They should also take part in external evaluations of their operations. There are separate Education Evaluation Councils conducting external evaluation, which are attached to the Ministry of Education and Culture. They are tasked with organising activities among networks within universities, the National Board of Education and other evaluation experts. From 2009-11, there were two large National Evaluations on Pre-School Education by the Finnish Education Evaluation Council, which include the issue of quality relative to the Core Curriculum for Pre-school.

- In **Mexico**, the Ministry of Social Affairs is monitoring the implementation of its services and their co-ordination with the health sector under *Evaluación de consistencia y de resultados del programa de guarderías y estancias infantiles*. This is being carried out by an external institution. The Ministry also conducted La educación preescolar en México. *Condiciones para la enseñanza y el aprendizaje*, which is the result of an over-three-year investigation of preschool education in Mexico. The evaluation includes various aspects of early childhood education, such as infrastructure, materials, organisation, staff professional training, financial resources and service processes.

- **Slovak Republic** has carried out inspections for kindergartens with regard to education, as well as institutional management, by the State School Inspectorate. The comprehensive inspection activities focus on the quality of education and related child outcomes; quality of ECEC provision and its management; co-operation with parents and other sectors (*e.g.*, primary school, special pedagogues, psychologists, doctors and seniors); working conditions of ECEC staff; and supplementary activities of kindergarten. Based upon the inspection results, kindergarten services take advantage of the following: 1) sharing updated goals and information; 2) establishing proper decision-making standards for kindergarten directors; 3) collaborating with advisory bodies to address professional issues; and 4) co-operating with various educational institutions.

- In **England** (**United Kingdom**), the Office for Standards in Education carries out regular inspections to evaluate the overall effectiveness of the provision in line with the principles and requirements of a curriculum framework called *Early Years Foundation Stage* (EYFS), which covers early learning and development and care. The inspection report makes judgements on the overall effectiveness of the provider (how well the setting meets the needs of the children in the EYFS), the effectiveness of the leadership and management, the quality of provision in the EYFS and outcomes for children in the EYFS.

-   In **Norway**, municipalities are responsible for the development and supervision of both private and municipal institutions and for ensuring that institutions are run according to goals set by the national government. The County Governor is inspecting municipalities to ensure that ECEC is in accordance with the Kindergarten Act. Reports show that there are differences in how municipalities carry out their role as local authorities. To tackle these challenges, the government invested NOK 4.5 million in 2011 to educational measures targeting municipal officials. Additionally, in 2011, a public committee will evaluate Norwegian ECEC legislation, inspection rules and guidelines.

-   In **Korea**, inspections for kindergarten and child care centre started in 2007 and 2005 respectively, jointly by the central and local authorities. All ECEC providers are obliged to undergo inspection, which takes place every three years and consists of self-evaluation reports as well as an external evaluation. Kindergartens and child care centres are evaluated for areas including environment, health, safety, management and curriculum – a very important aspect of evaluation. In 2011, the number of items and indicators to be evaluated was reduced by almost half, and the Local Offices of Education were given more autonomy to suggest their own indicators in addition to the nationally defined ones. Moreover, a central management system of evaluators was set up and shared among the local offices to exchange information among evaluators in different cities and provinces. Training was prepared to enhance the quality of the evaluators. The child care accreditation process, managed by the Korean Childcare Accreditation Council, focuses more on process quality rather than regulations. The number of target areas, items and indicators for evaluation has also been reduced for child care centres. The area "family and community involvement" was made embedded into the general management area, while another area, "interaction skills and pedagogies", was newly introduced. Until July 2011, 26 674 of all 39 181 child care centres (68.1%) have been accredited as a result of the inspection. Guidebooks and manuals for these two quality assurance frameworks were developed and have been disseminated to administrators and practitioners.

-   In the **French Community** of **Belgium**, *l'Office de la Naissance et de l'Enfance* (the Department for Birth and Childhood) conducts surveys on the quality of services it approves and subsidises. The Department has *coordinatrices accueil* (care co-ordinators) and *agents conseil* (inspection officers) who regularly visit *crèches* or the care givers as a way to monitor the quality of the services provided. In the education sector, inspectors, whose role was reviewed in 2007, are responsible for inspecting and advising the teaching staff regarding the various laws governing education. They contribute to reports that serve as the basis for more general evaluations and feed into steering education.

- In **Spain**, regional education authorities design and implement assessment plans, taking into consideration the specific socio-economic and cultural status of children and their families, as well as the school environment and available resources. The authorities also support self-evaluation processes in schools of management and staff in addition to the external inspections that take place.

*Developing monitoring tools and providing support for parents and staff*

- In **New Jersey** (**United States**), classroom quality is measured through structured observations using three instruments: the first measures general classroom quality with an emphasis on classroom environments for health, safety and provision of educational materials; another instrument assesses both general and specific materials and teacher activities and interactions that have been found to lead to increased oral language and literacy skills; and the final instrument provides information on the materials and teaching interactions across all the types of mathematical thinking and skills. Taken together, these criterion-referenced instruments provide information that is easily understood and used for programme improvement at the classroom, district and state levels.

- **Slovak Republic** intensified co-operation with the State School Inspectorate, which is mandated to monitor the implementation of the school educational programmes. Inspections are now conducted on a regular basis (yearly). Slovak Republic also developed self-evaluation kits for staff with which teachers and carers can assess their own knowledge and skills.

*Minimising the burden on unsubsidised providers*

- In the child care sector of **Flanders** (**Belgium**), subsidised facilities receive public funding, so they can be required to provide data on their services. However, independent facilities receive limited public funding, so it is not possible to obtain the same amount of data from them as from subsidised facilities. The current data collection and monitoring system produces an incomplete picture of child care services, so the government is assessing how to obtain missing data without placing too great of a burden on unsubsidised facilities.

*Obliging private providers to provide data and be audited*

- In **Australia**, child care provision has a significant proportion of private-for-profit providers. One provider in particular, ABC Developmental Learning Centres, had a wide reach across the country: it was founded in 1998, and by 2008, it made up 25% of the long day care market. ABC was a well-recognised brand, and its learning centres met accreditation standards, building standards, provided staff support, etc. However, it was an organisation reportedly with poor company financial records, a complex organisation and governance structure, complicated and expensive lease/building arrangements, and an acquisition policy funded primarily through debt. In 2008, the company was collapsing, and the government had to intervene to prevent the possibility of major social and economic disruption in many communities. The government provided significant financial support to keep centres operating while plans were being prepare for the sale, transfer or closure of centres. One development was the emergence of a not-for-profit syndicate interested in the acquisition of a significant portion of the former ABC centres. The government assisted this organisation through the provision of a fully repayable loan at no cost to taxpayers that created a new level of collaboration and co-operation between the government, the not-for-profit sector and private investors. Over 90% of the original ABC Learning Centres operating at the time of collapse are still operating today. The government now requires that new operators must demonstrate that they are suitable to operate a child care centre, and monitoring of child care centres has been strengthened. The Australian government has passed regulatory measures, which were announced in the 2010-11 Budget, to: 1) undertake annual assessments of the financial viability of large long day care providers with 25 or more services; and 2) engage an expert to carry out an independent audit where a provider is found to be experiencing significant financial difficulty.

## Challenge 6: Lack of feedback cycles

Providing relevant and timely feedback as a result of monitoring is a challenge in many countries. First, the effectiveness of monitoring for improvement depends on the capacity of those designing and undertaking the monitoring. The monitoring for improvement – if not solely for accountability – needs to consider the focus of the purpose at the design stage and plan how the feedback cycles could be embedded in delivering the results of the monitoring.

Second, the effective monitoring for improvement also depends on the skills and competencies of those who use the results. Even when the results are delivered with feedback cycles, there will be no change if the persons receiving the feedback will not take the message in a formative way or take actual actions to change their practices for improvement.

### *Encouraging the use of assessment for "reflection" and "improvement"*

- In **Scotland** (**United Kingdom**), the framework of quality indicators set out in *How Good is Our School?* and *Child at the Centre* provides a focus for self-reflecting on professional practice and curriculum for improvement in schools and centres. Additionally, external inspections are organised which monitor curriculum and practices. The Scottish government is working with education authorities and other partners to develop processes for sharing assessment information so that education authorities can use the data to learn about the work of their schools and centres and, where appropriate, support changes in curriculum.

- In **New Jersey** (**United States**), the New Jersey Department of Education formed a state-wide advisory council to develop *Abbott Preschool Program Implementation Guidelines*. This document forms the basis for the criteria included in the Self Assessment Validation System, which is used to assess compliance with the Guidelines and to implement the continuous improvement cycle as an annual process at the district level. Districts gather documentation to evaluate and rate their own implementation; this rating and documentation is periodically validated by peers and the state and used to inform the annual programme improvement plans.

- **Australia** is in the process of introducing a National Quality Standard Framework, including a new monitoring process. The monitoring process will be a consistent process of reflection and evaluation. It also enables services to gain an informed picture of current practice and the quality of education and care experienced by children and families. This "picture" of current practice can be used to recognise and confirm the service's particular strengths and be used as a starting point for planning to improve quality.

- In **Flanders** (**Belgium**), the Decree on Quality of Education allows an inspection to apply a differentiated approach instead of a standardised one. The scope and intensity of inspection is determined by specific school profiles, such as school policies and quality assurance practices. If schools receive negative inspection results, they can opt for an improvement trajectory in co-operation with the School Advisory Services. School principals are obliged to share the findings of the inspection report during a formal meeting with the personnel in the school.

- In the **United States**, Head Start grantees will be required to re-compete for their grants if they fall short of quality benchmarks, including classroom instruction and health and safety standards as well as financial accountability and integrity. Among the factors that will be considered is a classroom assessment that was developed by researchers at the University of Virginia and has been validated through rigorous research.

### *Providing support on how to use monitoring results*

- In 2011, **Korea** implemented "Kindergarten Consulting" after piloting it in 2010. Consultation is being carried out to enhance the quality of kindergartens through boosting their own capabilities. Upon request from individual kindergartens, professionals specialised in early childhood education analyse the challenges in kindergarten management and provide advice on how to address them. This consultation process focuses on six areas: 1) curriculum operation; 2) faculty/staff management; 3) financial management; 4) safety of facilities and meal service; 5) parental education; and 6) civil and legal affairs. Each Provincial Office of Education has to set up a "consulting support group" composed of two to three experts, while they may dispatch an independent consultant requested by the kindergarten to tackle more specific questions. In general, "Kindergarten Consulting" unfolds as follows: preparation, diagnosis, recommendations for solving problems, implementation/trouble shooting and conclusions, which are brought together in a report. Additionally, a satisfaction survey for the participating kindergarten has to be conducted.

- In the **French Community** of **Belgium**, *l'Office de la Naissance et de l'Enfance* (the Department for Birth and Childhood) has created a special job function called *conseillers pédagogiques* (pedagogic counsellors). They are tasked to supervise and assist teachers to reflect on their practices based on the results of the inspection in *maternelles*. They ensure the quality of care services by providing care professionals with information and answers to their questions on a regular basis.

- In the **Nordic countries**, pedagogical advisors work comprehensively at the local level to improve the quality of pedagogy in all services by providing up-to-date information on new forms of pedagogy and supporting the organisation on internal quality improvement processes, such as team-evaluation and documentation.

## RESEARCH

### Challenge 1: Need for more evidence on the effects of ECEC and cost-benefit analysis

The current research base on the effects of ECEC and cost-benefit analyses are mainly rooted in research carried out in the United States and the United Kingdom. Other countries often lack the rigour or means to collect data on the costs and financing on ECEC and/or to carry out policy/programme evaluations on ECEC.

Another challenge may be related to tensions between the use of qualitative and quantitative research on ECEC and measuring outcomes or processes. It is necessary to advance more quantitative research on ECEC, while recognising that both approaches are complementary and will enrich the research base on the effects of ECEC.

*Launching a longitudinal study at the national level*

- In **Flanders** (**Belgium**), the Ministry of Education and Training and the Ministry of Economy, Science and Innovation launched Study and School Careers under the Policy Research Centre to construct knowledge about students' experiences in school from pre-primary education into the labour market and to identify the impact and effectiveness of policy measures and educational innovations on these transitions. As a part of the study, they will explore the non-cognitive characteristics of pupils in the third year of preschool, in the first year of primary education and in subsequent years.

- In **Ireland**, the Department of Health and Children is conducting a longitudinal study, Growing up in Ireland, for the period 2006-12. The study aims to identify the factors influencing children's development and well-being from birth to adulthood. It will contribute to setting up effective policies and relevant services for children and families. The study provides an extensive range of reports, which are widely available to policy makers and researchers through various channels, including the Annual Growing Up in Ireland Research Conference.

- PreCOOL in the **Netherlands** is a large-scale national cohort study of about 5 000 children ages two to five assessing the short- and long-term effects of participation in different provisions of ECEC. The study is followed up by COOL 5-18. Pre-COOL has been set up by the Ministry of Education, Culture and Science in the Netherlands and is being conducted on request by the Dutch Organization of Academic Research.

- In **Norway**, the Norwegian Mother and Child Study (*MOBA*) is a general epidemiological study to identify causal factors of serious diseases among mothers and children. The ongoing study started in 1999. The *Language and Learning Study,* a sub-study of *MOBA*, explores the effects of activities in child care centres on child language development and behaviour. The preliminary results show that children who attended regular formal centre or family-based child care at ages one-and-a-half to three became less often late talkers than children who are looked after by parents or childminders. The second phase of this study will focus on the effect of quality in ECEC services on the development of language skills, social skills, behaviour disorders and emotional problems for five-year-olds. The part of the study related to ECEC is funded by the Ministry of Education and Research with, on average, NOK 2 million per year.

- Also in **Norway**, the Behaviour Outlook Norwegian Development Study (BONDS) is conducted to identify: 1) child behaviour and social skill development from six months of age onward; 2) influencing factors and conditions of family and ECEC services on child development; and 3) child social competence and behaviour development in kindergarten. The study is co-funded by the Norwegian Centre for Child Behaviour Development and the Ministry of Education and Research with, on average, NOK 651 057 per year.

- In **Korea**, the Korea Institute of Child Care and Education has launched the Panel Study of Korean Children (PSKC), a 13-year longitudinal study since 2006. It sampled 2 078 babies born between April and July 2008. PSKC covers prenatal through the ages of 7, 9 and 12. PSKC aims to provide comprehensive, cross-sectional data to contribute to identifying causal relationships between children's developmental outcomes and child rearing support. The focus of the analysis includes: 1) Korean children's developmental processes; 2) changes in parental child rearing values and practices over time; 3) effects of ECEC services; 4) impacts of ECEC policies; and 5) programme evaluations with experiments or quasi-experiments.

- **Slovenia** launched longitudinal research, Effects of Preschool on Child Development and School Achievement. The study follows children's development from an early stage up to the beginning of middle childhood and explores the relationship between preschool and school achievement in first grade. The results show that children who experienced an earlier entry into preschool experience less emotional problems have a more powerful will and have advanced social skills. Early entry into quality preschool also functioned as a protective factor of language development for children of low-educated parents. Data and results of the research were used in the preparation of the White Paper on Education (2011), which contributed to taking further steps in improving education, such as changes in initial and in-service training, laws and other regulations.

– The Mother-Child Training Foundation (*AÇEV*) in **Turkey** implemented the Turkish Early Enrichment Project from 1982-2005. The project examined the long-term effects of participation in different ECEC institutions and home-based intervention programmes. The research revealed that participation in ECEC and intervention programmes has long-term effects, including increased language skills and improved educational attainment, occupational status and integration into society.

– **Australia** conducted several relevant longitudinal studies, such as the Household Income and Labour Dynamics, the Longitudinal Study of Australian Children (LSAC), and the Longitudinal Study of Indigenous Children (LSIC). These research strands are still ongoing but, in the case of LSAC and LSIC, are already providing some useful insights into ECEC-related issues.

– The **United States** carries out many programme evaluations of large-scale samples, such as Head Start, High/Scope Preschool Program and the Chicago Child Parent Centre Program. This is partly because there is public pressure on presenting performance results and justifying public spending in the country and partly due to the accumulated knowledge and advancement of research on policy and programme evaluation.

– In the **United Kingdom**, there is a comprehensive programme of research that has evaluated Sure Start, including a study on the impacts of Sure Start local programmes on child development and families. The Department for Education has also carried out a longitudinal study (Effective Provision of Pre-School Education), analysing the impact of participation in different ECEC settings on young children's intellectual and social/behavioural development between ages three and seven. A longitudinal extension to this study (Effective Provision of Pre-School, Primary and Secondary Education) also analyses the impact of preschool and primary school on children's intellectual and social/behavioural development between the ages of three to fourteen.

– The federal government of **Canada**, the provincial government of **Manitoba** and community-based partners have been working in partnership since 1997 on a longitudinal study that follows children from preschool to school entry and beyond to measure how child care affects children's behaviour and development in the areas of social skills, problem solving, motor skills and school readiness. "The 1997 Manitoba Birth Cohort Study" follows 635 children born in 1997; and over time, the study will provide insight on how early child care and other experiences influence children's development. Several research findings have already been published, which support decisions and policies in this area, such as Manitoba's Early Learning and Child Care Curriculum and Manitoba's Family Choices Agenda.

*Establishing a national or provincial body dedicated to advancing research on ECEC*

– In **Korea**, the Korea Institute of Child Care and Education (KICCE), a national research institute, was established in December 2005 to take a systematic approach to advancing research on ECEC policy and support ECEC services more efficiently. Before its establishment, policy research on ECEC had been conducted separately by the Korea Educational Development Institute, Korea Women's Development Institute, and the Korea Institute of Health and Social Affairs. KICCE conducts a range of policy research on ECEC, serves as a databank and plays a role in bringing stakeholders from the education and the care sectors together to provide opportunities for dialogues. Recently, KICCE, as assigned by the central government, developed a common curriculum for five-year-olds (the *Nuri Curriculum*) and is in charge of training 20 000 teachers, developing supporting materials, providing consultation and monitoring curriculum use to ensure a successful implementation of the *Nuri Curriculum*.

- In **Australia**, the Australian Children's Education and Care Quality Authority (ACECQA), a new national body, will play a role in undertaking research and evaluation activities regarding ECEC. This will create a strong evidence base for informing and supporting ACECQA's functions and driving continuous quality improvement. It will also contribute to building the Australian evidence base on early childhood development, which will be used for policy and strategy development.

- The Child Care Coalition of **Manitoba** (**Canada**), a public education and advocacy organisation, has initiated research quantifying the economic and social impacts of child care across its province. Based on research findings, the coalition makes recommendations to the local government on issues, such as the need for more child care services, higher quality services, more affordable and accessible services, and a better supported and resourced labour force. The coalition invites member organisations to attend an annual general meeting and participate in campaigns and activities. Members include parents, the labour movement, women's groups, the child care community, educators and researchers, and organisations committed to social justice and community economic development, among others. The coalition works collaboratively with the national child care advocacy movement.

### Conducting or contracting research programmes that will inform policy and practice

- In **Ireland**, there are two actions taken to carry out policy-relevant research. First, a Scientific and Policy Advisory Committee has been established. Second, a Project Team and Steering Group comprised of key policy makers have been established to have operational and strategic oversight on a policy research agenda.

- In **Portugal**, the government often contracts research and external evaluations on ECEC out to the research departments of universities. The research and evaluations play a role in providing recommendations on various educational issues.

- In **Korea**, the Ministry of Education, Science and Technology commissions city and provincial Offices of Education, as well as seven Early Childhood Education and Development Institutes (ECEDI) across the country, to carry out practice-oriented research projects. The Ministry finances these projects with its budget for local special subsidies. City/provincial Offices of Education and ECEDIs develop and implement various programmes, such as extra-curricular activity programmes for full-day kindergartens and teacher training programmes, and disseminate audio-visual aids for promoting kindergarten curriculums to help practitioners implement curricula. The Ministry of Health and Welfare commissions the Korea Childcare Promotion Institute, one of its affiliated organisations, to conduct research on child care centre accreditation and child care teacher qualification management to inform policy and practice.

- In **Slovenia**, the government finances research programmes in the ECEC field. In the last decades, several researches have been conducted on: the daily routine in preschool institutions and the first year of schooling before and after the curricular reform; early development of early literacy and language; and self-evaluations of preschool education as a means to improve quality.

- In **British Columbia** (**Canada**), the provincial government has provided funding to a project set up by a university that focuses on Investigating Quality Early Learning Environments. This project broadened and deepened discussions related to quality in ECEC at the local, provincial, national and international levels. It promoted discussions on quality through various forums on ECEC as well as professional learning for early childhood educators.

- **England** (**United Kingdom**) has contracted the National Academy of Parenting Research on a five-year contract until March 2012 to conduct a programme of parenting and family research, examining and evaluating innovative parenting interventions that work with vulnerable families. Part of this includes a project on the Commissioning Toolkit, which describes many of the parenting programmes offered in England and highlights the programmes which are most effective.

- In **Finland**, the Academy of Finland's Research Programme (*SKIDI-KI`DS*) focuses on promoting children's health and welfare at the system level. The programme aims at supporting and encouraging multidisciplinary research approaches regarding risk management of children's health, welfare and environment. The programme consists of three themes: 1) the environment of early childhood growth; 2) service systems; and 3) challenges in improving children's health and welfare. The project Quality Interaction – Quality Learning: Nature of Medication and Interaction in Finnish Preschool and First Grade Setting has been carried out by the University of Helsinki. The main purpose of the study is to examine the nature of staff-child interactions in early learning settings.

- In the **United Kingdom**, the Innovation Unit conducts a research programme, Transforming Early Years, funded by the National Endowment for Science, Technology and the Arts. The programme aims to find better policy solutions for child-relevant services at lower costs to improve the lives of families with very young children. The Innovation Unit is closely supporting six localities to translate the Radical Efficiency model into a sequence of activities to design services that achieve better outcomes at lower costs than current services. This programme is expected to provide the localities with new perspectives on the challenges they face as well as potential solutions and to generate new service ideas for children.

- In **Norway**, the government finances, through the Research Council of Norway, research programmes, such as the Programme for Practice-based Educational Research (*PRAKUT*) (2010-14) and Educational Research towards 2020 (EDUCATION 2020) (2009-13). These programmes will enhance the knowledge base for policy making, public administration, professional education and professional practice. *PRAKUT* shall enhance the quality of ECEC, basic education and teacher education. The aim of this programme is to link closely between research and the field of practice. The aim of EDUCATION 2020 is to optimise development and learning for children, young people and adults. As part of this programme, the government is also financing a large, interdisciplinary, five-year research project about quality in Norwegian ECEC.

## Challenge 2: Under-researched areas or areas with newly growing interest

Identifying effective policy interventions for immigrant children has become a high policy interest in many OECD countries with the increasing number of immigrant children, both first-generation and second-generation. Despite the level of policy interest, this area is under-researched in ECEC.

Research on space and environments within ECEC provisions is also of high interest among policy makers. It can contribute to designing better, more development-appropriate and evidence-based standards and regulations. However, this is also an under-researched area.

### Advancing research on children under age three

- In **Norway**, the significant increase in the number of children under age three participating in ECEC raises the need for in-depth knowledge about the contents and the effects of kindergarten on young children. The new research, Programme for Practice-based Educational Research (*PRAKUT*) (2010-14), emphasises this, investigating the conditions that contribute to creating and maintaining optimal learning environments for all children in ECEC institutions.

- In **Finland**, the study "Environmental and intervention effects on stress regulation and development in young children" has been conducted in the Helsinki area. The research identified a model of dynamic stress regulation for children attending day care institutes. The research evaluated how the quality of day care provision moderates the effects of children's biological nature (temperament, gender and neuro-developmental risks) on physiological stress regulation and its impacts on socio-emotional and cognitive development. Results show that a lower level of stress among children is significantly correlated to a higher quality level of team planning and arrangement.

- The **French Community** of **Belgium**'s *Observatoire de l'enfance, de la jeunesse et de l'aide à la jeunesse* (Observatory for children, youth and youth welfare) is carrying out research to develop indicators for care for children ages zero to three. The results will be available in June 2012. Also in 2012, the Observatory will launch research on quality indicators of the care environment from the point of view of young children.

- In **Korea**, research on children under age three is often covered by research on children ages zero to five, thus including children under three. Policy recommendations often include the need for financial support, parental counselling, etc. Research on infants' language development is largely undertaken by individual researchers funded by the National Research Foundation of Korea.

## Conducting research on cultural aspects and socio-cultural analysis

- In **Finland**, the research project "Towards children's efficacious agency in formal and informal contexts" identified factors influencing children's efficacious agency during early childhood. The research hypothesised that young children are not merely reactive, passive and controlled by environmental or biological features; rather, they can make themselves more efficacious, proactive and self-regulating through the efficacious agency.

- In Korea, the Korea Institute of Child Care and Education is currently conducting research on a wide range of policy issues in different socio-cultural contexts. This includes research on child rearing support for multicultural families, the current status and values of child rearing among ethnic Koreans living overseas, supporting child rearing policies for families defected from North Korea, and comparative research on child rearing practices in South and North Korea to prepare future re-unification.

- In **Denmark**, recent research has been studying the relevance of staff background (immigrant background or gender) on child development of children with different backgrounds. A study on the effects of staff indicators, such as the share of male staff, staff-child ratio, share of non-native staff, staff stability and share of staff with a pedagogic education, found that the number of staff per child and the shares of male staff, pedagogic staff and non-native staff have a significant, positive impact on child development. The study found that boys benefit more from a higher number of staff per child and a higher share of male staff, whereas non-native children benefit from a higher stability of the staff body. This study indicates that preschool quality factors contribute to equalising outcomes for boys and non-native children.

## Researching children's spaces and learning environments

- In **Finland**, the Academy of Finland is conducting a research project to investigate what kind of space is offered for toddlers in ECEC. The preliminary results indicate that ECEC professionals use children's age as a determining factor to differentiated spatial-temporal practices in the group. The results also indicate that the best interests of the child are addressed in the form of age-related developmental tasks represented by certain orders and routines. The research implies that continuing professional education should be promoted to enhance reflective discussions on care and education for under-three-year-olds.

- Japan carries out a research project regarding the environment and space of nursery centres. The purpose of this study is to ensure children's well-being and safety and to help the development of a healthy body and sound mind.

- In Korea, a number of studies have been conducted on the development of ECEC facility standards and kindergarten design guidelines in an effort to define legal and regulatory requirements for ECEC facilities and to set optimal standards, which support young children's development. Such studies include research on optimal building design and learning spaces.

- In Norway, a research project "Kindergarten space – materiality, learning and meaning making" (Vestfold University College) is investigating pedagogical relevant dimensions in the physical environments in kindergartens and how children use and experience these spaces. The project is included in a larger multidisciplinary research involving different research institutions: "Places for learning, care and growth – a multi-method and interdisciplinary approach to kindergarten's physical environments".

### *Researching different pedagogical interventions*

- In **Denmark**, the current research project Knowledge-based Efforts for Socially Disadvantaged Children in Day-care (*VIDA*) explores the overall research question: How can Danish general day care improve socially disadvantaged children's opportunities in life? This comprehensive research project examines and documents which of two types of pedagogical interventions in general day care is most effective at improving the learning and well-being of socially disadvantaged children. The overall goal of this effort is to stimulate children's personal, linguistic and social competences as well as their logical understanding. The research project comprises some 6 000 children in 120 day care centres across four municipalities in Denmark. The intervention will be implemented in an inclusive environment; *i.e.*, the ordinary day care environment that is shared with other children. Two types of efforts are tested in this project. To be able to compare the two, the participating day care centres are divided into three groups. In one group, focus is on the children's well-being and learning (*i.e.*, the *VIDA* basis model programme). In another group, focus is on parental involvement as well as the children's well-being and learning (*i.e.*, the *VIDA* basis + parent model programme). A third group of day care centres is left to continue with their ordinary practice (*i.e.*, the control group). The project has been commissioned and is financed by the Danish Ministry of Social Affairs.

## Challenge 3: Lack of dissemination

Linking research to policy and to practice is a generic challenge for many OECD countries, not only in ECEC but also in education fields in general.

Researchers' main interest may focus on producing and publishing cutting-edge research findings – not necessarily to following through to communicate their findings to policy makers and practitioners. Not all policy makers and practitioners have the time or knowledge to read academic journals – written in highly-technical terms – to fill the knowledge gap.

Conscious efforts are required to systemically translate research findings into policy actions or practices on the ground. Such systemic dissemination efforts will require funding; however, budget is not easily allocated for "communication" or "dissemination" activities.

*Providing financial or in-kind support*

- In **Finland**, the Academy's Board allocated EUR 8.5 million to initiate research programmes in 2009 for 2010-13. This programme-based funding contributes to launching extensive interdisciplinary research projects, collecting scattered research resources and promoting the establishment of networks among national and international researchers. Also, the Advisory Board on ECEC, under the Ministry of Social Affairs and Health, organised a national seminar in November 2010 on ECEC research. At the seminar, relevant materials were shared. They are also available on the Ministry's website for a year.

*Enhancing links between research and policy*

- In **Finland**, Centres of Excellence on Social **Welfare** were established in 2002 to overcome challenges in linking research and practice. The objectives of the centres include: development and transmission of expertise needed in the social welfare sector; development and transmission of primary services, special services and expertise services; development of diverse connections among basic, postgraduate and further education; and development of research, experiment and development activities.

- In **Manitoba** (**Canada**), the Healthy Child Manitoba (HCM) Office monitors the HCM Strategy, which was implemented in 2000 and serves as a network of programmes and supports for children, youth and families. The Strategy was nationally recognised and set in legislation under the HCM Act in 2007. This Act commits the provincial government to evidence-based decision making and approaches to policy and programme development. The HCM Office reports regularly on children's development and evaluates whether programmes for children are working. The HCM Act states that the HCM Office is responsible for the development of Manitoba's Five-Year Status of Children's Outcomes Report, which will be released in 2012.

*Enhancing links between research and practitioners*

- In **Norway**, the Programme for Practice-based Research and Development (R&D) in Pre-School through Secondary Schools and Teacher Education (2006-10) generated research-based knowledge and promoted well-organised co-operation between teacher training institutions and school management groups. The new research programme, Programme for Practice-based Evaluation Research (*PRAKUT*) (2010-14), is designed to further develop and strengthen R&D expertise and the knowledge base in teacher education programmes. *PRAKUT* aims to increase the application of research-based knowledge in the field of practice with a view to ensure that teacher education and practice become more closely interlinked.

- In **Slovenia**, all preschools have adopted the *Preschool Curriculum* since 2001. The government applied two approaches to evaluate the implementation of the curriculum. The National Education Institute monitored institutional practices by using different methods, such as observation, semi-structured interviews and questionnaires. In the meantime, the advisors prepared semi-annual and annual reports for presentation to the Minister of Education and other responsible institutions. The findings were forwarded to the preschools and used for the preparation of the contents of professional training as a way for evaluation to inform practices.

### Creating a regional or international research network

- **Norway** organised the Nordic Research Conference in the field of ECEC in 2009 and 2011. The main purpose of these conferences was to consolidate the relationship between research, practice and policy through presentations and discussions on cutting-edge Nordic research findings. Policy makers and researchers from all Nordic countries and self-governed areas participated and contributed to the conferences. Additionally, a co-operation between **Denmark, Sweden** and **Norway** has been established to finance and disseminate a mapping of Scandinavian research in the field of ECEC.

- The **OECD Network on ECEC** aims to support participating countries in developing effective and efficient ECEC policies. At Network meetings, policy makers share their good practices, as well as challenges, with their concrete country experiences on ECEC policy issues. The meetings also serve as a clearing house of new policy research and to identify new areas for fruitful policy research, analysis and data development.

- The research network Diversity in Early Childhood Education and Training brings together researchers and practitioners interested in resolving issues regarding access to ECEC for families and children from diverse cultural backgrounds. Eight European countries are represented in the network: **Belgium**, **Germany**, **Greece**, **France**, **Ireland**, the **Netherlands**, **Spain** and the **United Kingdom** (**England** and **Scotland**). For example, in Flanders (Belgium), the network participated in diversity practices training for early childhood personnel. Training in diversity contributes to more effective dialogues between educators and parents and reduces stereotypical thinking and institutional discrimination.

- The **European Early Childhood Education Research Association**, launched in 1992, is an international association, which promotes and disseminates multi-disciplinary research on early childhood and its applications to policy and practice. It also encourages and supports cross-national collaborations and themed publications through its special interest groups.

- The **Pacific Early Childhood Education Research Association** (PECERA), founded in 2000, is an academic association dedicated to disseminating and supporting research in early childhood education within the Pacific area.

PECERA serves as a Pacific network of researchers and practitioners in order to facilitate communication and collaboration among them. The association holds annual conferences and publishes journals. There are 11 countries that are members of the association: Australia, China, Hong Kong, Japan, Korea, New Zealand, Philippines, Singapore, Taiwan, Thailand and the United States.

# ACTION AREA 4 – MANAGING RISKS: LEARNING FROM OTHER COUNTRIES' POLICY EXPERIENCES

This section summarises country experiences as lessons learned from:

- Advancing data collection, research and monitoring

It aims to be a quick read about challenges and risks to consider when implementing policy initiatives.

## ADVANCING DATA COLLECTION, RESEARCH AND MONITORING

### Lesson 1: Communicate progress to the wider public and disseminate knowledge through networks and workshops

**Australia**'s national, state and territory governments have prioritised the publication of annual reports on progress with implementing the National Partnership for Early Childhood Education towards achieving Universal Access to early childhood education by 2013. Even in its early stages, reporting from 2009 shows that progress is being made throughout the country: an increase has been observed in hours of attendance by children in most jurisdictions, and there has been an increase in participation by indigenous children in some of the larger jurisdictions.

**Mexico**'s experience with evaluating child outcomes has shown that children attending services provided by the National Council for the Development of Education (CONAFE) have better outcomes compared to children who do not attend these services. However, the government has also learnt that language and communication aspects of the services must be improved. Mexico's case is an example of how data collection on child development can highlight strengths of ECEC services but also reveal areas requiring improvement.

Through its Centres of Excellence on Social Welfare, **Finland** has created a mechanism for developing and transmitting expertise needed in the social welfare sector; ensuring diverse connections among basic, postgraduate and further education; and enabling research, experiment and development activities. Practice has proven that the centres have succeeded in networking regional and social actors.

Reports on findings from the longitudinal study Growing Up in **Ireland** are made available to policy makers and researchers through various mechanisms, one of which is the Annual Growing Up in Ireland Research Conference. Additionally, data from the study are made available for research purposes through databases; and the dissemination and use of data is encouraged through data workshops. Ireland finds that the dissemination of data enables children's development to be examined for stability and continuity over time and will allow development sequences to be identified. Factors protecting children from risk and creating resilience can also be illuminated. Based on experience, however, Ireland has learnt that dissemination of research to influence policy can be challenging if the research is not commissioned by the government and if it is based on pilot interventions which cannot be scaled up because of cost factors.

### Lesson 2: Link research findings and monitoring results to policies and practices

**Korea** established the Korea Institute of Child Care and Education (KICCE) in 2005, which is one of the few national research institutes in the work devoted specifically to the field of ECEC. The establishment of KICCE has had positive impacts on the development of ECEC policy research, planning and implementation. KICCE has conducted a total of 175 projects, including the integration of the care and education systems, a series of projects on the *Advancement of Early Childhood Education*, a national survey on child care, and the development of curriculum, workforce and quality assurance. The *Panel Study on Korean Children*, a longitudinal study, is expected to contribute to identifying the developmental mechanisms and outcomes of children as influences and resulted by the inputs of ECEC policies and services. Korea has never more strongly advocated research-based policy and intends to evaluate policy research regarding the feasibility and efficiency of numerous measures proposed based on research findings in order to bridge the gaps between policy, practice and research.

In **Norway**, monitoring through standardised annual reports from all kindergartens has revealed a need for more qualified staff and points to those regions experiencing the greatest difficulties with workforce quality. As a result, the government launched a plan to recruit preschool teachers, and they have designed targeted actions for certain regions. Based on the case of Norway, it is clear that data collection on workforce can serve as an evidence base for taking concrete action to improve the quality of ECEC services.

When **Slovenia** evaluated the implementation of its preschool curriculum, the findings were shared with education officials and institutions responsible for ECEC, and they were forwarded to preschools so that suggested improvements could be introduced throughout the system. In addition to improving the implementation of the curriculum, Slovenia notes that the findings proved to be important for the preparation of professional development training contents.

**Mexico** has learnt via data collection that while a majority of preschool children have achieved basic skills in language and mathematics, those who have not are concentrated in rural communities. As a result of this finding, Mexico has decided to create new pedagogical materials specifically for rural communities in an effort to help underachieving students perform at the same level as their peers. This is an example of how data on child development can be used to design evidence-based interventions and help children in need of special support.

Through its *Language and Learning Study*, **Norway** has found that children who attended regular formal centre or family-based child care at ages one-and-a-half to three became less often late talkers than children who are looked after by parents or childminders. The cause is not certain, so the government welcomes further research into kindergarten conditions that enhance language development; however, preliminary findings strengthen the rationale for kindergarten attendance both for majority and minority language children.

**Flanders** (**Belgium**) seeks to pursue an evidence-based policy orientation in education and has thus introduced a student monitoring system, which tracks individual student development. This is believed to offer insight into, among other things, the quality of educational institutions. Flanders also notes that decreasing research budgets coupled with an academic disinterest for policy makes it difficult to respond to increasingly more diverse policy issues.

## Lesson 3: Track financing and costs to justify education spending

For **Australia**, tracking financial spending on ECEC has shown that funding has led to an increase in the number of children enrolled in child care services from 2007-10 and a decrease in the cost to parents for long day care services from 2004-10. This is one example of how financial tracking and monitoring of outcomes can showcase proven results and accountability, which justify the educational funding.

**Portugal** has learnt that not having a systemic research agenda for ECEC leads to difficulties in the assessment of quality and makes it complicated to show the benefits of investing in ECEC.

## Lesson 4: Place key actors at the centre of monitoring, data collection and research

As **Australia** has introduced a National Quality Standard Framework, which includes a new monitoring process, governments at all levels are recognising the importance of creating opportunities for professionals to regularly assess their practice. Australia finds that the most effective improvements to service delivery are initiated from within the service, rather than imposed from the outside. Upon assessing the quality of practices and services, the next step is to determine where quality improvements can be made and plan effectively to implement them.

In **Flanders** (**Belgium**), a report is produced upon completion of an external inspection, and school principals are obligated to share the findings during a formal meeting with the school's personnel; however, teachers unions claim that this is not common practice. A lesson learnt from Flanders is that when a feedback cycle is put into place, all parties involved must participate as planned if the cycle is to function properly.

**British Columbia (Canada)**, **Japan** and **Slovenia** highlight the importance of having a programme or curriculum evaluated/assessed by persons related to the ECEC centre, such as parents and local residents. It increases the objectivity and transparency of the assessment, stimulates parent and community engagement, increases parental satisfaction and deepens the understanding of the stakeholders regarding ECEC centres.

**Ireland** highlights the importance of ensuring the following when conducting research: relevance of the policy study; minimal attrition; maximised data; minimal respondent burden; and child-centeredness, capturing the breadth of children's lives. A variety of measures have been taken to meet these challenges in Ireland; and one of the main lessons the government has learnt is that it is essential to involve all stakeholders from the outset, in particular policy makers and children.

## Lesson 5: Collect data on ECEC services consistently across providers, including those not subsidised by government

In the child care sector of **Flanders (Belgium)**, independent facilities receive limited public funding, so it is not possible to obtain the same amount of data from them as from subsidised facilities. As subsidised facilities receive public funding, they can be required to provide data. A key lesson learned from Flanders is that the overall picture of child care services is in incomplete when monitoring is not carried out consistently across all providers. With the current monitoring system, the government realises that they are lacking information, such as the profiles of users in all facilities, who pays how much of the total child care costs, who is not being reached by child care services, qualifications of personnel in all facilities, staff turnover rates and the age of staff. Flanders is assessing how to obtain missing data without placing too great of a burden on facilities and without invading the privacy of parents and children.

**Norway** collects data (administrative records) across public and non-public kindergartens on an annual basis, including information about the quality of ECEC provision (staff-child ratio, staff provisions and qualifications and gender); the organisation of kindergarten (ownership [public/private], opening hours); parents' fees (reduction for siblings, reductions for low-income families); the number of ECEC places and children in ECEC (ages, weekly attendance, etc., including minority language children and children with disabilities); and kindergarten co-operation with other institutions. By collecting this data from all kindergartens, Norway is able to create official statistics about ECEC services, which provide an in-depth, comprehensive picture of services provided throughout the country.

## Lesson 6: Consider both the advantages and disadvantages when giving local authorities the responsibility of monitoring quality

With regards to giving more autonomy to local authorities in monitoring the quality of ECEC services, **Japan**, **Mexico** and **Portugal** agree that it can be advantageous in that it promotes local-level initiatives; and local authorities tend to have a better understanding of the educational needs of the population, which could give shape to more rigorous monitoring and evaluation. However, these countries also concur that one of the disadvantages is that different authorities may establish different monitoring criteria. Another challenge is harmonising the collection and processing of data among local authorities. These issues make it difficult to consolidate data at the national level and maintain national standards for the quality of services. Additionally, Mexico finds that local authorities sometimes do not have the necessary training to manage resources for monitoring and data collection.

## Lesson 7: Use monitoring as an opportunity to effectuate compliance and process quality

For **British Columbia (Canada)**, monitoring class size across the province on an annual basis has resulted in universal compliance for kindergarten class size.

**Korea** learnt that a monitoring and quality assurance system can contribute to the enhancement of quality in ECEC, not only in terms of structural quality (*e.g.*, staff-child ratio, class size and space per child) but also in terms of less tangible processes such as staff-child interactions. Internal monitoring and self-supervision practiced among staff are acknowledged as more sustainable resources for the enhancement of quality.

# ACTION AREA 5 – REFLECTING ON THE CURRENT STATE OF PLAY

This sheet has been prepared based on international trends and is designed to facilitate reflection on where your country stands regarding:

- Data collection, research and monitoring

The aim is to raise awareness about new issues and identify areas where changes could be made; the aim is not to give marks on practices. Please reflect on the current state of play by circling a number on the scale from 1-5.

## DATA COLLECTION, RESEARCH AND MONITORING

| Data collection | Not at all | | | | Very well |
|---|---|---|---|---|---|
| 1. Critical policy questions have been defined that an ECEC data system should help answer. Futhermore, it is clear where data gaps exist and what linkages among ECEC programmes are needed to answer the policy questions. | 1 | 2 | 3 | 4 | 5 |
| 2. Currently collected ECEC indicators are well designed and can be used to inform policy and determine whether the overall ECEC goals are being met. | 1 | 2 | 3 | 4 | 5 |
| 3. The current data systems for ECEC indicators are aligned with school data systems. | 1 | 2 | 3 | 4 | 5 |
| 4. The currently collected data are presented and communicated in a user-friendly way. | 1 | 2 | 3 | 4 | 5 |
| 5. Data is currently collected on:<br>a) children (*e.g.*, actual numbers of children enrolled in ECEC services in each age cohort, their socio-economic backgrounds, gender, immigrant status). | 1 | 2 | 3 | 4 | 5 |

| | Not at all | | | | Very well |
|---|---|---|---|---|---|
| b) programmes (*e.g.*, different types and forms of services, including private and informal care arrangements). | 1 | 2 | 3 | 4 | 5 |
| c) workforce (*e.g.*, numbers of staff and their qualification levels, age, gender, immigrant status, salaries and developmental opportunities). | 1 | 2 | 3 | 4 | 5 |
| d) financing sources and cost information. | 1 | 2 | 3 | 4 | 5 |
| 6. Linkages can be made among the collected indicators, such as those identified in point 5. | 1 | 2 | 3 | 4 | 5 |
| 7. Sufficient funding has been allocated to improve data coverage and data quality to answer critical policy questions. | 1 | 2 | 3 | 4 | 5 |
| **Research** | Not at all | | | | Very well |
| 8. There is a stable infrastructure and long-term funding for ECEC research. | 1 | 2 | 3 | 4 | 5 |
| 9. The following types of research have been conducted:<br>a) country-specific policy evaluation and research | 1 | 2 | 3 | 4 | 5 |
| b) comparative, cross national research | 1 | 2 | 3 | 4 | 5 |
| c) longitudinal studies | 1 | 2 | 3 | 4 | 5 |
| d) cost-benefit analysis | 1 | 2 | 3 | 4 | 5 |
| e) large-scale programme evaluations with randomised controlled trials | 1 | 2 | 3 | 4 | 5 |
| f) neuroscience and brain research | 1 | 2 | 3 | 4 | 5 |
| g) socio-cultural analysis with ethnographic and qualitative methods | 1 | 2 | 3 | 4 | 5 |
| h) research on practice and process, such as action research | 1 | 2 | 3 | 4 | 5 |
| i) child-centred research with participant observation methods | 1 | 2 | 3 | 4 | 5 |
| j) parental needs | 1 | 2 | 3 | 4 | 5 |

| | | | | | |
|---|---|---|---|---|---|
| 10. The main gaps in research on ECEC:<br>a) have been identified. | 1 | 2 | 3 | 4 | 5 |
| b) are being addressed with concrete proposals. | 1 | 2 | 3 | 4 | 5 |
| 11. Research networks or other processes are in place to connect research communities with:<br>a) policy makers in the country. | 1 | 2 | 3 | 4 | 5 |
| b) practitioners in the country. | 1 | 2 | 3 | 4 | 5 |
| c) international audiences. | 1 | 2 | 3 | 4 | 5 |
| 12. There are sufficient university chairs, postgraduate programmes, dissertations and academic journals focusing on ECEC. | 1 | 2 | 3 | 4 | 5 |
| 13. Research is being used to shape initial education and professional development for ECEC staff. | 1 | 2 | 3 | 4 | 5 |
| 14. A multidisciplinary approach is being promoted for ECEC research, including anthropology, sociology, public policy, gender studies, learning theory and brain research. | 1 | 2 | 3 | 4 | 5 |
| **Monitoring** | Not at all | | | | Very well |
| 15. The purpose and methodologies of monitoring have been specified, agreed upon and communicated clearly to ECEC managers, practitioners and parents; and stakeholder buy-in for the monitoring (purpose, process and follow-up) has been established. | 1 | 2 | 3 | 4 | 5 |
| 16. It is clear who is responsible and who is involved in monitoring practices. An assessment has been made on the capacities needed to effectively implement monitoring before the actual implementation. | 1 | 2 | 3 | 4 | 5 |
| 17. The following indicators are being used to monitor quality:<br>a) structural quality (*e.g.*, staff qualifications, class size, staff-child ratios) | 1 | 2 | 3 | 4 | 5 |

| | 1 | 2 | 3 | 4 | 5 |
|---|---|---|---|---|---|
| b) process quality (*e.g.*, types of experiences children have in an ECEC setting, types of interactions with staff and their peers) | 1 | 2 | 3 | 4 | 5 |
| 18. The following methods are being used to monitor quality:<br><br>a) testing child outcomes | 1 | 2 | 3 | 4 | 5 |
| b) document and record | 1 | 2 | 3 | 4 | 5 |
| c) observation | 1 | 2 | 3 | 4 | 5 |
| d) interview | 1 | 2 | 3 | 4 | 5 |
| e) survey | 1 | 2 | 3 | 4 | 5 |
| f) programme review tools | 1 | 2 | 3 | 4 | 5 |
| e) quality rating | 1 | 2 | 3 | 4 | 5 |
| f) self-reports | 1 | 2 | 3 | 4 | 5 |
| g) others (specify) | 1 | 2 | 3 | 4 | 5 |
| 19. Enough attention has been paid to how to monitor less quantifiable child outcomes in comparison with easily measurable results such as math and literacy gains. | 1 | 2 | 3 | 4 | 5 |
| 20. Monitored data is used to underpin:<br><br>a) technical assistance for staff | 1 | 2 | 3 | 4 | 5 |
| b) staff professional development | 1 | 2 | 3 | 4 | 5 |
| c) corrective actions or sanctions | 1 | 2 | 3 | 4 | 5 |
| d) adjustments to curricula | 1 | 2 | 3 | 4 | 5 |
| f) mentoring | 1 | 2 | 3 | 4 | 5 |
| g) funding decisions | 1 | 2 | 3 | 4 | 5 |
| h) changes to policy | 1 | 2 | 3 | 4 | 5 |
| i) others (specify) | 1 | 2 | 3 | 4 | 5 |

# NOTES

1   Patton refers to this as "the problem of labelling the black box" (Patton, 2008, p. 142).

2   See, for example, Keystone STARS study (www.pakeys.org/uploadedContent/Docs/STARS/outreach/2010%20STARS.rpt.final.pdf) and RAND study (www.rand.org/pubs/research_briefs/RB9343/index1.html).

3   See http://ecedata.org/files/DQC%20ECDC%20brochure%202011%20Mar21.pdf.

4   For countries with an integrated ECEC system, when reported monitoring practices refer to children in the whole age range of ECEC (covering children from age zero to compulsory schooling age), the practices are included in monitoring practices for both child care and kindergarten/preschool, since these two provisions cover the whole ECEC age range. This does not indicate these countries have a split system for care and early education. They are included in both child care and kindergarten/preschool for comparative reasons, indicating that these countries have monitoring practices for the whole ECEC age range.

# ANNEX

## LIST OF NETWORK MEMBER CONTRIBUTORS

Contributors to this publication provided country data, country-specific policy information, comments on the drafts, etc. as members of the OECD Network on Early Childhood Education and Care (listed in alphabetical order).

| Country | Name | Organisation |
|---------|------|--------------|
| **Australia** | Ms. Jo CALDWELL | Department of Education, Employment and Workplace Relations |
| | Ms. Laura HIGGINS | Department of Education, Employment and Workplace Relations |
| | Ms. Margaret PEARCE | Australian Delegation to the OECD |
| | Ms. Robyn SHANNON | Department of Education, Employment and Workplace Relations |
| | Mr. Mark UNWIN | Australian Delegation to the OECD |
| | Dr. Mary WELSH | Department of Education, Employment and Workplace Relations |
| **Austria** | Ms. Marion GRATT | Permanent Delegation of Austria to the OECD |
| | Ms. Daniela HERTA | Permanent Delegation of Austria to the OECD |
| | Ms. Marisa KRENN-WACHE | Federal Training College for Kindergarten Pedagogues Klagenfurt |
| | Ms. Andrea SCHMÖLZER | Federal Ministry for Education, the Arts and Culture |
| | Ms. Christine SCHNEIDER | Federal Ministry for Education, the Arts and Culture |
| **Belgium** | Ms. Veronique ADRIAENS | Department of Education |
| | Ms. Bea BUYSSE | Formerly, Kind en Gezin (Child and Family) |
| | Ms. Dominique DELVAUX | Observatoire de l'enfance, de la jeunesse et de l'aide à la jeunesse (Fédération Wallonie-Bruxelles) |
| | Ms. Anne-Marie DIEU | Observatoire de l'enfance, de la jeunesse et de l'aide à la jeunesse (Fédération Wallonie-Bruxelles) |
| | Mr. Roger HOTERMANS | General Delegation of the French Community and the Walloon Region of Belgium |
| | Ms. Cathy MISSON-FIEVET | Permanent Delegation of Belgium to the OECD |
| | Ms. Christele van NIEUWENHUYZEN | Kind en Gezin (Child and Family) |
| | Ms. Myriam SOMMER | Office de la Naissance et de l'Enfance |
| | Ms. Linde VAN CUTSEM | Department of Education |

| | | |
|---|---|---|
| **Chile** | Ms. Eliana CHAMIZO ÁLVAREZ | Ministry of Education |
| | Ms. Jacqueline ARANEDA | Junta Nacional de Jardines Infantiles |
| | Ms. Irma BRANTTES | Junta Nacional de Jardines Infantiles |
| | Mr. Fabian GREDIG | Permanent Delegation of Chile to the OECD |
| **Czech Republic** | Dr. Irena BORKOVCOVÁ | Czech School Inspectorate |
| | Ms. Helena CIZKOVA | Permanent Delegation of the Czech Republic to the OECD |
| | Ms. Alena SPEJCHALOVA | Ministry of Education Youth and Sports |
| **Denmark** | Mr. Lars Hornung BAHN | Ministry of Children and Education |
| | Ms. Christina BARFOED-HØJ | Ministry of Children and Education |
| | Ms. Clara Albeck JAPSEN | Ministry of Children and Education |
| | Mr. Frode NEERGAARD | Permanent Delegation of Denmark to OECD |
| | Ms. Lene ØSTERGAARD | Ministry of Children and Education |
| **Estonia** | Ms. Tiina Peterson | Ministry of Education and Research |
| **Finland** | Ms. Tarja KAHILUOTO | Ministry of Social Affairs and Health |
| | Ms. Päivi LINDBERG | National Institute for Health and Welfare |
| | Ms. Kirsi LINDROOS | Permanent Delegation of Finland to the OECD |
| | Ms. Anna MIKANDER | Ministry of Education and Culture |
| | Ms. Maiju PAANANEN | National Institute for Health and Welfare |
| | Ms. Hely PARKKINEN | National Board of Education |
| **France** | Mr. Claude GIRARD | Permanent Delegation of France to the OECD |
| | Dr. Michael JANSEN | Ministère de l'Enseignement supérieur et de la recherche |
| **Germany** | Mr. Peter KLANDT | International Bureau of the Federal Ministry of Education and Research |
| | Dr. Philipp ROGGE | Federal Ministry for Family Affairs, Senior Citizens, Women and Youth |
| | Dr. Miriam SAATI | Federal Ministry for Family Affairs, Senior Citizens, Women and Youth |
| **Hungary** | Ms. Martina BEKE | Permanent Delegation of Hungary to the OECD |
| | Mr. László LIMBACHER | Ministry of National Resources |
| | Mr. Gergely VÁRKONYI | Permanent Delegation of Hungary to the OECD |
| **Ireland** | Mr. Darragh DOHERTY | Department of Health and Children |
| | Ms. Catherine HYNES | Department of Education and Science |
| | Mr. Michael O'TOOLE | Permanent Delegation of Ireland to the OECD |
| | Mr. Heino SCHONFELD | Centre for Early Childhood Development and Education |
| **Israel** | Ms. Sima HADDAD-MA-YAFIT | Ministry of Education |
| | Ms. Monica WINOKUR | Ministry of Education |
| | Ms. Martine WORMS | Ministry of Education |

| | | |
|---|---|---|
| **Italy** | Ms. Silvana MARRA | Ministry of Education, University and Research |
| | Dr. Angiolina PONZIANO | Ministry of Education, University and Research |
| **Japan** | Dr. Kiyomi AKITA | University of Tokyo |
| | Mr. Jugo IMAIZUMI | Permanent Delegation of Japan to the OECD |
| | Dr. Riyo KADOTA-KOROGI | Seinan Gakuin University |
| | Mr. Takuto MIYAMOTO | Former Deputy Director Early Childhood Education Division Ministry of Education, Culture, Sports, Science and Technology (MEXT) |
| | Mr. Keisuke OTANI | Former Director Early Childhood Education Division Ministry of Education, Culture, Sports, Science and Technology (MEXT) |
| | Ms. Maria OJIMI | Unit Chief Early Childhood Education Division Ministry of Education, Culture, Sports, Science and Technology (MEXT) |
| | Mr. Masatoshi SUZUKI | Hyogo University of Teacher Education |
| | Mr. Hiroshi UMEHARA | Former Deputy Director Early Childhood Education Division Ministry of Education, Culture, Sports, Science and Technology (MEXT) |
| **Korea** | Ms. Jeong-Eun AN | Ministry of Education, Science and Technology |
| | Ms. Yeonhee GU | Permanent Delegation of Korea to the OECD |
| | Dr. Mugyeong MOON | Korea Institute of Child Care and Education |
| **Luxembourg** | Mr. Manuel ACHTEN | Ministère de la Famille et de l'Intégration |
| | Ms. Claude SEVENIG | Ministère de l'Éducation nationale et de la Formation professionnelle |
| **Mexico** | Ms. Lucero NAVA BOLANOS | National Council for the Promotion of Education |
| | Mr. José Carlos ROCHA SILVA | National Council for the Promotion of Education |
| | Dr. Arturo SÁENZ FERRAL | National Council for the Promotion of Education |
| | Ms. Luisa SOLCHAGA | Permanent Delegation of Mexico to the OECD |
| | Ms. Valerie VON WOBESER SUÁREZ | National Council for the Promotion of Education |
| **Netherlands** | Ms. Wytske BOOMSMA | Ministry of Education, Culture and Science |
| | Mr. Jakob VAN DER WAARDEN | Ministry of Social Affairs and Labour |
| | Ms. Willeke VAN DER WERF | Ministry of Social Affairs |
| | Mr. Peter WINIA | Ministry of Education, Culture and Science |
| **New Zealand** | Ms. Natasha KUKA | Ministry of Education |
| | Ms. Te Rina LEONARD | Ministry of Education |
| | Mr. Karl LE QUESNE | Ministry of Education |
| | Mr. Richard WALLEY | Ministry of Education |

| | | |
|---|---|---|
| **Norway** | Ms. Kari JACOBSEN | Royal Norwegian Ministry of Education and Research |
| | Ms. Tove MOGSTAD SLINDE | Ministry of Education and Research |
| | Mr. Espen SOLBERG | Permanent Delegation of Norway to the OECD |
| | Ms. Marit SOLHEIM | Royal Norwegian Ministry of Education and Research |
| **Poland** | Ms. Iwona KRZESZEWSKA | Permanent Delegation of Poland to the OECD |
| | Ms. Katarzyna MALEC | Ministry of National Education |
| | Ms. Emilia RÓŻYCKA | Ministry of National Education |
| | Mr. Aleksander TYNELSKI | Ministry of National Education |
| | Ms. Olga WASILEWSKA | Educational Research Institute |
| **Portugal** | Mr. Fernando EGIDIO REIS | Ministry of Education |
| | Ms. Catarina FIGUEIREDO CARDOSO | Permanent Delegation of Portugal to the OECD |
| | Ms. Helena GIL | Ministry of Education |
| | Ms. Alexandra MARQUES | Ministry of Education |
| | Ms. Liliana MARQUES | Ministry of Education |
| | Ms. Luisa UCHA SILVA | Ministry of Education |
| **Singapore** | Mr. Charles CHAN | Ministry of Education |
| | Ms. Pik San LEONG | Ministry of Education |
| **Slovak Republic** | Ms. Viera HAJDUKOVA | Ministry of Education, Science, Research and Sport |
| | Ms. Marcela HANUSOVA | Permanent Delegation of the Slovak Republic to the OECD |
| **Slovenia** | Ms. Sabina MELAVC | Ministry of Education and Sport |
| | Ms. Nada POZAR MATIJASIC | Ministry of Education and Sport |
| **Spain** | Mr. Vicenç ARNAIZ | Gouvernement des Iles Baléares |
| | Mr. José Antonio BLANCO FERNANDEZ | Permanent Delegation of Spain to the OECD |
| | Mr. Rafael BONETE PERALES | Permanent Delegation of Spain to the OECD |
| | Mr. Manuel GÁLVEZ CARAVACA | Ministerio de educación |
| | Ms. María Luz OCAÑA HERREROS | Permanent Delegation of Spain to the OECD |
| **Sweden** | Mr. Hans-Åke ÖSTRÖM | Permanent Delegation of Sweden to the OECD |
| | Mr. Christer TOFTÉNIUS | Ministry of Education and Research |
| **Turkey** | Mr. Burak RENDE | Permanent Delegation of Turkey to the OECD |
| | Mr. Fatih TASTAN | Ministry of National Education of Turkey |

| | | |
|---|---|---|
| **United Kingdom** | Ms. Susan BOLT | The Scottish Government |
| | Ms. Kathryn CHISHOLM | The Scottish Government |
| | Mr. Peter DRUMMOND | DWP Joint International Unit |
| | Mr. Steve HAMILTON | Department for Children, Schools and Families |
| | Ms. Rosalyn HARPER | Department for Education |
| | Ms. Pauline JONES | Children's Workforce Development Council |
| | Mr. Jamie KELLY | Department for Education |
| | Mr. Jason LLOYD | The Scottish Government |
| | Mr. Adam MICKLETHWAITE | Department for Children, Schools and Families |
| | Ms. Helen MISTALA | Department for Education and Skills |
| | Ms. Karuna PERERA | Department for Education |
| | Ms. Anncris ROBERTS | The Scottish Government |
| | Ms. Gigi SANOTRA | Department for Education |
| | Mr. Simon SMITH | Department for Education |
| | Mr. Robert SPECTERMAN | HM Treasury |
| | Dr. Wendy VAN RIJSWIJK | The Scottish Government |
| | Ms. Ann WILSDON | Department for Children, Schools and Families |
| | Mr. Dudley WYBER | United Kingdom Delegation to the OECD |
| **United States** | Mr. Steven HICKS | United States Department of Education |
| | Dr. Jacqueline JONES | United States Department of Education |

# ORGANISATION FOR ECONOMIC CO-OPERATION AND DEVELOPMENT

The OECD is a unique forum where governments work together to address the economic, social and environmental challenges of globalisation. The OECD is also at the forefront of efforts to understand and to help governments respond to new developments and concerns, such as corporate governance, the information economy and the challenges of an ageing population. The Organisation provides a setting where governments can compare policy experiences, seek answers to common problems, identify good practice and work to co-ordinate domestic and international policies.

The OECD member countries are: Australia, Austria, Belgium, Canada, Chile, the Czech Republic, Denmark, Estonia, Finland, France, Germany, Greece, Hungary, Iceland, Ireland, Israel, Italy, Japan, Korea, Luxembourg, Mexico, the Netherlands, New Zealand, Norway, Poland, Portugal, the Slovak Republic, Slovenia, Spain, Sweden, Switzerland, Turkey, the United Kingdom and the United States. The European Union takes part in the work of the OECD.

OECD Publishing disseminates widely the results of the Organisation's statistics gathering and research on economic, social and environmental issues, as well as the conventions, guidelines and standards agreed by its members.

OECD PUBLISHING, 2, rue André-Pascal, 75775 PARIS CEDEX 16
(91 2012 01 1 P) ISBN 978-92-64-12325-0 – No. 59731 2011-02